How to Prepare for

The Real Estate Licensing Exam

and Have a Great Career

How to Prepare for
The Real Estate Licensing Exam

and Have a Great Career

HENRY S. HARRISON

WITH **BURTON S. LEE** AND **BARBARA L. DRISKO**

McGraw Hill

New York   Chicago   San Francisco   Lisbon   London
Madrid   Mexico City   Milan   New Delhi   San Juan
Seoul   Singapore   Sydney   Toronto

1 2 3 4 5 6 7 8 9 10   QPD/QPD   0 9 8 7

ISBN-13: 978-0-07-148091-8
MHID: 0-07-148091-9

This publication is designed to provide accurate and authoritative information in regard to the subject matter covered. It is sold with the understanding that neither the author nor the publisher is engaged in rendering legal, accounting, or other professional service. If legal advice or other expert assistance is required, the services of a competent professional person should be sought.
—From a Declaration of Principles jointly adopted by Committee of the American Bar Association and a Committee of Publishers.

McGraw-Hill books are available at special quantity discounts to use as premiums and sales promotions, or for use in corporate training programs. For more information, please write to the Director of Special Sales, McGraw-Hill Professional, Two Penn Plaza, New York, NY 10121-2298. Or contact your local bookstore.

*To our readers who choose to become real estate professionals and pass their real estate license exam.
Good luck and best wishes in your new career.*

CONTENTS

ACKNOWLEDGMENTS

I started my real estate career in 1956. It would take a separate book for me to acknowledge all the people who helped me along the way! All I can do at this point is say, "Thanks," because without them this book would never have been written.

Since that time, I have written over 20 books. As always when I write a book, many people play an important part in the process long before the final product is realized. I have learned to wait until the eleventh hour to write the acknowledgments page, hoping not to leave out anyone who has helped me either directly or indirectly with the book. (Based on my past experience, I will once again omit someone who should have been included. To them, I say, "I am sorry," in advance.)

First, I want to thank Neil Salkin, Ph.D., and Studio B Productions Inc., the literary agency that somehow decided and then convinced McGraw-Hill that I was the author who could write the book McGraw-Hill was planning to publish.

Some of the material included in the book was the result of a joint effort by my coauthor Barbara L. Drisko and myself to write a real estate book some years ago, for which we never found a national publisher. We drifted apart, and when I finally located her again she was serving as first selectwoman of Columbia, Maine. We are both delighted that the material we worked so hard to produce has been updated and has become part of this book.

My other coauthor, Burton S. Lee, and I are also partners in the Harrison & Lee Appraisal Education Company. Together, we are developing new classroom and online material for real estate appraisal education. Burton is also associated with VanEd Inc., an online real estate education company. He helped make sure that the material in this book is current, correct, and up to date. Both Barbara and Burton have been enthusiastic about the project, and I thank them for their support, professionalism, and friendship.

The staff at McGraw-Hill have been exceptional to work with. Mary Glenn (Editorial Director), Ed Chupak (Business Education Coordinator), and Daina Penikas (Editing Supervisor) are down-to-earth, smart, and a great team. Every interaction with them has reconfirmed my good opinion of their focus and dedication.

This book was produced by Ginny Carroll (copyediting), Jim Fogel (composition), and the staff at North Market Street Graphics. They set and then met every deadline. Their professionalism and creative problem-solving ability was amazing.

When I retired from real estate sales and became an honorary life member of the Greater New Haven Association of Realtors, I remained involved by creating the Real Estate Educational Foundation, Inc., (REEF) of which I am still the president. Roberta O'Hara, Executive Vice President of the Association, and her assistant Jeannine Mollica, keep the foundation running, helping support our important charitable work. Lynn Westerhoff is the new education director of the New Haven Real Estate School, which is the primary source of REEF's funding. I sincerely appreciate all their help.

A tip of my tennis hat to super coach Jim Cole, who kept me physically fit with tennis lessons throughout the long months of this project. Hopefully, I have inspired him to become an author, too.

I listened with interest as Gloria Coros reported to me the step-by-step process she just went through to obtain her real estate license. She is now starting her new adventures as a real estate salesperson. Good luck to her and all the others who follow in her footsteps.

My son-in-law Jason Gaines and my wife, Ruth Lambert, helped me prepare the manuscript. I thank them for their computer expertise and dedication to the task. Ruth and my four married children also deserve my special appreciation, as they and their families always sacrifice time with Dad (aka Poppa) whenever I am elbow-deep in a book project.

Henry S. Harrison
October 2007

HOW TO USE THIS BOOK

Use this book to help you decide whether to become a real estate professional.

Readers who are considering real estate as a profession will find in this book a great deal of information about what being a real estate professional is all about. There is a self-scoring quiz, with questions about yourself, that will help you decide if your personality is the type that tends to be happy and successful in our profession. The real estate profession is gigantic. The National Association of Realtors is the largest of many real estate trade organizations. It alone has about 1,400,000 members. Keep in mind that there are many types of people who are successful and happy in the real estate profession.

The majority of people starting out in real estate start as real estate sale professionals (RESPs). However, there are many other ways to make a living in real estate. Many RESPs open their own offices and become real estate brokers. These entrepreneurs hire other RESPs. Chapter 21 provides useful information about 14 other opportunities in real estate besides selling homes. Some of these career opportunities involve appraising; management; commercial, industrial, and investment property sales; insurance; and education.

In addition to this direct information about the real estate profession, many readers will also find it helpful to read the rest of the chapters in the book, which cover the body of knowledge needed to obtain a real estate sales license. Your interest in this information is another good indication of whether real estate is the right profession for you.

Use this book to help you pass the real estate license exam.

In our opinion, every real estate professional (even those choosing specialties such as insurance and appraisal, which do not require a real estate sales license) should obtain a real estate sales license. Almost all real estate professionals sooner or later have the opportunity to make a sale because of their exposure to the market. When this opportunity arises, it is too late to obtain a license. Even if you never intend to make a sale, what you learn by studying for a license will help you in whatever specialty you choose.

Every state now requires you to take one or more courses before you can take the real estate sales exam. This book has a proven system that will indicate to you whether you are ready to successfully take the exam. If you are not ready, it will help you get ready, without wasting time. The book does this by focusing you on what you don't know but need to know, rather than wasting time studying what you already know.

Here is how this proven system works. Chapters 5 through 19 cover the subjects that are on the real estate license exam. *Once you have read the book, do not read these chapters again.* Following these steps:

1. Take the exam at the end of Chapter 5.
2. Correct the exam using the answers that follow each exam.
3. Mark only the questions that you answered wrong. Ignore the questions you answered correctly.
4. On a piece of paper, write the chapter and page number shown next to each question you have missed.
5. Start studying by going to the first chapter and page number on your list. Find the icon that shows where the answer to the missed question is located in the text.
6. Study only that part of the text which contains the correct answer to the question you missed.
7. Repeat steps 5 and 6 until you have covered all the questions you missed in this chapter.
8. Go to the next chapter and repeat this process, proceeding through each chapter until you have completed Chapter 19.
9. Take the first practice exam in Chapter 23. If you answer at least 80 percent of the questions correctly, you are ready to take the national part of the real estate exam. (This book does not cover the state-specific questions on the exam.)
10. If you answer less than 80 percent correctly, study the answers to the questions that you missed and go back into the text to read more about the specific subjects pertaining to the questions you missed.
11. Repeat steps 9 and 10 using practice exam 2.
12. When you score 80 percent or higher, you should take the real estate license exam as soon as you can. Don't give up if you fail the first time. Review the text once more, covering only the information that pertains to your wrong answers.
13. Take the real estate license exam the second time. Congratulations if you pass. If you didn't, it indicates that you probably need to take another real estate course.

INTRODUCTION

All About the Real Estate License Examination

This book is designed to help you pass your real estate license examination the first time you take it. Though it is nice to get a high score, the only important thing is to pass. We will make this statement several other places in this book because we know whenever adults take an examination they become anxious. We know it is impossible to eliminate your anxiety, but we also know there is a lot this book can do to reduce it.

What makes many students anxious is coming across material that they just don't seem to be able to understand. They become so anxious about that material (often math) that it interferes with their studying the rest of the material. At the most, math comprises only 10 percent of the license exam. The passing percentage in most states is 70 percent, so even if you missed all of the math questions (which is highly unlikely), you still can miss a lot of other questions, too.

We have developed a method of studying that has been proven to be successful. Our appraisal examination book is very popular, and students who use it have a very high passing rate. Our unique system of studying really works!

The real estate license examination in most states is really two exams, which are often combined to look like only one. The biggest part of the

1

exam is the general real estate questions that the testing companies use in almost every state. The other questions pertain to specific rules and regulations that are relevant only to the state in which you are applying for a license.

This book alone is not sufficient to study for your real estate license examination. Either in a classroom setting or online, you will have to take and pass the training that is required by your state. During this training you will study both the general real estate material that is covered in this book and the special material that applies only to your state.

This book has three purposes (besides helping you decide if you want a career in real estate sales):

---

1. You can use it to get a head start on your training. This will go a long way toward reducing your anxiety and will make your classroom or online learning more meaningful and less stressful.

2. You can use it as a reference source during your required training. When you don't understand something, reading about it in this book can help to clarify the material.

3. This book is a proven review tool. When you use it as directed, you will substantially increase your chances of passing the real estate license exam on your first try. The same is true if you have to take the exam a second time.

HOW TO CONTACT YOUR STATE'S REAL ESTATE COMMISSION OR OTHER LICENSING AUTHORITY

The following information provides everything you need to find out exactly what your state's real estate license requirements are. These sites will also state all the other requirements for obtaining a real estate agent's license.

The following three sections list 25 things you can find out about the real estate license exams by contacting your state license authority. Information on how to contact them immediately follows the list.

Sometimes (but not very often) this information changes. If that happens, use Google. Enter your state's name and "real estate license, requirements." That should get you to the appropriate contact information. Don't get discouraged if it doesn't come up on the first page (which is filled with offers to sell you education and review products).

Questions About the Exam

1. Which testing service examination is given in your state? (There are four major testing services. Information about each of them follows the list of state contact information.)
2. What subjects are covered on the exam and what percentage of the exam is allocated to each subject? (This information is also included at the end of this chapter)
3. How many questions are on the exam?
4. How many general questions are there?
5. How many state-specific questions are there?
6. Are the exam questions multiple choice, true-or-false, essay, or some combination of these? (Most likely, the majority of the questions are multiple choice.)
7. Do you take the exam on paper or on a computer?
8. How long does the exam take?
9. Do you need a calculator, and if so, what kind is best?
10. How is the exam scored?
11. Is there any penalty for wrong answers? (If there is no penalty, you must answer every question even if the answer is a wild guess.)
12. What is the lowest passing score?
13. Is each section scored separately, or are all the questions scored together?

Questions About Taking the Exam

14. Where is the exam given?
15. When is the exam given (date)?
16. If necessary, can you reschedule the exam? If so, how much notice is needed?
17. At what time is the exam given, and when should you be there? (Whatever time they tell you, try to be at least a half hour early.)
18. How do you register for the exam?
19. What is the fee?
20. What are you required to bring to the exam?
21. What are you prohibited from bringing to the exam?
22. If the exam is given on a computer, when and where can you practice using the computer? (If practice is not permitted at the testing center, there may be an online practice site.)

Questions About the Exam Results and Retests

> **23.** When and how do you get the exam results?
>
> **24.** If you fail, how and when can you take a retest?

Special Needs

> **25.** If you have special needs, how will they be accommodated?

CONTACT INFORMATION FOR STATE AND TERRITORY REAL ESTATE COMMISSIONS AND LICENSE AUTHORITIES

ALABAMA
Alabama Real Estate Commission
1201 Carmichael Way
Montgomery, AL 36106-4350
Phone: 334-242-5544
Fax: 334-270-9118
www.arec.state.al.us

ALASKA
Division of Occupational Licensing
Real Estate Commission
550 W. 7th Avenue, Suite 1500
Anchorage, AK 99501-3567
Phone: 907-269-8160
Fax: 907-269-8156
www.dced.state.as.us./occ/prec.htm

ARIZONA
Department of Real Estate
2910 N. 44th Street, Suite 100
Phoenix, AZ 85018
Phone: 602-468-1414
Fax: 602-468-0562
www.re.state.az.us

ARKANSAS
Real Estate Commission
612 South Summit Street
Little Rock, AR 72201-4740
Phone: 501-683-8010
Fax: 501-683-8020
www.state.ar.us/arecweb.html

CALIFORNIA
State of California
Department of Real Estate
P.O. Box 187000
Sacramento, CA 95818-7000
Phone: 916-227-0931
Info Line: 916-227-0864
www.dre.cahwnet.gov

COLORADO
Department of Regulatory Agencies
Division of Real Estate
560 Broadway, Suite 925
Denver, CO 80202
Phone: 303-894-2166
Fax: 303-894-2683
www.dora.state.co.us/Real-Estate

CONNECTICUT
Department of Consumer Protection
Occupational and Professional Licensing Division
165 Capitol Avenue, Room 110
Hartford, CT 06106
Phone: 860-713-6150
Fax: 860-713-7239
www.ct-clic.com

DELAWARE
Real Estate Commission
861 Silver Lake Boulevard, Suite 203
Dover, DE 19904
Phone: 302-739-4522, Ext. 219
Fax: 302-739-2711
www.state.de.us/research/profreg/realcomm.htm

DISTRICT OF COLUMBIA
Board of Real Estate
941 North Capitol Street, NE, Room 7200
Washington, DC 20002
Phone: 202-442-4320
Fax: 202-442-4528

FLORIDA
Division of Real Estate
400 W. Robinson Street, Suite N309
Orlando, FL 32802-1900
(P.O. Box 1900
Orlando, FL 32802-1900)
Phone: 407-245-0800
Fax: 407-317-7245
www.state.fl.us/dbpr/re/index.shtml

GEORGIA
Real Estate Commission
Suite 1000—International Tower
229 Peachtree Street NE
Atlanta, GA 30303-1605
Phone: 404-656-3916
Fax: 404-656-6650
www.grec.state.ga.us/

GUAM
Department of Revenue and Taxation
P.O. Box 23607
GMF Barrigada, Guam 96921
Phone: 671-475-1843
Fax: 671-472-2643

HAWAII
Real Estate Commission
King Kalakaua Building
335 Merchant Street, Room 333
Honolulu, HI 96813
Phone: 808-586-2643
Fax: 808-586-2650
www.state.hi.us/hirec

IDAHO
Real Estate Commission
P.O. Box 83720

Boise, ID 83720-0077
Phone: 800-447-5411
Fax: 208-334-2050
www.idahorealestatecommission.com

ILLINOIS
Office of Banks and Real Estate
500 East Monroe Street, Suite 200
Springfield, IL 62701
Phone: 217-785-9300
Fax: 217-782-3390
www.obre.state.il.us/realest/realmain.htm

INDIANA
Professional Licensing Agency
302 W. Washington Street, Room EO34
Indianapolis, IN 46204
Phone: 317-234-3009
Fax: 317-232-2312
www.in.gov/pla/bandc/estate/

IOWA
Real Estate Commission
1920 SE Hulsizer Avenue
Ankeny, IA 50021-3941
Phone: 515-281-7393
Fax: 515-281-7411
www.state.ia.us/government/com/prof/realesta/

KANSAS
Real Estate Commission
Three Townsite Plaza, Suite 200
120 SE 6th Avenue
Topeka, KS 66603-3511
Phone: 785-296-3411
Fax: 785-296-1771
www.ink.org/public/krec

KENTUCKY
Real Estate Commission
10200 Linn Station Road, Suite 201
Louisville, KY 40223
Phone: 502-425-4273
Fax: 502-426-2717
www.krec.net

LOUISIANA
Real Estate Commission
P.O. Box 14785
Baton Rouge, LA 70898-4785
Phone: 225-925-4771
Fax: 225-925-4431
www.irec.state.la.us

MAINE
Real Estate Commission
35 State House Station
Augusta, ME 04333-0035
Phone: 207-624-8603
Fax: 207-624-8637
www.state.me.us/pfr/olr

MARYLAND
Real Estate Commission
500 N. Calvert Street
Baltimore, MD 21202-3651
Phone: 410-230-6200
Fax: 410-333-0023
www.dllr.state.md.us/license/occprof/recomm.html

MASSACHUSETTS
Real Estate Board
239 Causeway Street, Suite 500
Boston, MA 02114
Phone: 617-727-2373
Fax: 617-727-2669
www.state.ma.us/reg/boards/re/default.htm

MICHIGAN
Department of Consumer and Industry Services
Bureau of Commercial Services
P.O. Box 30243
Lansing, MI 48909
Phone: 517-241-9288
Fax: 517-241-9280
www.michigan.gov/cis/

MINNESOTA
Department of Commerce
133 East 7th Street
St. Paul, MN 55101

Phone: 651-296-6694
www.commerce.state.mn.us/

MISSISSIPPI
Real Estate Commission
P.O. Box 12685
Jackson, MS 39236-2685
Phone: 601-932-9191
Fax: 601-932-2990
www.mrec.state.ms.us/

MISSOURI
Real Estate Commission
P.O. Box 1339
3605 Missouri Boulevard
Jefferson City, MO 65102
Phone: 573-751-2628
Fax: 573-751-2777
www.ecodev.state.mo.us/pr/restate/

MONTANA
Board of Realty Regulation
P.O. Box 200513
301 South Park
Helena, MT 59620-0513
Phone: 406-444-2961
Fax: 406-841-2323
http://mt.gov/govt/agencylisting.asp

NEBRASKA
Real Estate Commission
P.O. Box 94667
Lincoln, NE 68509-4667
Phone: 402-471-2004
Fax: 402-471-4492
www.nrec.state.ne.us/

NEVADA
Department of Business and Industry
Real Estate Division
2501 E. Sahara Avenue, Suite 102
Las Vegas, NV 89104-4137
Phone: 702-486-4033
Fax: 702-486-4275
www.red.state.nv.us/

NEW HAMPSHIRE
Real Estate Commission
State House Annex
25 Capitol Street, Room 435
Concord, NH 03301-6312
Phone: 603-271-2701
Fax: 603-271-1039
www.state.nh.us/nhrec/license.html

NEW JERSEY
Real Estate Commission
20 West State Street
P.O. Box 328
Trenton, NJ 08625-0328
Phone: 609-292-8280
Fax: 609-292-0944
www.nj.gov/dobi/rec_lic.htm

NEW MEXICO
Real Estate Commission
5200 Oakland Avenue NE, Suite B
Albuquerque, NM 87113
Phone: 505-222-9820 or 800-801-7505
Fax: 505-222-9886
www.state.nm.us/nmrec/

NEW YORK
Division of Licensing Services
84 Holland Avenue
Albany, NY 12208-3490
Phone: 518-474-4429
Fax: 518-473-2730
www.dos.state.ny.us/lcns/realest.html

NORTH CAROLINA
Real Estate Commission
P.O. Box 17100
Raleigh, NC 27619-7100
Phone: 919-875-3700
Fax: 919-872-0038
www.ncrec.state.nc.us/

NORTH DAKOTA
Real Estate Commission
200 East Main Avenue

Bismark, ND 58502-0727
Phone: 701-328-9749
Fax: 701-328-9750
www.governor.state.nd.us/boards/

OHIO
Division of Real Estate and Professional Licensing
77 South High Street, 20th Floor
Columbus, OH 43215-6133
Phone: 614-466-4100
Fax: 614-644-0584
www.com.state.oh.us/real/

OKLAHOMA
Real Estate Commission
Shepherd Mall
2401 N.W. 23rd Street, Suite 18
Oklahoma City, OK 73107
Phone: 405-521-3387 or 866-521-3389 toll-free
Fax: 405-521-2189
www.state.ok.us/orec/

OREGON
Real Estate Agency
1177 Center Street NE
Salem, OR 97301-2505
Phone: 503-378-4170
Fax: 503-378-2491
www.rea.state.or.us/

PENNSYLVANIA
Real Estate Commission
P.O. Box 2649
Harrisburg, PA 17105-2649
Phone: 717-783-3658
Fax: 717-787-0250
www.dos.state.pa.us/bpoa/site/default.asp

PUERTO RICO
Real Estate Board
P.O. Box 9023271
San Juan, PR 00902-3271
Phone: 787-722-0136 or 787-722-2122
Fax: 787-722-4818

RHODE ISLAND
Department of Business Regulation
233 Richmond Street, Suite 230
Providence, RI 02903
Phone: 401-222-2255
Fax: 401-222-6654
www.dbr.state.ri.us/

SOUTH CAROLINA
Department of Labor Licensing and Regulation
Real Estate Commission
P.O. Box 11847
Columbia, SC 29211-1847
Phone: 803-896-4400
Fax: 803-896-4404
www.llr.state.sc.us/POL/Realestatecommission/

SOUTH DAKOTA
Real Estate Commission
425 E. Capitol
Pierre, SD 57501
Phone: 605-773-3600
Fax: 605-773-4356
www.state.sd.us/dcr/realestate

TENNESSEE
Real Estate Commission
500 James Robertson Parkway
Davy Crockett Tower, Suite 180
Nashville, TN 37243-1151
Phone: 615-741-2273
Fax: 615-741-0313
www.state.tn.us/commerce/boards/trec/index.html

UTAH
Division of Real Estate
P.O. Box 146711
Salt Lake City, UT 84114-6711
Phone: 801-530-6747
Fax: 801-530-6749
www.commerce.utah.gov/dre/index.html

VERMONT
Office of Professional Regulation
Real Estate Commission

81 River Street, Drawer 9
Montpelier, VT 05609-1106
Phone: 802-828-3228
Fax: 802-828-2368
www.vtprofessionals.org/opr1/real_estate/

VIRGIN ISLANDS
Department of Licensing and Consumer Affairs
Golden Rock Shopping Center
Christiansted, St. Croix 00820, VI
Phone: 340-773-2226
Fax: 340-778-8250
www.dlca.gov.vi/forms/VI_REALESTATE_App.htm

VIRGINIA
Department of Professional and Occupational Regulation
3600 West Broad Street
Richmond, VA 23230
Phone: 804-367-8526
Fax: 804-367-2475
www.dba.state.va.us/licenses/

WEST VIRGINIA
Real Estate Commission
300 Capitol Street, Suite 400
Charleston, WV 25301
Phone: 304-558-3555
Fax: 304-558-6442
www.state.wv.us/wvrec

WISCONSIN
Bureau of Direct Licensing and Real Estate
1400 E. Washington Avenue
Box 8935
Madison, WI 53708
http://drl.wi.gov/prof/apps.htm

WYOMING
Real Estate Commission
2020 Carey Avenue, Suite 100
Cheyenne, WY 82002
Phone: 307-777-7141
Fax: 307-777-3796
http://realestate.state.wy.us/

Currently every state requires an applicant for a real estate sales license to pass an exam. Most of the states use one of the national testing companies to administer the tests. California is a major exception.

The national testing companies usually, but not always, administer the test on a testing computer. We recommend that you find out where you can practice using a testing computer (see question 22 in the preceding section, "Questions About Taking the Exam"). If you cannot get this information from the state, you should be able to obtain it from wherever you take the required classroom or online training. We highly recommend that you practice on a testing computer before you take the exam. Many students who fail the test attribute their failure to the stress caused by using a testing computer for the first time.

Here is information about the four major testing companies and California.

Applied Measurement Professionals, Inc. (AMP)
18000 W. 105th Street
Olathe, KS 66061-7543
Phone: 800-345-6559 or 913-895-4600
Fax: 913-895-4650
www.goamp.com

Subjects Covered	Number of Questions
Listing property	34
Selling property	22
Property management	12
Settlement/transfer of Ownership	17
Financing	12
Professional responsibilities/ fair practice/administration	3
	100

Note: At least 10 percent of the questions require mathematical calculation.

The exam may include additional (unidentified) questions that are being pretested and are not included in the scoring of the exam.

State of California
P.O. Box 187003
Sacramento, CA 95818-7003
Phone: 916-227-0931
Fax: 916-227-0925
www.dre.cahwnet.gov/licstats.htm

Subjects Covered	Number of Questions
Legal aspects	Unknown
Encumbrances	Unknown
Real estate law	Unknown
Financing escrow	Unknown
Contracts	Unknown
Taxation	Unknown
Subdivision	Unknown
Land descriptions	Unknown
Arithmetic	Unknown
Appraisal	Unknown
Definitions	Unknown

Note: At least 10 percent of the questions require mathematical calculation.

Thompson Prometrics (formerly Experior)
Metro Center
One Station Place
Stamford, CT 06902
Phone: 203-539-8000
Fax: 203-539-7734
www.prometric.com/default.htm

Subjects Covered (Different for Each State)	Percentage of Questions
Business practice and ethics	21%
Agency	15%
Property	17%
Property valuation and the appraisal process	6%
Real estate sales contracts	17%
Financing	9%
Closing/settlement and transferring title	10%
Property	5%
	100%

Note: At least 10 percent of the questions require mathematical calculation.
The exam may include additional (unidentified) questions that are being pretested and are not included in the scoring of the exam.

Promissor, Inc.
3 Bala Plaza West, Suite 300
Bala Cynwyd, PA 19004-3481
Phone: 610-617-9300
www.promissor.com

Subjects Covered	Number of Questions
Real property characteristics, definitions, ownership, restrictions, and transfer	16
Property valuation and appraisal process	6
Contracts and agency relationships with buyers and sellers	21
Property conditions and disclosures	6
Financing the transaction and settlement	17
Federal laws governing real estate activities (e.g., Federal Fair Housing Act, Americans with Disabilities Act, antitrust, marketing controls	6
Leases, rents, and property management	6
Brokerage operation	2
	80

Note: In addition to these national questions there will be up to 30 additional questions about state laws, rules, and regulations.

Note: At least 10 percent of the questions require mathematical calculation.
The exam may include additional (unidentified) questions that are being pretested and are not included in the scoring of the exam.

Psychological Services, Inc. (PSI)
100 West Broadway, Suite 1100
Glendale, CA 91210-1202
Phone: 800-733 9267
www.psiexams.com

Subjects Covered	Number of Questions
Property ownership	7
Land-use controls and regulations	7
Valuation and market analysis	7
Financing	8
Laws of agency	10
Mandated disclosures	6
Contracts	10
Transfer of property	7
Mathematics	5
Speciality areas (management, commercial, etc.)	3
Practice of real estate	10
	80

The exam may include additional (unidentified) questions that are being pretested and are not included in the scoring of the exam.

SUMMARY

An important purpose of this book and our unique test preparation system is to help you pass your real estate sales agent license exam. The important thing is to pass and not make yourself anxious because you do not think you know the answers to all the questions. Most states require only 70 percent of the questions to be answered correctly to pass. Many states do not release the scores of those people who pass.

Before you can take the examination you will need to take one or more courses as prescribed by your state. In those courses you will learn about the laws, regulations, and rules that apply to your state. There will be state-specific questions, usually mixed in with the other questions.

As soon as you decide to further consider getting a real estate agent's license, you should go to your state's Web site and obtain all the information you will need to qualify for the license.

Every year, well over 100,000 people pass their real estate license examinations. When you use this book as instructed, the chances are excellent that you will join them. Good luck!

CHAPTER 1

Test-Taking Tips

Test taking is not an everyday activity for most real estate professionals. Therefore, this chapter has been included to help you understand how best to prepare for your state's real estate agent's license examination. Be forewarned: There is no easy, secret, surefire, can't-miss, guaranteed-pass method for taking the test. Good preparation involves commitment, some hard work, and significant time expenditure.

The chapter is organized chronologically to focus on specific areas to keep in mind before, during, and after the exam. Nevertheless, it is a good idea to read all the material now and then review the recommendations for the actual test day as it approaches.

BEFORE THE TEST: BE PREPARED

The old Boy Scout motto is never more appropriate than when you are anticipating a test. There is, of course, no substitute for thorough knowledge and review of the subject matter on which you will be tested.

Your first step is to gather all the information that was covered in the Introduction. When you have the information you need, sit down and plan your time. Register for a test date that will allow you ample time to prepare and *sign up early.* In many places, certain test dates and centers fill up early and you might be assigned to a less convenient test date or location.

Now you need to consider two basic aspects of preparation, which are equally important. First, you need to know the material you will be tested on, and second, you need to acquire good test-taking skills.

STUDY—THERE IS *NO* SUBSTITUTE

To learn the material, you need to study. Again, the best approach is to start early. Assess your strengths and weaknesses honestly and overestimate the time you think you will need. Try to set aside a regular time for preparation, and stick to it. Most people who have trouble with exams overestimate their own knowledge and skill with standardized tests or underestimate the difficulty of the exam. So don't assume you know it all—review the material thoroughly.

Use as many information sources as you can. This helps reinforce what you already know and makes sure you cover all the material. Here are some suggestions for materials to review:

- The material covered in this book, including a review of the glossary of real estate terms so you are familiar with the appropriate jargon.
- Your real estate course(s)—reread this text, class notes, study guides, outlines, problem sets, test questions, and so on.
- Any information you have obtained from the testing or state licensing agency.
- Special prelicensing review courses—some people find these crash courses to be useful supplements, but most people find them unnecessary.

PRACTICE TEST-TAKING SKILLS

While you are studying your review material, you also need to be learning and fine-tuning specific test-taking skills. One of the best ways to do this is to take practice tests. These are available after each chapter in this book that covers material that is on the exams and in the special section containing additional practice examinations.

You should not use test taking as a substitute for studying. It is probably not wise to memorize test questions and answers, because they are only examples. No matter where you get the questions, they are not likely to be duplicated on an actual exam.

It is helpful to practice under conditions similar to those that will exist on test day. Apply the hints cited in the section entitled "During the Test" while you take each practice test. Practice budgeting your time so that you can finish the whole test, and when you have finished, spend some time reviewing your work. Learn from your errors, but also read the answers to the questions you answered correctly to reaffirm and expand your knowledge.

The overall objective is to develop a strategy for test day that works best for you as an individual. Use the practice tests to identify your strengths and weaknesses. For example, you might find that you make frequent math errors. In that case, you can practice using your calculator more slowly and carefully. It also might be worthwhile to double-check these answers. On the other hand, you might find the questions about titles and liens easy. In that case, you can confidently focus your studying on other material.

THE DAY OF THE TEST

The best thing you can do on test day is be *early;* if you arrive late, at best you will feel extra pressure and at worst you may not be allowed to take the exam as scheduled. Go to bed *early* the night before, so you are well rested. Get up *early,* so you are relaxed and not rushed. Eat a healthy breakfast, so your brain has plenty of energy, but don't overeat—it tends to make you sleepy.

Before you leave home, make sure you have everything you need. Generally, this includes:

- Exam entrance ticket
- Required identification
- Extra pencils with erasers
- Calculator (with extra fresh batteries!)
- Wristwatch
- Glasses or contact lenses

Leave for the test *early.* Test proctors hear the most amazing excuses for why examinees are late: getting lost, being unable to park, forgetting exam tickets, having a flat tire, getting stuck in heavy traffic, losing keys, encountering a broken elevator, and so on. Certainly you should get good directions to the test center (including where to park and how to get into the building), but the bottom line is, if you are early, all of these problems can usually be avoided or circumvented.

If you arrive early, you have time to relax, get coffee, read the newspaper, and do whatever else you need to put yourself into a positive frame of mind. To save time and prevent anguish during the test, it is also a good idea to locate and use the bathroom when you arrive.

BEFORE STARTING THE TEST

Try to find a seat that is comfortable, accommodates erect posture, is situated away from heating or cooling ducts, and offers adequate light. Many testing sites are located in modern buildings with modern furniture. However, some states give the tests in poorly lit rooms that are often too hot or too cold.

Listen to and follow the proctor's instructions carefully, even though you may be familiar with them from your practice tests. Remember that this is the best time to ask questions if anything is confusing. Fill in your name and other required information legibly and carefully.

Finally, when the proctor says to start, make note of the start and finish times on your scratch paper, so you can budget your time appropriately. Also, preview the whole test, noting how many and what types of questions there are. Make sure you aren't missing any of the test or its appendixes.

DURING THE TEST

Work Quickly and Carefully

It is important to be relaxed and confident. You have prepared well, and it does not help to worry now. You will achieve the best score by getting all the questions you know right and making good guesses on the ones you are unsure of. It is surprising how frequently stupid mistakes are made: marking "A," when you meant "B," reading the question or one of the answers incorrectly, filling in the wrong number on the answer sheet or computer, hitting the wrong button on your calculator, or the like. To prevent such errors, do not rush. Proceed as quickly as you can, and check your work as thoroughly as possible as you go.

Read Questions Thoroughly

Many errors are the result of rushing and skimming. For example, you might read *trustor* as *trustee* or *efficiency* as *deficiency* or be thinking of gross income when the question asks about net income. After you read each question, stop and think a moment before answering. By doing this, you will better understand what the question is asking and in most instances be able to look through the answer choices to find the one you want. This helps you avoid selecting a misleading answer.

Watch for Key Words

Frequently, questions will contain words such as *except, not, incorrect, must, best, normally,* and the like, in capital letters or bold or italic type. These are emphasized for a reason; they are vital clues in determining the correct answer and should set off an alarm in your head, telling you to focus on them. Be especially careful about negative questions to prevent common errors like picking a correct answer when the question asks for the *incorrect* one.

Read All the Answers

Remember that it is your job to pick the *best* answer. Don't get caught picking the first answer you read that sounds good—the next one might be better. Sometimes, this is straightforward, as in the case of numerical answers, because only one answer can be correct. However, often the best answer that you know is not one of the choices or several of the answers are at least partially correct. In that case, you have to use your judgment to pick the answer that is the most reasonable. It usually helps to start by ruling out the answers that are obviously wrong and get to the best one by a process of elimination.

Use Your Scratch Paper

The only thing that is graded is your answer sheet, so take advantage of your scratch paper and test book to make any notes or calculations that might help you. Underline important words; cross out wrong answers; circle correct ones; mark answers that are guesses; leave notes to yourself in the margins. All of these strategies can help you avoid careless mistakes, remind you of important words, and improve your reviewing skills if you have extra time.

The Answer Sheet or Screen

It is the answer sheet or the answers on the computer screen that will be graded, so fill in the blanks carefully and completely using the correct pencil or carefully enter the correct answers into the computer. You can avoid losing points by completely erasing any answers you change and leaving no stray marks. Fill in the answer sheet or computer screen as you go, so that you don't accidentally run out of time before transferring correct answers from your test book. This also keeps you from accidentally skipping an answer and entering answers out of sequence.

If the test is given on an automatic test-taking computer terminal, be sure you understand how the computer works. Most students like the computer test machines. Some states require you to use them when they are available. Other states permit you to request to use pencil and paper. You should check on your state's policy prior to the day of the test and not make this decision at the last minute. Unless you are truly afraid of the test-taking terminal, you should elect to use it.

It is important to ignore patterns on the answer sheet—for example, that the last seven answers have been "D" or there has not been an "A" in a long time. Answer the questions as asked and don't try to make your answers fit a pattern. One incorrect answer can alter a pattern and completely confuse you if you are looking for patterns.

Be careful when transferring answers from the test book to the answer sheet or the test terminal. Get in the habit of checking the question number against the number you are filling in and don't mark "B" when you mean to mark "C."

Guessing

Guessing is an art, but it can be practiced successfully. There are some tricks that can help. The first rule is not to lose your cool. There are always going to be some questions for which you can't determine the right answer, so don't panic, get sidetracked, and waste time. Instead, give yourself 20 or 30 seconds to try one of the approaches discussed next.

The Web site for your state's real estate authority will usually tell you whether you will be penalized for wrong answers. Most state tests do not penalize for wrong answers. When this is the case, you should answer every question, even if you make a wild guess.

Educated Guesses

Almost always there will be one or more answers given that are obviously wrong. Eliminating these will give you much-improved odds of guessing correctly. Also use other questions on the exam to help you. Frequently, the same subject matter will be tested with several questions and you may get a clue about the answer to one question from something you see later on.

Use the Answers

Some examinees are unfamiliar with multiple choice questions. Never forget that the answer *is* listed on the sheet in front of you. Simply reading all the answers and using common sense will often help. Also remember that only one answer is right, so if two of them say the same thing, both must be incorrect.

Absolute Words

Words like *all, none, always, never, must, cannot, every, no, absolutely, impossible, totally,* and *unique* have the effect of strengthening statements. When you see such words in an answer, it is *less likely* to be correct, because it refers to an absolute case. In contrast, qualifiers tend to generalize a statement and make it more likely to be true. These words include *may, possibly, often, sometimes,* and *usually.* Watch out for questions that ask for an *incorrect* statement; in that case, an absolute word in an answer would make that answer *more likely* to be the *correct* one.

If you are still stuck after trying these things, make a random guess and go on. There is nothing to gain and a lot to lose if you waste time puzzling about one answer. Remember that you get no points for blank spaces, so fill in something on your answer sheet.

As of this printing, none of these tests penalize for incorrect answers. However, to avoid being penalized for random guessing, check the exam you are taking to make sure this is still true.

Budget Your Time

As noted previously, it is a good idea to note the start and finish time for your exam. It is also helpful to reassess, every 15 minutes or so, where you stand. If you are ahead of pace, great! Keep going. If you are behind, don't panic; simply try to be more efficient. To catch up, focus on your strengths and answer all of the questions in those subjects, while skipping those in your weak areas. Remember that all the questions count the same, no matter how long they take to answer. Answer the brief or easy ones first, and leave the ones requiring a lot of reading, analysis, or calculation for later, especially if time is short.

The biggest trap to avoid is spending excessive time on a single question. Set an imaginary alarm clock in your mind to warn you when you have spent more than a minute or two on any question. If, after that time, an answer is not immediately forthcoming, force yourself to guess and go on. The question will still be there if you have time to come back to it. It is very likely that there are plenty of easy ones still to come and it would be tragic not to have time to answer those.

Another thing to keep in the back of your mind is that the questions on the exam are designed to be answered in a short period of time, usually about 90 seconds at the most. Therefore, *before* you embark on any long, involved calculations that will consume several minutes of valuable time, stop and think. There may be a simpler, shorter way to get to the answer. If you don't see it, guess and go on.

NUMERICAL ANSWERS

Questions that require a number for the answer have a slightly different spin that you should keep in mind. As noted previously, there is no best answer in such cases; one number is correct and the others are wrong. Often you will find that several of the answers are similar—they differ by only a decimal place or two of the digits are reversed. These are the traps set to catch those who are sloppy with their math, so be extra careful.

Rounding Off

Many questions will ask you to make calculations of things like mortgage payments or property taxes. Frequently the answer you calculate will not be a round dollar figure, but the answer choices will all be in whole dollars. In these cases, the test makers should not be trying to confuse you by giving as answer choices two quantities that are very close together. For example, if you calculate the annual debt service on a loan to be $867.56, the correct answer might be $867 or $868 or even $870, but not more than one of these would be a choice among the possible answers listed. If two answers are very close to the number you calculate, it is more likely that you have made an error in calculation than that only one of them is the correct answer.

Estimate

This is a quick and simple way to get the right answer in math problems or at least eliminate some of the answers. For example, a question might ask you to figure the mean selling price for five homes priced at $65,000, $66,000, $67,500, $68,000, and $75,000. A rough estimate would be about $68,000, since most of the values are at the low end of the range and you could certainly eliminate all the answers above, say, $70,000 or below $66,000. Another example would be a question that asked you to calculate a homeowner's equity after the person has made half of the mortgage payments. At any realistic interest rate, you could guess that the equity would be less than half the mortgage, because you know that the amount of a mortgage decreases at a greater rate at the end of the mortgage than at the beginning.

USE THE INFORMATION GIVEN

Many times, examinees neglect to use all the available data. If there are compound interest tables, diagrams, maps, or other materials attached to the test, use them.

IGNORE THOSE AROUND YOU

Do not concern yourself if the person next to you flips pages faster than you, makes more notes than you, uses a calculator more or less frequently than you, or leaves halfway through the exam. The last thing you want to do is anything a proctor might construe as cheating. Focus on your work, and use your time fully.

EXTRA TIME

There is nothing to gain by leaving the exam early. Since you have spent a lot of time, energy, and money to prepare for this day, make the most of it. The difference between passing and failing is only one point, and most people who fail miss passing by only a few points. Very few people score far below the passing level, so one or two points is really worth the extra few minutes it may take.

CHECK ANSWERS

It is worthwhile to review any questions you can, regardless of whether you guessed or feel absolutely sure you got the right answer. On the questions you feel confident about, simply make sure you did not make a stupid error. Review any notes or calculations you made on your scratch paper or on the test book to make sure you were approaching the question correctly and re-member the *key words*.

Probably the best ways to confirm an answer are to either work backward or try a different approach. Working backward means looking at the answer first and then seeing if it fits the question. In math problems, you can calcu-late backward and make sure you come out with the original numbers given in the question stem. Trying a different approach works similarly. If you made a simple mistake or an erroneous assumption in getting the original an-swer, you might avoid that pitfall by taking a different path. For example, in a math problem, you might try estimating to see if your final answer is in the right ballpark.

UNANSWERED QUESTIONS

Looking at things from a different angle or sometimes simply coming back to a question after a break may shed a whole new light on the problem. In these cases, you may be able to answer some questions you skipped or guessed about previously. If you are still stuck, make a reasonable guess.

One student who reported failing by two questions admitted leaving 10 questions (mostly math) unanswered. Had the person guessed on all 10, the odds are very much in favor of getting at least two correct and thus passing the test.

CHANGING ANSWERS

There is an important myth about changing answers that is important to dispel. Many of your colleagues, teachers, or even other texts will tell you to *always* stick with your first impression. This is *not* the best way to proceed, for several reasons. First, you often find a glaring error in your approach to a question. Furthermore, recent psychological testing has shown that when examinees change their answers for any substantiated reason, their scores tend to improve. The hesitation to change comes from the fact that when test answers are reviewed, examinees tend to focus on the few answers they changed from correct to incorrect, while forgetting or ignoring those changes that turned out to be correct. This is not to say that you should change answers for the sake of changing, but if you find an error, do not hesitate to correct it.

THE LAST FEW MINUTES

Most proctors will give you a warning when time is running out. However, don't simply assume they will. Keep track of the time left yourself. At this juncture, your time is usually best spent checking your answers. Make sure you have filled in all the blanks. Quickly double-check that you have been transcribing answers correctly from the test book to the answer sheet or terminal, and fully erase any stray marks.

AFTER THE TEST

Before leaving the exam room, if it is a written test, review your answer sheet one more time. Make sure your name is written legibly and there are no stray marks. If you need to correct or erase something after time has been called (for example, your address or telephone number), confer with the proctor first so you are not accused of irregular activity. Finally, make sure you have turned in all your exam materials.

SUMMARY

Test taking is difficult and a cause of worry and apprehension for most adults. By far the best thing you can do before a test is study the material. Go over the many review questions in this text. Concentrate on areas that are difficult for you or that you don't know thoroughly. Don't waste your time studying material you know well.

Get to the examination place early. Don't rush. Review your work. Good luck!

Congratulations! More than likely you will pass your exam and be well on the road to successfully meeting the requirements for a real estate agent's license. However, if you do fail, do not despair; it is not the end of the world. Consider your experience as practice, so when you retake the exam you will be in a better position to pass. A very high percentage of people who fail an examination the first time they take it pass it on the second try. Be sure to follow the instructions in the Introduction of this book for how to use it to review the material and focus on what you do not know.

CHAPTER 2

Do You Have What It Takes to Sell a House?

Fortunately for you it is not a simple thing to sell a house. If it were, everyone would sell their own house and avoid paying a substantial commission.

Because it takes a variety of skills, knowledge, and experience to sell a house, most houses are sold by licensed and trained real estate agents and brokers. The difference between a real estate agent and a real estate broker is covered in Chapter 4. For the purposes of this chapter, we will call them all *real estate sales professionals* (RESPs). When you become an RESP your official title depends on which state you are in and whom you choose to represent in each transaction in which you become involved.

The National Association of Realtors (NAR) is the largest trade organization in the United States. It has over 1 million members who make selling houses their career. Each year they sell millions of houses (there are over 100 million houses in the United States). Almost half of all the licensed agents and brokers belong to the NAR. Only members of the NAR can call themselves Realtors because the term is a registered trademark owned by the organization.

Is every RESP successful? Of course not! If they were all successful there would be no room in the real estate sales profession for you.

People who succeed in real estate sales will tell you they have discovered that there are not many other things they could do that are as challenging and exciting as a career in real estate. People who choose real estate as a career are people who want meaningful work that pays well.

It is common for someone considering real estate sales as a career to ask what makes a successful RESP. Unfortunately, there does not seem to be a simple answer to this question. One thing for sure is that RESPs come from very widely divergent backgrounds.

We have met successful RESPs who formerly were taxi drivers, supermarket cashiers, beauticians, medical doctors, nurse's aides, retired military personnel, and so on. The backgrounds of the over 1 million Realtors most likely include just about every known job description and profession.

Another way to look at it is that there are four broad groups of people who enter the real estate profession at a rate of about 250,000 new people each year.

- Group #1: People who are just out of school and choose real estate as their career. They range from students who have studied little or nothing about real estate as part of their general education to those who have advanced college degrees in real estate or real estate–related subjects. Another group of first career seekers are those who prepared for some other career while in school and then decided to try real estate instead.
- Group #2: Currently employed men and women who have spent time in a career and then decide to make a career change into real estate.
- Group #3: Men and women who have dropped out of the workforce for a variety of reasons and then decide to return to work later in their lives in a new career in real estate
- Group #4: Retirees who, for a variety of reasons, have decided to reenter the workforce either full- or part-time.

There is no significant study indicating which of these groups is most successful in the real estate profession.

IS A CAREER IN REAL ESTATE FOR ME?

Here are 10 questions to ask yourself to determine if a career in real estate is for you. If you score less than five correct answers you may want to think twice before choosing a career in real estate sales.

1. Do I like to sell things? (Yes or No)

2. Do I like to receive a paycheck each week? (Yes or No)

3. Do I deal well with rejection? (Yes or No)

4. Does my lifestyle make it easy for me to work on weekends? (Yes or No)

5. Do I mind taking telephone calls at home in the evening? (Yes or No)

6. Am I able to ask embarrassing questions when I need information or do I tend to ask others to get it for me? (Yes or No)

7. Can I tell a friend "No, thank you" when the person offers to do something for me but I'd rather that they didn't? (Yes or No)

8. Am I often afraid to give people advice because I fear that if the advice is taken it could turn out to be bad advice? (Yes or No)

9. Do I often ask friends and relatives to help me? (Yes or No)

10. Have I ever used a calculator for anything other than adding and subtracting? (Yes or No)

The answers that indicate you are suitable for selling real estate are: 1. Yes, 2. No, 3. Yes, 4. Yes, 5. No, 6. Yes, 7. Yes, 8. No, 9. Yes, 10. Yes

The more correct answers you have the more likely you are cut out to be a successful and happy RESP.

SELLING REAL ESTATE IS A LIFESTYLE, NOT A JOB

Most successful RESPs love to make sales. What makes them happiest is putting together a successful transaction. Conversely, when a deal falls through, they brush it off, do not take it personally, and move on to the next transaction. Most of them have no idea how many potential deals they failed to close. They only count the sales they make.

If you are the type who tells your friends, "It does not matter if you win or lose, it only matters how you play the game," this may be an indication that a real estate sales career is not for you.

However, even this rule has its exceptions. One of the most successful RESPs we know worked only from nine to five and never on weekends or holidays. His theory was that only serious buyers and sellers would use him because of the inconvenient hours. This strategy worked for him, but he was probably the exception that proves the rule. Most successful RESPs are available 24/7/365 and don't care how much it takes to close a transaction.

SELF-MOTIVATION

The accepted wisdom is that to be a successful RESP you need to be self-motivated. There is little doubt that being self-motivated is helpful. However, if only self-motivated people succeed, why are there so many weekly sales motivation meetings at the big real estate offices and why do motivational speakers draw such large audiences?

HARD WORK

Common wisdom also holds that you have to be a hard worker to succeed as an RESP. Certainly hard work can't hurt—or maybe it can.

It is possible for RESPs to make an excellent living without killing themselves. When asked how, they usually reply that the trick is to work smart, not hard.

It is very easy to waste a lot of time in real estate sales. Probably the biggest waste of time is an overpriced listing. There is an old myth believed by many people that if you wait long enough someone will come along and give an owner of an overpriced listing what they are asking for the property. Nothing can be further from the truth. Most overpriced listings do not sell until the owner reduces the asking price.

The question you have to ask yourself is whether you can say "No, thank you" to friends or relatives when they offer you an overpriced listing, thinking that they are helping you in your new career.

THE ABILITY TO WORK WITH EVERYONE

Another skill that successful RESPs are supposed to have is the ability to work with all kinds of people. As nice as this sounds, it is not necessarily true.

There are successful RESPs who limit their business to working only with segments of the population they want to work with—for example, retired military personnel, young couples, gay couples, millionaires, or first-time home buyers. One of the nice things about real estate is that you get to choose whom you want to work with. However, there is one limitation: your choice cannot be based on discrimination as defined in the antidiscrimination laws.

SUMMARY

The first step in starting a real estate sales career is to obtain a real estate sales license. A substantial portion of this book is designed to help you accomplish this task. What you will officially be called when you pass your license exam will depend on the state in which you are located. Real estate licensing and selling is regulated individually by each of the 50 states.

Although not everyone agrees, there are many advantages to immediately becoming employed by a broker who is a member of the NAR. There are likewise many advantages for you to join the NAR as soon as you are eligible.

Real estate sales is an exciting and rewarding career that pays well if you are successful. What makes a successful RESP is hard to define because successful RESPs are so diverse. Thousands of people from the four categories we've identified in this chapter get their real estate sales licenses each year and go on to become successful RESPs, although a substantial number of people who obtain their real estate sales licenses go to work for a broker and leave the real estate field within a year. It is likely that if some of these people had had the financial ability to stick it out for a second year, they too would have been successful.

The 10-question self-grading quiz presented in this chapter may help you decide whether real estate sales is for you. There is no passing or failing score; this test simply points out personality characteristics that might be an indication of your future success.

Real estate is more than a job; it's a way of life. Friends and relatives will identify you as being in real estate.

Self-motivation, hard work, and the ability to work with all kinds of people are characteristics that many successful RESPs possess—although there are many exceptions.

The authors of this book (who are very different types of people) have had successful real estate careers and love what they do. Henry S. Harrison, for example, started in 1956 and has no intention of retiring soon. Real estate has been really good to him and his family. We hope it will do the same for you.

CHAPTER 3

Becoming a Successful Real Estate Agent

The first step you need to take after you have passed the real estate license examination is to find a real estate broker to work for who will assume the responsibility for all your real estate activities. In most states, you have to physically hang your license in the broker's office. Some brokers recruit potential real estate sales agents before they obtain their licenses. Some offer free training to potential licensees who indicate that they want to become real estate agents.

Before you start working, you need to have an agreement that at a minimum covers whether you are an employee or an independent contractor. Most real estate salespeople are independent contractors. This means that they are paid a commission that is based on their sales. An independent contractor can be given a weekly draw against future sales they make. Theoretically, they could be required to pay back any draw they received in excess of their earned commissions, but this is not the typical arrangement.

An employee must be paid based on the number of hours worked, and the amount of pay must be at least the minimum wage required in the state where they are located. They must also be paid overtime for any work they do over 40 hours per week. They can be paid bonuses based on sales they make.

Whichever status is elected (employee or independent contactor), there should be a written contract between the real estate sales agent and the broker about how commissions that are earned as a result of the real estate sales agent's efforts will be divided between the broker and the real estate sales agent. The agreement should also include what expenses can be deducted from the commission before it is divided between the real estate sales agent and the broker. The employment contract arrangement between the selling agent and the real estate broker may cover a variety of other items, such as what expenses are paid by the listing agent and the selling agent. The listing agent may have to pay for advertising, telephone, office overhead, transportation, health insurance, and so on. The selling agent may have to pay for telephone, office overhead, transportation, health insurance, gifts to buyers and sellers, and so on.

The contract may also cover work rules such as the requirement that the sales agent work full-time, conform to a dress code, cover the office during specified hours (also known as floor time), and so on.

SPLITTING COMMISSIONS

Commission-splitting arrangements must cover all the possible commissions received by the broker as a result of the work of the real estate sales agent. This must include commissions received from other brokers who sold a listing for the real estate sales agent as well as commissions received because they sold a listing from another broker's office.

Following are some examples of how the commission might be split on the sale of a $200,000 house. The Federal Trade Commission (FTC) has strict rules against any group getting together to fix commission rates or commission-splitting arrangements. The FTC requires that every commission and fee-splitting arrangement be individually negotiated. The commissions and fee-splitting arrangements used in these examples have been arbitrarily selected by the authors and are not represented to be typical commissions or fee-splitting arrangements.

Example #1

An RESP lists a house and sells it for $200,000. The negotiated commission is 6 percent. The commission-splitting arrangement between the RESP and the broker is 50 percent of the commission to the selling agent and 50 percent to the broker:

Sales price: $200,000
Commission: 6%
Total commission: $200,000 × .06 = $12,000
RESP's share: 50% or $12,000 × .50 = $6,000
Broker's share: 50% or $12,000 × .50 = $6,000

Example #2

An RESP sells a house for $200,000 that was listed by another broker's office. The total negotiated commission paid by the seller is 6 percent. The commission-splitting arrangement between the listing broker's office and the selling broker's office is 50 percent of the commission each. The commission-splitting arrangement between the real estate salesperson in the selling broker's office and the broker is 50 percent of the commission to the RESP and 50 percent to the broker:

Sales price: $200,000
Commission: 6%
Total commission: $200,000 × .06 = $12,000
Selling broker's office: 50% = $12,000 × .50 = $6,000
Listing broker's office: 50% = $12,000 × .50 = $6,000
Selling broker's 50% is $6,000 × .50 = $3,000
RESP's 50% of their broker's office commission is $6,000 × .50 = $3,000

Example #3

An RESP lists a house for $200,000 that is sold by another RESP in the same broker's office. The commission-splitting arrangement between the RESP in the broker's office and the broker is 25 percent of the commission to the listing agent and 25 percent to the selling RESP:

Sales price: $200,000
Commission: 6%
Total commission: $200,000 × .06 = $12,000
Broker's office receives 100% = $12,000
Selling RESP's 25% is $12,000 × .25 = $3,000
Listing RESP's 25% is $12,000 × .25 = $3,000

These three examples demonstrate that when the RESP's arrangement with the broker is 50 percent of the commission the broker receives, the RESP usually receives 25 percent of the commission unless the RESP sells his or her own listing, in which case the RESP receives 50 percent of the commission.

WHAT IT TAKES TO SELL A HOUSE

Getting Your Own Listings

The single best thing RESPs can do to ensure success is to obtain their own listings where the asking price is within 10 percent of what the ultimate selling price will be.

The best sources of new listings are friends and relatives. When a very successful broker with a large office was asked why it didn't disturb him that so many sales agents lasted for only a year, his reply was that even during the first year, he had made a profit from many of the new agents. He further explained that they were a good source of new listings and clients for the office because their relatives and friends tried to help them get started by giving them listings and finding good listings for them from among their wider circle of friends and acquaintances.

Many positive things happen when you obtain a good listing. Right away, other agents and brokers in your office recognize your accomplishment and focus on selling your listing to their customers.

When you list a property with a multiple listing service (MLS), other agents and brokers in your market area will show the property, and often they will sell it.

When you advertise the property, you will meet potential buyers. Even if they do not buy the house, they will provide you with a base of new customers to whom to show other houses that are not your listings. No matter who sells the house, you will earn a commission. You will have to share the commission with the selling broker, but half a loaf is better than no bread at all, as the saying goes.

One of the best ways to get a new listing is to sell the one you have. That is why successful RESPs try to leave their SOLD signs up for as long as possible in front of properties that have been sold. This basically constitutes free advertising about an agent's successful activity on behalf of the seller, and anyone who drives or walks by the house will see that.

It is often said that each house an RESP sells leads to two new listings.

MULTIPLE LISTING SERVICES

A multiple listing service (MLS) is an operation often run by a local organization that is part of the NAR. A recent change in the real estate business is the growth of independent MLS systems. The other recent change is access to MLS systems through the Internet.

MLS systems operated by Realtors tend to be well run and tightly controlled. In the past, only members of the local real estate board had access to Realtor-operated MLS systems. This exclusivity is being challenged in the courts, and some MLS systems have already open access to nonmembers and the public.

Traditionally, in the pre-Internet days, information about listed properties was published in books that were distributed as often as weekly. Some MLS systems still use books. However, most MLS systems are now computerized.

One of the best ways to use the MLS system, besides putting your own listing on it, is to find listed houses that would be suitable for potential customers who had looked at your listing but did not buy it. Knowing what your potential client wants gives you an edge in trying to find something they will like.

In the process of showing customers your listing, you have an opportunity to develop a relationship. You must learn how to distinguish serious buyers from lookers, or you may find yourself wasting a lot of time.

You should ask those potential customers who seem like serious buyers if you can show them some houses you think might be suitable for them. Then you can use the MLS to find houses they might be interested in seeing.

Smart RESPs create an extensive database of every client and potential client with whom they have spent time showing their own and other listings. Follow-up calls, cards, and other methods can help you "farm" this ever-increasing pool of potential business. (More details on farming are provided later in this chapter.)

FINDING THE RIGHT BUYER

Not everyone who looks at a house for sale is what is known as a *qualified buyer*. Many are just lookers who will waste your time because looking at houses is a form of recreation for them. Like Sunday drivers, they can tie you up in nonproductive "traffic."

Qualifying Buyers

Other buyers are serious about buying a house but do not realize they cannot afford to buy the type of house they desire. When they find a house they want and make an offer that is accepted, it may turn out that they will not be able to obtain the mortgage they need. Not only does this waste your time, it also distresses the sellers, who fault you for taking their house off the market during the mortgage application process. Instead of being a source of future recommendation for you, they bad-mouth you to their friends and relatives. You should avoid this situation if at all possible. As in many other personal service businesses, word of mouth about your reputation and skills is probably the single most important result of your involvement with clients and potential clients. A good reputation is like money in the bank.

Many RESPs have trouble qualifying potential buyers because they find it embarrassing to ask for the personal financial information that is required. If you can't do it yourself, you must get someone else to do it for you. You cannot afford to waste time on unqualified buyers.

Once you have qualified potential buyers, you should know how much they can afford to spend for a house. Showing them houses that are more expensive than they can afford is a waste of your time and theirs.

Generally, buyers tell you the truth, but not always. For example, during the qualifying process, they might forget to tell you that their in-laws are providing the down payment, or they might be reluctant to tell you about alimony payments or that they have large credit card debt. You need to probe carefully to be sure you have a complete financial picture so that you can work appropriately for your clients, and for yourself.

Helping the Buyers Make an Offer

Successful RESPs often have to use some psychology to get prospective buyers to make an offer on a house they are considering.

Keep in mind that buying a house is usually the biggest financial decision people make. There are a lot of psychological factors that get in the way of buyers making an offer. To help them overcome their fears, RESPs need to demonstrate a very positive attitude about the house the buyers are considering.

Studies show that people do not want to overpay for something they buy and that this has little to do with the actual money involved. It is more a matter of self-esteem. Most houses can be bought for less than the asking price, so buyers should be encouraged to make a reasonable offer. Keep in mind that the initial offer is often refused and more often than not you will have to get the buyers to increase their offer. Each time you have to go back and forth between buyers and sellers, the harder it becomes to consummate the sale.

Without lying, you should remind your clients that by procrastinating they run the risk of losing the house to some other buyer. You should share your enthusiasm for the house as an appropriate choice for their needs.

Persuading the Sellers to Accept the Offer

A moment of truth arrives when you have received a reasonable offer from a qualified buyer and it is up to you to close the deal. Some agents have told me that the adrenaline rush they experience when this happens is what keeps them in the business.

Agents and brokers must be careful to keep in mind where their primary loyalty lies. This depends on whether they are buyers' agents or sellers' agents.

It is in everyone's best interest to make the sale at a fair price. You are the catalyst that can make this happen.

Deals cool off like hot coffee left on the table; it is your job to keep them hot. You do this by hustling. As soon as you obtain the signed offer with a deposit, you should contact the sellers or listing brokers and tell them with excitement in your voice what a great offer you have just received. Don't wait!

Present the offer as soon as you receive it. Emphasize that time is of the essence and you don't want the buyer to cool off.

Remind sellers, if this is their first offer, that every RESP has horror stories to tell about sellers who turn down a first offer only to regret in the future that they did not accept it. Sooner or later you will probably lose a sale because you did not act fast enough. Then you will know firsthand how important speed and tenacity are in real estate transactions.

Helping Buyers Obtain a Mortgage

How difficult it will be for the buyers to obtain a mortgage depends mostly on where in the mortgage lending cycle the economy is at the time. In the early 2000s, lenders were falling over themselves to make mortgages. Brokers and agents were doing a favor for those to whom they steered their customers. It was up to the lenders to make the mortgages; otherwise, they would stop getting the agent's or broker's business.

At the time this book was written, the mortgage market was beginning to tighten up, making it necessary for RESPs to be knowledgeable about which lenders were most suitable for particular buyers. Lenders who prefer to make loans to wealthy people with large down payments may not be suitable for first-time buyers with small down payments. A different lender might be best for buyers with less-than-perfect credit histories. It is up to the RESPs to determine where to send their clients for help. You don't want to lose a sale because the loan application was turned down. When a potential sale cools off, it often cannot be reheated.

Getting Ready for the Closing

The manner in which closings are handled depends on where the RESP is located. RESPs need to be familiar with the closing procedures throughout the market in which they are operating. Sometimes they are the same statewide. In other places, such as Connecticut, the process varies from town to town.

As an RESP, you need to know the steps required to arrange a closing and the materials that all parties must have ready in order for the closing to take place smoothly and without extra stress.

Don't just sit around and wait for the closing to happen. Be proactive and arrange for it to take place as soon as possible. Don't let the sale get cold! A condition known as "buyers' remorse" often sets in as soon as a contract is signed. To avoid this, keep in close communication with all parties to the transaction. In particular, let your clients feel your concern for them and your enthusiasm for the deal—don't underestimate how contagious your feelings can be. Also, making sure that you are easily accessible can head off any potential problems before they get in the way. Don't abandon your clients once they've signed the contract. Your goal is to move them to a speedy closing that results in a completed sale.

You should have a list of everything needed for the closing and who will be bringing the documents and payments involved. It is your job to make sure *everyone* produces what is needed in a timely, professional, and non-frantic manner.

WHAT THE SALES AGENT OFFERS THE PUBLIC

Even today with the Internet and the public's access to many MLS systems, it is still difficult for owners to sell their own house.

Experience has shown that new RESPs can usually obtain listings from their friends, neighbors, and relatives soon after they go into business. New listings are a great beginning for a new RESP. Other agents in their office recognize their accomplishment in signing up new clients. The clients to whom you show your listing become potential customers for other houses listed through your office and/or available on the MLS.

The sale of one listing often leads to other listings from people who are aware of the sale and recognize your success in accomplishing it.

Psychological Reinforcement

One of the most important services RESPs provide that cannot be provided by owners trying to sell their own house is the psychological reinforcement many buyers need to make an offer, enter negotiations with the sellers, come to an agreement, and close the deal.

Arranging Financing

Many buyers also need help in obtaining financing. RESPs develop ongoing relationships with lending sources in the community to help point their clients in the right direction for loans that meet their needs.

Keeping Buyers Enthusiastic

Deals tend to cool off. The RESP's enthusiasm helps keep the sale from becoming cold. It is not a given that once a sales contract has been signed by all parties, the sale will close. A variety of problems can arise and become deal breakers. Keeping buyers enthusiastic about their purchase can head off buyers' remorse and help make the RESP successful in closing the sale.

Bringing Professionalism to the Process

One of the best sources of new business is a closing from which everyone emerges happy. When we sold our house a few years ago, the RESP arrived with a dozen long-stem French roses for both the buyer and the seller. My wife immediately went to work to find her another listing. Developing a reputation for being a class act can help you build on your successes.

WHAT IT (REALLY) TAKES TO SELL A HOUSE

Obtaining a Listing

Many real estate professionals believe that the most profitable way RESPs can spend their time is obtaining good listings. There is an old saying in the real estate business: "If you list, you last."

We believe that the single best thing RESPs can do to ensure their success is to try to obtain listings where the asking price is within 10 percent of what the ultimate selling price will be.

Listings are to the real estate business what merchandise is to a retail store. The problem is that it is very easy to waste a lot of time on an overpriced listing. Clients and potential clients do not feel confident if their RESP shows them obviously overpriced houses that are beyond their means or not in keeping with the market. Make sure to let your clients know that you have other listings you would be happy to show them.

New agents should always ask the office manager (or their supervisor) if any salespeople have left the office and gone out of the real estate business. It is possible that their listings—both active and expired—have already been turned over to another agent. However, quite often this has not happened and new agents are allowed to follow up on these listings.

RESPs shouldn't be afraid to follow up on expired listings, either. Often owners who have allowed listings to lapse will try to sell their houses unsuccessfully themselves and will come to the conclusion that they are going to need help. Since they already know the office, it is quite possible that a new agent who asks them to relist their property will meet with success. Sometimes this second listing is better than the first one, as the sellers may be highly motivated to negotiate price at this point. Prior disappointment can be the basis for active and energetic RESPs to make their clients very happy by effectively marketing and selling their properties.

Other Sources of New Listings

Absentee Homeowners

In many localities it is relatively easy to produce a list of houses that are not owner occupied and that have *absentee owners*. The assessor or tax collector is a good source for contact information about these owners.

Builders and Remodelers

Small builders and remodelers often become disenchanted with their existing agent, especially when the market is slowing down. The fact that you have contacted them may convince them that you are aggressive enough to do a good job selling their houses.

Employees

You or members of your family may have employees. Without pressuring them, you can let them know that you are in the real estate sales business and would appreciate their patronage.

Expired Listings

Every time you show a house, you should keep notes on what you saw inside it. When the listing expires (there are a variety of ways to determine when a listing expires) you can contact the owners, remind them that you have shown their house, and also tell them that you think you can sell it for them.

Some of the reasons you can give them are that you are active in the market area and have a backlog of clients who are potential buyers for their house. Explain the advantages of listing a house through the MLS system. Remind them that you can provide the psychological reinforcement the potential buyers need to make an offer and to keep up their enthusiasm during the time of the offer to the final closing so that they don't cool off. Finally, point out that you have the skills needed to obtain the necessary financing.

Friends and Relatives

Be sure to let your friends and relatives know that you are in the real estate business. Everyone likes to be helpful. Don't be afraid to ask them for their help—nobody is insulted by this. That is why we take the time to give complete strangers directions!

Houses for Sale by Their Owners (FSBOs)

Whenever a house becomes FSBO on your farm, you should immediately contact the sellers and tell them you have buyers looking for houses in their neighborhood. If you have done a good job of farming, they will already know about you. Fortunately for RESPs, many FSBOs do not succeed and the owners end up using an agent when they fail to get results on their own.

Recommendations from Potential Buyers Who Liked You and Your Service

It should become part of your standard practice to ask all potential buyers to whom you show houses whether they know anyone else who might list their house with you. If they like you, they can be a good source of business. Be sure to give them your business card and maybe a small gift inscribed with your contact information—for example, a refrigerator magnet—so that they will know where to find you if they want to contact you in the future.

The Importance of Farming: An Overview

Many of the topics discussed in this chapter are aspects of *farming*. Here is the big picture of how it is done.

Stake Out Your Farm

First, select an area on which you want to focus your efforts. The basis of this selection may include where your friends live, the type of houses in the area, the school district, the languages spoken there, or any of a variety of factors.

Make a Map

Create a map of your potential farm using a reliable Internet source such as Google Earth. Don't make your farm too large. A good start would be 250 to 300 houses. You can always expand it.

Keep Good Records

Thorough and accurate record keeping is the secret of good farming. You should have a card or computer record of every house on your farm (this is why the number of properties should not be too big). Each record should include the name of the owner, contact information, information about the property's last sale, and any current listings. Whenever you meet owners, speak to them on the phone, fax, or e-mail them, make a record of it. Whenever you have any spare time, farm. You do this by sending letters, dropping off flyers, and making cold calls during which you introduce yourself and explain that you are a real estate professional specializing in their neighborhood.

Cold-Calling to Prospective Seller Lists

It is a good idea to study a map and decide on a territory where you will specialize. This is the first step in farming. Using a cross-reference telephone directory, online directory, or other information sources available in your market area, compile a list of homes. Then call each of the homes in your area to introduce yourself and ask if the house is for sale. You may receive any of a variety of different replies. Regardless of the replies you receive, you need to be creative in answering them.

Cold-Calling Phone Responses

Here are some scenarios you might encounter when you are cold-calling, and how you should respond in each case.

"I don't take calls from strangers." Follow up with a letter introducing yourself, and then soon after that, make another call asking whether they received the letter and if you can talk to them about selling their house.

"I am just visiting." Ask who the owner is and when it is a good time to reach them.

"I am not the owner; I just rent." Ask who the owner is and how they can be contacted. Keep in mind that you can also get this information from the town hall assessor or tax collector's office.

"The house is listed with another agent." Ask when the listing expires and call back then, or wait a month or so and call back.

"I don't want to sell my house." Ask whether they know of any neighbors or friends who want to sell, mentioning that you have buyers looking for houses in their neighborhood.

OTHER CONSIDERATIONS

How to Choose a Company to Work For

Offices have reputations just as RESPs do, and it is important to try to associate with a company that is well known in your community for professionalism and effectiveness. When you are choosing an office to work for, one of the things to consider is how much training and help the personnel there is willing to give you. How knowledgeable is the rest of the staff? Is there high turnover? Have the managing partners been with the company for many years? What is the atmosphere of the office? Is it frantic or well organized, attractive, and orderly? Where is the main office located? Is the geographic area that the office serves going to be convenient and accessible for you?

Maximize Use of the MLS

Many MLS systems store data about both properties that are currently being offered in the market and properties that were sold, rented, exchanged, optioned, or withdrawn. This information is very useful in helping to make a competitive market analysis (CMA), which the RESP uses as a tool to help property owners determine the best listing price for their property. It can also provide data that will allow you to forecast trends in your farming area and offer your clients the most current properties to review.

Computers have the capability to screen every property in the MLS and select those that meet highly specific criteria, based on information about the client's specific needs. The more clearly you help your clients identify their needs and wishes, the more useful the MLS can be in helping to find their future home.

SUMMARY

Choosing to become an RESP means the beginning of a fascinating, exciting, and rewarding career. It also has been the route to personal prosperity for millions of people.

A home is usually the largest purchase most people ever undertake. Being an RESP means helping people realize their dream of homeownership. It can be frustrating at times, and it is not an easy living, but it can also be very satisfying to become a knowledgeable, reputable, and successful RESP.

CHAPTER 4

Becoming a Real Estate Broker

In most states real estate agents have to work for a real estate broker for several years before they are eligible to take the broker examination that permits them to become a real estate broker.

Real estate agents are salespeople who spend the bulk of their time and energy obtaining listings and selling real estate.

Real estate brokers are businesspeople who run businesses that sell real estate and offer other real estate services. They rely heavily on real estate sales agents to do the bulk of the selling. It is common for the broker to perform other real estate–related functions such as leasing, management, appraising, and insurance (appraising and insurance require separate licenses and certifications). They often hire and supervise real estate sales agents who focus primarily on selling houses and other types of real estate.

STARTING A BROKERAGE OFFICE

Typically, after a few sales have been made, the selling agents ask themselves, "Would I not be better off in my own office? If I had my own office, I would receive a bigger share of the commissions I have earned." In order to help answer this question the following is a brief description of the real estate brokerage business.

Real Estate Brokerage

Most real estate brokerage firms are small businesses. These include those using such well-known names as Century 21, ReMax, and Coldwell Banker. These well-known national names are primarily franchises to independent brokerage firms who use their national names and avail themselves of the many other services the franchisor provides the individual broker (franchisee). Some of the franchisors own some of the brokerage offices within their system.

Running a small business has its rewards and challenges. It requires an additional set of skills to run a real estate brokerage office besides being able to sell real estate.

Franchise Office versus Unaffiliated Brokerage Business

National real estate franchises offer many services to a real estate broker. They play an important role in the real estate industry. It is estimated that over 25 percent of real estate brokerage offices are now affiliated with a national franchise. Most of them either operate under the name of the national franchise or combine the national franchise name with their own name.

Here are a few of the things that a national franchise does for its franchisees:

- Help locate and set up offices
- Provide advertising and promotion help
- Provide training
- Give the brokerage office name recognition
- Provide relocation customer leads

History of Real Estate Brokerage

Prior to World War II brokerage offices typically were small independent offices with small staffs and often a family enterprise. Most states did not require a real estate license to either sell real estate or run a brokerage office.

The general pattern of a residential sales office (most offices were primarily residential sales offices) was simple. The real estate broker obtained a listing, advertised it, showed it to prospective customers and some of the time obtained an offer and deposit, negotiated the sale with the seller, eventually brought both parties into an agreement, arranged for a closing, and collected a commission at the closing.

In those days it was relatively clear that legally the broker was an agent of the seller and was supposed to represent the seller's best interests throughout the transaction. This included trying to obtain the highest price possible for the seller. The commonlaw doctrine of *caveat emptor* (let the buyer beware) was the rule.

Based on our experience and observations, this often was not how the process really worked. The broker was primarily interested in making the sale. The broker would disclose information about the seller's circumstances and the seller's property that was not in the best interest of the seller. This information often would allow the buyer to negotiate a price lower than what would have been possible without knowing the disclosed information. The seller's agent might, for example, reveal that the seller was being transferred to another location and was anxious to sell the house before moving.

Multiple listing service (MLS) systems, where brokerage offices shared information about their listing and offered to share their commission with brokers or their sales agents who sold the property, were mostly run by NAR affiliates called Real Estate Boards (now called Associations of Realtors). Only Realtor members had access to the listings. Therefore, unless sales agents began their careers working for a Realtor, they did not have access to the listings on the MLS systems. Until the introduction of computers and the wide use of the Internet, the MLS systems published books (often as frequently as weekly) showing all the properties that were listed for sale.

Today the real estate business is going through many changes. The consumer movement ended the fiction of the brokers only representing the sellers. States are now changing their laws to distinguish between brokers and their sales agents who represent the sellers and those who represent the buyers. Chapter 5 discusses in more detail the different and more complex types of agencies, and how they affect the relationship between the brokers and the buyers and sellers.

Ownership Structures of Brokerage Businesses

Today a real estate brokerage business may be a sole proprietorship (a single owner), one of several types of partnerships, or one of several different kinds of corporations.

Many brokerage businesses consist of a single office or one with a few branch offices. Larger operations have many offices and may operate in more than one state. Many specialize in selling homes; others offer a wide variety of services. Many today operate as franchises of large national corporations.

What most of these brokerages have in common is that they are small businesses. Most of the people who own these offices also sell real estate. However, they must also run a business, which consumes a good deal of their time and energy.

When real estate salespeople consider becoming brokers they should consider the following four items:

> **1.** The need to study for and pass a broker license examination
>
> **2.** The need to open an office
>
> **3.** Their responsibility to pay all the expenses associated with running a small business
>
> **4.** The time and effort it takes to recruit, supervise, and motivate sales agents.

The economics of running a one-person office is such that many sole operators discover that their income does not exceed what they made when they were working as sales agents for other brokers. They conclude that only by hiring more sales agents will they be able to increase their income.

As soon as they hire sales agents, they assume a responsibility for the success of these sales agents. This means the brokers must spend time training them and helping them obtain listings and make sales. This leaves less time for the brokers to make their own sales. They discover that, in addition to being salespeople, they must also be business managers.

It is beyond the scope of this book to go into greater depth about the pros and cons of being a real estate agent working for a broker versus a real estate broker running an office. You have to become a licensed real estate salesperson in most states before you can become a licensed broker.

Assuming you decide to stay in the real estate field, you will have time to consider whether you are better off remaining a real estate salesperson or becoming a broker and owning your office. Another alternative is to become involved in one of the many other real estate career fields. See Chapter 21 for information about many other real estate career opportunities.

SUMMARY

Many RESPs remain as sales agents working for brokers through their careers and are successful and happy doing this because they like to sell and do not want the responsibilities associated with running a brokerage office.

Many others decide that just selling is not enough and they want to be part of the American dream of being an entrepreneur. They are prepared to assume the responsibilities of running an office and most likely supervising other people who will act as RESPs and support help. Once in the brokerage business it is common to expand the office into other real estate–related fields such as property management, appraising, or insurance.

In order to become a broker it is necessary to pass a real estate broker exam. One of the main differences between a sales license exam and a broker license exam is that the broker exam contains many more mathematical questions and problems.

When you decide to open a brokerage office, one of the first decisions you may make is whether to obtain a national franchise. One of the advantages of making this decision quickly is, if you go the franchise route, the franchisor will provide you with a lot of help setting up your office.

It is beyond the scope of this book to go into all the advantages and disadvantages of going the franchise route. My only advice is to give it serious consideration before you open up your own office.

The laws of agency have been around for hundreds of years. However, what was true in the past is rapidly changing, and these changes are far from over.

A brokerage office may have RESPs who are representing sellers, RESPs who are buyers' agents, and other RESPs who are dual agents. All of this now is governed both by common law and state law. When you are the broker, it is your responsibility to make sure your RESPs are acting within the law. The misdeeds of RESPs can get their brokers fined or suspended, have their licenses terminated, and, in extreme cases, put in jail.

The brokerage business of tomorrow is going to be very different from the brokerage business of today because the customer now has access to so much more information about what is being offered for sale. The Internet is making sellers more confident that they can sell their own houses. The services RESPs will have to provide to be successful will be much more than just providing information.

Brokerage firms run from single office sole proprietorships to multioffice corporations. Some use the name of the owner. Others use a franchise name.

Our final advice is look before you leap. Being an RESP is very different from being a broker. Which you choose should depend on your own personality, skills, and needs.

CHAPTER 5

Agency Law

Let every eye negotiate for itself
And trust no agent.

—KING HENRY V IN *MUCH ADO ABOUT NOTHING*
WILLIAM SHAKESPEARE

THE NATURE OF THE AGENCY RELATIONSHIP

5.1→ The relationship between parties where one party is authorized to act on behalf of the other party is known as an *agency* relationship. Agency is based on a long history of common law and specific state statutes.

Every professional sports player has an agent. The same is true of most people in the entertainment business. Any author who tries to get a book published without an agent is probably doomed to failure. Unlike in real estate, these agent-client relationships probably have few, if any, laws that regulate the relationship, yet people who have agents representing them have little doubt in their mind about what the agent is supposed to do. In fact, if the agents do not perform correctly, they can be taken to court and held accountable. This is because the agent-client relationship is hundreds of years old, and there is a vast number of court decisions based on the commonlaw relationship.

Generally an *agent* is anyone who represents the interests of another person. The purpose of an agency relationship is to allow one or more people (called the client or *principal*) to utilize the services of one or more people (who are called agents) to accomplish what they cannot or do not wish to accomplish themselves.

In real estate (and essentially in other agency relationships, too), the agent is regarded as an expert on whom the client relies for expert professional advice and services.

Most real estate agency relationships involve property and money, and the agents have a special responsibility to their clients or principals called *fiduciary responsibility*. Being a *fiduciary* means that the agents must act in the principals' best interests throughout the period of time that the agency relationship exists. The agents are also responsible to be certain any other agents (known as *subagents*) also act in the best interests of their clients.

It is assumed, as far as real estate is concerned, that the agents have skills and expertise that may give them an advantage over the principals. An important foundation of an agency relationship is the right of the principal to expect the agent to be trustworthy and act in the principal's best interests.

TYPES OF AGENTS

The four different principal-agent relationships are:

> **1.** Universal agency
>
> **2.** General agency
>
> **3.** Special agency
>
> **4.** Agency by *estoppel* (ostensible agency)

Universal Agency

Universal agency exists when the principal gives the agent broad authority to act on the principal's behalf. This authority might include the power to actually sell the principal's property, borrow money, and almost any other function one may legally delegate to an agent. Universal agency is rarely used in real estate. Before brokers accept the responsibility of universal agency, they should consult an attorney to be certain they are complying with all the applicable state laws and that they understand the responsibility they are taking on.

General Agency

General agency exists when the principal gives the agent power to bind the principal in specified business transactions. General agency is the agency created between brokers and their sales associates.

Special Agency

5.6➤
5.7➤

Special agency (also called specific agency) exists when the agent is authorized to perform specific limited functions for the principal. It is the typical relationship between a property owner and the listing broker. The listing agreement spells out what functions the broker can perform as agent on behalf of the principal, who is the property owner. These specified powers are known as the *actual authority* confirmed by the principal on the agent. These functions often include advertising the property for sale or for rent, showing the property to prospective buyers and tenants, taking offers and deposits, hiring subagents, listing the property on an MLS system, and so on. Most listing agreements do not authorize special agents to accept an offer on behalf of the principal.

Agency by Estoppel
(Ostensible Agency)

5.8➤
5.9➤

Property owners and others must be careful not to create an agency known as *agency by estoppel* (ostensible agency) by their actions as observed by third parties. When a third party has reason to believe that the principal has given someone agency powers, based on the actions of the principal and the agent, they may act as if the agency has been created and is a valid agency. When a third party may reasonably assume a person has *ostensible authority,* based on the actions of the principal and the agent, which act as ratification of the agent's authority, the courts will *estoppel* the principal from trying not to be bound by the ostensible agent's actions.

All 50 states have laws that require anyone who acts as an agent in a real estate transaction to have a license (some states make an exception for attorneys, trust officers, etc.). To become a real estate agent you have to comply specifically with your state's laws.

POWER OF ATTORNEY

5.10➤
5.11➤
5.12➤

A *power of attorney* is a document that attests to the fact that a person has been made an agent by a principal, and having become an *attorney in fact*, is authorized to act on behalf of the principal. A *special power of attorney* gives an agent authority to carry out a specific act or acts. A *general power of attorney* authorizes an agent to carry out all the business of the principal.

SUBAGENTS

5.13➤

It is common practice in real estate brokerage for brokers who become agents for property owners to delegate some or all of their authority to a *subagent* who may be a salesperson or sales associate, or a licensed broker. What can and cannot be delegated is often spelled out in the listing agreement.

5.14→ Many listing agreements permit listing brokers to offer subagencies to other *cooperating brokers* (cobrokers). The listing brokers split their commissions with the cooperating brokers when the cooperating brokers are instrumental in consummating the sale or rental of the listed property.

Recently, the problems created by the use of subagency have been increasing. Some subagents fail to make it clear to buyers and prospective tenants that they are not the agents of the buyer or prospective tenants, and therefore their loyalty is not to the buyer or prospective tenant. They often fail to disclose that they are primarily concerned about the property owner's interests. Many states have changed their laws to permit RESPs to become agents for buyers or to represent both the buyer and the seller, which is known as dual agency.

Confusion Caused by Historical Real Estate Agency Relationships

Real estate agents have probably been around for thousands of years. During most of this time, common law required that they be agents of their clients, the sellers. The fact that they spent the majority of their time with buyers and often encouraged buyers to make offers lower than what the seller wanted did not seem to bother too many people until recently.

It was naïve not to recognize that often the agents actually were agents for themselves in that all they were really interested in was making the sale and earning a commission. The following are the fiduciary responsibilities agents are supposed to have to their clients.

FIDUCIARY RESPONSIBILITIES

There are six basic fiduciary responsibilities of agents to their clients and principals:

1. Duty of loyalty
2. Duty of confidentiality
3. Duty of disclosure
4. Duty of obedience
5. Duty of reasonable skill and care
6. Duty of honest accounting

Duty of Loyalty

An agent's *duty of loyalty* requires that agents must always act in the best interests of their principals, even when it is not in their own best interest.

When brokers obtain listings, they become the listing brokers and it becomes their responsibility to make sure that their sales associates (and any cooperating brokers and their sales associates) also act in the best interest of **5.15 ➤** the property owner. None of these parties can have an undisclosed *conflict of interest,* such as being related to the buyer, without disclosing this fact to the property owner.

A common problem occurs when a property is shown by a cooperating broker who tries to help the buyer obtain the property as cheaply as possible. Unless the cooperating broker is going to be paid by the buyer, and therefore is an agent of the buyer (see "Dual Agency," later in this chapter, and "Buyer Representative," in Chapter 11), it is the duty of the cooperating broker to help the listing broker obtain the best price and terms for the property being shown, and not to help the buyer obtain the property at the lowest price possible.

One of the most common violations of the agency relationship is advising a buyer to offer less than the asking price. Both the listing agents and their salespeople and the subagents who show the property are obligated to help the seller or landlord obtain the highest possible price and best terms. Suggesting to a buyer or tenant that the listing price is too high is a breach of this responsibility. A proper response by seller's agents when asked if the price is too high is to say either that they feel the property is worth the asking price or that they do not know what the value of the property is. They should also say that they do not know what price the seller or landlord will accept.

Duty of Confidentiality

5.16 ➤ Agents' *duty of confidentiality* obliges them to keep confidential any information they receive from their clients that should not be revealed to potential buyers or tenants. However, not all the information they receive must be kept confidential.

An example of confidential information is the reason why the seller wants to sell, such as financial or marital problems, sickness, or pending job changes. The agent must also keep confidential any remarks made by the client that indicate how much below the asking price an acceptable offer would be.

Examples of information that cannot be kept confidential are information about known but unapparent physical problems existing on the property, the presence of environmental hazards, or known pending changes taking place in the neighborhood or community.

Duty of Disclosure

5.17 ➤ The opposite of confidentiality is an agent's *duty of disclosure*. All brokers, sales associates, and cobrokers are required to disclose to the client of the listing agent any relationship they have to any other party in the transaction. For example, cobrokers must disclose if they are related to potential buyers or tenants.

Other typical relationships that should be disclosed to clients are that the brokers, salespersons, or subagents have been promised a listing by the buyers or tenants if they are able to successfully purchase or rent the clients' property.

In addition, any business relationships, close friendships, and other financial connections such as the broker, sales associate, or cobroker loaning money or receiving a loan from the buyer or tenant should be disclosed.

Any referral fees received by the broker, sales associate, or cobroker from lenders, relocation companies, attorneys, inspectors, and so on, must also be disclosed.

Agents must disclose to the client the existence of any other offers, even if the offers are lower than another offer that is in the process of being presented to the client.

Agents must disclose the exact status of any deposit. They must disclose when they actually have the deposit, and if it is cash, personal check, bank check, certified check, or the like. If the deposit is a regular personal check, they must disclose whether they have taken any steps to determine if it is good, or if the buyer or tenant has said something to the effect that they will make the check good when the offer is accepted.

Known information about the financial status of the buyer or tenant must be revealed to the client. For example, the agent may be aware that the buyer has failed to qualify for a mortgage on another property.

When agents have a supported opinion of value such as an appraisal of the client's property, this must be told to the client. Sometimes the agents, because of their expertise, know that a property is worth more than the listing price proposed by the property owner. The agents must advise the client about their opinion of the true worth of the property.

The property owner is entitled to know how the commission is being split between the listing broker, sales associates, and cobrokers, and if any of the commission is being rebated to the buyer or the tenant (this practice is prohibited in some states).

The most important thing to remember about disclosure is that any known information must be disclosed, regardless of the consequences to the pending sale or rental. This means that even if the disclosure will kill the deal, the disclosure must be made to the principal by the agent. This disclosure requirement also applies to their sales associates and cobrokers.

Duty of Obedience

Agents must obey the instructions they receive from their principals, even when they do not agree with these instructions. However, there are some instructions in spite of the agent's *duty of obedience* that an agent may not have to carry out. For example, property owners cannot tell the agents not to show their property to a member of a minority group. Property owners cannot instruct the agents not to tell potential buyers or tenants about known but unapparent defects in the property.

5.18→

A principal could instruct an agent not to accept any offer that was not accompanied by a deposit for a specified amount. However, the agent would be obligated to disclose to the principal information about any other offer that was made, even if it did not meet the principal's criteria.

Duty to Use Reasonable Skill and Care

When agents accept listings from property owners, they have a *duty to use reasonable skill and care* when marketing the properties, showing the properties, and presenting offers.

When listing properties, the brokers must be careful that the listing information is accurate and the listing agreement and MLS contract are properly and completely filled out and filed with the MLS office within the required time. When the listing broker thinks that the listing price is too high or too low, this opinion must be transmitted to the property owner.

Once a property is listed, it must be marketed in a professional manner. Any promises made to the property owner about how the property will be marketed and advertised must be fulfilled. Advertisements must be accurate and written in such a way as to promote the sale or rental of the property. Any agreed-on signs must be erected and maintained on the property. When the listing agreement calls for listing with the MLS service, all the MLS requirements must be promptly met. One of the most common complaints clients have about their agents is that the agents do not professionally market their property.

A common problem occurs when an RESP or cooperating broker shows a property without taking the time and effort to learn about it. An unfortunate very common example is when cooperating brokers take clients alone to properties to which they have obtained keys and to which they have never been before. This is a case of the blind leading the blind through the property.

Since the brokers, RESPs, and cooperating brokers are agents of the seller or landlord, they should take steps to qualify potential buyers and tenants to determine that there is a reasonable possibility they can make the purchase or rental they are seeking.

When an offer is being made, it is the responsibility of the broker to determine that the offer form is completely and correctly filled out and signed by the prospective buyer or tenant.

When brokers feel the clients should seek the expert advice of an appraiser, attorney, tax consultant, and so on, they are obligated to make this recommendation to their clients. They are not obligated to make this recommendation to the prospective buyers or tenants.

Once an offer has been accepted by the clients, it becomes the responsibility of the brokers to help them do whatever is necessary to close the transaction. This includes help in obtaining whatever inspections are required, arranging financing, and any other advice or help they may need to close.

- The broker, sales associates, and cobrokers must hold themselves to high professional standards, so that the property owner receives services that meet the standards set in their community. For example, if a typical agency would advertise this type of property weekly in the local newspaper and hold open houses biweekly, the listing broker should be offering similar services to their property owners.

Duty of Honest Accounting

All states now have strict rules governing how brokers handle and account for the principal's funds. Some states require that these monies be held in special bank accounts, which are protected by the state and accrue interest for the buyer or tenant while they are held. When there is no specific state statute that controls how the funds are to be handled, what happens to the deposit should be specified in the offer. When not otherwise specified, it is good practice to place the funds in a special escrow depository account or in a trust fund account set up for the specific purpose of handling deposits. It is common practice in some states for a broker to hold a deposit check until an offer is accepted, unless specifically instructed not to do so by the principal.

Some states require that separate accounts be kept for rental deposit funds. These states often have regulations that provide for how much interest must be paid to the tenant on deposit monies held by the landlord or their agent.

5.19➤ In all states the real estate broker must be very careful not to commingle deposits (or any client funds) with their own funds. This automatically oc-
5.20➤ curs if the agents place the funds in their own personal or business checking accounts, even if they designate on their records what is client money. It is absolutely necessary to maintain separate bank accounts for funds that belong to principals, tenants, and buyers in order to prevent commingling of the funds.

Failure to comply with these requirements can lead to loss of the broker's real estate license, fines, and even a jail sentence.

AGENTS' DUTIES TO OTHERS (THIRD PARTIES)

Agents' primary duty is to their principals. However, agents also have some responsibilities and duties to other parties to any transaction. These duties and responsibilities can be broken into four groups:

1. The responsibility to disclose known hidden defects and other known material information about the property being sold or rented. Most state laws require RESPs and brokers to disclose known information about hidden defects and problems, including defects in the property, environmental hazards, and known problems (current and future) in the neighborhood.

For example, if RESPs or brokers knew about a proposed interstate highway to be constructed near a property, they would have to disclose this information to prospective buyers and tenants. They would also have to disclose any information they possess about environmental hazards on or off the site that may affect the property.

2. RESPs and brokers are required to act honestly and fairly with all parties to a transaction. For example, it would not be honest to tell a prospective buyer that someone else is about to make an offer when, in fact, they know this is not true.

3. RESPs and brokers need to act with skill and care at all times.

For example, if a prospective buyer asks questions about a property's mechanical systems, the broker, sales associate, or cobroker must obtain accurate information rather than just gloss over the questions, implying that they are all adequate and in good working condition.

4. RESPs, brokers, and cobrokers need to comply with all applicable laws and regulations. They must comply with the fair housing laws and all the other state and federal laws that apply to real estate. New environmental regulations should be studied and understood so that the RESPs, brokers or cobrokers do not sell or rent a property with significant undisclosed environmental problems. It is often good practice to recommend that environmental inspections be made prior to the closing, and that the sales or rental listing agreement contain a clause making the transaction contingent upon a satisfactory environmental report.

PUFFING, MISREPRESENTATION AND FRAUD

5.21→ There is a fine line between *puffing,* which is legal, and misrepresentation, which is illegal. Puffing refers to the exaggeration of the benefits and qualities of a property. *Black's Law Dictionary* defines puffing as "an expression of opinion . . . not made as a representation of fact. Exaggeration by a salesperson concerning qualities of goods (not considered a legally binding promise); usually concerns opinions rather than facts." Some examples of statements that probably can be classified as puffing are: "This is the most beautiful house in the neighborhood" or "Your friends will be envious of the great deal you are about to make." To say that a 60-ampere electrical service is adequate may not be true in many markets today. To say that a house has no environmental problems, when you are aware of a radon test that indicates a level of 40 picocuries per liter, is probably misrepresentation or fraud. The practice of puffing should therefore be avoided.

DUAL AGENCY

5.22→ *Dual agency* (sometimes called limited agency) finally tries to recognize and deal with a practice that has existed for years. Theoretically, brokers are the agents of the property owner and all sales associates and cobrokers also act as agents for the property owner. Government and other surveys have confirmed that many buyers and tenants did not understand the roles of the RESPs, brokers, and cobrokers in transactions in which they were involved. The buyers and tenants often thought that one or more of the RESPs, brokers, or cobrokers were representing them rather than the property owner. Interestingly, they maintained this wrong impression even when they knew that the RESPs, brokers, and cobrokers were being paid by the property owner and not by them.

These surveys further point out that property owners often feel that RESPs, brokers, and cobrokers are not loyal to them. They often feel that the RESPs, brokers, or cobrokers encouraged the buyer or tenant to offer an amount less than the asking price or rent.

The temptation to shift loyalties from the property owner to the buyer or tenant has often been too strong for many RESPs, brokers, or cobrokers to resist.

For example, when potential buyers or tenants asked what price the RESPs, brokers, or cobrokers thought the property owner would accept, they often received answers that were below the prices in the listing agreements. A proper answer for someone 100 percent loyal to the property owner would have been that the listing price was a fair price for the property and what the property owner expected to receive. It probably would be acceptable to remind the buyers or tenants that they had the right to make any offer and that the brokers, sales associates, or cobrokers would submit their offer. However, to encourage them to do so may not be in the seller's best interest.

Dual agency is designed to permit the RESPs, brokers, or cobrokers to represent both parties. The keystone of dual agency is disclosure to all parties that the RESPs, brokers, or cobrokers intend to act as dual agents and that they obtain permission from all the parties to do so.

There is a clear distinction between dual agency and when regular agents breach their agency responsibility to their clients and attempt to represent both parties in order to make the sale or rental transaction go through. The latter is a breach of the agency relationship and subjects the agents to ethical and legal disciplinary measures. Dual agency, when implemented correctly with full disclosure, is permitted by law in some states and by the National Association of Realtors Code of Ethics.

The most common creation of dual agency takes place when brokers, sales associates, or cobrokers are working for buyers or tenants. The buyers' agents find a property (often through the MLS system) and show it to their customer.

The RESPs, brokers, or cobrokers in this very common situation must make a clear choice. Either they notify the seller or landlord (through their listing broker) that they are the buyers' or tenants' agents and will be paid by the buyers or tenants or they notify the buyers or tenants that they are no longer their agents and they are becoming *subagents* for the selling or rental agent who has the listing. Then they will share the commission with the brokers for the sellers or landlords. It is common for brokers and sales associates to tell buyers and tenants this when they start looking for them, saying that they do not expect to be paid a commission by them and that they will split a commission from the selling or rental brokers. The problem that has occurred is that the buyers' or tenants' brokers or sales associates do not make it clear to the buyers or tenants that by taking a commission from the selling or rental brokers, they become subagents of the selling or rental brokers, and therefore represent the sellers or landlords and not the buyers or tenants.

The key is that whenever RESPs, brokers, or cobrokers are a buyer's or tenant's agent or a dual agent, all parties to the transaction are notified in advance and give their permission. Failure to make this disclosure and obtain the needed permissions exposes the brokers, sales associates, or cobrokers to forfeiture of their commission and license suspension.

Since this disclosure is so important and susceptible to misunderstanding, it almost always should be in writing. Some states have mandatory agency disclosure forms that are signed by all parties to every transaction and clearly spell out all of the agents' relationships to all the parties.

It is not always possible to get property owners or the prospective buyers or tenants to sign a dual agency disclosure and permission form. Once they clearly understand that they are giving up the loyalty of the RESP, broker, or cobroker, they may become dissatisfied with the arrangement. Often, they do not understand why they cannot get good advice on how much to offer or how much to accept.

Recently many real estate commissions have increased their enforcement of undisclosed dual agency relationships. They have been revoking or suspending the licenses of dual agency disclosure and permission violators.

The best way for brokers, sales associates, and cobrokers to protect themselves is to obtain acknowledgement of disclosure and confirmation of permission *in writing* from all the parties to a transaction, both at the beginning of the transaction and again at the closing, when the sale or rental is consummated.

Dual agency presents special problems to you when you take your license examination. First of all, you must know your own state laws on dual agency. Some states do not permit dual agency. Unfortunately, there is a substantial lack of uniformity among states. Second, you can expect several questions on your exam that will test your understanding of your state's laws and how they are enforced.

TERMINATION OF A PRINCIPLE/ AGENT RELATIONSHIP

There are a variety of ways the agency relationship between an agent and a principal may be terminated.

5.23→ Either the principal or the broker may terminate an agency relationship at any time by giving the other party written notice. Written notice must also be given to any known third parties with whom the principal or agent are dealing at the time of the termination.

The early termination may make the party who terminates the contract liable for damages. For example, a seller or landlord who prematurely terminates a listing agreement may be liable to the agent for expenses and time expended by the brokers, sales associates, or cobrokers in attempting to sell or rent the property prior to the termination of the listing.

Many listing agreements spell out the parties' obligations to each other when the listing agreement is terminated by either party prior to its stated expiration date.

The agent/principal relationship ends on the *listing expiration date* stated in the listing agreement. Some listing agreements have automatic extension provisions. These provisions *are not permitted* in many states.

5.24→ When the broker sells or rents the property, the agency relationship is terminated. Usually the property owner then pays the broker a commission or fee.

When either party to an agency agreement dies, the contract is automatically terminated, unless the listing agreement specifically spells out some method of continuation in the event of the death of the broker or the principal.

An agency agreement is also terminated when the property is substantially destroyed by fire or some other natural disaster.

ESCROW OR TRUST ACCOUNTS

Most states require that all monies received by a broker, sales associate, or cobroker as earnest money, binder deposits, or advanced fees be immediately deposited in a specially designated account in a type of institution acceptable to the state. These institutions usually include commercial banks, mutual savings banks, savings and loan associations, and, in some states, title insurance company escrow accounts.

Some states permit the money to be placed in interest-bearing accounts, and these states have regulations that determine who gets the interest earned on the account.

A general rule that applies to all states is that none of the broker's own money may be deposited in the escrow account, which usually constitutes an illegal practice called *commingling*.

5.25→

RESPs and cobrokers are required to promptly turn over all escrow money they receive to a broker. Unless there is a dual agency arrangement or a buyer's agent arrangement, the money should be promptly turned over to the property owner's broker.

An escrowed deposit remains under the control of the buyers or tenants (even though it is deposited with the property owner's broker) until their offer is accepted. They can ask for, and should receive, the return of their deposit anytime before their offer is accepted or when their offer is rejected.

When the offer is accepted, the control of the escrow deposit is transferred to the property owners, who may then be entitled to the money unless the sales contract specifies that the deposit will be held in escrow until the closing or transfer of title.

When the broker, property owner, and buyer or tenant do not agree about how the deposit should be disposed of, the escrowing broker has several courses of action available to resolve the problem.

1. In some states the real estate commission has a procedure to resolve the problem.

2. Both parties may be convinced that an arbitrator be appointed (or the sales contract may provide for this) and an arbitration hearing can be held to resolve the problem.

3. The broker who holds the escrowed deposit, by filing an *interpleader action,* may ask the court to decide what to do with the money. It is not a good idea to go to court without a lawyer (although some people do so success-

fully). Usually when the court hears an interpleader action, the court will award attorney's fees to the broker who brought the action, so that the attorney will be paid for by the parties to the transaction and not the broker who brought the action.

SUMMARY

The relationship where one party is authorized to act on behalf of another party has existed for thousands of years. For most of this time it has been governed by common law.

An agent has a fiduciary responsibility to his or her client.

There are four different types of agents: universal agents, general agents, special agents, and agents created by estoppel.

A power of attorney is a written document that gives one person the power to act on behalf of another person. A general power of attorney authorizes the agent to carry out all the business of the principle. A special power of attorney gives the agent the power to carry out only specific acts for the client.

When brokers become agents for sellers, it is common practice for brokers to delegate some of their powers to RESPs or cobrokers.

In spite of recent laws in some states, there is still substantial confusion between how brokers and their subagent act when they represent a seller and what they do in practice.

There are six basic fiduciary responsibilities of agents to their clients and principals: duty of loyalty, duty of confidentiality, duty of disclosure, duty of obedience, duty of reasonable skill and care, and duty of honest accounting.

Real estate agents have some duties to third parties. They include the duty to disclose known but unapparent defects of the property they are selling, to act honestly and fairly with all the parties to a transaction, to act with skill and care at all times, and to comply with all applicable laws and regulations.

There is a fine line between puffing, which is legal, and misrepresentation, which is illegal.

Dual agency is when an agent represents both parties to a transaction. Some states prohibit the practice. Others require written permission from all parties involved in the transaction.

There are a variety of ways an agency agreement can be terminated. Many states do not permit the automatic extension of an agency agreement.

REVIEW QUESTIONS

5.1 An agency relationship is one where the agent is:

A. Always paid a fee to accept the responsibility of becoming an agent

B. Based only on common law

C. Based only on statutory law

D. None of the above

5.2 Fiduciary responsibility means that the agent must:

A. Always act trustworthy with the client

B. Act in the principal's best interest during the time an agency relationship exists

C. Be certain subagents also act in the client's best interest

D. All of the above

5.3 Being a fiduciary means that:

A. A broker must not advertise a property without permission

B. A broker can not split a commission with a sales associate

C. An agent must act in the principal's best interest

D. All of the above

5.4 Universal agency exists when:

A. The principal gives the agent broad authority to act on the principal's behalf

B. The principal lists a property for rent with an agent

C. A sales associate becomes affiliated with a broker

D. All of the above

5.5 General agency exists when:

A. The principal gives the agent broad authority to act on the principal's behalf

B. The principal lists a property for rent with an agent

C. A sales associate becomes affiliated with a broker

D. All of the above

5.6 Special (specific) agency exists when:

A. The principal gives the agent broad authority to act on the principal's behalf

B. The principal lists a property for rent with an agent

C. A sales associate becomes affiliated with a broker

D. All of the above

5.7 Principals who have engaged brokers to be their agent typically give the agent the actual authority to:

A. Advertise the property for sale or for rent

B. Show the property to prospective buyers or tenants

C. Take offers and deposits

D. All of the above

5.8 Estoppel is a legal concept that describes an agency relationship:

A. Where the broker and the property owner are related

B. Created by the actions of the property owner and the agent

C. Created when a sales associate tries to directly represent a property owner

D. None of the above

5.9 Agency by estoppel (ostensible agency) is created when:

A. A broker gets a signed listing

B. A sales associate takes an offer from a seller

C. A broker hires a sales associate

D. None of the above

5.10 A power of attorney is:

A. The power an attorney has to act as a closing agent

B. A document signed by a principal

C. A document signed by an agent

D. None of the above

5.11 An *attorney in fact* is:

A. An attorney who has passed the bar examination

B. An attorney who acts on behalf of their client

C. Anyone who has been made an agent by a principal according to a signed power of attorney

D. None of the above

5.12 A general power of attorney exists when:

A. A broker lists a property owned by the principal

B. A broker hires a sales associate

C. A document authorizes an agent to carry out all the business of a principal

D. None of the above

5.13 A subagent may be a:

A. Licensed real estate broker

B. Licensed real estate sales person

C. Both of the above

D. None of the above

5.14 A cobroker must be a:

A. Licensed real estate broker

B. Licensed real estate salesperson

C. Both of the above

D. None of the above

5.15 Which of the following might be considered a conflict of interest?

A. The buyer is a relative of the property owner's broker

B. The property owner's broker owns the property next door

C. Both of the above

D. None of the above

5.16 An agent's duty of confidentiality obliges the agent to:

A. Keep confidential all information about a property told by the principal to the agent

B. Keep personal information about why the property owner wants to sell confidential

C. Keep confidential the results of a radon test if they indicate the radon level is above minimum EPA standards

D. None of the above

5.17 An agent's duty of disclosure obliges the agent to:

A. Disclose to the property owner that a deposit check is not good, but the buyer will make it good if the offer is accepted

B. Disclose negative information they learn about the buyer, such as a poor credit rating, to the property owner

C. Disclose to the property owner that the buyer has promised them a listing on their house if the deal goes through

D. All of the above

5.18 An agent has a duty of obedience to their principal. Which of the following must they do even if they disagree with the action?

A. Refrain from showing the property to specified minority groups

B. Refrain from telling a prospective buyer about known hidden defects in the property

C. Refrain from telling a prospective tenant about a known environmental problem

D. None of the above

5.19 When a sales associate takes a deposit from a customer who is making an offer on a house listed by the sales associate's broker, what should the sales associate do with the deposit check?

A. Attach it to the sales contract and present them to the seller

B. Tell the seller that they have the deposit check and ask for instructions about its disposition

C. Deposit the check in the sales associate's escrow account

D. None of the above

5.20 An agent's duty of honest accounting includes:

    A. Keeping a separate account for deposit funds received with offers

    B. A requirement that the agent keep all the records in a safe

    C. A requirement that the broker keep accurate records of how many hours each sales associate works

    D. All of the above

5.21 Puffing by brokers, sales associates, or cobrokers is:

    A. Illegal in all states

    B. The exaggeration of the benefits and qualities of a property

    C. A fact that makes a property seem more desirable

    D. None of the above

5.22 Dual agency is:

    A. A new practice recently written into many state laws

    B. An old practice that is finally being recognized

    C. A practice well understood by the public

    D. None of the above

5.23 A listing on a property is terminated:

    A. When the property owner gives the broker written notice that it is terminated

    B. When the broker gives the property owner written notice that it is terminated

    C. When the listing expiration date has been passed

    D. All of the above

5.24 A listing on a property is terminated when:

    A. The property is sold or rented

    B. Whenever there is a fire

    C. If married property owners become divorced

    D. None of the above

5.25 Prohibition of commingling prevents:

    A. Two brokers, sales associates, or cobrokers showing a property at the same time

    B. A broker working for two clients who are related at the same time

    C. Putting the broker's funds and the client's funds in the same escrow account

    D. All of the above

ANSWERS

The answer to each question is indicated by the letters A, B, C, or D. The explanation of the answer is indicated by the page number and an arrow that points to the appropriate paragraph on the page.

Q 5.1	D	Page 57	Q 5.6	B	Page 59	Q 5.11	C	Page 59	Q 5.16	B	Page 61	Q 5.21	B	Page 66
Q 5.2	D	Page 58	Q 5.7	D	Page 59	Q 5.12	C	Page 59	Q 5.17	D	Page 62	Q 5.22	B	Page 66
Q 5.3	C	Page 58	Q 5.8	B	Page 59	Q 5.13	C	Page 59	Q 5.18	D	Page 63	Q 5.23	D	Page 68
Q 5.4	A	Page 58	Q 5.9	D	Page 59	Q 5.14	A	Page 60	Q 5.19	D	Page 64	Q 5.24	A	Page 68
Q 5.5	C	Page 58	Q 5.10	B	Page 59	Q 5.15	C	Page 61	Q 5.20	A	Page 64	Q 5.25	C	Page 69

CHAPTER 6

The Importance of Fair Housing Laws

THE IMPORTANCE OF FAIR HOUSING

All real estate professionals have an important role to play in making sure that their actions comply with all of the fair housing and antidiscrimination laws. This will not be as easy as it sounds. Unfortunately, some of their clients and potential buyers and tenants will not be familiar with the fair housing and antidiscrimination laws. Some of the things they want you to do may be in violation of these laws.

Under no circumstances should you violate these laws, as you may put your career in jeopardy. You are expected to know all these laws that apply to real estate, and the license examination will have questions on it to test your knowledge. This book covers only the federal fair housing laws. In addition, you must be familiar with your state, county, and local fair housing laws.

It is your responsibility as a real estate professional not only to comply with all these laws but also to make sure your clients comply with the laws. Unfortunately, the illegal actions of your clients and customers may reflect upon you even if you are not directly involved.

To protect yourself, you need to determine if your clients and customer are familiar with the laws. If they are not, it is up to you to educate them. If you discover that they are not complying with the laws, you need to warn them that this is not acceptable. If they continue to violate the laws, our advice to you is to terminate your relationship with them.

FAIR HOUSING LAWS

It is illegal according to federal law to discriminate:

<table>
<tr><td>

1. In the sale or rental of housing or residential lots
2. In advertising the sale or rental of housing
3. In the financing of housing
4. In the provision of real estate brokerage services
5. In the appraisal of housing
6. By engaging in *blockbusting*—the practice of inducing panic selling in a neighborhood for financial gain by spreading information that the values in the neighborhood are going down because houses are being sold to people of other races, religions, or nationalities
7. By representing that a dwelling is unavailable when it is available
8. By channeling a home buyer to or away from any neighborhood in an attempt to limit their choices—a practice called *steering*
9. As a commercial lender in house financing in the terms or conditions of such financing, including loans for the purchase, construction, repair, or maintenance of a dwelling
10. By denying access to, or membership in, a multiple listing service or real estate brokers' organization, or to discriminate in the terms and conditions of such access or membership
11. By threatening or interfering with a person's exercise or enjoyment of their Title VIII rights or with a person who has aided or encouraged someone else in the exercise or enjoyment of their Title VIII rights

</td></tr>
</table>

6.1➤

HISTORY OF FAIR HOUSING LAWS

The following is a summary of the history of fair housing laws.

1. The Civil Rights Act of 1866 prohibits discrimination in housing based on race without any exceptions.

2. The Housing Act of 1954 was the first federal legislation to specifically address the special needs of minorities.

3. Executive Order No. 11063, signed in 1962, prohibits discrimination in housing funded by FHA- or VA-insured loans.

6.2→ 4. The *Civil Rights Act of 1964* prohibits discrimination in any housing that is federally funded.

6.3→ 5. Title VIII of the *Civil Rights Act of 1968,* known as the Federal Fair Housing Act, prohibits discrimination in any housing based on race, color, religion, or national origin. There are exceptions to this act:
   a. The sale or rental of a single-family home is exempt when the home is exempt, when the home is owned by an individual who does not own more than three such homes at one time, and when a broker or salesperson is not used and discriminatory advertising is not used. If the owner is not living in the dwelling at the time of the transaction or was not the most recent occupant, only one such sale by an individual is exempt from the law within any 24-month period.

6.4→   b. The rental of rooms or units is exempted in an owner-occupied one- to four-family dwelling.
   c. Dwelling units owned by religious organizations may be restricted to people of the same religion if membership in the organization is not restricted on the basis of race, color, national origin, handicap, or *familial status.*
   d. A private club that is not open to the public may restrict the rental or occupancy of lodgings it owns to its members, as long as the lodgings are not operated commercially.

6. Title VIII of the 1968 Civil Rights Acts, as amended in 1974, extends the prohibitions to discriminate in housing based on sex.

7. Section 109 of the 1974 Housing and Community Development Act prohibits discrimination in HUD-assisted community development programs on the basis of race, color, national origin, or sex.

8. The Equal Credit Opportunity Act of 1974, amended in 1976, extends to lenders the prohibitions of discrimination in housing loans based on sex and marital status.

9. The 1974 Equal Credit Opportunity Act of 1974, amended in 1976, extends coverage to include prohibition of credit discrimination in housing on the basis of race, color, religion, national origin, or because the applicant's income derives from a public assistance program. It indirectly prohibits the
6.5→ practice of *redlining,* which is the refusal to make loans in certain neighborhoods regardless of the quality of the structure or the ability of the borrower

to repay the loan. (Red lining refers to the practice of lenders having maps with the prohibited neighborhoods outlined in red.)

10. Section 109 of 1974 Housing and Community Development Act, amended in 1981, extends coverage to include prohibition of discrimination on the basis of age or handicap.

MAJOR FEDERAL FAIR HOUSING LAWS

1866 Civil Rights Act

At the end of the Civil War, the U.S. Congress passed the *Civil Rights Act of 1866.* It prohibited discrimination in the purchase, sale, leasing, and conveyance of property (real estate and personal property). It prohibited discrimination based on race or color. The act said in very strong language that, when it comes to property, everyone has the same rights regardless of their race or color. It made noncompliance with the law a federal offense so that, when an action was taken against someone for noncompliance, it was tried in a federal court.

There was an important case in 1968 (*Jones v. Alfred H. Mayer Company*) that affirmed the 1866 act. The importance of this act today and the court case is that, unlike some of our current fair housing laws, it did not contain any exceptions.

The Civil Rights Act of 1968 is often called the Federal Fair Housing Act. It prohibited discrimination in housing based on race, color, religion, or national origin. It contained the statement, "All citizens of the United States shall have the same right in every State and Territory, as is enjoyed by white citizens thereof to inherit, purchase, lease, sell, hold, and convey real and personal property."

FAIR HOUSING AMENDMENTS ACT OF 1988

The Fair Housing Amendments Act of 1988 extends protection to covered persons to include discrimination on the basis of familial status and *handicapped* status.

6.6→   Handicapped is defined in the amendment as:

1. Having a physical or mental impairment which substantially limits one or more major life activities
2. Having a record of having such an impairment
3. Being regarded as having such an impairment

How these prohibitions of discrimination against the handicapped will affect real estate and the public is still not fully understood. Handicapped people are going to be allowed to make reasonable modifications to their living units. It is now unlawful for landlords or their agents to refuse to make reasonable accommodations, rules, policies, practices, and services when necessary to afford handicapped people an equal opportunity to use and enjoy their dwelling. New multifamily dwellings of more than four units now being built must be accessible to handicapped people.

6.7→ The term *protected class* is used to describe all those classifications of people who are protected under the various civil rights, fair housing, and fair credit laws.

6.8→ *Familial status* is defined as one or more individuals (who have not obtained the age of 18 years) being domiciled with a parent or other person having legal custody of such individual or individuals or the designee of such parent or other person having custody, with the written permission of such parent or other person. These protections also apply to any person who is pregnant or is in the process of securing legal custody of any individual who has not obtained the age of 18 years.

This means that all homeowner association properties, apartment projects, cooperatives, and condominiums now have to have facilities adapted for children and cannot discriminate against anyone on the basis of familial status when leasing, selling, or renting properties unless they are specifically exempted from this portion of the law. Many adult apartment projects, cooperatives, and condominiums may lose their ability to keep out children unless they meet one of the following exceptions:

1. The development provides housing under a state or federal program that the secretary of Housing and Urban Development determines to be specifi-
6.9→ cally designed and operated to assist elderly persons known as *housing for the elderly* or *housing for older persons*.

2. The development provides housing intended for and is generally occupied only by persons 62 years old or older.

3. The development provides housing generally intended and operated for at least one person 55 years of age or older per unit and meets certain other regulations adopted by the secretary of Housing and Urban Development.

The penalties for violation of these federal statutes are quite severe. A first offense can result in fines up to $50,000. Subsequent offenses may be fined up to $100,000. These fines are in addition to civil damages, potential injunctions, attorney fees, and other defense costs.

DISCRIMINATORY ADVERTISING

All discriminatory advertising is prohibited. HUD has provided guidelines to help you avoid inadvertently creating a discriminatory advertisement.

What you have to be careful of is not to use words, phrases, pictures, or any other visual image that could be construed to be discriminatory. For example, if there are people in the pictures, they should not all be alike. A good mix of color, sex, and ages will keep you out of trouble. Don't show pictures of the church next door.

Where you advertise can also be a problem. If the only advertisements you run are in media that specialize in one type of readership or one limited location, it could be a problem. You can advertise in these types of media, but it must be offset with advertisements in media that serve the general population.

HUD guidelines help understand what words may have double discriminatory meanings or are considered to be code words or catch words. These words often appear on license examinations.

For examination purposes you should consider all of these words and phrases as being discriminatory:

6.10 ➤
- Integrated neighborhood
- Exclusive (whatever)
- Pride of ownership
- Any word that describes a color as it relates to race or ethnicity (this is true even if you are trying to say that everyone is welcome)
- Familial status
- Children
- Handicapped people unless to say that the property is handicapped accessible
- National origin, race, religion, sex, or gender (there are some exceptions for people who want to share an apartment or house)

This is not to be considered a complete list.

STATE AND LOCAL FAIR HOUSING LAWS

Many states, counties, and communities have there own fair housing laws. Their legislative bodies decided that the federal laws were either not broad enough or not clear enough. They often wished to put into codified law what was being done at the federal level as a result of the Supreme Court interpretations of the Constitution. State, county, and community laws can never restrict federal laws and Supreme Court interpretations of the Constitution. All they can do is expand them and clarify them.

SUMMARY

Everyone involved with the sale, rental, and financing of real estate must comply with all the fair housing and antidiscrimination laws. They must avoid complying with the wishes of their buyers, sellers, and landlords who may not be aware of all the provisions of these laws.

Violation of these laws can put your career in jeopardy and subject you to severe penalties. You must watch that your buyers, sellers, and landlords are not discriminating behind your back. If they are caught, you run the risk of being implicated. If they can not be educated and controlled, you should consider terminating your relationship with them.

The Civil Rights Act of 1866 was the first American antidiscrimination law.

The Housing Act of 1954 was the first federal legislation to specifically apply to minorities.

Title VIII of the Civil Rights Act of 1968 prohibits discrimination in any housing based on race, color, religion, or national origin.

Discrimination in HUD-assisted community development programs on the basis of race, color, national origin, or sex and discrimination in housing loans were prohibited in 1974 and 1976 as was credit, age, and handicap discrimination.

All discrimination in advertising is also prohibited. This includes the use of words, phrases, pictures, or any other visual image that could be construed to be discriminatory.

States, counties, and communities passed there own fair housing laws to expand coverage and provide clarification.

REVIEW QUESTIONS

6.1 Blockbusting is the illegal practice of:

A. Lenders designating blocks where they will not make loans

B. Real estate brokers spreading rumors that a neighborhood is going to be ruined by the introduction of minority people in the neighborhood

C. Both of the above

D. None of the above

6.2 The Civil Rights Act of 1964 prohibits discrimination in any housing:

A. That is federally funded

B. Because of sex

C. Because of a person's handicap

D. All of the above

6.3 The Civil Rights Act of 1968 prohibits discrimination in any housing:

A. That is federally funded

B. Because of sex

C. Because of a person's handicap

D. All of the above

6.4 An exception to the 1968 Federal Housing Act is:

A. The rental of rooms or units in an owner-occupied one-to-four family dwelling

B. Pets weighing under 10 pounds

C. Dwellings owned by people over 85 years old

D. None of the above

6.5 Redlining is the illegal practice of:

A. Lenders designating blocks where they will not make loans

B. Real estate brokers spreading rumors that a neighborhood is going to be ruined by an influx of minority people

C. Both of the above

D. None of the above

6.6 The Federal Housing Acts now provide protection for the handicapped, who are defined as people:

A. Having physical or mental impairment which substantially limits one or more major life activities

B. Having a record of having a physical or mental impairment

C. Being regarded as having a physical or mental impairment

D. All of the above

6.7 A protected class of people are people who are:

A. Poor

B. On welfare

C. On Title XXII

D. None of the above

6.8 The term *familial status* is defined as one or more individuals:

A. Who are elderly and reside with their children

B. Under the age of 18 being domiciled with a parent

C. Living in an elderly housing project with one's spouse, who is not 55 years old

D. None of the above

6.9 Children under the age of 18 can be legally prohibited from moving into a:

A. Housing for the elderly project

B. Housing for older persons project

C. Both of the above

D. None of the above

6.10 The following words are considered to be discriminatory when used in real estate:

A. Integrated neighborhood

B. Pride of ownership

C. Exclusive

D. All of the above

ANSWERS

The answer to each question is indicated by the letters A, B, C, or D. The explanation of the answer is indicated by the page number and an arrow that points to the appropriate paragraph on the page.

Q 6.1	B	Page 76	Q 6.3	D	Page 77	Q 6.5	A	Page 77	Q 6.7	D	Page 79	Q 6.9	C	Page 79
Q 6.2	A	Page 77	Q 6.4	A	Page 77	Q 6.6	A	Page 78	Q 6.8	B	Page 79	Q 6.10	D	Page 80

CHAPTER 7

Types and Forms of Ownership

BUNDLE OF RIGHTS AND INTERESTS

The *bundle of rights* theory holds that the ownership of real property may be compared to a bundle of sticks, wherein each stick represents a distinct and separate right or privilege of ownership. These rights, inherent in ownership of real property and guaranteed by law but subject to certain limitations and restrictions, include the right to occupy and to use real property, to sell it in whole or in part, to bequeath it, to lease it, or to transfer by contract for specified periods of time the benefits to be derived by occupancy and use ("beneficial interests"), or to do nothing at all with it.

The bundle of rights is often illustrated as it is in Figure 7.1 by a bundle of sticks. Each stick in the bundle represents a separate right or interest inherent in ownership. These individual rights can be separated from the bundle by sale, lease, mortgage, donation, or other means of title transfer. The complete bundle of rights, called the *private rights,* is often divided as follows:

- The right to sell one or more of the interests in the property
- The right to occupy the property

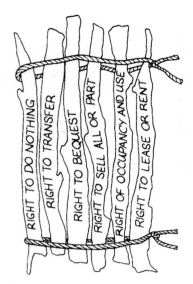

Figure 7.1 Bundle of rights.

7.1➤
- The right to lease property to someone other than the owner of the property
- The right to mortgage the property
- The right to give away (donate) all or part of the property
- The right to do none of the above things

GOVERNMENT RIGHTS (POWERS)

All of the private rights of ownership are subject to the government's rights and powers. They are covered in more detail in Chapter 9, "All Those Government Lending Institution and Land Use Regulations."

Ad Valorem Taxation

7.8➤

7.9➤

The right of the state to levy and collect a tax varying with the assessed value of the property is called *ad valorem taxation*. It is a compulsory contribution exacted from all owners of real estate for the general support of the state and for the maintenance of public services. Also included are *special assessments* that may be levied against certain real estate benefiting from public improvements, usually to directly offset the cost of such improvements. A common example is when a group of residences are subject to a special assessment to pay for new sewer lines serving their house.

Eminent Domain

7.10➤ *Eminent domain* is the right reserved by government to force an involuntary conveyance or taking of title to private land through the process of condemnation for public benefit, provided just compensation is paid. The concept of what constitutes public benefit has been extended to quasi-government or public bodies such as housing authorities and public utilities. A recent U.S. Supreme Court decision upholding the states' broad power of eminent domain has caused a review of these statutes in many states.

Police Power

The right to regulate property to promote the safety, health, morals, and general welfare of the community via zoning ordinances, building codes, traffic regulations, and other restrictions such as fair housing laws is called *police power.*

Escheat

The reversion to the state of property ownership if the owner dies without a will and with no known legal heirs is called *escheat.*

FORMS OF OWNERSHIP

In the United States there are two kinds of estates in land:

7.2➤ 1. *Freehold estates,* which are ownership for an undetermined period of time

7.11➤ 2. *Nonfreehold estates or leasehold estates,* which signify possession of a property with a determinable end.

Fee Simple Ownership (Freehold Estate)

7.12➤ In a typical year, over 5 million homes, which are owned in some form of *fee simple* ownership, are sold annually in the United States. Add to these the many commercial, industrial, and special-purpose properties that are also owned in fee simple and you realize the importance of this type of ownership.

There are three basic ways a fee simple ownership can be held:

1. In severalty

7.3→ 2. By co-owners

3. In trust

Fee Simple Ownership in Severalty

This legal word looks like "several" and ought to mean ownership by more than one person. However, this is not the case.

7.4→ *Ownership in severalty* is ownership by one person. When we say that a person owns a property in severalty, we mean that the person owns it all by him- or herself. (It is possible that a spouse will have an interest in the property through *dower* or *curtesy,* but the ownership is still called ownership in severalty.)

Joint Ownership

Fee Simple Ownership by Co-Owners

When two or more individuals, companies, or organizations own a piece of real estate together, they are known as co-owners. This is a general word that describes many types of ownership by more than one person.

Division of earnings or productivity occurs when ownership is in undivided interests such as either tenancy-in-common or joint tenancy. Co-ownership, also called concurrent ownership in real estate, has several different forms. The rights of the co-owners and their creditors vary depending on the type of co-ownership.

Some co-ownerships are formed to control the transfer from one owner to the other upon the death of one of them. Others permit the pooling of resources by several individuals to buy real estate that none of them could afford individually.

Co-ownership can result even without the co-owners intending to be co-owners. They can result from inheriting real estate from one who dies intestate. It may also occur when tenancy by a husband and wife is converted upon divorce to a tenancy in common. The dollar value of such interests is usually less than the numerical percentage of the portion of ownership, particularly where the ownership is less than 50 percent in the property.

There is an almost infinite number of possible combinations and forms of co-ownership. However, most co-ownerships are in one of the following forms or some combination of them:

- Tenancy in common
- Joint tenancy
- Community property
- Tenancy by the entirety
- Partnerships
  - General partnerships
  - Limited partnerships

Tenancy in Common

7.13➤ *Tenancy in common* is the most prevalent type of joint ownership. It is permitted in almost every state. In most states, when two or more unmarried people take title to a property and no form of ownership is specified in the deed, a tenancy in common is automatically established.

There are two distinct characteristics to ownership by tenancy in common:

> **1.** Each owner has an undivided interest in the property.
>
> **2.** Each owner holds title in severalty and therefore can sell, mortgage, exchange, option, or pass their ownership interests on to their heirs without permission from the other owner(s).

Another distinguishing characteristic is that the percentage of ownership each owner has does not have to be the same. One owner can own 75 percent and the other owner 25 percent, or any other combination that adds up to 100 percent. When no fraction or percentage is specified in the deed, it is presumed that the owners have equal shares.

Unlike some other forms of ownership, the owners of a tenancy in common clearly do not have any survivorship rights in the interests of the other owners. When one or more of the owners die, their interests pass on to their own heirs, and not to the surviving owners.

Tenants in common contribute to the property's expenses and share in the property's profits proportionate to their share of ownership.

A unique feature of tenancy in common is that each owner has the right of possession and use of 100 percent of the property. Obviously, this form of ownership creates problems when the owners do not all get along with each other.

A tenancy in common is created when property is inherited by more than one person and no other ownership form is specified.

When problems arise because the tenants in common cannot agree on the use or management of the property, they can institute a legal action to have the property partitioned so that each owner has a specific and divided portion of the property. The court may decide that such a partition is impossible and order that the property be sold instead and the proceeds divided among the owners, according to their percentage of ownership interest.

Joint Tenancy

Joint tenancy is a form of ownership by two or more persons with the right of survivorship.

On the death of a joint tenant owner, that person's interest passes on to the surviving joint tenants and not to the person's own heirs. Because no interest passes to any heirs after death, there is no need for probate. The surviving owner(s) receive the deceased's property.

The potential for problems and inequities to occur upon the death of one or more joint tenant owners is substantial. Therefore, most states have passed the Universal Simultaneous Death Act, which defines how property interests will be allocated upon the simultaneous deaths of two or more partners.

Joint tenancy ownership must be specifically created by the owners. In order to create a joint tenancy, traditionally four unities (requirements) must be met:

> **1.** Unity of time
> **2.** Unity of title
> **3.** Unity of interest
> **4.** Unity of possession

UNITY OF TIME

The unity of time requirement states that all interests of the joint tenant owners must be acquired at the same moment in time.

In order to accomplish this requirement, it is necessary for an owner of a property who wants to convey part of the ownership to one or more new owners (who will share the ownership with the original owner) to convey the property to some other third party (known as a "straw man" or "straw woman") who then simultaneously conveys the property back to the original owner and the new owners. Some states recognize the unnecessary complexity of this process and allow the original owner to create a joint tenancy without the use of straw people.

UNITY OF TITLE

The unity of title requirement states that a joint tenancy must be created by a single conveying instrument. The traditional wording that creates a joint tenancy is: "The real estate is hereby conveyed to (name of the joint tenants) equally as joint tenants with the right of survivorship and not as tenants in common."

A corporation cannot be a joint tenant because a corporation has perpetual existence and, in a legal sense, never dies. (As a matter of practicality, there are lots of dead corporations.)

When there are only two owners and one owner sells or otherwise conveys their interest to a third party, the joint tenancy is terminated and the new owners become tenants in common.

When there are three or more joint tenant owners and one sells their interest to a third party, it does not automatically terminate the joint tenancy. Rather, the new owner becomes a tenant in common with the remaining owners, who still hold their original ownership interest as joint tenants.

UNITY OF INTEREST

The requirement of unity of interest states that each joint tenant must have the same estate and an equal fractional share in the property. If there are two owners, each must have 50 percent. If there are three owners, each must have 33⅓ percent, and four owners each must have 25 percent ownership. There is no limit to the number of owners as long as they each have the same percentage of ownership.

UNITY OF POSSESSION

The joint tenancy requirement of unity of possession gives each owner the right to 100 percent of the use and possession of the whole property. If all the owners cannot agree how to share the use and possession of the property, they must either voluntarily convert to another form of ownership or liquidate the property. If they are unable to agree on how to accomplish this, any one of the owners can ask the courts to partition or liquidate the property.

It is a popular misconception that joint tenancy protects owners from their creditors. Creditors have the right to attach an owner's interest in a joint tenancy and take the owner to court to force partition.

Community Property

At the time this book was being written, about eight states had *community property* laws, which vary widely. Generally, in a community property state, any property acquired while a couple is married to each other is the property of both spouses, no matter whose name appears on the deed (see "Joint Tenancy"). When the property is sold, it is necessary to obtain both spouses' signatures on the new deed, no matter whose name appears on the deed that gave either of them title to the property. Many lawyers in these community property states require both spouses' signatures on all deeds conveying the property of married couples (even for those properties held in joint tenancy that should not be affected by the community property laws) to protect themselves and their clients from the possibility that there might be a defect in the joint tenancy such that the property may actually be owned by tenants in common. In this event, it would be susceptible to the dower and curtesy provisions of the state's community property laws.

Tenancy by the Entirety

About half the states permit *tenancy by the entirety.* It operates similarly to a joint tenancy with the following special requirements:

- The owners must be married to each other.
- Neither party can sever their legal interest in the property without permission of the other or by order of the court (which is very hard to obtain).
- A tenancy by the entirety becomes a tenancy in common when the parties are divorced.
- Upon the death of either party, while they are still married to each other, the interest of the decedent automatically passes to the survivor.

There are five unities required to create a tenancy by the entirety:

---

1. Unity of time

2. Unity of title

3. Unity of interest

4. Unity of possession

5. Unity of marriage of the owners to each other

There are several advantages to a tenancy by the entirety:

- It protects each spouse from the other spouse conveying or mortgaging the property without the other spouse's permission.
- In some states it prevents one spouse's creditors from forcing the sale of the property to satisfy that spouse's debts (because to do so would infringe on the ownership by the other spouse).
- It provides for automatic survivorship.

Fee Simple Ownership in Trust

A trust is an arrangement whereby a trustee takes over the ownership of a property upon the direction of the property owner (called the *trustor*) for the benefit of one or more beneficiaries.

Trustees get their power to act from a trust agreement created and executed by the trustor or beneficiaries. It spells out exactly what the trustees are empowered to do on behalf of the beneficiaries of the trust. A trust is a fiduciary relationship between the trustees and the beneficiaries of the trust.

There are three common types of trusts:

> **1.** Living trusts
> **2.** Testamentary trusts
> **3.** Land trusts

Living Trusts

A *living trust* is created by a trust agreement executed during the trustor's (property owner's) lifetime.

The *trustor* conveys ownership of property to a trustee (who can be an individual, lending institution, corporation, and so on) who manages the property for the benefit of the designated beneficiaries.

Testamentary Trusts

Testamentary trusts are usually established by a will after the death of a property owner, to manage the property for the benefit of the heirs, who become the beneficiaries of the trust.

Land Trusts

Only a few states still permit the use of *land trusts*. One of the primary purposes of a land trust is to hide the true identity of the property owner. This is possible in some states where the land records do not have to indicate the identity of the beneficiary of a land trust. This can be very useful when a developer is trying to create an assemblage to be used to develop a project. If the true identity of the developer were known, it would most likely have the effect of increasing the selling price on the remaining land needed to be acquired for development. Another advantage is that a beneficial interest can be assigned without the formality of a recorded deed that reveals the selling price.

A complex tax reason for land trusts is that the beneficiary's interest is personal and will pass at the beneficiary's death under the law of the state in which the beneficiary resided rather than the laws of the state where the property is located. This is especially helpful if the property is located in several different states.

Individuals are usually the only ones who can create land trusts. However, corporations and individuals can be the beneficiaries. A land trust ordinarily continues for a definite term such as 25 years. The trust expires if it is not extended, and depending on the provisions of the trust, the trustee either distributes the assets to the beneficiaries or sells the assets and distributes the proceeds to the beneficiaries.

JOINT OWNERSHIP

Cooperative Ownership

Cooperative ownership is a form of ownership in which a corporation or land trust is established to hold title to an entire property, usually financed with a blanket mortgage, which covers the entire property.

7.5→ When buyers want to own cooperative units, they cannot buy the unit directly. Instead, they buy stock in the cooperative corporation which owns the property. They and the other stockholders are given a proprietary lease on a specific unit, subject to certain conditions and obligations as to its use, subleasing rights, and sale.

Usually the sale of stock and the proprietary lease are subject to the approval of the board of directors of the cooperative. When the proposed sale and lease are approved, a stock subscription agreement and lease are signed. The obligations of the cooperative unit owner include payment of a proportionate share of the expenses incurred by the corporation for maintenance, property taxes, and debt service.

One disadvantage is that, as the balance of the blanket cooperative mortgage decreases (as it is paid off), the amount of cash required to purchase a unit increases. Fortunately, innovative cooperative loans made available by some lenders help reduce this problem.

In some states, a securities license is required to sell a cooperative.

In spite of the technical differences between cooperative ownership and condominium ownership, the public tends to view them as being similar. Often they directly compete with each other for customers.

Condominium Ownership

A condominium is a form of ownership which involves a separation of property into individual ownership elements and common elements. A *condominium*
7.6→ *ownership* is established by a declaration or master deed. Each owner of a unit receives fee simple title in a unit deed, finances the unit with an individual mortgage, and pays his or her share of the common charges. The owners own their unit but do not own the land or any of the other common elements.

A *homeowners' association* (HOA) is responsible for the governance of the condominium and maintenance of the land, common areas, and elements. Common elements are those portions of the community property owned *pro rata* on an undivided basis by the owners of the individual units. State statutes that permit the creation of the condominium form of real property ownership are called horizontal property acts. They permit ownership of a specified horizontal layer of airspace as opposed to the traditional vertical ownership from the earth below to the sky above.

Condominiums are often confused with planned unit development (PUD).

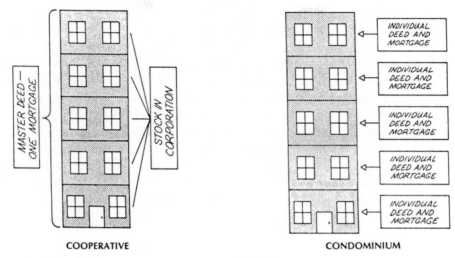

Figure 7.2 Types of ownership (cooperative and condominium).

One of the big differences is that, in a PUD, the individual owner owns the land under and around his or her unit. Checking the deed will clearly indicate what form of ownership the property is.

Timesharing

Fractional interests created by *timesharing* have been marketed extensively in recent years, especially in resort areas. Timesharing is the sale of limited ownership interests in residential apartments or hotel rooms. Multiple purchasers buy interests in the same unit. They buy a segment of time (usually one or more weeks).

A timeshare estate consists of a fee simple interest. Once the property has been developed and sold, each unit owner's occupancy and use of the property is limited to a specified period of time during the year or there may be floating time that varies each year. Many timeshare projects designate the specified period by week number. Timeshare weeks traditionally run from Friday to Friday, Saturday to Saturday, or Sunday to Sunday. The weeks normally start about 3:00 p.m. and end about 11:00 a.m. The hours in between are used by the staff of the management company to clean the unit and make it ready for the next occupant.

A timeshare estate interest runs forever. However, improvements do not last that long and what happens when the improvements become old is not clear, because this form of ownership is relatively new. In most cases, the multiple timeshare owners will contribute to upkeep and replacement of furnishings on a *pro rata* basis.

Anticipating this problem, another type of timeshare ownership has developed called a *timeshare use*. Instead of fee simple, the buyer gets the use of the unit for a long period of time (usually 30 or more years). At the end of that time, the project again belongs to the developer.

Organizations like Resorts Condominium International (RCI) allow timeshare owners to trade their weeks with timeshare owners in other facilities. Rather than making a direct trade, units are put into a common computer space bank of units. This system seems to work quite well, and many timeshare owners enjoy using units all over the world.

With few exceptions, timeshares have not proven to be good financial investments. Owners who wish to liquidate their shares in a unit find them hard to sell, and often must take a substantial loss. They continue to be popular because many buyers do not buy them as an investment. They are looking for a lifestyle benefit.

OTHER BUSINESS OWNERSHIPS

Partnerships

General Partnerships

Most states have passed the Uniform Partnership Act. It is designed to encourage *general partnerships* used for business relationships. It provides that partners may own partnership real estate in their own individual names or in the name of the partnership itself.

The Uniform Partnership Act also creates a special type of ownership called tenancy in partnership. These are some of its special provisions:

- Consent is required of all the general partners to sell, assign or mortgage the property.
- The creditors of one partner cannot attach an individual interest in the property. In order to attach the property, a debt must be of the partnership and not just the individual partner.
- A partner's legal interest in the partnership property is not subject to dower, curtesy or homestead protection and it is not inheritable.

Generally when a partner dies, his or her interest in the property goes to the surviving partners and not to the heirs of the deceased partner.

Limited Partnerships

Limited partnerships are an investment vehicle designed to allow passive investors to invest in real estate development and other projects. The original purpose of limited partnerships was to develop an ownership form with the tax advantages of the partnership form of ownership and the same protection from creditors that investors have when they buy stock in a corporation.

A limited partnership consists of at least one general partner, who under certain circumstances in some states is a corporation, and one or more limited partners. To be classified as a limited partner, the limited partner cannot have any control over the day-to-day operations of the partnership.

Unless the general partners commit fraud or fail to pay their taxes, they shoulder all the risk of the investment beyond the amount of capital supplied by the limited partners. An exception is that some limited partnerships have a provision for the limited partners to be called on to make additional capital contributions under certain specified circumstances and for specified limited amounts. Failure to meet these additional capital calls subjects the limited partners to forfeiture of their partnership interests, but that is the extent of their liability.

Many states and the federal government classify larger limited partnerships as security investments and require them to be registered under the provisions of their security laws. Many states require that brokers have a security license in order to sell interests in limited partnerships.

The typical limited partnership is used to sell real estate investments to wealthy people. Often investors are required to demonstrate that they have the required assets and income before they are permitted to invest. Typically, the general partners conceive and structure the investment opportunity and then raise money from the limited partners. This money is used to purchase land and construct and rent the improvements. Any profits are divided among the partners. Usually, the general partners have first claim on the profits to reimburse them for their investment start-up costs. Additional profits are then split (usually unequally) among the general and limited partners.

People who sell or invest in limited partnerships should seek advice from their attorney before they sign any papers or offer any shares for sale.

Limited liability limited partnerships are frequently used by real estate businesses. Technically they are a type of limited partnership. Similar to a traditional limited partnership, they can have one or more general partners and one or more limited partners. The general partners manage the business and the limited partners only invest in the business.

Unlike a traditional limited partnership, in a limited liability limited partnership the general partners can be protected from personal liability of the operating entity. This is one of the primary motivations for this type of ownership.

The limited partner liability connected with the traditional limited partnership and the limited liability limited partnership cannot exceed the amount of money invested into the enterprise.

Corporate Ownership

7.7→ A *corporation* is an artificial being granted a charter, usually by a state and occasionally by the federal government, called a certificate of incorporation. There is no such thing as a commonlaw corporation. State and federal statutes require corporations to do certain things and file specified reports with the state or federal government. Failure to meet the state's or federal government's requirements will cause the corporation to be dissolved and go out of existence.

A corporation doing business within the state where it was incorporated is called a domestic corporation. When they engage in business in another state, they are called foreign corporations.

Corporations can only do what they are empowered to do in their charters. Most corporations have very broad powers (but some have only limited powers, which may not include real estate functions). These powers often include the power to develop, buy, sell, rent, and exchange real estate just as an individual or partnership would. Most corporations can mortgage property in order to borrow money.

There are four different types of corporations that often own real estate:

> **1.** Public corporations
>
> **2.** For-profit corporations
>
> **3.** Not-for-profit corporations
>
> **4.** Limited liability companies

Public Corporations

Public corporations are various government corporations such as cities, towns, counties, school districts, port and highway authorities, public improvement corporations, and so on, organized to perform government functions.

For-Profit Corporations

For-profit corporations are created to run businesses and engage in a wide variety of other activities. The stock of for-profit corporations can be publicly traded or privately owned. Small for-profit corporations can elect to be taxed as partnerships. These are called Subchapter S corporations. They can only engage in limited real estate activities.

The circumstances under which the corporation may engage in real estate transactions and who must sign the required documents are spelled out in the corporation charter or articles of incorporation and bylaws. These expressly state how directors and officers are elected, what powers they have, and which officers, directors, or other persons must sign real estate transaction documents. One of the disadvantages of corporate ownership of real estate is that depreciation for income tax purposes cannot always be passed through directly to the owner of the corporate stock. Income received by the stockholders of a corporation is therefore often subject to double taxation.

Not-for-Profit Corporations

Not-for-profit corporations are often churches, fraternal organizations, foundations, educational institutions, health care facilities, and a wide variety of other corporations whose purpose it is to perform a public service outside the functions of government. Many not-for-profit corporations are exempt from federal and some local taxes. Tax exemption is not automatic and must be applied for and approved by the taxing authority.

Limited Liability Company

A *limited liability company* is similar to a corporation in that it provides liability protection to the owners. It is best suited for businesses with a limited number of owners. Owners are known as members. The rights of one or more classes of members are described in an operating agreement.

When there is more than one owner, the entity is treated as a partnership for tax purposes. This avoids double taxation that can occur with corporations. Another advantage of a limited liability company is that there is no requirement for an annual meeting of the shareholders.

Syndications

A *syndication* is a private or public partnership, corporation, or any other ownership form that pools funds for the acquisition and development of real estate projects. Syndications are established when an individual or group purchases interests in real estate for the purpose of transferring (syndicating) those interests to a larger number of people, who will be the investors. The syndicators will be the managers. A syndicate comes under the state and federal syndication laws. Many of the rules applying to limited partnerships also apply to syndications.

Joint Ventures

A *joint venture* is a combination of two or more entities that join to undertake a specific project. They often take the form of a general partnership or limited partnership. It differs from a syndication or partnership in that it is usually intended to be temporary and project specific. There usually is a separate agreement for each project.

Real Estate Investment Trusts (REITs)

In 1967 changes to the IRS code went into effect that permitted the formation of *real estate investment trusts* (*REITs*). The purpose of this change was to permit the formation of public trusts that could invest in real estate like a corporation but pass the profits and losses directly to their investors (without being double taxed). The stated purpose of these special tax provisions was to allow and encourage small investors to pool their money to participate in larger real estate transactions and thereby make a new source of financing available to large real estate developments.

REITs generally invest their money in one of two ways:

> **1.** They lend money for interest income generation. These REITs are called mortgage REITs.
>
> **2.** They buy, rent, sell, and develop property. These REITs are called equity REITs.

The REIT is allowed to earn income from its real estate investment and pass the income along to the shareholders (who are technically trust beneficiaries) of the REIT without the REIT paying any federal income taxes. The REIT shareholders pay tax on the income they receive at their own tax rates. To avoid paying taxes, a REIT must distribute 90 percent of its income annually.

FRACTIONAL OWNERSHIP (APPURTENANCES)

A fractional ownership or interest is a division of the physical use of a property. A leasehold and leased fee interest represent common examples of fractional interests. Some are called appurtenances, and these are automatic rights that go along with the ownership of real estate. Air rights, water rights, and subsurface rights are some examples of appurtenances. Following are the most common types of fractional ownerships and appurtenances.

Horizontal Subdivision

A *horizontal subdivision* is the description of the surface area boundaries of a property. It is used primarily to describe an individual ownership of a unit in a multistory condominium building.

Vertical Subdivision

A *vertical subdivision* refers to the division of *air rights* and *subsurface rights*. Subsurface rights in the form of oil or mineral rights are commonly leased or sold. Their exclusion may have little effect on surface land values if the terms of conveyance protect the surface from interference. Subsurface rights may also involve accommodation of underground pipes and cable lines.

Air Rights

Within the distances normally encompassed above the land surface, real estate ownership may be considered to be between vertical boundaries above the site. This means that a 100- by 100-foot parcel of land is not a square surface but a cube. Accordingly, this cube may be divided not only vertically but also horizontally as in the individual layers of the cake. The useful height of the cube (number of stories) is limited only by the practicalities of engineering, economics (highest and best use), and zoning. When air rights are divided from a property and sold or leased (or an easement is granted), the portion that is divided off is called an *air lot*.

   With the advent of air travel, the right to total control air space has been limited to the space that the owner of the property could reasonably expect to use. Space above that is shared by the public. The space where satellites fly is now considered to be international space.

Water Rights (Riparian Rights)

Land bordering on flowing bodies of water such as rivers and streams enjoy the right to use the water, along with owners of other contiguous portions of the same body of water. Such water rights are referred to as *riparian rights*. Land bordering on large bodies of water, such as a lake or a sea, carries with it littoral rights, which allow the owners use and enjoyment of an adjacent body of water.

Mineral Rights

Like air and other rights, *mineral rights* may be owned, sold, bought, and transferred to another party for profit. Within the distances normally encompassed below the land surface, real estate ownership may be considered to be between vertical boundaries below the site. This means that a 100-foot by

100-foot parcel of land is not a square surface but a cube. Accordingly, this cube may be divided not only vertically, but also horizontally, as in the individual layers of a cake. The useful depth of this cube is limited only by the practicalities of mining engineering. In areas where there are minerals under the land, the ownership of the surface is often different from the ownership of the subsurface.

Transferable Development Rights (TDRs)

Transferable development rights (TDRs) emerged in the real estate industry during the 1970s. A transferable development right is a development right that cannot be used by the landowner, but can be sold to landowners in another location. Some TDRs are used to preserve property for agricultural production, open space, or historic buildings.

LESSER ESTATES (NONFREEHOLD ESTATES)

Leasehold

A *leasehold* estate is known as a lessee's estate or tenant's estate.

Leasehold Interest

A lease between the fee simple property owner and a tenant usually is a contract that transfers some of the fee simple property owner's rights to the tenant in exchange for the payment of rent by the tenant to the fee simple property owner. The interest that the tenant acquires is called a *leasehold interest.*

Leased Fee Interest (Estate)

An owner may lease real estate, thereby relinquishing the right of occupancy but retaining the title to the fee, subject to the lease, including the recovery of use at the expiration of the lease, known as the reversionary rights. The value of a *leased fee* estate interest is profoundly affected by its length and terms, which may cover a wide range of provisions agreed on between the parties. Generally, a long lease for commercial or residential property will develop leasehold value as other rentals in the area increase, unless it has adequate rent adjustment provisions.

OTHER INTERESTS

Leasehold Estate—Estate for Years (Fixed Termination)

A leasehold estate that exists for a specified period of time is called a *leasehold estate for years*. The word *years* is not interpreted strictly and the period of time can be any specified period of time. Unless otherwise specified in the lease, at the end of the specified time the tenant is supposed to move out and surrender the property to the property owner in the same condition, less normal wear and tear.

Normally, a lease is not terminated on the death of the landlord or the tenant, and the heirs of either party are bound by the terms of the lease.

The basic principle of a lease is that the owner of the property gives up the right to use the property to a tenant, and in return, receives rent.

Not all states require that leases for over a year must be in writing. Many states do require that they be recorded. When a property is sold, it is normally sold subject to any existing lease.

Sandwich Lease

A *sandwich lease* is a lease held by a lessee who sublets all or part of his or her interest, thereby becoming a lessor. Typically, the sandwich leaseholder is neither the owner of the fee estate nor the user of the property. The sandwich lessee tries to profit from the rent differential of the other leases.

Leasehold Estate—Estate from Period to Period (Periodic Tenancy)

A leasehold estate from period to period (*periodic tenancy*) is a lease for a specified period of time that automatically renews itself, without the landlord or the tenant having to notify the other that they wish to continue. If either party wishes to terminate the lease, they have to give notice to the other party in a manner and at a time specified in the lease. Failure to give timely, correct notice automatically extends the lease into the next period.

A week-to-week or month-to-month tenancy is generally created when the tenant takes possession of a property and pays rent on a weekly or monthly basis. Normally the amount of notice that is required by either the tenant or the landlord is the normal period for which rent is paid.

Leasehold Estate—Estate at Will

A *leasehold estate at will* gives the tenant the right to occupy the property for an unspecified amount of time.

A common type of "at will" arrangement is when a landlord lets a tenant stay in possession until some event at an unspecified time in the future takes place. A common example is the completion of a new building for the tenant to move into.

Leasehold Estate— Estate at Sufferance

A *leasehold estate at sufferance* is created when a tenant, who originally legally occupied the property, continues to occupy the property after they are supposed to move out according to their lease arrangements. They continue to hold possession of the property without the consent of the landlord, that is, at sufferance.

Life Estate

A *life estate* consists of the total rights of use, occupancy, and control of a property that is limited to the lifetime of a designated party. The designated party is known as the *life tenant*. Usually it is the obligation of a life tenant to maintain the property and to pay the taxes during the period of the life estate.

During the period of a life estate there are two separate interests in the property:

> **1.** The interest of the life tenant
>
> **2.** The interest of the owner of the fee who is called the *re-maindeman* during the period that the life estate is in effect

There are a variety of way life estates can be created. The most common are:

- By operation of law
- By will
- By a deed of conveyance

Types of Life Estates

Life Estate (Not Inheritable)—Conventional Life Estate–Ordinary with Remainder

A *life estate* (*not inheritable*) is ownership, possession, and control for the life of an individual. When the person dies, the ownership, possession, and control go to someone else. When the life that controls the ownership is the life of the grantee, it is called a life estate ordinary. If the estate then passes on to a third party, it is called a life estate ordinary with remainder.

An example of a life estate ordinary with remainder is when a property passes on to the children of the owner on the owner's death.

Life Estate (Not Inheritable)—Conventional Life Estate–Ordinary with Reversion

This is the same as a life estate–ordinary with remainder except if the estate passes back to the grantor or their heirs, it is called a life estate–ordinary with reversion.

An example of this type of estate is when a property is deeded to a grantor's wife, and when she dies the property passes back to the grantor if he is still alive, or on to his heirs rather than to his wife's heirs if he is deceased.

Life Estate (Not Inheritable)—Conventional Life Estate–pur autre vie with Remainder

This is a life estate (not inheritable) where ownership, possession, and control are for the life of someone other than the person who has the ownership, possession, and control. When the third person dies, the ownership, possession, and control go to someone else. When the life that controls the ownership *is not* the life of the grantee, it is called *pur autre vie*. If the estate passes on to someone other than the grantor, it is called a life estate *pur autre vie* with remainder.

Life Estate (Not Inheritable)—Conventional Life Estate–pur autre vie with Reversion

This is a life estate (not inheritable) where ownership, possession, and control are for the life of someone other than the person who has the ownership, possession, and control. When the third person dies, the ownership, possession, and control go to someone else. When the life that controls the ownership *is not* the life of the grantee, it is called *pur autre vie*. If the estate passes on to the grantor, it is called a life estate *pur autre vie* with reversion.

Life Estate (Not Inheritable)—Legal Life Estate–Dower

Dower is the life estate a wife has in the estate of her deceased husband. It still exists in a few states. The applicable state statutes provide that the surviving wife has from a one-third to a one-half interest in the property owned by her husband, even if her name does not appear in the title to the property.

In states where dower rights exist, it is important to have the wife of a property owner also sign the deed in order to prevent a dower claim in the future.

Life Estate (Not Inheritable)—Legal Life Estate–Curtesy

Curtesy is the life estate a husband has in the estate of his deceased wife. It exists only in a few states. The applicable state statutes provide that the surviving husband has from a one-third to a one-half interest in the property owned by his wife, even if his name does not appear in the title to the property.

In states where curtesy rights exist, it is required to have the husband of a property owner also sign the deed in order to prevent a curtesy claim in the future.

Life Estate (Not Inheritable)—Legal Life Estate–Homestead

A *homestead* is a property that is used as a family home. In some states with homestead laws, all or part of the property is shielded from the claims of creditors. This exemption applies only for unsecured loans. It does not apply to mortgages, tax liens, or mechanic's liens. Homestead laws differ widely, especially as to how much is protected, which ranges from the whole value of the homestead to some specified dollar amount.

SUMMARY

What gives real property its value is its ability to satisfy the needs and desires of human beings. In order to estimate the value of property it is necessary to understand some value theory.

The terms *real estate*, *real property*, *chattels*, and *fixtures* have different meanings, which must be understood in order to use them correctly.

Most appraisals made by real estate appraisers include an estimate of value only of the real estate even when some non–real estate items may be included in the sale. When business assets or items of personal property are included in the estimated value, this must be clearly explained in the appraisal report.

The characteristics of immobility, indestructibility, and uniqueness make land different from most other commodities that are bought and sold in a market. The four concepts that relate to land are geographic, legal, social, and economic.

The bundle of rights theory illustrates the rights of real estate ownership, which are the rights to sell, occupy, lease, mortgage, donate, and do nothing with your property.

The government has rights and powers that affect real estate. They are the rights to take the property for the benefit of the public and to exercise police powers to promote the safety, health, morals, and general welfare of the community. Property without an identifiable private owner reverts to the government through the power of escheat.

There are two forms of private ownership in the United States called freehold estates and nonfreehold estates. There are many forms of joint ownership including corporate, condominium, and cooperative ownership. Corporations are artificial beings that can own real estate.

Syndications are formed so that many investors can pool their resources to buy real estate they could not afford to own as individuals. A popular form of syndication is a real estate investment trust (REIT), many of which issue stock that is publicly traded.

REVIEW QUESTIONS

7.1 Which of the following is not one of the bundle of rights?
   A. The right to give the property to the government without their permission
   B. The right to do nothing with the property
   C. The right to donate it to your aunt
   D. The right to lease it to an American Indian

7.2 A freehold estate is ownership:
   A. That was free because it was inherited
   B. For a short period of time
   C. For a long period of time
   D. An ownership for an undetermined period of time

7.3 Which is a way a fee simple estate can be held?
   A. In severalty
   B. In trust
   C. By co-owners
   D. All of the above

7.4 Ownership in severalty is ownership by:
   A. One person
   B. Two people
   C. Several people
   D. None of the above

7.5 In a cooperative form of ownership the ownership of the real estate is:
   A. A partnership of all the tenant
   B. A corporation or land trust
   C. A trust company
   D. None of the above

7.6 In a condominium each owner receives:
   A. Fee simple ownership of their individual unit
   B. Curtesy ownership of their individual unit
   C. A leasehold interest in their individual unit
   D. A life estate interest in their individual unit

7.7 A corporation is:
   A. A common law entity
   B. At least 10 or more people acting together
   C. An artificial being
   D. None of the above

7.8 Ad valorem taxation is based on the:
   A. Income of the property owner
   B. Value of the furniture plus the value of the real estate
   C. Value to the property owner of their special public improvements
   D. Value of the whole property

7.9 Special assessments:
 A. Have been ruled by the courts to be discriminatory
 B. Are assessed annually based on their changing value to the owners
 C. Are used to pay for public improvements
 D. None of the above

7.10 Eminent domain is:
 A. The right of the state to use a property it does not own
 B. The power of the government to take property it needs
 C. The requirement of the approval of the voters for each taking
 D. None of the above

7.11 Freehold estates are:
 A. The same thing as leasehold estates
 B. Different from leasehold estates
 C. Created when a person dies without an estate
 D. None of the above

7.12 Fee Simple ownership is:
 A. The most common form of ownership in the United States
 B. Not allowed in community property states
 C. Only ownership by a single person
 D. None of the above

7.13 The most prevalent type of joint ownership in the United States is:
 A. Fee double
 B. General partnerships
 C. Limited partnerships
 D. None of the above

ANSWERS

The answer to each question is indicated by the letters A, B, C, or D. The explanation of the answer is indicated by the page number and an arrow points to the appropriate paragraph on the page.

Q 7.1	A	Page 86	Q 7.4	A	Page 88	Q 7.7	C	Page 98	Q 7.10	B	Page 87	Q 7.13	D	Page 89
Q 7.2	D	Page 87	Q 7.5	B	Page 94	Q 7.8	D	Page 86	Q 7.11	A	Page 87			
Q 7.3	C	Page 88	Q 7.6	A	Page 94	Q 7.9	C	Page 86	Q 7.12	A	Page 87			

CHAPTER 8

Private Restrictions: Easements, Liens, and Encroachments

PRIVATE RESTRICTIONS

A property's legal owner and type of ownership can be ascertained from public records, which are maintained by the government. RESPs must know where the records are maintained for each community in which they operate and how, when, and where they can be accessed. Local title or abstract companies may also provide this information.

8.1➔ The most common form of property ownership is ownership in *fee simple*. If a property is not in fee simple, the elements of title that are to be excluded must be indicated and carefully analyzed so that they are not misrepresented to potential buyers.

OWNERSHIP RESTRICTIONS

Covenants, Conditions Restrictions (CC&Rs)

Covenants, conditions, and restrictions (CC&Rs) are a statement of all these items that affect the use of a parcel of land (also known as a *declaration of restrictions*). A subdivider may note the restrictions on the map or plan when recording the subdivision plat. If the restrictions are numerous, the subdivider may also prepare a separate document called a declaration, listing all the restrictions, and then record this declaration. The restrictions usually aim at a general plan of development and require all lot owners to comply with certain building standards and conform to certain other restrictions. For example, the CC&Rs may require lot owners to construct homes valued at more than 1,800 square feet or to obtain prior design approval from a designated architectural control committee. Once recorded, the restrictions in the declaration run with the land and bind all future lot owners. Any owner can enforce the restrictions against any other owner who violates any of them. A declaration of restrictions can be terminated by lapse of a specified time period or by agreement of all benefited parties.

The following are typical provisions in a declaration of restrictions:

- "Each building or other structure shall be constructed, erected, and maintained in strict accordance with the approved plans and specifications."
- "No building shall be located on any lot nearer than 35 feet to the street lot line, nearer than 30 feet to the rear lot line, or nearer than 10 feet to the side lot lines."
- "No building or structure shall be more than 25 feet in height as measured from the highest natural grade at any point on the perimeter of the foundation of the structure to the highest point of the roof."
- "No animals, livestock, or poultry of any kind shall be raised, bred, or kept on any land in the subdivision except by special permit issued by the board of directors. However, a reasonable number of dogs, cats, or other common household pets may be kept without the necessity of obtaining such permit."

"Lawsuits frequently arise over interpretation of questionable language in a declaration of restrictions. For example, if trailers are prohibited, does that also exclude mobile homes? Or does the word *structure* include a swimming pool or fence? Restrictions should be carefully drafted to avoid ambiguity"

(*The Language of Real Estate*, 5th edition, Real Estate Education Company, Chicago, IL 2000).

Deed Restrictions

8.3→ Certain limitations may be placed on the use of land by a property owner and will run with the title to the land as it passes on to future owners. *Deed restrictions* are contractual and are usually imposed by the deeds used to convey title. Sometimes deed restrictions are imposed on an entire tract by the developer of the land. Usually, the goal of such restrictions is to protect the value of all properties in the development.

At one time, racial and religious *restrictive covenants* were not unusual in single-family subdivisions. In the 1930s and 1940s, the Federal Housing Administration sometimes required such restrictions as a condition for granting mortgage insurance. Restrictions of this kind have been unlawful for many years, following a 1948 decision of the Supreme Court, and now violate many federal, state, and local fair housing laws. Occasionally, deeds containing such restrictive covenants still surface, but this type of restriction is not enforceable.

EASEMENTS

8.4→ An *easement* is a nonpossessing interest held by one person (the benefited party) in the land of another person (the burdened party) whereby the first person is accorded partial use of such land for a specific purpose. Easements are created to allow access to property, whether it be from public or private land. An easement may be vertical, horizontal, or both, such as in the case of underground utility line easements.

The party who is the beneficiary of an easement owns a dominant estate relative to the land included in the easement. The party who grants an easement has a servient estate relative to the land included in the easement. The rights of both the dominant estate and the servient estate are defined in the grant of easement document.

Other easements give nonowners the right to use the air over a property or subsurface rights for utility installations, soil removal, flood control, or mineral extraction. RESPs must consider the effect of an easement on the value of the property.

When an easement is granted to allow specific access to or through a property, it may be called a right-of-way. The owner of the property is not dispossessed from the property, but rather coexists side-by-side with the holder of the easement, sharing the use of the property.

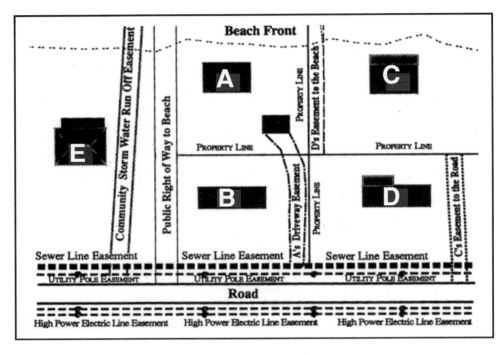

Figure 8.1 Types of easements.

The following are illustrated in Figure 8.1:

- A has an easement over B for a driveway to the street.
- The high power electric lines, utility lines, and sewer lines have utility easements.
- D has an easement over C to the beach.
- The community has a storm water run off easement over E.
- C has an easement over D to get to the city road.
- There is a public right-of-way on the border between E on one side and A and B on the other.

Affirmative and Negative Easements

8.5➤ An *affirmative easement* permits one to use someone else's property. A *negative easement* is used to prevent the use of a property in some way. Examples of negative easements are light and air easements, which prohibit construction of improvements that would block the light and air of another property in a manner described in the easement. A common type of negative easement is a *scenic easement* that prevents building in a manner that would block a view.

Common Types of Easements

There are four general classifications of easements:

> 1. Easements appurtenant
> 2. Easements in gross
> 3. Party wall easements
> 4. Easement by prescription

Easement Appurtenant

An *easement appurtenant* is a right acquired by the owner of one parcel of land to use the adjacent land of another owner for a special purpose. It always requires two parcels of property owned by different people. The property that benefits from the easement is known as the dominant tenement and the property that is subject to the easement is known as the servient easement. The owner that benefits from the easement has a dominant estate and the owner who grants the easement has a servient estate.

Easement in Gross

An *easement in gross* is the right to use the land of another without the existence or necessity of an adjacent or dominant estate. One type of easement in gross is a personal easement, where the rights do not run with the land. A personal easement in gross is not inheritable and it cannot be mortgaged or transferred to a third party.

The other type of easement in gross is a *commercial easement.* It is one of the most common types of easements. Examples are easements to put up advertising billboards on the land and rights-of-way for utility lines. Commercial easements in gross are inheritable and may be mortgaged, sold, or otherwise transferred.

Party Wall Easements

A *party wall easement* is typically a cross-easement providing two parties an easement for the exterior of their common party wall to serve both properties. The easement could exist as a result of a party wall agreement or a grant of easement (implied or explicit). The party wall easement or party wall agreement should be in writing and it should identify the rights and responsibilities of each party.

The rights might include the ability to rely on the wall for structural support for the benefit of the balance of the improvement. The responsibilities might include sharing the responsibility and cost of maintaining the wall or avoiding all activities that could damage the wall.

Easement by Prescription

Easements by prescription, also called prescriptive easements, are implied easements that give the easement holder a right to use another person's property for the purpose the easement holder has used the property for a certain number of years, which varies from state to state. Prescriptive easement doctrine is not the same as adverse possession doctrine, which allows someone to acquire ownership of the title to a property by asserting possession of the property for the legally required period; in some states, additional requirements apply. For example, in California, the adverse possession statute requires the "adverse possessor" to assert possession of the property *and* pay all property taxes for at least five years. Prescriptive easements are a type of implied easement, in that they arise even though they are not expressly created or recorded. Unlike other implied easements, however, prescriptive easements are hostile (i.e., without the consent of the true property owner). Prescriptive easements do not convey the title to the property in question, only the right to utilize the property for a particular purpose. They often require less strict requirements of proof than fee simple adverse possession.

Once they become legally binding, easements by prescription hold the same legal weight as written or implied easements. Before they become binding, they hold no legal weight and are broken if the true property owner acts to defend his or her ownership rights. Easement by prescription is typically found in legal systems based on common law, although other legal systems may also allow easement by prescription.

Creating an Easement

An easement may be created by:

- Agreement
- Express grant in a deed
- Reservation in a deed
- Necessity
- Condemnation
- Prescription

Creating an Easement by Agreement

Creating an *easement by agreement* is accomplished when the parties make clear their intention to create the easement. A party wall, party driveway, and use of water rights are examples of easements that are often created by agreement.

Creating an Easement by an Express Grant in a Deed

To create an *easement by express grant* in a deed, the owner of a property prepares a deed that delineates the easement being given, executes the deed, and delivers it. The deed should also be recorded.

Creating an Easement by Reservation in a Deed

An *easement by reservation* (or easement by exception) in a deed is created when the owner of a property deeds the property to someone else and reserves in the deed the right to use some portion of the land.

Creating an Easement by Necessity

An *easement by necessity* is an easement created by operation of law rather than the express intention of the parties affected by the easement. The requisite elements for creation of an easement by necessity or implication are:

- One owner owns two parcels of land.
- The owner uses one of the parcels in a way that benefits the other parcel.
- The beneficial use is apparent and obvious.
- The beneficial use is continuous.
- The beneficial use is necessary.
- At some time after the above conditions have been met, the owner transfers title to one of the parcels to another owner, without mentioning the easement that has been created.

An example of an easement of necessity is where a property owner owns a house and an adjacent lot. A driveway is built with half on each lot. When the extra lot is sold off without the benefit of a survey or mention of the fact that the driveway is half on the lot being sold and half on the lot being retained, an easement by necessity is created.

Creating an Easement by Condemnation

An *easement by condemnation* is created by a legal action of the government, when the government exercises its right of eminent domain. When the government condemns a property for public use, it has a choice of taking the whole fee or just acquiring an easement for the intended use. Since the government must pay fair value for the property rights it takes, it may elect to take only an easement in order to reduce the amount of money it will have to pay the property owner for the taking.

Creating an Easement by Prescription

Easements by prescription, also called prescriptive easements, are implied easements that give the easement holder a right to use another person's property for the purpose the easement holder has used the property for a certain number of years, which varies from state to state.

Unlike other implied easements, however, prescriptive easements are hostile (i.e., without the consent of the true property owner). Prescriptive easements do not convey the title to the property in question, only the right to utilize the property for a particular purpose. They often require less strict requirements of proof than fee simple adverse possession.

Once they become legally binding, easements by prescription hold the same legal weight as written or implied easements. Before they become binding, they hold no legal weight and are broken if the true property owner acts to defend his ownership rights. Easement by prescription is typically found in legal systems based on common law, although other legal systems may also allow easement by prescription.

Termination of an Easement

An easement may be terminated by:

- Release of the easement by the owner of the easement
- Combining the dominant and servient property into one property
- Abandonment of the easement by the owner of the easement
- The purpose of the easement ceasing to exist
- Expiration of a specified time period for which the easement was created
- Excessive use (such as when a residential walkway is converted to a commercial use)
- Lawsuit

Maintenance and Repair of an Easement

Unless the document creating an easement specifically requires it, the owner of the servient estate has no duty to make the easement ready for use, repair it, or do any other act for the benefit of the easement owner. On the other hand, the owner of the easement (benefited party) has the right to take any measures necessary to make the easement reasonably usable.

PROFIT À PRENDRE (PROFIT)

A right to take part of the soil, gravel, water, minerals, coal, gas, oil, timber, and game off the land of another is called a *profit à prendre.*

LICENSE

A *license* is a personal right given by contract to enter the property of another. It usually includes the right to do something, such as park a car, hunt, or otherwise enjoy the use of the property for a specified purpose. A license does not encumber the title to real property. It is revoked on the death of the property owner or the person who has the license.

LIENS

A *lien* is a legally recognized claim or charge on a property that encumbers the property and makes it security for the payment of a debt or the taxes of the property owner. Liens are established as either voluntary or involuntary. Liens may be specific liens (in *rem*) or general liens (in *personam*). The party who owes the money is called the *lienor* and the party to whom the money is owed the *lienee*.

Types of Liens (Legal Basis)

There are three classifications of liens that indicate the legal basis of their creation:

> **1.** Contractual liens
> **2.** Statutory liens
> **3.** Equitable liens

Contractual Liens

A *contractual lien* is created by agreement of the parties. A common example is a mortgage lien.

Statutory Lien

A *statutory lien* is created by a specific statute. The most common is a real estate tax lien. They are involuntary and require no action by the property owner.

Equitable Lien

An *equitable lien* is created when justice and fairness would require a court of equity to declare that such a lien exists or when the conduct of the parties implies that a lien was intended.

Types of Liens
(Voluntary and Involuntary)

Liens are also classified as:

• Voluntary liens
• Involuntary liens

Voluntary Lien

A *voluntary lien* is created by the property owner. The most common voluntary lien in real estate is a mortgage. It is voluntary because it is contracted by the agreement of both of the parties.

Involuntary Lien

An *involuntary lien* is created by statute and is also called a *statutory lien*.

Types of Liens
(General and Specific)

Liens are also classified as *general liens*, which are liens on all the property owned by the debtor within the jurisdiction of the court that orders the lien and *specific liens*, which are liens on a specific property.

• General Liens
    • Judgment
    • Federal tax liens (IRS)
    • Estate and inheritance tax liens
    • Descendant's liens

• Specific Liens
    • Mortgage lien
    • Vendor's lien
    • Vendee's lien
    • Real property tax lien
    • Special assessment tax lien
    • Mechanic's and materialman's lien
    • Attachment lien
    • Bail bond lien
    • Corporation franchise tax lien
    • Municipal utility lien
    • Decedent's debts lien

Judgment Liens

A *judgment lien* arises from lawsuits for which money damages are awarded. The law permits a judgment lien, which is an involuntary lien, to be placed against the real estate of the parties who lose the law suit. There are restrictions upon what type of real estate the court will enter a judgment lien against. Often it must be in the county where the court has jurisdiction. For example, a state court cannot place a lien on property out of the state. When the loser of the court action does not pay the judgment voluntarily, the winner can ask the court to issue a *writ of execution* that directs the sheriff to seize and sell a sufficient amount of the loser's property to pay the judgment and the expenses of the sheriff.

Federal Tax Liens (IRS)

The U.S. Internal Revenue Service (IRS) can lien a person, partnership, or corporation property for failure to pay taxes such as income tax or taxes due on employees' payroll. A *federal tax lien* (IRS) is a general, statutory, involuntary lien. These liens are a claim against all the delinquent's real estate and personal property. Unlike a property tax lien, an IRS lien *does not* have a priority over any other lien. Its priority is based on the date when it was filed.

Estate and Inheritance Tax Liens

An *estate and inheritance tax lien* is a general, statutory, involuntary lien. By statute, the state acquires a lien on the assets of a deceased person, so that the assets cannot be sold until all the taxes and debts are paid. The deed given by the person ordered to do so by the court does not guarantee the title, so it is important to get title insurance when buying property going through the probate process, as it is hard to be certain that all the estate and inheritance taxes have been paid.

Mortgage Lien

A *mortgage lien* is a voluntary lien executed by the property owner to borrow money, using the property as security. The property owner signs a mortgage note that becomes part of the mortgage lien against the property. When the mortgage is paid off, the lien is discharged by the lender filing a release. If the mortgage payments are not made when due, the mortgagee can institute a legal action called a *foreclosure.*

There can be more than one mortgage lien against a property at the same time. Their priority of claim against the proceeds of a foreclosure sale are in the order that they were filed. A mortgage can be (and often is) transferred by the lender (mortgagee) to another party by assignment of the mortgage and mortgage note.

Vendor's Lien (Seller's Lien or Purchase Money Mortgage)

A vendor's lien (seller's lien or *purchase money mortgage*) arises when the seller of property, instead of receiving the purchase price all in cash, takes a note and mortgage for part of the purchase price. This is a lien on the property that was sold for the unpaid balance of the purchase price.

Vendee's Lien

A *vendee's lien* is created in some states when a sales contract is executed for the sale of a parcel of property, and the seller defaults.

The buyer obtains a lien (in some states, this requires a court order) against the property. This prevents the seller from selling the property to someone else, until after the defaulted sale is resolved. The lien is for any deposit money the seller possesses plus any money expended by the buyer in the process of purchasing the property. If a broker was used, the deposit would be held in trust until the dispute was resolved. The seller can also try to collect damages for lost profits caused by the failure of the transaction to close.

Real Property Tax Lien

When property taxes are not paid, they become an involuntary, specific tax lien against the property on which the property taxes were levied. *Real property tax liens* have a priority and come before most other liens, regardless of when they are filed.

Special Assessment Tax Lien

When special assessment taxes are not paid, they become an involuntary, specific tax lien against the property on which the property taxes were levied. *Special assessment tax liens* have a priority and come before most other liens, regardless of when they are filed.

Mechanic's and Materialman's Liens

A *mechanic's lien* or *materialman's lien* is a specific lien that may be filed by such people as a contractor, subcontractor or individual carpenter, plumber, electrician, or almost anyone who has provided labor or service used in the construction, improvement, or repair of real estate.

All states have special statutes that not only give these parties the right to place a lien against a property where they supplied labor, services, or supplies, but also provide for a priority position against all other types of liens except property tax and special assessment liens.

In some states, proof must be shown that those filing the lien were hired by the property owner. In other states it is only necessary to show that the work was done and the property owner did not object to it being done.

The rights subcontractors have to file liens vary from state to state. The problem arises when the contractor is paid by the property owners, but then fails to pay the subcontractor or the material supplier. Many states impose an obligation on the property owners to determine that everyone who worked on the property has been paid. This is usually accomplished by having the subcontractors provide affidavits, releases, or other proof that they have been paid in full. The property owners hold some money back from the general contractor until they receive the proofs of payment. An alternative way for property owners to protect themselves is to require that the general contractor post a security bond to guarantee the payments to subcontractors or material suppliers and the performance of work for which they are paid.

8.10 ➤ A mechanic's lien is backdated to the time when the work was completed. Each state has a window of time (three months is typical) within which a mechanic's or materialman's lien can be filed and be given a back-dated priority.

DISCHARGE OF A MECHANIC'S OR MATERIALMAN'S LIEN
There are four common ways a mechanic's lien or materialman's lien may be removed from a property:

1. The property owner pays the amount owed and receives a *certificate of execution, satisfaction of lien* or *release of lien* from the parties who filed the lien.

2. The lien expires. Each state has a statutory period in which the lien holders must start a foreclosure action or the lien will expire.

3. The property owner can post a bond in the amount of the lien. The property is then released and the amount that is owed is determined later, when the case comes to trial (or the statutory period expires).

4. The property owner may disagree with the lien and have the lien claimant served with notice to commence action or foreclose within a short period of time (usually 30 days). This forces the claim into court. If the lien claimant fails to pursue the claim in court within the statutory time, the court will discharge the lien without a trial.

Bail Bond Lien

A *bail bond* is security that is posted with the court to guarantee that a person who is accused of a crime will appear for his or her trial. Many courts will accept a lien on real estate called a *bail bond lien* as collateral instead of a cash bond. When the charged person appears at his or her trial as promised, the property lien is released by a certificate obtained from an official of the court.

Corporate Franchise Tax Lien

A state can lien a person, partnership, or corporation property for failure to pay state corporation franchise taxes. A state *corporation franchise tax lien* is a general, statutory, involuntary lien. These liens are a claim against all the delinquent's real estate and personal property. Unlike a property tax lien, a state lien *does not* have a priority over any other lien. Its priority is based on the date when it was filed.

Municipal Utility Lien

Some states now give public utilities the right to file a *municipal utility lien* against a property when utility bills have not been paid. In some states, the lien can be filed when the bill is due from a tenant. A state tax lien is a general, statutory, involuntary lien. In most states, they do not have a priority position.

Decedent's Debts Lien

When a person dies, his or her assets are subject to prior liens and new liens that often are filed when creditors receive notice of the debtor's death. These *decedent's debts liens* are general, statutory, involuntary liens. Generally, the probate court will try to pay the taxes and debts claimed against an estate out of the proceeds of the sale of personal property. If that is not sufficient, the court will order that the real estate be sold to raise money to pay the taxes and debts. When the court sells the real estate, a deed is given by a person ordered to do so by the court. These deeds do not guarantee the title, so it is important for a buyer to obtain title insurance when buying property going through the probate process, as it is hard to be certain that all the debts have been paid and the title is clear.

LIS PENDENS

8.9► *Lis pendens* (Latin for *litigation pending*) is a device that allows potential lien holders to establish their priority before that actual lien is filed. It is commonly used in litigation, where the parties who are filing the suit (which may not be tried for many years) are able to get their priority set back in time to the date that the lis pendens was filed. A property that was purchased (or a lien that was filed) after the date that the lis pendens was filed would be subject to the lien described in the lis pendens when it is filed, even if the original property owners no longer own the property.

ENCROACHMENTS

8.7➤ There are two types of encroachments. Either the improvement may extend over the property line onto abutting properties or the improvements on abutting properties may encroach onto the subject site.

An encroachment is a trespass onto the land of another owner that is created by a tree, shrub, part of a building, fence, or some other object going across the boundary line of the property being encroached upon.

In Figure 8.2, the shrubs, tree, fence, and garage from Property A encroach onto Property B, a vacant lot. The boundary line between the two properties is shown as a dotted line.

8.8➤ The encroaching owner is a *trespasser.* In many encroachment situations, the *encroachment* is not understood, unintentional, or accidental. Some encroachments are very obvious and others can be detected only by a survey.

It does not matter that an encroachment is not understood, unintentional, or accidental; it is still an encumbrance. In most states, if a trespass or encroachment continues for a prescribed period of time (which is specified in the state statutes), it may become an easement by prescription. Before the expiration of the statutory prescribed time, the property owner who is being encroached upon may bring a court action to remove the encroachment and collect damages for any harm that was done by the encroachment.

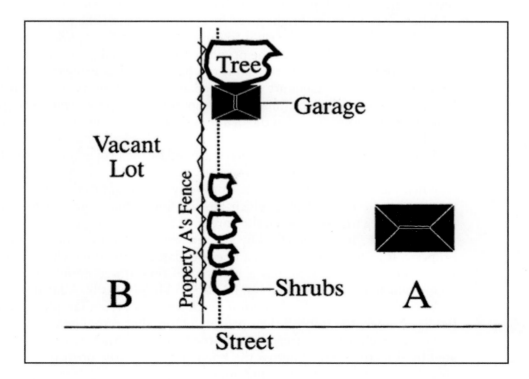

Figure 8.2 Types of encroachments.

SUMMARY

RESPs must be knowledgeable about what kind of title is being offered for sale. They must be able to explain to buyers what title problems exist if they are aware of them. There is nothing more frustrating to an RESP than to get all the way to a closing, only to discover that there are title problems that have not been solved and the sale is not going to close.

Covenants, conditions, and restrictions (CC&Rs) are a statement of all these items that affect the use of a parcel of land (also known as declarations of restrictions).

Deed restrictions are limitations that may be placed on the use of land by a property owner and will run the title to the land as it passes on to future owners.

Racial and religious restrictive covenants are no longer enforceable.

An easement is the right a nonowner has to use another person's property without paying rent. Some easements give nonowners the right to use the air over a property or subsurface rights for utility installations, soil removal, flood control, or mineral extraction. The RESP must consider the effect of an easement on the value of the property.

There are four general classifications of easements: easements appurtenant, easements in gross, party wall easements, and easement by prescription.

An easement may be created by an agreement express grant in a deed, reservation in a deed, necessity, condemnation, and prescription.

A license is a personal right given by contract to enter the property of another. It usually includes the right to do something such as park a car, hunt, or otherwise enjoy the use of the property for a specified purpose.

Liens are legally recognized claims or charges upon a property which encumber the property. Liens are established as either voluntary or involuntary. Liens may be specific liens (in *rem*) or general liens (in *personam*). The party that owes the money is called the *lienor* and the party to whom the money is owed the *lienee*.

A *mortgage lien* is a voluntary lien executed by the property owner to borrow money, using the property as security.

When the owners do not pay their property tax a *real property tax lien* can be filed by the tax collector which has a priority that comes before most other liens, regardless of when they are filed.

A mechanic's lien can be filed by anyone who does construction work on a property. It is unique because it can be backdated to the time when the work was completed. Each state has a window of time (three months is typical) within which a mechanic's lien can be filed and be given a backdated priority.

A *lis pendens* (Latin for *litigation pending*) is a device that allows potential lien holders to establish their priority before that actual lien is filed.

An encroachment is a trespass onto the land of another owner that is created by something going across the boundary line of the property being encroached upon from an adjoining nonowned property.

REVIEW QUESTIONS

8.1 What is the least limited form of real estate ownership?

   A. Fee complete

   B. Fee without easements

   C. Fee simple

   D. None of the above

8.2 Who usually creates the covenants, conditions and restrictions?

   A. An aggrieved homeowner

   B. The initial developer

   C. The zoning board

   D. None of the above

8.3 Deed restrictions are usually:

   A. Limitations on use

   B. Exceptions to zoning

   C. Allowed because of the police power of the state

   D. All of the above

8.4 Easements may be:

   A. Vertical

   B. Horizontal

   C. Both of the above

   D. None of the above

8.5 An affirmative easement permits:

   A. Someone to use your property

   B. No blocking a view

   C. Both of the above

   D. None of the above

8.6 Which of these is a common type of easement?

   A. Easement appurtenant

   B. Easement gross

   C. Party wall easement

   D. All of the above

8.7 An encroachment is when:

   A. An improvement extends over an adjoining now owned property

   B. Improvements from an abutting property extend on an adjoining property

   C. Both of the above

   D. None of the above

8.8 Which of the following excuses a trespasser making an encroachment?

   A. When they did not understand they were encroaching

   B. When the encroachment was unintentional

   C. Both of the above

   D. None of the above

8.9 Lis pendens means:

   A. A lease has been signed but not recorded

   B. No signed lease exists for the subject space

   C. The lease is conditional upon a credit check of the pending tenant

   D. None of the above

8.10 What makes a mechanic's lien different from most other liens?

A. There is no limit on how much the lien may be for

B. The lien may be backdated to when the work was completed

C. There is no time limit as to when it can be filed

D. None of the above

CHAPTER 9

Government Lending Institution and Land Use Regulations

The use of the land in most areas is regulated by the federal, state, county, and municipal government. Governments have a variety of ways to regulate land use, which are covered in this chapter. Fair housing laws and environmental regulations are covered in separate chapters.

FEDERAL GOVERNMENT REGULATION

9.1➤ The U.S. government primarily uses five agencies to regulate the lending institutions and to manipulate the supply and cost of money:

1. Federal Reserve System (the Fed)
2. U.S. Treasury (the Treasury)
3. Federal Deposit Insurance Corporation (FDIC)
4. Federal Home Loan Bank (FHLBanks)
5. Office of Thrift Supervision (OTS)

Federal Reserve System (the Fed)

9.2→ The *Federal Reserve System* (the Fed) is the central bank of the United States. It was founded by Congress in 1913 to provide the nation with a safer, more flexible, and more stable monetary and financial system. Over the years, its role in banking and the economy has expanded.

Today, the Federal Reserve's duties fall into four general areas:

9.3→
1. Conducting the nation's monetary policy by influencing the monetary and credit conditions in the economy in pursuit of maximum employment, stable prices, and moderate long-term interest rates

2. Supervising and regulating banking institutions to ensure the safety and soundness of the nation's banking and financial system and to protect the credit rights of consumers

3. Maintaining the stability of the financial system and containing systemic risk that may arise in financial markets

4. Providing financial services to depository institutions, the U.S. government, and foreign official institutions, including playing a major role in operating the nation's payments system

9.4→ The Federal Reserve System is composed of 12 Federal Reserve districts and run by a seven-member Board of Governors, who are nominated by the president of the United States and confirmed by the Senate. A full term is 14 years. A new term begins every two years. A member who serves a full term may not be reappointed.

Currently, the chairman is Ben Bernanke, appointed by President George W. Bush and sworn into office on February 1, 2006, for a term lasting until 2010. Bernanke succeeded Alan Greenspan, who served for more than 18 years under four U.S. presidents.

All federally chartered commercial banks and many state-chartered banks become members of the Federal Reserve System by buying stock in the Fed's district bank in the region where the lender is located. The institutions clear their checks through the Fed's check-clearing system. They maintain the cash 9.5→ reserves required by the Fed and can borrow short-term money from the Fed without collateral. The interest rate that they are charged is called the *federal fund rate*. Every time the Fed raises or lowers the federal fund rate, it makes newspaper headlines. It usually also has an effect on the stock and bond markets and on mortgage interest rates.

This is one of the Fed's methods for controlling the amount of money in circulation. Higher interest rates decrease borrowing by business and industry, and lower interest rates tend to increase borrowing and the money supply.

Regulation Z (Truth in Lending Act)

Members of the Federal Reserve System must comply with the Fed's regulatory policies, one of which is *Regulation Z*, required by the *Truth in Lending Act*. The heart of Regulation Z is the requirement that all lenders disclose to borrowers the true cost of their loan. The *annual percentage rate* (APR) is calculated based on all the costs of obtaining the loan, not on just the money borrowed. It is calculated on the net amount of money the borrower receives, after deducting all the costs of acquiring the loan. The intent of this law is to help consumers shop for the lowest interest rate available by giving them a standardized measure of comparison. In addition, the act requires that a disclosure statement be given to the borrower either before the loan closes or at the loan closing. The disclosure statement must include:

- The annual percentage rate (APR)
- The lenders' identity
- The amount of finance charges
- A complete schedule of payments, with due dates and payment amounts
- Notice of the right to receive an itemization of what is being borrowed
- Late payment fees
- Prepayment penalties
- A description of what is being taken as security
- Assumption rights

An important provision is the right of some borrowers to rescind the loan within three business days following their receipt of the disclosure statement. Since this statement is rarely delivered in advance, what usually happens is that the disbursement of the funds is held up until three days after the loan documents are signed. Fortunately for real estate professionals, there is an exclusion of this provision that applies to the purchase of a principal residence.

The Truth in Lending Act also contains loan advertising guidelines.

U.S. Treasury (the Treasury)

The *U.S. Department of the Treasury* is a cabinet department. It was established by an act of Congress in 1789 to manage government revenue. The first secretary of the treasury was Alexander Hamilton. President George Washington asked Hamilton after first having asked Robert Morris. Hamilton almost single-handedly worked out the national financial system, and for several years he was a force behind Washington's administration as well.

The Treasury is administered by the U.S. Secretary of the Treasury and the Treasurer of the United States, who receive and keep the money of the United States. The Treasury prints and mints all paper currency and coins in circulation through the Bureau of Engraving and Printing and the U.S. Mint. It also collects all federal taxes through the Internal Revenue Service (IRS).

9.8➤

Federal Deposit Insurance Corporation (FDIC)

9.9➤

The *Federal Deposit Insurance Corporation* (FDIC) is a U.S. government corporation created by the Glass-Steagall Act of 1933. The vast number of bank failures during the Great Depression spurred the U.S. Congress into creating an institution that would guarantee banks, inspired by the Commonwealth of Massachusetts and its Deposit Insurance Fund (DIF). The FDIC provides deposit insurance, which currently guarantees checking and savings deposits in member banks up to $100,000 per depositor. A higher amount is guaranteed for IRA accounts.

Federal Home Loan Bank (FHLBanks)

The *Federal Home Loan Bank* (FHLBanks) is a regional cooperative of 12 FHLBanks. Their 8,100-member lenders are the largest source of residential mortgage and community development credit in the United States. Each regional FHLBank manages and is responsive to its customer relationships, while the 12 FHLBanks use their combined size and strength to obtain the necessary funding at the lowest possible cost.

FHLBanks help communities by providing billions of dollars of primary liquidity to approximately 80 percent of the nation's financial institutions. This allows member institutions to remain active lenders, in all economic cycles, to help their local economies grow.

The mission of the FHLBanks is to provide cost-effective funding to members for use in housing, community, and economic development; to provide regional affordable housing programs, which create housing opportunities for low- and moderate-income families; to support housing finance through advances and mortgage programs; and to serve as a reliable source of liquidity for its membership.

To raise money, FHLBanks issue debt to institutional investors through the Office of Finance. FHLBank debt is the joint and several liability of all the FHLBanks.

Office of Thrift Supervision (OTS)

The *Office of Thrift Supervision* (OTS) is part of the U.S. Treasury. Its mission is to supervise savings associations and their holding companies in order to maintain their safety and soundness and compliance with consumer laws, and to encourage a competitive industry that meets America's financial services needs.

Interstate Land Sales

9.10→ Real estate is primarily regulated by the individual states. However, based on the federal government's constitutional right to regulate interstate commerce, the U.S. Congress has passed legislation allowing the federal government to regulate *interstate land sales*.

Congress passed The *Federal Interstate Land Sales Full Disclosure Act,* which regulates interstate land sales of unimproved lots. It became effective in 1969 and was made more restrictive by a 1980 amendment. This act is administered by the Secretary of Housing and Urban Development (HUD) through the Office of Interstate Land Sales Registration. Its purpose is to prevent fraudulent marketing schemes that may transpire when land is sold "sight unseen." The act requires that a developer file a statement of record with HUD before offering unimproved lots in interstate commerce by telephone or through the mail. The statement of record requires disclosure of specific information about the property.

Developers of these properties are also required to provide each purchaser or lessee of such property with a printed property report, which discloses specific information about the land before the purchaser or lessee signs a purchase contract or lease. Information required on these property reports includes things such as the type of title a buyer will receive, number of homes currently occupied, available recreation facilities, distance to nearby communities, utility services and charges, and soil or other foundation problems in construction. If the purchaser or lessee does not receive a copy of the property report prior to signing a purchase contract or lease, the purchaser will likely have grounds to void the contract.

9.11→ The act provides for several exemptions, the most important of which are:

- Subdivisions in which the lots are of five acres or more
- Subdivisions consisting of fewer than 25 lots
- Lots offered for sale exclusively to building contractors
- Lots on which a building exists or where a contract obligates the lot seller to construct a building within two years

If a developer offers only part of the total tract owned and thereby limits the subdivision to fewer than 25 lots to acquire an exemption, the developer may not sell additional lots within the tract later. HUD considers these additional lots to be part of a "common plan" for development and marketing, thereby eliminating the opportunity for several exemptions for the developer as a result of piecemeal development of a large tract in sections of fewer than 25 lots at a time.

The act provides severe penalties for violation by a developer or a real estate licensee who participates in marketing such a property improperly. The developer or the real estate licensee, or both, may be sued by a purchaser or a lessee for damages and is potentially subject to criminal penalty of fines up to $5,000 or imprisonment for up to five years or both. Therefore, prior to acting as an agent for a developer in marketing interstate property, both real estate brokers and sales associates must be certain that the developer has complied with the act or is exempt from the act.

ZONING

A History of Zoning

Zoning gives the public the right to control the uses of private property for the benefit of the entire community. Zoning is part of the police power of the government. Zoning as it is today did not exist during the nineteenth century, which was the major development period for most American cities. As a result of this lack of control and planning, cities developed with congested streets, overcrowded buildings, poor light and air, and a poor mixture of uses, each negatively affecting the others. From this disorganization came the deteriorated commercial areas, slums, and urban blight of today. The population density increased, resulting in housing pressures and the construction of large apartment houses that were built to the boundaries of their lots. People with enough money to do so fled the cities into newly developing suburbs. As city redevelopment continues, this trend is reversing. Starting in the 1980s there was a trend to move back into city centers with better access to culture, education, and employment. In many cities the trend continues today.

9.12→

In the early 1900s, Los Angeles and Boston passed laws that controlled the use of land. In 1916, New York City passed the first truly comprehensive zoning ordinance. It included use districts, control of building heights, and lot area coverage regulations. Shortly thereafter, other cities passed zoning ordinances that stood up against many court challenges. By the middle of the 1920s, the constitutionality of zoning laws, based on the government's right to use its police power to regulate private property, was well established in legal precedent.

9.13→

The zoning ordinances of the 1920s were primarily concerned with height regulations and front, side, and rear yard requirements, to ensure that the population had adequate light and air. By the late 1920s, zoning regulations began to emphasize the separation of residential neighborhoods from commercial and industrial uses. Also, high-density apartments were segregated from low-density single-family areas.

New Thrust in City Zoning

Since World War II, a new thrust in city zoning has occurred. These newer zoning regulations emphasize direct control of development and design in an effort to prevent further spread of urban congestion and decay.

Zoning often restricts the use of a site that would be physically possible and economically feasible to develop. Residential properties are often bought and sold subject to the success of an application for zone change, such as from residential to more intensive apartment use or from residential to industrial or business use.

Some suburban communities have attempted to use zoning as a method of preventing further growth, by increasing the minimum lot requirements to sizes greater than necessary for orderly growth. Other requirements making it economically impossible to develop vacant land have been imposed in some areas, but growing social and legal pressures are being applied to stop the use of punitive "exclusionary" zoning to restrict community growth and prevent specific development such as low-income or elderly housing.

Ideally, zoning should be used to regulate and promote orderly and consistent development but should not be used to stop expansion. Good zoning fosters sound values, sufficient municipal services such as schools and parks, and a climate of orderly growth without the stagnation of highly restrictive regulation.

Planned Unit Development (PUD)

Planned unit developments (PUDs) are a new type of zoning classification that are increasing in popularity. Lots are grouped in clusters, with part of the land dedicated to open space for use by everyone. Ownership in the common land may be held by an owners' association or by the community. In its most advanced form, the PUD can actually be an entire city, where some of the nonresidential land is reserved for future commercial and industrial development as well as recreational and open-space uses. In order to encourage developers to create PUDs, the developer is usually allowed to build more houses in the development than would be allowed by the existing zoning.

9.14-➤

Houston a Community without Zoning

Not every community has resorted to zoning to control its development. There are vast areas of the country that are not governed by zoning regulations. Many of these areas are rural or sparsely populated. However, one of the best arguments against government control by zoning is the metropolitan center of Houston, Texas. Without zoning, Houston has developed into one of our most modern, exciting cities. The citizens of Houston have voted several times to remain a community without zoning.

The key to Houston's orderly development has been the use of deed restrictions and the enforcement of a rigid building code that includes control of density. By a special act of the Texas legislature, the enforcement of deed restrictions is the responsibility of the city attorney rather than the individual property owner. Deed restrictions are also enforced by the local lending institutions, which refuse to loan money for purposes that violate deed restrictions. In addition, Houston's civic clubs help enforce and police deed restrictions.

There are some problems, of course. Federal funds for urban renewal were withheld for a time, and in many areas the mixture of uses has caused severe losses in value for adjoining properties. Older residential areas tend to be hastened through the last phase of their life cycle. Still, advocates of no-zoning make a strong case that land values and land uses should depend on the natural highest and best use of property, and not on the misguided whims or outright self-interest of local political appointees who traditionally sit on zoning boards.

Building Codes, Fire Codes, and Health and Safety Laws

9.15 ➤ *Building codes, fire codes,* and *health and safety laws* are specific restrictions that, like zoning regulations, are based on police power. State and local governments, recognizing the need to protect public health and safety, have enacted building codes, fire codes, and health and safety laws for this purpose. They provide design control of permitted buildings and delineate the types of materials that may be used. In addition to a general building code, many states and communities have separate electric and plumbing codes, based on considerations of health and safety.

Before a *building permit* is granted, the design of a proposed new structure or the addition or alteration of an existing structure must meet the building code requirements. During construction, local building department inspectors visit the construction site to make certain all the codes are being observed. When the building is finished, a certificate of occupancy is issued to **9.16 ➤** the property owner to show that the building meets the codes. Without a certificate of occupancy, the building cannot be legally occupied or used.

Traditionally, the establishment of building codes has been delegated by the states to individual communities or counties. The result in many areas has been a lack of uniformity in enforcement from one area to another. Also there are increased costs of construction as builders, engineers, and architects have to adapt to each community where they are working. The trend now is toward statewide building codes.

Historical Restrictions and Preservation

Laws that regulated historic properties were first passed in the United States before World War II. They are based on the same police power of the government that is the basis for all zoning laws. The purpose of these laws is to preserve buildings and areas that contain historical and architecturally significant buildings.

9.17→ The most common technique used to accomplish this goal is to create a historic district, which is an area designated to retain and preserve its historic quality. In 1966 Congress passed the Historic Preservation Act, which defined the federal government's role in historic preservation. Most states have passed legislation authorizing local governments within the state to establish historic districts.

The federal government has established a process to certify historic districts. It consists of stringent requirements that must be met before the certification is obtained, including compliance with the criteria of the National Register of Historic Places. There are a variety of tax credits available to developers and investors who renovate buildings in a federally designated historic district.

EMINENT DOMAIN

Property Rights Required for Public Use

A judicial or administrative proceeding to exercise the power of *eminent domain* is the power of the government (federal, state, local, or improvement **9.18→** district) to take private property for public use or quasi-public use such as a redevelopment project. The agency taking the property is the *condemnor*. The owner whose property is taken is called the *condemnee*. In the taking of private property for public use, a fee simple estate or any lesser right, such as an easement, may be acquired. A common example of condemnation is the taking of an owner's access to a street entrance when the county builds a highway or dedicates the area for county use.

Just Compensation

The actual market value of the property at the date of the summons is generally the measure of valuation used to determine the amount of *just compensation*. However, there is often disagreement about the appropriate market value or damages to the remainder, and this becomes the basis for most condemnation lawsuits.

Certain items are not considered in determining the value of condemned property, such as loss of goodwill, relocation expenses, inconvenience, and the value of the improvements added to the property after the date of the summons being served on the property owners to notify them that their property is going to be taken.

In many cases of eminent domain, government officials and community leaders work with developers to propose a plan to seize property and make improvements to encourage economic development. Once local government approves the plan, the town offers to compensate displaced property owners. Though the town cuts the checks, the compensation typically comes out of the developer's pocket. In some cases, property owners may be able to swap their existing property for a unit in the new development.

If a business is operating from the condemned real estate, the owner is ordinarily entitled to compensation for the loss or disruption of the business resulting from the condemnation. In a minority of jurisdictions, the owner may also be entitled to compensation for loss of *goodwill,* the value of the business in excess of fair market value due to such factors as its location, reputation, or good customer relations. If the business does not own the land, but leases the premises from which it operates, it would ordinarily be entitled to compensation for the value of its lease, for any fixtures it has installed in the premises, and for any loss or diminishment of value in the business.

Due Process of Law

The right of eminent domain is limited by the Fifth Amendment to the U.S. Constitution, which states: "No person shall be deprived of life, liberty, or property without due process of law; nor shall private property be taken for public use without just compensation." Private property may be taken without the consent of the owner, whose claim may be that the land was not taken for a sufficient public use or, as is more frequently the case, that just compensation was not paid.

A 2006 U.S. Supreme Court case, *Kelo et al. v. City of New London et al.,* upheld the right of the city of New London, Connecticut, to take a property that was in good condition to be used for part of a new commercial development. The Supreme Court said it was up to the state legislature to limit what constituted "public use" if they wanted it to be something less than what is permitted by the U.S. Constitution in the Fifth Amendment's taking clause.

Property rights advocates contend that abuses of the exercise of these powers in the past require substantial safeguards to the public today, including requirements to force the various government units that use eminent domain to document the need for it and allow the public access to and comment on the proceedings before the real property can be seized. Federal statutes require complete relocation programs to be administered by the various states in order to receive federal participation in the costs of the improvements (often 80 percent) and further require full certification that the public process and benefits were offered to the claimants and that the benefits were actually paid to the correct claimants and displacees.

The use of eminent domain has slowed dramatically nationwide as the full build-out of the Interstate Highway System approaches and reflects the fact that needs in the future will be for projects of a local nature such as schools, roads, and other local improvements.

Determining Need for Taking

The modern trend of the courts is to define the term *public use* broadly to include not only public facilities such as streets, roads, schools, and parks, but also property that would provide intangible public benefits, such as scenic easements. It is up to the state's legislature to reduce these broad powers if they see fit to do so.

Notification

When a property is being taken, the taking authority must notify the owner that the property is going to be taken and what their rights are. Often the notification is in the form of a summons served by a sheriff or process server. The date of the notification in many jurisdictions is the date of taking used in the appraisal.

Determination of Compensation

The amount of money to be received by property owners for the taking of their property under the power of eminent domain is called *just compensation*. A property owner can either accept the offer of compensation made by the taking authority or request and receive a court hearing for determining the appropriate amount of compensation.

Negotiation

Eminent domain law and legal procedures vary, sometimes significantly, between jurisdictions. Usually, when a unit of government wishes to acquire privately held land, the following steps (or a similar procedure) are followed:

1. The government attempts to negotiate the purchase of the property for fair value (just compensation).

2. If the owner does not wish to sell, the government files a court action to exercise eminent domain and serves or publishes notice of the hearing as required by law.

3. A hearing is scheduled, at which the government must demonstrate that it engaged in good-faith negotiations to purchase the property but that no agreement was reached. The government must also demonstrate that the taking of the property is for a public use, as defined by law. The property owner is given the opportunity to respond to the government's claims.

4. If the government is successful in its petition, the government takes possession of the property and subsequent proceedings are held to establish the fair market value of the property. Any payment to the owner is first used to satisfy any mortgages, liens, and encumbrances on the property, with any remaining balance paid to the owner. The government obtains title.

5. If the government is not successful, or if the property owner is not satisfied with the outcome, either side may appeal the decision.

Whole versus Partial Taking

Many condemnations do not take the whole property. For example, when a street is widened, the state may take only a small strip of land from the front of the property. This is called a *partial taking*. This could result in anything from a severe loss of value to just a nominal loss.

Most jurisdictions require that the value of the taking be determined by the before-and-after technique. An appraiser determines the value of the property before it was taken and the value of the remainder of the property after the taking. The difference between these two values is the damages caused by the taking.

ESCHEAT

Escheat is the reversion of property to the state or county, as provided by state law, in cases where a property owner dies intestate and there are no

9.19➤ known heirs. It is against public policy to have a piece of property that is not owned by anyone, because the results is a property that nobody is responsible for taking care of.

Each jurisdiction has regulations about the steps that must be taken before the government can take ownership of a property by *escheat*.

SUMMARY

The U.S. federal government primarily uses five agencies to regulate the lending institutions and to manipulate the supply and cost of money. They are the

Federal Reserve System (the Fed), U.S. Treasury (the Treasury), Federal Deposit Insurance Corporation (FDIC), Federal Home Loan Bank (FHLBanks), and the Office of Thrift Supervision (OTS).

The Truth in Lending Act, known as Regulation Z, requires that lenders disclose to borrowers in their advertising and directly to the borrower at the time the loan is made what the annual rate of interest is (APR) is on their loan. The requirement that this information must be given to most borrowers three days in advance of the loan being made does not apply to the purchase of a principal home.

The sale of vacant land in a state other than where the buyer resides is called an interstate land sale and is subject to federal regulation based on the interstate commerce clause in the U.S. Constitution. Developers must provide the potential buyer complete, accurate details about the land being purchased prior to the sale. Failure to do so is grounds for the buyer to void the sale. The principal exemptions from these requirements are subdivisions in which the lots are of five acres or more, subdivisions consisting of fewer than 25 lots, lots offered for sale exclusively to building contractors, and lots on which a building exists or where a contract obligates the lot seller to construct a building within two years. Both the developers and their real estate sales agents are subject to severe penalties for a violation of these requirements.

Zoning is part of the police power of the government and gives the public the right to control the uses of private property for the benefit of the entire community. Zoning regulations are local in nature. There are few state and no federal zoning regulations.

A type of zoning classification that is increasing in popularity is planned unit developments (PUDs). Lots are grouped in clusters, with part of the land dedicated to open space for use by everyone. Ownership in the common land may be held by an one owners' association or by the community. Houston is a large community that has not resorted to zoning to control its development. The key to Houston's orderly development is the use of deed restrictions and the enforcement of a rigid building code. Houston has had many problems as a result of its lack of zoning. However, no-zoning remains popular, and several elections ratifying it have been successful.

Building codes, fire codes, health codes, and fire and safety laws recognize the need to protect public health and safety. Before a building permit is granted, the design of a proposed new structure or the addition or alteration of an existing structure must meet the code requirements. When the work is completed, a building department official must issue a certificate of occupancy before the property can be occupied.

The purpose of historical restrictions and preservation laws is to preserve areas that contain historical and architecturally significant buildings. The historic district has become an important tool in historic preservation.

Eminent domain is the power of the government to take private property for public use. The government that takes the property must pay the owner just compensation, which is often considered to be fair market value. Businesses operating from the property being taken are also often entitled to compensation.

The government does not have to take the whole property. They can take just the piece they need. The amount of compensation to the owner of the taken property is the difference between what the property was worth before the taking and its fair market value after the taking. It is not the value of the part that was taken.

Escheat is a provision of state law that when an owner dies, and there are no known heirs, the title of the property reverts to the government.

REVIEW QUESTIONS

9.1 Which of these federal government agencies is not used to regulate lending institutions?

   A. Federal Housing Administration

   B. Office of Thrift Supervision

   C. Federal Deposit Insurance Corporation

   D. None of the above

9.2 The central bank of the United States is:

   A. Bank of America (BA)

   B. Federal Reserve System (FED)

   C. Federal Deposit Insurance Corporation

   D. None of the above

9.3 The duties of the Federal Reserve System include:

   A. Conducting the nation's monetary policy

   B. Influencing interest rates

   C. Both of the above

   D. None of the above

9.4 The Federal Reserve System is composed of how many districts?

   A. 10

   B. 12

   C. 48

   D. 50

9.5 One of the ways the Federal Reserve System controls interest rates is to:

   A. Publish a monthly interest rate directive

   B. Recommend periodically that Congress change the rate

   C. Borrow money from the U.S. Treasury

   D. None of the above

9.6 Regulation Z is also called:

   A. The Truth in Lending Act

   B. The Federal Interest Control Act

   C. HUD Borrower's Information Act

   D. None of the above

9.7 The annual percentage rate (APR):

   A. Is the nominal interest rate of the loan

   B. Is calculated on the amount of money the borrower actually receives

   C. Applies to all loans made by federally regulated lenders

   D. None of the above

9.8 The Internal Revenue Service is:
   A. Part of the Treasury Department
   B. A separate cabinet-level department
   C. In charge of printing U.S. currency
   D. None of the above

9.9 The Federal Deposit Insurance Corporation was created:
   A. By Alexander Hamilton, the first secretary of the treasury
   B. To stabilize the currency right after the Civil War
   C. As a result of the Great Depression
   D. None of the above

9.10 Real estate is primarily regulated by the:
   A. Federal government
   B. Department of the Treasury
   C. Individual states
   D. Secretary of the treasury

9.11 The Federal Interstate Land Sales Full Disclosure Act regulates all:
   A. Real estate sold interstate
   B. FHA- and VA-insured houses
   C. Vacant land sold interstate
   D. None of the above

9.12 Zoning is based on the government's:
   A. Health and safety laws
   B. Police power
   C. Interstate commerce clause powers
   D. None of the above

9.13 The first zoning laws in the United States were passed:
   A. Right after the Civil War
   B. In the early 1900s
   C. After World War I
   D. None of the above

9.14 Most planned unit developments (PUDs) permit:
   A. The same number of homes in a subdivision as would be permitted by the existing zoning
   B. A greater number of homes in a subdivision than would be permitted by the existing zoning
   C. Fewer homes in a subdivision than would be permitted by the existing zoning
   D. None of the above

9.15 Building codes are based on the government's:
   A. Health and safety laws
   B. Police power
   C. Interstate commerce clause powers
   D. None of the above

9.16 A certificate of occupancy is usually issued:

   A. At the same time as the building permit

   B. After the construction is completed and inspected

   C. After the roof and all the mechanical systems have been installed and inspected

   D. None of the above

9.17 The Historic Preservation Act was passed:

   A. Soon after the Civil War to prevent historic houses from being torn down

   B. Right after World War II to prevent houses from the 1800s from being torn down.

   C. In 1966 to allow states to create historic districts

   D. None of the above

9.18 The government's right of eminent domain is its power to take land:

   A. For any purpose as long as they pay the owner just compensation

   B. For any purpose that is approved by the state's legislative body

   C. For the sole purpose of being for public use or quasi-public use

   D. None of the above

9.19 Escheat is when property:

   A. Is taken by the government for unpaid taxes

   B. Reverts to government ownership when no known heirs exist

   C. Is taken by the government for public use

   D. None of the above

CHAPTER 10

How Real Estate Ownership Is Transferred

Some real estate salespeople study the title transfer process in order to pass their license examination and then never use the information again throughout their entire careers. This is because usually the title transfer is done by attorneys, title companies, or some combination to the two. Successful agents realize that it is not enough to get the buyer and seller together and have them sign a sales contract. From bitter experience they have learned that things can go wrong and kill a sale after the sales contract has been signed and before the end of the closing process.

10.1 →

With knowledge about how title is transferred, RESPs can facilitate the closing and sometimes sidestep what might have become a deal-breaking issue.

A HISTORY OF TITLE TRANSFER

Throughout history, wars have been fought primarily over the possession and control of land. The monarch who had control of the land gave portions of it to lords and other favored people, who in turn shared it by various means with people who worked the land and paid rent and taxes (often in the form of a portion of the crops). These people also shared responsibility for defending the land from claims by others who wanted it.

10.2→ In 1677, England passed the first statute of frauds. It required all transfers of real estate to be in writing, and signed, in order to be enforceable. From this requirement developed the deed as we know it today. In the United States today, all 50 states and territories have a statute of frauds, which requires that all transfers of real estate and leases over one year in duration be in writing and signed.

In the United States, private title to land was originally acquired in one of two ways: by grant from the federal government or by grant from a foreign government. (See Figure 10.1.) Therefore, a recorded history of title to a given parcel of land should reveal a series of voluntary (or involuntary) transfers involving private individuals, partnerships, trusts, and corporations as well as political and quasi-public units.

The history of title to a parcel of land is called its *chain of title*. When it is compiled in written form (usually in chronological order of transfers) together with a statement of all liens and other recorded liabilities to which the title may be subject, it is referred to as an *abstract of title*.

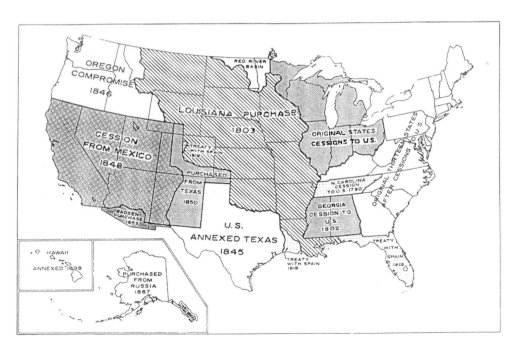

Source: History of Public Land Law Development (Washington, DC: U.S. Gov. Pinting Office, 1968), p.76 Prepared by the Bureau of Land Managment

Figure 10.1 Map of U.S. territory acquisition.

METHODS OF TITLE TRANSFER

10.3➤ Today each state has its own laws and customs governing the transfer of real estate. Generally, in most states title can be transferred one of five ways:

---

1. Voluntary alienation by deed

2. Involuntary alienation

3. Will

4. Descent

5. Dedication

Voluntary Alienation by Deed

10.4➤ Transfer of title by voluntary alienation is made by sale or gift. To voluntarily transfer a property during the life of the owner requires that the owner use some kind of written document to make the transfer. Most transfers are made using one of the many types of deed described later in this chapter.

Deed Requirements

Title in the United States is now transferred by a written and signed document known as a *deed*. The requirements of a valid deed are not the same in all states. However, there are certain basic requirements that apply to most deeds, which usually include:

10.5➤
- Grantor (seller)
- Grantee (buyer or other party receiving the property)
- Consideration (something of value)
- Granting clause (words creating the conveyance)
- Habendum clause (a clause defining the ownership taken by the grantee)
- Limitations (if any on the title)
- Legal description (of the property being transferred)
- Signature of the grantor (and sometimes a seal)
- Delivery and acceptance (by the grantee in order to pass title)
- Acknowledgment
- Recording

GRANTOR

The *grantor* is the owner of the property being conveyed or someone else who has the authority to convey the property. A deed is a form of contract, and the laws and customs that generally apply to contracts also apply to deeds.

10.6 →   The grantor must be of sound mind. It is generally held that the test of sound mind is the capacity to understand the action. A person can be temporarily not of sound mind because he or she is under the influence of drugs or alcohol. A deed executed by a person not of sound mind is voidable.

The grantor must be of lawful age, which is 18 years or older in most states. A grantor under 18 years old is a minor. As with any contract, the acts of a minor may be rescinded. Therefore, generally, minors do not have the legal capacity to transfer property. In order for a minor or legally incompetent person to convey property it is necessary to obtain permission from the court (in most states, the probate court). In states with *dower* or *curtesy*, the grantor's spouse must also sign the deed, thereby giving up marital and homestead rights.

The grantor's name must be spelled correctly and there must be no variation between the name on the new deed and the name on the deed giving the grantor title to the property. When the grantor's name has changed or is spelled differently than on the old deed, the grantor should sign the deed twice, once with his or her current name and once with the old or incorrect name that appeared on the old deed.

GRANTEE

It must be clear who the *grantee* is. It is not permissible in most states to deed a property to a fictitious person or organization.

CONSIDERATION

The same *consideration* rules apply to deeds as to contracts. For a deed to be valid, some consideration (which is something of value) must be recited in the deed. Contract law does not require that the consideration be adequate to be valid. Often, where permitted, the deed will use a nominal amount of consideration such as "$1.00 and other valuable consideration." Some states permit terms such as "love and affection" to be used for consideration. Most states require that the actual amount paid be recited in the deed. Some states go so far as to make it a criminal offense to state an incorrect consideration. This is done to facilitate the work of assessors.

GRANTING CLAUSE

The *granting clause* spells out the grantor's intention to convey the property. Terminology such as *grant*, *bargain and sell*, and *convey and warrant* may be used, depending on the state and the type of deed.

When there is more than one grantee, the granting clause often spells out the relationship of the parties to each other, if such a relationship exists. The relationship could also be that of joint tenants or tenants-in-common.

The granting clause also states the type of title that is being conveyed, such as fee simple or something other than fee simple. This is where the wording necessary to create a life estate would be included.

HABENDUM CLAUSE

The *habendum clause* usually follows the granting clause. *Habendum* means "to have and to hold" and it reaffirms the extent of the own̅ ̅ ̅hip. Its provisions must agree with those set down i̅ ̅ ̅ ̅ ̅ ̅ ̅ ̅ ̅ ̅ ̅ ̅or example, when conveying a condominium or time̅ ̅ ̅ ̅ ̅ ̅ ̅ther interest that is less than fee simple, the habendum̅ ̅ ̅ ̅ ̅ ̅he rights the owner is̅ entitled to, as well as how they a̅

LIMITATIONS CLAUSE

The *limitations clause* is also called the *ex̅ ̅ ̅ ̅ ̅ ̅ ̅ns clause*. Grantors may reserve one or more of the bu̅ ̅ ̅ ̅ ̅ ̅ ̅elves. This might be a use easement or some restriction̅ ̅ ̅ ̅w the land may be used or developed. These are commonly known as *deed restrictions*.

LEGAL DESCRIPTION

A deed should contain a *legal description* of the property. It should be in a form that allows a registered surveyor to locate the property. If the description does not meet this test, the deed may not be valid.

SIGNATURES OF THE GRANTORS

The *signature of the grantor* must appear in the deed. All of the property owners must sign the deed, including those with dower, curtesy, and homestead rights. If the grantor cannot write his or her name, the person may sign with an "X." It is then usually necessary to have witnesses sign that they have seen the grantor affix the "X." When the deed is from a corporation, it is signed by an officer of the corporation or other authorized person. A corporate seal is usually required.

10.7→

DELIVERY AND ACCEPTANCE

Before title transfers there must be *delivery* to and *acceptance* by the person receiving the property (the grantee). Delivery can be made by the grantor, by the grantor's parties (known as *escrow holders*), or by certified mail. Title does not pass until the deed is delivered. Recording of the deed is often evidence that the deed has been delivered. It is not acceptable to make a deed and have it held until the grantor dies and then deliver it to the grantee. The delivery must take place during the lifetime of the grantor.

ACKNOWLEDGMENT

Many states require *acknowledgment* of a deed, which means that the grantor's signature is acknowledged (sworn to under oath). In some states, the acknowledgment can be taken only by a notary public. In many states, attorneys, judges, justices of the peace, and military commanding officers can take the acknowledgment.

10.8→

RECORDING

Recording a deed is required in some states, and it is good basic practice in all states. Recording provides protection for the owner's title against claims of the past that were not recorded and therefore were unknown when the title was searched. Buyers of a property who rely on the recorded deed and are unaware of an unrecorded prior document are called a *bona fide purchasers* (BFP), and their real estate title is protected because of the recording.

Involuntary Alienation

The opposite of voluntary alienation is involuntary alienation, which is the relinquishing of property without the owner's consent. There are five kinds of involuntary alienation:

> **1.** Escheat
>
> **2.** Eminent domain (through a condemnation action)
>
> **3.** Foreclosure
>
> **4.** Adverse possession
>
> **5.** Natural forces

Escheat

Under the system of land ownership used in the United States, escheat does not limit land ownership, but where no owner can be found, it does provide for the reversion of the land to the state because the owner of record has died and there are no known heirs. As a matter of practicality, this does not happen very often. The rationale for *escheat* is that it is against the public interest for land to be owned by no one.

Eminent Domain (through a Condemnation Action)

The right of *eminent domain* is the power of the government to acquire an owner's land when it is needed for public use or the public good. The taking authority must pay the owner of the taken property at least its fair market value.

Foreclosure

Each state has a process by which a lender or a creditor may place a lien on a property and through a court action either take over the property by *strict foreclosure* or force its sale, which is called *foreclosure by sale,* and receive the proceeds of the sale to satisfy the debt.

Adverse Possession

Adverse possession is the acquisition of title to someone's real estate by means of open, notorious, hostile, and continuous possession for a period of time, established by statute in each state and territory.

In order to claim title by adverse possession, the claim must be made by the possessor and it is necessary for the possessor to show that all four conditions have been met. In practice, getting title by adverse possession is quite complex. What usually happens is that the people who claim title by adverse possession end up instead with some type of easement.

Natural Forces

People who had houses built on the sand dunes of the East Coast know all too well that property can be washed away by the waves via a process called *avulsion.* When property washes away more slowly, the process is called *erosion.* These are examples of involuntary alienation by *natural forces.*

Transfer of Title by Will

A will is a formal written document that allows a person to direct the distribution of his or her property after he or she dies. In most states, to be legal a will must be in writing, signed, witnessed, and attested to. Failure to follow the exact requirements of a state's statutes on how a will must be made and executed can result in an invalid will. A written amendment to a will is called a *codicil.* A person who dies without a will or with an invalid will is said to have died *intestate.* If a person's will is valid, the person has died *testate.*

The person who makes a will is called the *testator* (male) or *testatrix* (female). Real estate that is willed is called a *devise.* Whoever receives the real estate is called the *devisee.* The person who willed the property is the *devisor.* People who are in charge of carrying out the conditions of a will have various names in different states. They can be called an *executor* (male), *executrix* (female), *administrator,* or *personal representative.*

When personal property is being willed it is called a *legacy* or *bequest* and the person who receives it is a *legatee.* The parties named in a will have no rights prior to the death of the writer of the will, who can change the will whenever he or she wants.

Most states have a law that the will must be filed in a court (usually called a *probate court*) and that the probate judge must approve the conditions of the will prior to the distribution of any assets. Distribution of real estate is made with the approval of the court by one of the types of deeds discussed previously in this chapter.

Transfer of Title by Descent

When a person dies without leaving a valid will, the person has died intestate. The person's property passes to his or her heirs by *descent*. The laws of inheritance are state laws and they vary from state to state. It is assumed that people who die without a valid will want their property to go to their heirs. How the heirs split up the property is spelled out in state statutes.

In many states, the surviving spouse gets from one-third to one-half of the property. In the community property states, the surviving spouse usually gets all the property that was acquired during the marriage. When there is no surviving spouse, the children usually are the heirs to the estate. Any valid claims against the estate for the debts of the deceased are usually paid first.

Transfer of Title by Dedication

10.13 ➤ When a private owner wishes to transfer property to a public body as a gift, the process is called a gift by *dedication*. It is necessary to get an authorized public official to accept the gift on behalf of the public body.

When a new subdivision is created, it is common for the developer/subdivider to dedicate the right-of-way for the streets to the local municipality. Typically, as a condition of accepting the rights-of-way, the municipality will enter into an agreement with the developer that requires the developer to post a bond to secure the completion of the roads to the standards that are required by the municipality. The developer is responsible for the cost of the streets. Once the improvements are completed to the standards defined by the municipality and they are accepted by the municipality, the municipality becomes responsible for the maintenance of the dedicated property.

In addition to streets, title by dedication might include land for park sites, school sites, firehouses, and other community uses. Title by dedication frequently involves some level of negotiation between the grantor and the grantee.

TYPES OF DEEDS

There are a variety of types of deeds. States require different types of deeds for different purposes. Common deeds are:

- General warranty deed (warranty deed, full covenant and warranty deed)
- Special warranty deed

- Grant deed
- Bargain and sale deed
- Quitclaim deed
- Deed of trust
- Judicial deed (sheriff's deed, referee's deed in foreclosure, commissioner's deed, referee's deed in partition, executor's deed, administrator's deed, tax deed, guardian's deed)
- Correction deed (deed of conformation)
- Cession deed
- Director's deed
- Gift deed
- Interspousal deed
- Deed of release
- Deed of surrender
- Deed of reconveyance

General Warranty Deed (Warranty Deed, Full Covenant and Warranty Deed)

A *general warranty deed,* also called a *warranty deed* or *full covenant and warranty deed,* is used to convey the highest and most complete ownership

10.14→ of a parcel of real estate. The grantors personally warrant and guarantee forever the title against the whole world. They are guaranteeing to the grantee that the property is free and clear of all liens, and they are relinquishing all rights for themselves, their heirs, and predecessors to the property. A general warranty deed usually contains six covenants or promises. There is no standard national wording for them.

> **1.** Covenant of seisen
>
> **2.** Covenant of right to convey
>
> **3.** Covenant against encumbrances
>
> **4.** Covenant of quiet enjoyment
>
> **5.** Covenant of further assurances
>
> **6.** Covenant of warranty

Covenant of Seisen

The *covenant of seisen* is a statement by the grantors that they hold the title they specify in the deed and that they convey it to the grantee.

Covenant of Right to Convey

The *covenant of right to convey* usually follows the covenant of seisen. It restates that the grantor owns the title being conveyed and asserts that the grantor has the legal capacity to convey the title.

Covenant against Encumbrances

The *covenant against encumbrances* is a statement by the grantor that there are no encumbrances against the title, except those that are stated in the deed.

Covenant of Quiet Enjoyment

The *covenant of quiet enjoyment* is an assurance by the grantor that the grantee and his or her heirs and assigns shall have quiet possession of the property being conveyed and will not be disturbed in the use and enjoyment of the property because of a defect in the title. (This is not a general warranty of quiet enjoyment and does not protect the grantee from noise made by neighbors, traffic, etc.)

Covenant of Further Assurances

The *covenant of further assurances* is a promise made by the grantors that they will perform any acts necessary to correct any defects in the title being conveyed and any errors or deficiencies in the deed itself.

Covenant of Warranty

The *covenant of warranty* provides that the grantor will warrant and defend the title to the grantee against the lawful claims of all persons whomsoever. This is the best form of warranty for protecting the grantee and contains no limitations as to possible claimants it protects against. The covenant of warranty is the most important of all the covenants.

If the covenant of seisen or the covenant of warranty is broken, grantees may recover damages from the grantors long after the property is sold. Generally, they are limited in the amount they can recover, which is the price paid for the property. If they have to pay off an encumbrance, they can collect for the amount of the payoff, as long as it does not exceed the price of the property.

As a matter of practicality, when a defect appears in a title, the grantees first try to collect from the title insurance company (assuming there is title insurance that protects the grantees). They can also seek to recover from whoever did the title search and certified the title.

Special Warranty Deed

A *special warranty deed* contains the same covenants, expressed or implied, as a general warranty deed, except that the grantor covenants against claims made only for defects of title which arose during the time the grantor possessed title to the property. Often included are special words of conveyance, such as *warranty special*. In some states, the word *grant* (when used) creates a special warranty deed. The special warranty deed is commonly used in some states by guardians, trustees, executors, administrators, or grantors who have acquired the property via a foreclosure or other judicial sale.

Grant Deed

Currently, California, Idaho, and North Dakota use *grant deeds* instead of warranty deeds. There are some warranties in a grant deed, but they are not as broad as the warranties in a warranty deed. The typical warranties in a grant deed are as follows:

- The grantor has not previously conveyed the property to someone else.
- The grantor has not encumbered the property, except as noted in the deed.
- The grantor will convey to the grantee (at no cost) any additional interest he or she acquires in the property at a later date.

In general, a grant deed limits the responsibility of the grantors to whatever happened to the property while they owned it and relieves the grantors of any responsibility for anything that happened prior to their ownership. The grant deed became popular in California because of early widespread use of title insurance, which shifts the burden of warranting the title from the grantors to the title insurance company.

Bargain and Sale Deed

A *bargain and sale deed* was originally used instead of a sales contract in some areas. The idea was that title passed as soon as the document was executed, rather than later at a closing or escrow. Current versions of the bargain and sale deed are used by some trustees, fiduciaries, executors, and officers of the court. When used in this manner, it is really a judicial deed. There are usually few (if any) warranties in these deeds other than that the grantor has an interest in the property and the authority to sell it to the grantee. It may also state that the grantor has knowingly done nothing to damage the title to the property.

Quitclaim Deed

By giving a *quitclaim deed,* the grantors convey to the grantees every interest they have in the property, if any. No warranties or representations are made as to the interests the grantees have in the property. In fact, a quitclaim deed is sometimes used when the grantees have little or no interest in the property, just to protect the buyers against the remote possibility that the grantors had an interest. It is also used to remove a cloud on the title, which is a claim or encumbrance on the title that might injure the owner's title if it were not removed. In some states, it is the primary type of deed used to convey title. (The grant deed is used in California, Idaho, and North Dakota instead of a quitclaim deed, which is very similar.)

Many large corporations and utilities will sell only by quitclaim deed, believing this is the only way to avoid carrying a contingent liability on their books for claims that might be made against them in the future because of a warranty deed they signed in the past. Since the grantees receive no protection via a quitclaim deed, they usually purchase title insurance to provide the protection they need.

Deed of Trust

A *deed of trust* is a legal document that secures the repayment of a promissory note. It is an alternative to a mortgage. A deed of trust transfers title from the borrower (trustor) to a third-party trustee. The beneficiary of the trust is the lender. Once the debt is paid in full, a release of deed of trust or deed of reconveyance transfers title back to the borrower (trustor).

In the event of default by the borrower per the terms of the promissory note, the lender contacts the trustee to initiate a foreclosure. Although the mechanics of a foreclosure vary by state, either the lender's debt is paid in full or the lender takes title to the property.

The difference between a mortgage and a deed of trust is that with a deed of trust the title of the property transfers to the trustee, and in most states with a mortgage there is no transfer of title. A promissory note is sometimes called a mortgage when used in the context of real estate. Typically, state statutes provide for a mortgage to secure the note or a deed of trust to secure the note.

Mortgage Deed

A *mortgage deed* is a legal document that secures the repayment of a mortgage note. Generally, it is a lien against the title of a property. The mortgagor is the borrower, and the mortgagee is the lender. Once the debt is paid in full, a release of mortgage or satisfaction of mortgage is provided to the borrower for recording.

In the event of default by the borrower, per the terms of the mortgage note, the mortgagee initiates foreclosure. Although the mechanics of a foreclosure vary by state, either the lender's debt is paid in full or the lender takes title to the property.

The difference between a mortgage and a deed of trust is that with a deed of trust the title of the property transfers to the trustee, and in most states with a mortgage there is no transfer of title. A promissory note is sometimes called a mortgage when used in the context of real estate.

Judicial Deed

The execution of a *judicial deed* results from a court order to the official in charge of executing deeds for the court. The various types of judicial deeds described here are the most common ones and derive their names from the officials who are ordered to execute them. Judicial deeds, like quitclaim deeds, contain no warranties.

Sheriff's Deed

A *sheriff's deed* is used in those states where foreclosed property is sold at a sheriff's sale. The sheriff acts upon a court order whereby the court approves the sale. The sheriff acts as a public official, so the only warranty in the deed is that the sheriff is authorized to sell the property to the grantee.

Referee's Deed in Foreclosure

A *referee's deed in foreclosure* is used in those states where the court appoints a referee to sell a property in foreclosure. The referee acts as a public official, so that the only warranty in the deed is that the referee is authorized to sell the property to the grantee.

Commissioner's Deed

A *commissioner's deed* is used in those states where the court appoints a commissioner to sell a property in foreclosure. The commissioner acts as a public official so that the only warranty in the deed is that the commissioner is authorized to sell the property to the grantee.

Referee's Deed in Partition

A *referee's deed in partition* is used in those states where the court appoints a referee to partition or liquidate a property, often one held in joint tenancy. The referee acts as a public official, so that the only warranty in the deed is that the referee is authorized to sell the property to the grantee.

Executor's Deed

An *executor's deed* is used by the executor of an estate to sell the estate's property with the approval (or upon order) of the court. It carries no warranty other than the fact that the executor is authorized to sell the property. An executor's deed usually recites the selling price.

Administrator's Deed

An *administrator's deed* is used by the administrator of an estate to sell the estate's property with the approval (or upon order) of the court. It carries no warranty other than the fact that the administrator is authorized to sell the property. The administrator's deed usually recites the selling price.

Tax Deed

A *tax deed* is used to convey title to real estate that has been sold by the government because of nonpayment of taxes.

Guardian's Deed

A *guardian's deed* is used in some states to convey a minor's interest in a parcel of real estate. Generally it is used to state that neither the guardian nor the minor has encumbered the property. The deed must state which legal authority permits the guardian to convey the minor's interest, usually by court order.

Correction Deed (Deed of Conformation)

A *correction deed* (also called in some places a *deed of conformation*) is used to correct an error in a previously executed and delivered deed. Common errors that are corrected with correction deeds are misspelled names and mistakes in the property description. It is a special type of quitclaim deed.

Cession Deed

A *cession deed* is a form of quitclaim deed whereby a property owner conveys street rights to a municipality or the state.

Director's Deed

A *director's deed* is used in some areas when a public agency sells surplus land.

Gift Deed

A *gift deed* is a special deed used in some areas to give away real estate during the lifetime of the grantor. It is also used by charitable organizations, religious institutions, and government entities. Because valuable consideration is one of the required elements of a contract, a gift deed substitutes the term *good consideration* or *love and affection* in place of something material such as money. Some gift deeds also state a nominal money consideration, such as $1.00.

Interspousal Deed

10.15➤ An *interspousal deed* is used in some states to transfer title to real property between spouses, both of whom must be alive at the time of the transfer.

Deed of Release

A *deed of release* is used primarily to release a title from the lien of a mortgage when the debt secured by the mortgage has been paid in full or, in the case of a blanket mortgage, to release individual parcel of property from the lien of the blanket mortgage. In dower and curtesy states, it is sometimes used to release the interest of the husband or wife.

Deed of Surrender

A *deed of surrender* is used in some states by life tenants to convey their life tenant estate or their reversionary interest or their remainder interest. In other states, a quitclaim deed is used for the same purpose.

Deed of Reconveyance

A *deed of reconveyance* is like a deed of release and is used primarily to release a title from the lien of a mortgage when the debt secured by the mortgage has been paid in full. It is used by third-party trustees who originally received title to the property in a deed of trust to be reconveyed when the debt has been paid.

TITLE INSURANCE

Title insurance is a form of insurance that protects the policyholder from undisclosed defects in the title that occurred prior to the issuance of the policy. For example, if a property is purchased and the seller had borrowed against the property, the commitment for title insurance would disclose that the lender has a claim against the property. If the loan was not identified until after the closing, an owner's title insurance policy would protect the owner against the claim.

Prior to the issuance of a title insurance policy, the title company searches the public records to identify all matters of record that might have an impact on the title. When the commitment of title insurance is issued, it identifies all of the matters of record that might have an impact on the title that are excluded from the title insurance. Beneficiaries of the title insurance should review the exceptions to ensure that they are willing to take responsibility for the title considerations that will be excluded from the title insurance policy.

There are numerous types of title insurance policies and the most common ones are an owner's title insurance policy and a mortgagee's title insurance policy. An owner's title insurance policy is typically issued at the time a property is acquired, and the maximum amount of the insurance is the purchase price of the property. A mortgagee's title insurance policy protects the lender. The amount of the mortgagee's title insurance policy is the amount of the loan. A new mortgagee's title insurance policy is typically required for each refinance of the property.

FRAUDULENT TRANSACTIONS

An increasing concern in the real estate market is associated with fraudulent transactions. The fraud could be associated with the parties to the ownership transfer, the true price of the transfer, or the loan that supports a transfer. Anything abnormal that is associated with a transaction should raise concern that some level of fraud might be occurring. All parties associated with a fraudulent transaction are investigated as being part of the fraud.

In some of these situations identity theft could be involved. The identity theft could be associated with anyone connected to the real estate transaction. Anytime there is fraud involved in a real estate transaction, it is a federal offense, which could involve the Federal Bureau of Investigation.

SUMMARY

Title to most of the land in the United States goes back to monarchs who controlled the land prior to the creation of states and territories. The monarchs claimed they had original title to all land. They did not recognize ownership land claimed by the Native American Indians. The transfer of property has deep historical roots. Today in the United States, property is owned and transferred according to a statute of frauds in each state. Generally, in most states, title can be transferred in one of five ways: voluntary alienation by deed, involuntary alienation, will, descent, and dedication.

The opposite of voluntary alienation is involuntary alienation, which is the relinquishing of property without the owner's consent. There are five kinds of involuntary alienation: escheat, eminent domain (through a condemnation action), foreclosure, adverse possession, and natural forces.

Escheat is based on the concept that it is in the public interest that all land be owned by somebody and that owner will be responsible for it. Eminent domain is the right of the government to take land from private owners when it is needed for the public good. What constitutes the public good is up to the individual state legislatures and Congress to decide. Foreclosure is the process of taking title to property that was used as security for a debt that is in default. Adverse possession is a way defined by individual states that someone can obtain title to land by taking possession of it for long periods of time and meeting other state requirements. Avulsion and erosion are examples of how it is possible to lose private property by natural forces.

How property is transferred depends on which state you are in. The most common type of deed is a warranty deed. However, there are many other kinds of deed in common use, and they are different from state to state. The federal government has some limited rights to transfer property it owns.

REVIEW QUESTIONS

10.1 Most conveyances of real estate are concluded at closings conducted by:

A. Attorneys

B. Title companies

C. Both of the above

D. None of the above

10.2 The first statute of frauds was passed by the:

A. Greeks in around 500 BC

B. Romans in around 70 AD

C. English in the 1600s

D. Americans in 1776

10.3 Title laws are:

A. Based on federal guidelines

B. Similar in most states

C. Both of the above

D. None of the above

10.4 Transfer of title by voluntary alienation is made by a:

A. Sale

B. Gift

C. Both of the above

D. None of the above

10.5 Most deeds require:

A. Consideration

B. Granting words

C. Delivery and acceptance

D. All of the above

10.6 In most states the grantor must be:

A. Of sound mind

B. Of lawful age

C. The owner of the property or someone authorized to act for the owner

D. All of the above

10.7 In addition to the owners of the property, which of the following must also sign the deed?

A. Anyone with dower rights

B. Anyone with curtesy

C. Both of the above

D. None of the above

10.8 An acknowledgment of a deed means:

A. The closing attorney is familiar with the property being conveyed

B. There are two or more witnesses to the signing of the deed

C. The grantee's signature was sworn to under oath to be the person's free act and deed

D. None of the above

10.9 Recording of a deed:
  A. Is required in all the states
  B. Is never required
  C. Protects the seller from future claims
  D. None of the above

10.10 Involuntary alienation is when owners give up their property:
  A. With their consent
  B. Without their consent
  C. When they commit a felony
  D. None of the above

10.11 Escheat means the transfer of property to:
  A. Close relatives
  B. A lender in lieu of foreclosure
  C. The government
  D. None of the above

10.12 Eminent domain is the:
  A. Sale of a property to an abutting property owner
  B. Taking of a property by the government
  C. Foreclosure of a property without a sale
  D. None of the above

10.13 When private property owners give their property to the government, the process is called gift by:
  A. Dedication
  B. Escheat
  C. Descent
  D. None of the above

10.14 The deed that conveys the highest and most complete ownership is a:
  A. Quitclaim deed
  B. Warranty deed
  C. Full guarantee deed
  D. None of the above

10.15 An interspousal deed is used in some states to transfer property between spouses:
  A. When both are alive
  B. After one spouse dies
  C. After both spouses die
  D. None of the above

CHAPTER 11

Making and Breaking Contracts

RESPs need to know about both the basic concepts behind contracts, which are explained in this chapter, and the specific types of real estate contracts, which are covered in Chapter 12.

A contract is an agreement between two or more parties to do the things they have agreed on. It becomes legally enforceable by common law and statutory law only if it contains all the required elements of a contract, such as competent parties, a meeting of the minds (mutual agreement), consideration (something of value), and legal purpose. It also must meet the other requirements of a valid contract, depending on the type of contract and the specific laws that cover that type of contract.

TYPES OF CONTRACTS

There are a variety of ways to classify contracts. We use these classifications:

- Express contracts
- Implied contracts

- Unilateral contracts
- Bilateral contracts
- Executory contracts
- Executed contracts

Express Contracts

11.1 ➤ A contract that is in writing is usually called an *express contract,* because both parties have declared their intentions. A verbal contract can also be an express contract if both parties specifically agree with each other on the terms of the contract.

Implied Contracts

11.2 ➤ An *implied contract* is one that is understood to exist because of the actions of the parties to the contract. For example, when a person is hired to do some work without discussion of pay, it is implied that they will receive fair compensation for their work.

Unilateral Contracts

11.3 ➤ A *unilateral contract* is based on a promise exchanged for an act. The distinguishing characteristic is that one party makes a promise, often to pay the other party some consideration, if the other party does something (the act). However, the party who makes the promise is obligated to keep the promise only if the other party performs the act. The other party is not obligated to perform the act. An open listing is a unilateral contract whereby the property owner promises to pay the broker a commission if the property is sold and the broker has not made any promise in return. If the broker promises to advertise the property or try to sell it, the contract becomes bilateral.

Bilateral Contracts

11.4 ➤ A promise made by one party in exchange for a promise from another party is called a *bilateral contract.* An exclusive listing agreement is a bilateral contract because the property owner promises to pay a commission to the broker and the broker promises to make the best effort to sell or rent the property.

Executory Contracts

11.5→ When all the terms of a contract have not been fulfilled, the contract is said to be executory. A lease that has not expired is an *executory contract*. A sales contract after the acceptance of the offer and before the closing is an executory contract.

Executed Contracts

11.6→ When all the terms of a contract have been fulfilled, the contract is executed. A sales contract becomes an executed contract after the title to the property has been transferred.

VALID CONTRACTS

11.7→ When a contract complies with all the requirements of contract law it is a valid, enforceable contract. To be valid and enforceable, it must meet five (and sometimes six) requirements. The requirements of a valid contract are:

11.8→
> **1.** Mutual agreement
>
> **2.** Consideration
>
> **3.** Competent parties
>
> **4.** Absence of undue influence, duress, and misrepresentation
>
> **5.** Legal purpose
>
> **6.** In writing (not always required)

Mutual Agreement

An offer and acceptance is considered to be a mutual agreement. One party to the contract (the *offeror*) makes an offer, and the other party (the *offeree*) accepts it exactly as it is presented. If the acceptance alters the original offer in any way, it is not an acceptance, but it becomes a counteroffer. For a meeting of the minds to take place, the counteroffer must be accepted exactly as it was made. The offer-and-counteroffer process may be repeated many times before an offer is finally accepted without reservation or alteration. The offer and acceptance must be clear and precise. One of the ways people are able to get out of a contract is by successfully claiming that the contract was unclear or ambiguous.

Consideration

11.9 ➤ Consideration is always something of value. Money is commonly used as consideration but is not the only valid consideration. Consideration may be a promise to do something (or not to do something) at a future time. It can be personal services or something else given in exchange. The mere promise to pay money in the future is valid consideration. It is not necessary to have a deposit to make a valid contract, but it is a good idea. It is also not necessary that the consideration be adequate, fair, sufficient, or otherwise related to what is agreed on in the contract. The amount of $1.00, $10.00, or some other nominal number and the phrase "and other valuable consideration" is permitted to be used in some states where the amount of actual consideration is not required.

Competent Parties

All parties to a contract must have both the legal capacity and the mental capacity to enter into the contract. Generally, minors and people with mental illness are not considered legally competent parties for purposes of making a contract.

Minors

Minors (also legally called infants), in most states, are defined as those under the age of 18. They have very limited ability to make valid contracts that cannot be voided in the future by the minor. A contract with a minor for his or her necessities (food and clothing) is usually valid. Most other contracts with minors can be voided by the minor without a valid reason anytime before the minor reaches majority and for a reasonable time thereafter. Some states have statutes that prohibit minors from making specific types of contracts. When a contract with a minor is necessary, as it would be if the minor owned property that needed to be sold, the probate court must authorize someone who is not a minor to execute the contract on behalf of the minor.

People with Mental Illness

When any of the parties to a contract is mentally ill, the contract is probably voidable. Mentally ill people fall into two categories: those declared insane or mentally incompetent by the courts and those who have not been so declared but who are, in reality, mentally ill or incompetent. A contract with anyone who has been declared mentally ill or incompetent by the court is void from its inception. Voiding a contract with someone on the basis of incompetency or mental illness who has not been declared so by a court depends on proving their incompetency in court. It must be proved that the mental condition of the person was such that the person did not understand the nature and consequences of the transaction.

Absence of Undue Influence, Duress, and Misrepresentation

Contracts may be voidable if it can be proved that the people who entered into them did so because of undue influence, duress, or misrepresentation. Common types of claims are that the parties were irrational, sick, in great distress, or under the influence of alcohol or drugs. Any type of threat can also be introduced as evidence that the parties did not sign of their free will and accord, which is necessary for a contract to be valid.

Legal Purpose

A valid contract must be for a legal purpose. A contract for an illegal purpose is not enforceable. Ignorance of what is legal or illegal is no excuse. For example, a contract to have an unlicensed person act as an agent to sell a property is illegal. A contract to bribe a public official is illegal.

In Writing (Not Always Required)

In all 50 states and territories, most real estate sales contracts must be in writing, because each of the states and territories has a law called the statute of frauds, which requires that specified contracts must be in writing to be valid and enforceable. All of these statutes of frauds require that most real estate sales contracts meet the "in writing" requirement.

Each state has a slightly different statute of frauds. However, they have many elements that are similar. All of these statutes cover three types of contracts that are important to brokers and sales associates, as well as anyone who deals in real estate:

1. Contracts for the sale of real estate
2. Contracts that cannot be performed within one year
3. Contracts for specified amounts of personal property

Contracts for the Sale of Real Estate

Generally, any contract that affects any of the private ownership rights of real estate must be in writing to be enforceable. This includes, but is not limited to, contracts for listing properties for sale; offers; binders; sales contracts; grants of rights to remove oil, gas, minerals, or gravel; and all other grants and reservations.

The exception, in some states, is if one of the parties ratifies an oral contract by his or her actions. For example, an oral sales contract might be ratified if the seller accepts a deposit and then the buyer moves in and makes improvements to the property, all with the witnessed consent of the seller.

Contracts That Cannot Be Performed within One Year

Leases for less than a year do not have to be in writing. Leases for more than a year must be in writing to be enforceable. An exception can be made based on performance. For example, if a tenant paid two years' rent in advance, the tenant may have ratified an oral two-year lease. This is up to a court to decide. It applies not only to real estate but to many other transactions as well.

Contracts for Specified Amounts of Personal Property

Most statutes of frauds require that any contract for the sale of anything for $500 or more must be in writing. This is very important in real estate transactions. Sellers may agree to sell personal property for a reduced price as part of a sale that is worth over $500, but the sellers do not put it in writing. If the sellers change their minds prior to the closing, there is little the buyers can do to enforce the sale of the personal property. However, once the sellers have accepted payment and the buyers have taken possession of the personal property, the sale is probably ratified.

Real estate brokers and sales associates soon learn that all contracts should be in writing. The person who says "my word is my bond" may be telling the truth, but it still is better to get people to put their promises in writing.

UNENFORCEABLE CONTRACTS

There are three basic reasons why an otherwise legal contract might be unenforceable:

1. The contract does not comply with the statute of limitations.
2. The contract does not comply with laches.
3. The contract does not comply with estoppel.

Statute of Limitations

Various state statutes provide for a period of time during which different types of legal actions must be filed in court. If they are not filed within the specified time, they are precluded from being filed. For example, many states require that any claim for damages as a result of an accident or a claim of negligence be filed within one or two years of the date when the party was injured in the accident.

Generally the *statute of limitations* starts on the date an obligation is due. If no payment is made or no legal action is taken during the period prescribed in the statute, the right to enforce the agreement is lost.

Laches

The effect of *laches* is similar to that of the statute of limitations. The difference is that the period of time to file an action is not specified in a statute. Instead it is determined by the court on the basis of whether or not the action was filed in a reasonable period of time, and if by being filed late, it worked to the detriment of the other party. A typical example of laches is when property owners become aware that something being built on an adjacent property encroaches on their property. The property owners must promptly file an action to stop the encroachment rather than wait until the structure is completed.

Estoppel

Parties can be prevented from taking legal action based on a previous action or statement they made. For example, when a mortgage is assigned, lenders provide a certificate stating the balance of the mortgage on the date of the assignment. When the person who takes over the mortgage relies on this *estoppel* certificate, the lender cannot at a later date claim that a different balance was due. Another example is that when a party represents someone as their agent, they cannot later try to avoid responsibility to a third party for the acts of their agent.

VOID CONTRACTS

11.10→ A *void contract* is one whose subject matter or performance is against public policy. It is not recognized as a contract in the eyes of the law and is unenforceable.

VOIDABLE CONTRACTS

A *voidable contract* remains in existence until the party who has the power to rescind the contract takes affirmative action to do so. One example is a minor who signs a contract for things other than necessities and then at a later date decides to rescind the contract. The contract remains valid if nobody tries to void it based on the fact that the party was a minor.

Also, people who sign contracts when they are intoxicated have a reasonable time after they become sober and aware of the nature of the contract to rescind it.

REMEDIES UPON BREACH OF CONTRACT

When a contract is breached and the breaching party is unable to prove that there is a valid reason for the breach or that the contract is void or voidable, the wronged or innocent parties have six breach-of-contract remedies available to them. They may:

11.13→

1. Accept partial performance
2. Rescind the contract unilaterally
3. Sue for specific performance
4. Sue for money damages
5. Accept liquidated money damages
6. Mutually rescind the contract

Accept Partial Performance

Aggrieved parties may decide to accept partial performance for a variety of reasons:

- It is too much trouble to sue.
- They feel sorry for the other party to the contract.
- What they didn't get is not very important.
- It's easier to correct the problems themselves than to sue.
- The other party has disappeared or is out of business.
- The other party doesn't have any assets, so that even if a suit is brought and won, they will not be able to collect the judgment.

Rescind the Contract Unilaterally

The innocent parties take the position that if the other party won't perform, they won't either. A common real estate example is when a tenant withholds rent because the landlord fails to repair the premises. *Unilateral recision* can backfire and should not be undertaken without legal advice.

Sue for Specific Performance

When parties do not do what they promised to do in a contract, the aggrieved parties may institute a court action to make them keep their promise and perform. Generally, the courts would rather award monetary damages, as explained next, because that is easier to monitor. For example, when a contractor does not finish a job or does it poorly, it is difficult for the court to determine when the job is finished or when the poor work is brought up to an acceptable standard.

The exception is when someone contracts to purchase or lease a piece of property. It is well established that no two properties are the same. Therefore, it follows that when parties have a contract for specific properties, they may not be made whole by receiving money with which to buy other, substitute properties.

When a *specific performance* lawsuit of this type is won, the court forces the other party to deliver the property and execute the necessary papers. People who refuse such a court order can be held in contempt of court and jailed until they do what the court has ordered.

Sue for Money Damages (Compensatory Damages)

When a contract is breached, the innocent parties usually can show that they suffered a monetary loss as a result. The amount of money they can prove they have lost is called *compensatory damages* and is the amount that the court is asked to award.

The court determines the amount of compensatory damages that should be sufficient to put the innocent parties in the same economic position they would have been in if the contract had been performed as agreed on by the parties to the contract.

The calculation of compensatory damages is often misunderstood. For example, if a tenant moves out and does not pay the $5,000 still due on the lease, the compensatory damages would not necessarily be the whole $5,000. The court might reduce this amount by any rent the landlord was able to collect from a substitute tenant (which the landlord has an obligation to try to secure) and any utility and other expenses the landlord did not have to incur because the property was vacant.

Accept Liquidated Money Damages

11.12➤ Some contracts spell out the remedies each party has if the other party breaches the contract. These specified remedies are called *liquidated damages*. Many real estate contracts have liquidated damage clauses. A common one is that buyers forfeit their deposit if they fail to go through with the purchase.

The courts do not like to enforce liquidated damage payments that appear to be punitive. To be collectible, the liquidated damages must be reasonable as compared to the damage caused by the breach of contract.

Mutually Rescind the Contract

11.11➤ When one party notifies the other party to a contract that they do not intend to go through with the contract, the other party may simply agree to terminate the contract and let it go at that. They may decide this for many of the same reasons they would accept partial performance. Most mutually rescinded contracts are either torn up, left in limbo until the statute of limitations runs out, or formally terminated by the signing of releases.

SUMMARY

When two or more people, partnerships, or corporations, or any combination of them, agree to do something together, they can turn the agreement into a contract. To do this they have to meet all of the common laws or statutory laws that apply in the state where the agreement is made. If they do not meet all of these requirements, their agreement is not a contract and it is not enforceable.

Contracts can be classified as express or implied contracts, unilateral or bilateral contracts, and executed or executory contracts.

A valid contract is created when a contract complies with all the requirements of contract law. To be valid and enforceable it must meet these five requirements: mutual agreement; consideration; competent parties; absence of undue influence, duress, and misrepresentation; and legal purpose. If it is for the sale of real estate, a rental for over one year, or includes over $500 (the amount varies from state to state) of personal property, it must be in writing, as required by each state's statute of frauds. A contract may be unenforceable because it does not comply with the statute of limitations, laches, or estoppel.

A contract may be void if it is against public policy. A contract may be voidable when one of the parties did not have the legal capacity to sign the contract because of age or being under the influence of alcohol, drugs, undue influence, or fraud.

When a contract is breached without a valid reason, the wronged or innocent parties have six remedies available to them: accept partial performance, rescind the contract unilaterally, sue for specific performance, sue for money damages, accept liquidated money damages, or mutually rescind the contract.

Contract law is a complex subject. RESPs should be careful not to give opinions about contracts to their clients and friends, as this may constitute the practice of law. Should the advice turn out to be incorrect, you may be subjecting yourself to criticism, lawsuits, and/or criminal action. This does not stop RESPs from preparing contracts that are specifically for the real estate transactions that they are licensed to make.

REVIEW QUESTIONS

11.1 An express contract is one that is:

A. Prepared overnight

B. Delivered by express mail

C. In writing

D. None of the above

11.2 An implied contract is:

A. In writing

B. Created by actions of the parties

C. Both of the above

D. None of the above

11.3 A unilateral contract is:

A. Always in writing

B. Never in writing

C. Made when one party promises to do something only if the other party acts

D. None of the above

11.4 A bilateral contract is where:

A. Neither party promises to do anything

B. Both parties promise to do something

C. Both parties are in default

D. None of the above

11.5 An executory contract is where:

A. All of the terms of the contract have been fulfilled

B. One or more of the terms of the contract have not been fulfilled

C. A lease has expired

D. None of the above

11.6 An executed contract is a contract that has been:

A. Terminated

B. Stopped

C. Killed

D. Fulfilled

11.7 A valid contract must meet which of the following requirements?

A. Mutual agreement

B. Consideration

C. Competent parties

D. All of the above

11.8 For a contract to be valid there must be an absence of:

A. Undue influence

B. Duress

C. Misrepresentation

D. All of the above

11.9 Consideration can be:
   A. Money
   B. A promise to do something
   C. A partridge in a pear tree
   D. All of the above

11.10 A contract that is against public policy is:
   A. Void
   B. Voidable
   C. Both of the above
   D. None of the above

11.11 A mutually rescinded contract is a contract that:
   A. Does not contain a meeting of the minds
   B. Is illegal
   C. Violates the statute of frauds
   D. None of the above

11.12 Liquidated damages:
   A. Are specific remedies the parties agree on in their contract
   B. May not exceed the value of the property
   C. Are limited in most states by the statute of limitations
   D. Are equal to the amount of the deposit

11.13 When a contract is breached, the innocent party may sue for:
   A. Damages
   B. Specific performance
   C. Both of the above
   D. None of the above

ANSWERS

The answer to each question is indicated by the letter A, B, C, or D. The explanation of the answer is indicated by the page number and an arrow that points to the appropriate paragraph on the page.

Q 11.1 C Page 168	Q 11.4 B Page 168	Q 11.7 D Page 169	Q 11.10 A Page 173	Q 11.13 C Page 174
Q 11.2 B Page 168	Q 11.5 B Page 169	Q 11.8 D Page 169	Q 11.11 D Page 176	
Q 11.3 C Page 168	Q 11.6 D Page 169	Q 11.9 D Page 170	Q 11.12 A Page 176	

CHAPTER 12

Listing, Buyer Agency, and Sales Contracts

There are many different kind of real estate contracts. This chapter covers the following type of contracts:

Listing agreements
- Exclusive right to sell
- Exclusive agency
- Open listings
- Net listings
- Option listings

Buyer representative
- Exclusive right to represent (exclusive buyer agency agreement)
- Exclusive agency buyer agency agreement
- Open buyer agency agreement

Dual agency
- Dual agency consent agreements
- Dual agency disclosure agreements

Deposit receipts and offers to purchase
- Deposit receipts
- Offers to purchase

Sales contracts
- Contract for purchase and sale
- Purchase agreement
- Purchase contract
- Earnest money agreement

Installment land contracts
- Contract for deed
- Land contract
- Bond for deed
- Installment contract

Options and rights of first refusal
- Options
- Rights of first refusal

Contract for exchange of real estate

LISTING AGREEMENTS

Introduction

To represent a seller or landlord, a written agreement must be entered into. The agreement must be entered into before the broker or agent attempts to negotiate on behalf of the seller or landlord. Three basic types of listing agreements are recognized in many states: exclusive right to sell, exclusive agency, and open listing. Net listings and option listings are still permitted in some states.

12.1 ➤ A listing agreement is a contract between the owner of a property and a real estate broker that employs the broker and the broker's sales associates to act as the owner's agent to perform a service for the owner. Services to be performed are usually to sell, rent, lease, exchange, or option the property.

License laws in all 50 states require that only a licensed broker enter into a listing agreement with a property owner. The broker may use licensed sales associates to help perform the services called for in the listing agreement.

A unique characteristic of most listing agreements is that it establishes an agency relationship between the property owner and the broker. The owner authorizes the broker (and the licensed sales associates employed by the broker as subagents) to show the property to potential buyers, tenants, exchangers, or optionees, provide them with information about the property, and convey any offer they make to the property owner for acceptance or rejection. The broker is also permitted to accept a deposit along with an offer.

The relationship between the broker and the property owner is regulated by the state's real estate license laws, the state statute of frauds and the rules and regulations of the NAR and its local affiliates, and the multiple listing service if the broker is a member of the NAR.

Exclusive Right to Sell

12.3➤ The most desirable type of listing contract from the broker's point of view is the *exclusive right to sell listing.* One broker (sales associate or cooperating broker) is given the exclusive right to show the property and offer it for sale, rental, lease, option, or exchange. The owner must pay the broker the agreed-on commission or fee whenever the property is sold, leased, rented, exchanged, or optioned, *even if* the broker was *not the procuring cause* of the sale, rental, lease, option, or exchange.

Brokers like this type of listing best because they know if they spend time and money on a listing, they are going to be paid when a sale, rental, lease, option, or exchange is made. Therefore, they will spend more time and money to facilitate the transaction, which is in everyone's best interest.

Exclusive Agency

12.2➤ An *exclusive agency listing* agreement permits the broker, sales associate, or cooperating broker to show the owner's property, provide information about it and accept offers and deposits to be conveyed to the owner for acceptance or rejection. The important distinguishing characteristic of an exclusive agency listing agreement is that the property owner is obligated to pay a commission to the broker *only* if the broker (sales associate or cooperating broker) is the *procuring cause* of the sale, rental, lease, exchange, or option. If the owner sells, rents, leases, exchanges, or options the property without using the services of the broker to effect the specific transaction that is consummated, the owner is not obligated to pay the broker a commission or other fee for services.

Open Listings

12.5➤ Property owners may enter into as many *open listings* (also known as *nonexclusive listings* or *general listings*) as they desire because they are only obligated to pay a commission to the broker (sales associate or cooperating broker) who successfully sells, rents, leases, options, or exchanges the property or produces a buyer, tenant, exchange, or option that meets all the terms and conditions of the offer being made by the property owners.

When property owners sell, rent, lease, exchange, or option their property without the help of any of the brokers who hold open listings, they are *not* obligated to pay anyone a commission.

An open listing serves many useful purposes. Many states require some type of a written listing before a broker, sales associate, or cooperating broker can show a property. The open listing sets forth the terms of the offer being made by the owner and establishes the amount of commission that will be paid if the broker (sales associate or cooperating broker) produces someone who is ready, willing, and able to meet all the conditions of the owner's offer. Often an owner's offer has special conditions attached to it—for example, special available financing, occupancy requirements, or personal property included in the sale. These special conditions are spelled out in the open listing.

Formerly it was common for property owners to advertise their own properties, and the advertisement would state "Brokers Protected." If a broker showed the property and was the *procuring cause* of a sale, rental, lease, exchange, or option, the broker would be entitled to a commission. If the broker produced a buyer or tenant who was *ready, willing, and able* to meet the offer being made by the property owner, a commission would also be payable. Now many state laws require that brokers obtain an open listing *before* they show the property. Among other things, this open listing states the asking price and terms and what commission the broker will be paid if a sale, lease, rental, option, or exchange is consummated.

Net Listings

12.4→ A *net listing* states an amount of money the owners will take to sell, rent, lease, option, or exchange their property. Anything in excess of this amount is paid to the broker as a commission. Net listings used to be a very popular type of listing. Unfortunately, net listings inherently can lead to abuse and fraud. They also allow brokers to take unfair advantage of property owners who may not know (for a variety of reasons) the true value of their property. Net listings are now prohibited by many states. Where they are not illegal, they are discouraged.

Option Listings

12.6→ Like the net listing, the option listing is losing its popularity because of the high potential for fraud associated with it. An *option listing* gives the broker the option to buy the property at a stipulated price. If the broker is able to obtain a buyer or tenant at a higher price, the broker has the option to purchase the property at the previously agreed-on price. Unfortunately, like net listings, option listings inherently can lead to abuse and fraud. They also allow brokers to take unfair advantage of property owners who may not know (for a variety of reasons) the true value of their property. Option listings are now prohibited by many states. Where they are not illegal, they are also discouraged.

Contents of Listing Agreements

There are no national listing agreements and few, if any, statewide agreements. Some brokers have their own agreements, many real estate boards and MLSs have standard agreements, and some state associations have their own agreements. Some include factual information about the property being offered and others provide for this information on a separate sheet. In spite of the wide variety of listing agreements being used, most of them contain the following information in one form or another.

Names(s) and Address(es) of the Owners

Some states require that all owners sign the listing agreement. This is always a good idea, though it is not always possible. When all the owners do not sign the listing agreement, there is a risk that one or more of the owners will claim they did not agree to list the property and to the conditions of the listing agreement. This often leads to costly litigation, which is rarely beneficial to the broker. In many states, one spouse has rights to property owned by the other spouse, even if the first spouse's name does not appear on the deed as an owner of record. Therefore, it is a good idea to have the spouse sign the listing agreement or a release, whichever is customary in your state. Obtaining the addresses of the owners is required in some states, and it is always a good idea.

Address of the Property Being Listed

Sometimes a simple street name and number is sufficient. This is especially true in cities, where the lots are regular in shape. In rural areas and in subdivisions, a more detailed address may be needed. When all the property contiguously owned by the listing owners is not being offered, the listing agreement must be clear as to exactly what is being listed.

Physical Description of the Property

Many listing agreements have a separate page on which to describe the property being listed. Most MLSs have their own standard form. Be careful not to guess about the age and size of a property, as you may later be accused of false representation. Try not to get carried away with the adjectives you use.

Information about Existing Mortgages and Whether They Can Be Assumed

A favorable mortgage that can be assumed adds value to the property.

Potential Owner Financing

Owners, for a variety of reasons, may be willing to take back a purchase money mortgage that will have the effect of reducing the interest, reducing the amount of the monthly payments, and/or reducing the amount of the down payment required to purchase the property.

Unpaid Special Assessments

When sewers and other improvements are installed, the government sometimes levies a special assessment against the properties that benefit from the improvement. Often, these charges can be deferred by making monthly payments over an extended period of time. These assessments can be paid off at the closing or passed on to the buyer. How they will be handled should be stated in the listing agreement, as this will affect the value of the property.

How the Property Is Zoned

The listing should state the zoning classification and whether the property is conforming or nonconforming to the current zoning requirements.

Any Significant Deed or Other Restrictions and/or Encumbrances

A significant deed restriction or encumbrance, such as an environmental or other condition, may affect the value of the property.

Assessment and Taxes

The current assessment and taxes should be stated when known. When the current taxes are not known, the last known figure should be shown and identified.

Neighborhood and Community Information

Here is an opportunity to inform anyone interested in the property about desirable (and undesirable) features of the neighborhood and community that may not be obvious to anyone not familiar with them.

Directions to the Property

Clear directions to the property are helpful to anyone who shows the property and those who are unfamiliar with the area.

Anything Classified as Real Estate Not to Be Included

Unless there is a specific agreement to exclude it, buyers and tenants have a right to assume that they will get all the real estate on the premises. Common items that cause later disputes are chandeliers, satellite dishes, above-ground pools, and wall-to-wall carpets.

Any Personal Property to Be Included

The owners have the right to remove their personal property unless it is agreed that it will be included in the sale. Buyers and tenants sometimes wrongfully expect to get refrigerators, washers and dryers, and other personal property they see on the premises.

Any Other Special Conditions

Included in this category are purchase money mortgages held by the owner, occupancy of the premises by the buyer before the closing or the owner after the closing, personal property included in the sale, and any real estate not included in the sale.

Unique and Special Features of the Property

It is a good idea to ask the owners to tell you anything they believe is special about the property and to itemize these items on the listing agreement. (If the list is long, you can always use an addendum page.) You can add anything else you observe that is unique or special to the list, too.

Disclosure Concerning the Property and Agency Representation

Many states now have mandatory disclosure laws that cover title, physical characteristics of the property, and environmental problems. The NAR is advocating mandatory disclosure by property owners. You must become familiar with your state's laws, local and state rules and customs, and your MLS requirements. Because owner disclosure reduces potential professional lawsuits, many brokers are requiring owner disclosure even when it is not required by any other authority.

Type of Agency

Every listing agreement must clearly state what type of agency is being given by the owner to the broker.

Broker's Authority

Part of the broker's authority is indicated by the type of agency. However, the owner may extend or limit the broker's authority to place signs on the property, have open houses, use lockboxes, permit showings, make representations, accept deposits, set the time required for the owner to accept or reject an offer, and so on.

Owner Cooperation, Access, Sign, and Lockbox

See "Broker's Authority."

Name and Address of Broker

A listing agreement is a type of employment contract. The broker cannot assign it without the permission of the owner. It should be clear whether the contract is with a firm or an individual broker.

Listing Price

The initial listing price should be stated, as well as by what mechanism the owners will be able to change the asking price if they wish to do so.

Closing Requirements and Conditions and How They Are Paid For

Customs and traditions vary from place to place for how property is closed and who will pay for the various elements of the closing. Since buyers and tenants often come from other areas, they should be informed about local customs regarding closing costs and requirements when they are making an offer. This will prevent disputes and misunderstandings later. Sometimes, owners wish to handle the closing and closing cost apportionment differently than is the custom of the area where the property is located. This is usually permitted, as long as all the parties to the transaction agree.

Type of Deed, Lease, Option, or Other Contract That Will Be Offered

There are no national standard leases, deeds, options, or exchange agreements. In many areas, it is customary for residential properties to be transferred with warranty deeds. Many large corporations only give quitclaim deeds. The listing agreement should state what type of deed, lease, option, or exchange agreement will be offered by the owner.

Date of Possession

As part of the offer, occupancy of the premises by the buyer before the closing or the owner after the closing must be agreed on. Unless agreed on otherwise, the buyer has the right to expect the owner to have vacated the property before the closing, and for the premises to be "broom clean." The buyer has the right to inspect the property immediately prior to the closing to determine its condition and the fact that it is vacant.

Warranties and Guarantees

There are two common types of warranties and guarantees available to buyers. The most common is an *existing home warranty insurance policy* that can be assigned to the buyer or may be available to the buyer as part of a marketing program, or may be purchasable from a home warranty company. The other is the title warrant.

Commission Agreement—Negotiations (Antitrust Representations)

In spite of a massive education effort by the NAR (based on anti trust lawsuits brought against the NAR, state and local Realtor boards, and individual Realtors and brokers), the public still often thinks commissions are fixed and not subject to negotiation. Brokers must protect themselves against future lawsuits and state license law violation by making it crystal clear in their listing agreements that the commission has been negotiated between the property owner and the broker. The listing agreement should state what the commission is (a percentage, flat fee, or net) and under what circumstances it will be paid. It should also state by whom it will be paid and when (the most common arrangement is to have it paid at the time of the closing by the person handling the closing).

Termination Date

Many state laws require that all listing agreements have a fixed termination date. Some state laws and MLS rules prohibit automatic extension clauses. In other areas, they are common.

12.7➤

    Brokers are concerned that the owner will be tempted (especially toward the end of a listing agreement) to wait until after the listing has expired and then try to make a deal with someone introduced by the broker (sales associate or cooperating broker) and thus avoid paying a commission. A broker protection clause attempts to eliminate this problem by adding wording to the listing that requires a commission to be paid to a broker (sales associate or cooperating broker) if a deal is made with anyone introduced by the broker, sales associate, or cooperating broker, even after the listing has expired. Ideally, this protection would last forever, but experience has shown that the clause is more enforceable if it has a termination date (six months is common).

Hold Harmless (Indemnification Agreement)

In some areas it is customary for broker and owner to hold each other harmless for incorrect information, misrepresentations, warranties, and so on, made by either party that result in the other party being sued for damages.

Equal Opportunity (Nondiscrimination) Clause

Both federal and local laws and the NAR's Code of Ethics prohibit discrimination. All properties must be shown, sold, leased, optioned, and exchanged with anyone regardless of their race, color, creed or religious preference, national origin, sex, sexual orientation, age, handicap, source of income, health, and so on. Not all property owners are aware of these laws and the Realtor's Code of Ethics. This wording in the listing agreement informs them that the broker is not going to discriminate in any way.

Premature Termination Clause

The listing should state what happens if either the owner or the broker terminates the listing agreement prior to the expiration of the listing. Will the broker be paid for the time and expenses incurred in marketing the property? What will happen if the property is sold, leased, rented, exchanged, or optioned after the premature termination?

How Offers Are Taken and Presented

The listing agreement should state how, and which, offers are to be presented. Does the broker have to present verbal offers, offers without deposits, offers below the listing price, offers below previous offers that were rejected by the owner, or offers made while another offer is pending? The are state laws and MLS regulations that sometimes set guidelines and/or requirements.

Deposits

Many states now have laws that direct how deposits will be handled. Some allow the broker and the property owner to make their own agreement.

Enforcement of Contract, Arbitration, and Attorney's Fees

The listing agreement should state how either party can enforce the agreement. Will it be by a lawsuit or required binding arbitration? (And who will be the arbitrator?) There can also be a provision covering who will pay the costs of enforcement.

Construction of Listing Language

The customary technical wording for this provision varies from area to area. Whatever is customary in your area should be included in the listing agreement.

Entire Agreement Provision

This is another technical provision whose wording varies from area to area and also should be included in the listing.

FIRPTA

There are certificates that must be filed in some situations to comply with the Foreign Investment in Real Property Tax Act (FIRPTA). The owner should agree to file these certificates if they are required.

Recommendations

Many brokers provide recommendations to listing property owners for how the property can be improved in order to make it more marketable. They also may recommend contractors to do the suggested work. The listing agreement should contain a clause saying that by offering this service, the broker does not become responsible for the cost of the work done or the effect of the work being done.

Multiple Listing Service (MLS)

12.9 ➤

If the property is going to be listed through an MLS, this should be stated in the listing agreement in the form of a *multiple listing clause*. Many MLSs have required language that must be included in the listing agreement if the property is to be listed through it. Some MLSs require that their standard listing agreement be used. Some MLSs require that all properties listed by member brokers go through the MLS; other MLSs make this optional. Failure to list a property through an MLS when the broker represents to the owner that it will be so listed can result in a damage lawsuit.

Receipt of Copy Acknowledgment

One of the common defenses used when people try to get out of a contract is to claim that they never received a copy. Many state laws and MLS regulations require that an executed copy of the contract be delivered to all parties (this may mean every owner). The best proof that you have delivered the required copies is to have everyone sign a release stating that they have received a copy.

Listing Termination

Most states require that all listings have a specific termination date. In the past, many listings contained an *automatic extension clause* that extended the period of the listing automatically unless the owner or broker notified the other party (usually in writing) that the listing was not being automatically extended. Most states now prohibit this practice, too. Where it is not prohibited by law, it is discouraged.

There are at least seven ways a listing may terminate prior to its specified termination date:

> **1.** Listings may be terminated by mutual consent. Often property owners will compensate brokers for their expenses and possibly for their time.
>
> **2.** The property is condemned. Again, sometimes brokers are compensated for their time and expenses.
>
> **3.** Foreclosure in many states terminates any listing agreements.
>
> **4.** Bankruptcy of the owner usually terminates any listing agreements.
>
> **5.** Significant destruction of the property by fire or other hazards will terminate any listing agreements.
>
> **6.** Death or incapacity of the owner or broker will terminate any listing agreements.
>
> **7.** The property owner or broker breeches the listing contract. Common breeches are when the owner will not permit the broker to show the property or when the broker fails to advertise the property or list it through the MLS as agreed. Often when a listing agreement is breached, the broker and the owner end up suing each other for damages.

Unlike many contracts, a listing agreement cannot be assigned to another broker without permission of the owner. This is because it is a *personal services contract*. Owners have the right to the specific service of the broker with whom they listed the property.

Broker Protection Clause

In states where it is not prohibited, a listing agreement may contain a *broker protection clause.* This clause states that the property owner will pay the broker the commission called for in the expired listing agreement if, within a specified period of time after the expiration of the listing, the property is sold, leased, rented, optioned, or exchanged to anyone who was introduced to the property during the listing period by the broker, sales associate, or co-operating broker. This is intended to prevent owners from waiting for a listing to expire and then making a deal on their own with someone who was introduced to the property by the broker, sales associate, or cooperating broker.

This clause exposes the property owners to the possibility of having to pay two commissions, in the event they enter into another exclusive listing agreement at the end of the expired listing, with a different broker. To prevent this from happening, many broker protection clauses contain a provision stating that they are void if the property is relisted with another broker.

BUYER'S REPRESENTATIVE

Buyer Agency Agreements

- Exclusive right to represent (exclusive buyer agency agreement)
- Exclusive buyer agency agreement
- Open buyer agency agreement

Prior to World War II, the RESP's life was simple when it came to agency. Technically, all RESPs represented the seller, even one they never met. The rule of agency that was followed was that when an agent had a potential buyer and showed the buyer a property listed by another agent, the first agent became a subagent of the listing agent and was paid by the seller.

With the widespread use of the multiple listing services, this system became misunderstood, especially by buyers who often thought that the agent who showed them another agent's listing was actually representing the buyers and trying to get them the best deal possible. Legally, these agents were subagents of the seller and obligated to try to obtain the best deal for the seller. Real estate agents did little to inform buyers of their true status and often violated their fiduciary responsibility to the seller by giving the buyer information about the seller that was not in the seller's best interest. The agent who had the buyer often encouraged the buyer to make an offer, implying that it was the agent's opinion that the price was too high.

In the late 1980s the FTC discovered that the majority of buyers who were shown MLS properties by a nonlisting agent thought that the agent who was showing them the property was representing them and not the seller. The FTC encouraged states to pass legislation that required disclosure of who each agent represented in a transaction. Thus, three possibilities developed. The agent could represent the seller, the buyer, or both parties (dual agency).

When the agent is representing the buyer, three common contracts are used: exclusive right to represent (exclusive buyer agency agreement), exclusive buyer agency agreement, and open buyer agency agreement. Since these vary from state to state, real estate students must learn what is being used in their respective state. Almost all license exams have several questions about **12.17➤** buyer representation. One thing they have in common is that the terms must be in writing.

DUAL AGENCY

Dual Agency Agreements

- Dual agency consent agreements
- Dual agency disclosure agreements

Dual agency finally recognizes and deals with a practice that has existed for years. Theoretically, brokers are the agents of the property owner and all sales associates and cooperating brokers also act as agents for the property owner. Another government survey reconfirmed that many buyers and tenants did not understand the roles of the brokers, sales associates, and cooperating brokers in transactions in which they were involved. The buyers and tenants often thought that one or more of the brokers, sales associates, or cooperating brokers were representing them rather than the property owner. Interestingly, they maintained this wrong impression even when they knew that the brokers, sales associates, or cooperating brokers were being paid by the property owner and not by them.

These surveys further point out that property owners often feel that brokers, sales associates, or cooperating brokers are not loyal to them. They often feel that the brokers, sales associates, or cooperating brokers encourage the buyer or tenant to offer an amount less than the asking price or rent.

The temptation to shift loyalties from the property owner to the buyer or tenant has often been too strong for many brokers, sales associates, or cooperating brokers to resist. For example, when potential buyers or tenants asked what price the brokers, sales associates, or cooperating brokers thought the property owner would accept, they often received answers that were below the prices in the listing agreements. A proper answer for someone 100 percent loyal to the property owners would have been that the listing price was a fair price for the property and what the property owners expected to receive. It probably would be acceptable to remind the buyers or tenants that they had the right to make any offer and that the brokers, sales associates, or cooperating brokers would submit their offer.

Dual agency is designed to permit the brokers, sales associates, or cooperating brokers to represent both parties. The keystone of dual agency is disclosure to all parties that the brokers, sales associates, or cooperating brokers intend to act as dual agents and that they obtain permission from all the parties to do so.

There is a clear distinction between dual agency and when regular agents breach their agency responsibility to their clients and attempt to represent both parties in order to make the sale or rental transaction go through. The latter is a breach of the agency relationship and subjects the agents to ethical and legal disciplinary measures. Dual agency, when implemented correctly with full disclosure, is permitted by law in some states and by the Realtor's Code of Ethics.

The most common creation of dual agency takes place when brokers, sales associates, or cooperating brokers are working for buyers or tenants. The buyers' agent finds a property (often through the MLS system) and shows it to the customer.

The brokers, sales associates, or cooperating brokers in this very common situation must make a clear choice. Either they notify the sellers or landlords (through their listing broker) that they are the buyers' or tenants' agent and will be paid by the buyers or tenants or they notify the buyers or tenants that they are no longer their agent and they are becoming subagents for the selling or rental agents who have the listing. Then they will share the commission with the brokers for the sellers or landlords. It is common for brokers and sales associates to tell buyers and tenants this when they start looking for them, saying that they do not expect to be paid a commission by them and that they will split a commission from the selling or rental broker. The problem that has occurred is that the buyers' or tenants' brokers or sales associates do not make it clear to the buyers or tenants that by taking a commission from the selling or rental brokers, they become subagents of the selling or rental brokers and therefore represent the sellers or landlords and not the buyers or tenants.

The key is that whenever brokers, sales associates, or cooperating brokers are buyers' or tenants' agents or dual agents, all parties to the transaction are notified in advance and give their permission. Failure to make this disclosure and obtain the needed permissions exposes the brokers, sales associates, or cooperating brokers to forfeiture of their commissions and license suspension.

Since this disclosure is so important and susceptible to misunderstanding, it almost always should be in writing. Some states, like California, have mandatory agency disclosure forms that are signed by all parties to every transaction, clearly spelling out all the agents' relationships to all the parties.

It is not always possible to get the property owners or the prospective buyers or tenants to sign a dual agency disclosure and permission form. Once they clearly understand that they are giving up the loyalty of the brokers, sales associates, or cooperating brokers, they may become dissatisfied with the arrangement. They often do not understand why they cannot get good advice on how much to offer or how much to accept.

Recently many real estate commissions have increased their enforcement of undisclosed dual agency relationships. They have been revoking or suspending the licenses of dual agency disclosure and permission violators.

The best way for brokers, sales associates, and cooperating brokers to protect themselves is to obtain acknowledgment of disclosure and confirmation of permission in writing from all the parties to a transaction, both at the beginning of the transaction and again at the closing, when the sale or rental is consummated.

When the agent is representing the buyer, two common contracts are used: dual agency consent agreements and dual agency disclosure agreements. Since these also vary from state to state, real estate students must learn what is being used in their respective state. Almost all license exams have several questions about dual agency representation.

DEPOSIT RECEIPTS AND OFFERS TO PURCHASE

The way a sale is negotiated is fairly standard throughout the United States. However, the paperwork used in the process is not standard. Sometimes oral offers and acceptances are made, in spite of the fact that they are often not legally enforceable because of the statute of frauds.

A printed form called a *deposit receipt* or *offer to purchase* is used in many areas. These forms should contain all the elements of a contract. In theory, these forms can be initiated by either the buyer or the seller. More often they are initiated by the broker who gets the potential buyer to sign it and accompany it with a deposit check. Then the signed form is taken to the seller for his or her signature. However, this is not the only way a seller can accept an offer. Other ways a contract is created are by letter, check, telegram, fax, e-mail, memorandum, verbally, or any combination of these methods of communication.

Typical items included in a deposit receipt are:

- Receipt for the deposit
- Description of the property
- Terms of the sale
- Conditions to be met prior to the sale
- Identification of the parties to the transaction

- Contingencies
- Signatures

There is no law that spells out how much the deposit should be nor that it has to be reasonable. However, experienced brokers, sales associates, and co-brokers know that the bigger the deposit, the more likely it is that the transaction will close.

A deposit check can become earnest money upon acceptance of a contract. Earnest money represents an assurance from prospective buyers to the sellers that they are genuinely interested in purchasing the property. At the closing, the earnest money reduces the amount that the buyers are required to pay to complete the transaction. In the event the transaction does not close as a result of a default on the part of the buyers, the sellers frequently receive the earnest money for taking the property off the market for a period of time.

SALES CONTRACTS

The paperwork required to document a sales agreement between a buyer and a seller of real estate not only varies from state to state but also varies within the same state. What serves as a sales contract is variously called *contract for purchase and sale, purchase agreement, purchase contract,* or *earnest money agreement,* just to mention a few of the most common names. Obviously, potential licensees must learn which documents are used in their respective state and what provisions they claim. The following are some of the provisions that are found in many sales contracts.

A real estate sales contract is an agreement between the owner of a property and the buyer of the property, for the owner to sell and the buyer to buy. It contains all the details of the proposed sale. It is also called an *offer to purchase, contract for purchase and sale, purchase agreement, earnest money agreement,* or *deposit receipt,* which has already been described.

A real estate sales contract is often used as an offer to purchase by having the potential buyer sign it first and then having the seller accept the offer and sign it. If the seller accepts the offer exactly as it was presented, the offer becomes, or "ripens into," a valid contract. If the seller makes any alterations to the contract, it becomes a counteroffer and the buyer has to accept all the proposed alterations without exception to make it a valid contract. This process can go back and forth many times until both sides reach a 100 percent agreement.

The real estate sales contract is the most important document that most real estate professionals deal with. Brokers, sales associates, and cobrokers should be familiar with the sales contracts used in their area and know under which circumstances they are customarily used. They should also be familiar with the circumstances under which it is customary to use printed forms and those under which it is customary for buyers and sellers to have an attorney draw up the contract. Regardless of the custom in your area, you should use extreme caution about advising people not to use an attorney. Such advice may provide the basis for a professional liability suit. It may also result in disciplinary action from the real estate commission and possible loss or suspension of your license.

In all 50 states and territories, every real estate sales contract must be in writing because all the states and territories have statutes of frauds, which specifically include almost all real estate sales contracts.

The following is a list of items with brief explanations of the provisions that appear in many real estate sales contracts. The order in which these items appear varies from area to area and not all of these items appear in every contract. Also, there are many special provisions customarily used in certain states or areas that are not included in this list.

- Identification of the parties to the contract, which may be only the names of all the buyers and sellers, or may include their addresses.
- A statement of the purchaser's intention to purchase the property.
- The type of deed that will be used to transfer the title from the seller to the buyer.
- The amount of the *earnest money deposit* that will be required.
- How, when, and where the closing will take place. When the date for closing is important and a delay will impose a hardship on one or both parties, a *time is of the essence* provision is added to the contract.
- Who will conduct the closing or determine who will conduct it.
- How the closing costs will be paid.
- A description of what is being sold and purchased. This varies from a simple street address to a complete legal description.
- What personal property is included in the sale.
- What fixtures (for example, a dining room chandelier) are not included in the sale and when these fixtures will be removed by the seller.
- Who will search the title and provide "evidence of marketable title" by an abstract, legal opinion, certificate of title, or Torrens certificate.
- Who will issue the mortgagee's title insurance policy.
- Whether an owner's title insurance policy will be required and, if so, who will issue it (usually the same company that issues the mortgagee's title insurance policy).
- How the proration of insurance, taxes, rent, fuel, and so on, will be handled.
- What will happen if the property is damaged by fire or other causes between the time the sales contract is signed and the title is transferred.
- What will happen if either party defaults (liquidated damages, arbitration, notice, etc.).
- A statement that time is of the essence and what will happen if the closing or settlement is delayed for reasons such as financing, problems in clearing title, death or illness, and so on.

- If the existing insurance policies will be assigned and prorated, or whether the buyer will obtain new insurance.
- How any outstanding special assessments will be adjusted.
- Whether there will be any home warranty insurance or any other warranties made by the seller about the property that will survive the closing, or a statement that there are no warranties that will survive the closing.
- Any inspections on which the contract is conditional, when they will be made, who will make them, who will pay for them, and what happens if they have negative results. Typical inspections include termite, mechanical systems, environmental, well, septic system, habitability report, and other engineering inspections. A statement should be included that if the brokers recommend any of these services, they are not responsible for the results.
- A disclosure about the condition of the property or an agreement that the property is being sold *as is,* which means that the seller is not responsible for the condition of the property.
- Financing contingency—a special VA or FHA contingency statement when either of these types of financing will be used.
- Appraisal contingency: A special Veterans Administration (VA) or Federal Housing Administration (FHA) contingency statement when either of these types of financing will be used.
- The buyer's right to inspect the property immediately prior to the closing, called a *walk-through.*
- The buyer's right to rescind the contract within an agreed-upon time period or within a statutory time period.
- Whether a survey will be made, and if so, who will pay for it.
- Any work the seller is required to do to the property, either before or after the closing or settlement.
- What documents the buyer and seller will have to provide prior to and at the closing or settlement.
- A provision that allows the buyers to sell their home prior to the closing.
- A statement as to who the brokers are, who will pay their commission, and that there are no other brokers involved in the sale, as well as permission for the brokers to report the sale price and other conditions of the sale publicly.
- A severability statement saying that if one provision of the contract is defective, the rest of the contract remains in force.
- Signatures of every party to the transaction.
- Acknowledgment and witnessing of the signatures.

These are only some of the most common clauses that appear in sales contracts. There are many others that are used in different areas and under special circumstances.

INSTALLMENT LAND CONTRACTS

12.10→ The *installment land contract* is called, in different places, a *contract for deed, land contract, bond for deed,* or *installment contract.* These contracts are most commonly used when the sellers are going to finance the purchase. They are often used when the buyers are unable to obtain satisfactory financing from a traditional lender and the sellers are willing to, in effect, provide the financing that will allow the transaction to be completed.

12.11→ Such contracts provide for the sellers to retain title to the property as security that a series of promised payments by the buyers will be made. The buyers become the beneficial owners upon signing the contract and paying the deposit or first payment. However, the buyers do not receive a complete deed until the full purchase price has been paid and any other obligations of the buyers spelled out in the contract have been fulfilled.

When the buyers are entitled to possession is also spelled out in the contract. It may be as soon as the contract is signed, after an agreed-on number of payments have been made, at some specified date, after some specified occurrence, or when all of the payments have been made. When the buyers take possession of the property, they also take control of the property. However, they do not have the same rights as if they owned it outright. In such cases, the buyers must pay the taxes but may not remove or damage the property, nor may they materially change the property without permission of the sellers.

Most of the other provisions of an *installment sale* are the same as those in a standard sales contract. Traditionally, these contracts provide that the buyers lose all of their payments if they default. These are kept by the sellers as liquidated damages.

One of the problems with these types of sales is that when the buyers default and the sellers reclaim the property, there is a cloud on the title caused by the recorded contract. To clear the title, it is necessary to get a release or quitclaim deed from the buyers. If this is not obtainable (which it often isn't), it becomes necessary to clear the title with a foreclosure action or a court ac-
12.12→ tion to quiet title.

OPTIONS AND RIGHTS OF FIRST REFUSAL

Options

An option is a contract that keeps an offer to sell or lease open to a specific
12.13→ party (optioner) for a specified period of time. When the option is exercised, the property owner must sell the property to the optionee for the price and terms contained in the option. During this period of time, the optionee has the
12.15→ right to buy or lease the optioned property at a specified price. Customarily the optionee pays the property owner some consideration for granting the option.

12.14➤ A common option in real estate is a lease with an option to buy, also known as a *lease option*. This option allows tenants to buy the property they lease at a preset price. To be valid, all the terms and conditions of the purchase must be spelled out in the option.

To encourage buyers and tenants to exercise their options, it is common for the option consideration or part of the rent to be applied to the purchase price of the property.

An important characteristic of all options is that they bind only one party. In real estate, the bound party is usually the property owner.

It is very common for large residential development corporations to obtain options on land they will need for future development if the housing market continues to be strong in the area.

Rights of First Refusal

A *right of first refusal* is rarely contained in a document of its own. It is usually part of the condominium association, cooperative project, or lease documents. The essence of such clauses is that the entity with the right of first refusal has the opportunity to match any offer made by anyone on the property covered by the right of first refusal.

Typically, tenants who take out a long lease want an opportunity to buy their home or the location of their business when the owners of the property are willing to sell it. Often, the property owners are unwilling to grant the tenants an option because this requires the owners to determine what the value of the property will be when the option is exercised.

The right of first refusal solves the value-setting dilemma. The only significant downside it has is that it may delay a sale or actually prevent a sale when the potential buyers are unwilling to wait while the tenants or other holders of the right of first refusal decide whether or not to exercise their right to buy the property for the same terms and conditions as the potential buyers are willing to buy it for.

In reality, the many condominium associations and cooperative corporations that have the right of first refusal on all the units in their development rarely exercise their first refusal rights. Therefore, the additional cost involved in drawing up the papers needed to give the holders of the first refusal rights the notice they are entitled to is wasted.

CONTRACTS FOR EXCHANGE OF REAL ESTATE

12.16➤ Property exchanges take advantage of tax regulations. There are tax advantages to exchanging one property for another rather than each owner selling his or her property and using the proceeds to buy another property. This advantage is usually the deferral of taxes, not the elimination of taxes. Another advantage of exchanging property is that it may reduce the amount of cash needed to complete the transactions.

There are complex federal requirements for a tax-deferred exchange. Professional help is strongly recommended. Some real estate professionals specialize in tax-deferred exchanges. Great care must be taken with the preparation of all the contracts involved in a tax-deferred exchange.

To qualify as a *tax-deferred exchange,* both of the properties must be of "like kind." Since this is going to be a tax question, it is advisable to consult an accountant or other expert on tax-free exchanges to determine whether a proposed exchange meets the applicable tax codes. Since two properties are rarely equal in value, one owner is usually required to add something else to the exchange, typically in the form of money or property, which is called the *boot.* The party receiving the boot is taxed on it in the year the exchange takes place.

Section 1031 of the Internal Revenue Code establishes the basis on which property exchanges occur. They are referred to as 1031 exchanges. In addition to a simultaneous exchange between property owners, it is possible to sell a property at one point in time and purchase another property within a relatively short period of time and enjoy the tax benefits of an exchange. There are a number of specific rules that must be met in order to qualify, but the tax savings could be substantial.

REVIEW QUESTIONS

12.1 A listing agreement is:

A. A contract between a sales agent and a property owner

B. Not valid when signed by someone who has a written power of attorney from the property owner

C. A contract between a property owner and a broker

D. All of the above

12.2 An exclusive agency listing:

A. Permits the brokers, sales associates, and cooperating brokers to show the owner's property

B. Permits the brokers to accept deposits made with offers to buy and rent

C. Provides for payment to the brokers only when the brokers, sales associates, or cooperating brokers are the procuring cause of a transaction

D. All of the above

12.3 An exclusive right to sell listing:

A. Permits the listing broker, sales associates, and cooperating brokers to show the owner's property

B. Permits the listing broker to accept deposits made with offers to buy and rent

C. Provides for payment to the listing broker only when any broker, sales associate, or cooperating broker is the procuring cause of the transaction

D. All of the above

12.4 Net listings:

A. Guarantee that the listing broker will receive a commission when the property is sold by any broker, their sales associate, or cooperating broker

B. Pay the listing broker a commission consisting of 50 percent of everything received above a specified amount

C. Are increasing in popularity because property owners often pay only a very small commission

D. None of the above

12.5 An open listing:

 A. Is also known as a nonexclusive listing

 B. Is also known as a general listing

 C. Usually specifies the asking price

 D. Is all of the above

12.6 An option listing:

 A. Is becoming more popular because it gives both the property owner and the broker several desirable options

 B. Is an option that gives the property owner the right to cancel the listing without any penalty

 C. Gives the broker the option to buy the property at a stipulated price

 D. Is none of the above

12.7 A listing with an automatic extension clause:

 A. Is prohibited by many states

 B. Extends the period of the listing beyond its specified termination date

 C. Is discouraged where not prohibited by law

 D. All of the above

12.8 A broker's protection clause protects the broker:

 A. From commission claims made by other brokers

 B. From the property owner allowing other brokers to show the property

 C. Against the property owner trying to avoid paying a commission by trying to sell or rent the property to people shown the property when the listing was in effect during the listing period

 D. All of the above

12.9 A multiple listing service:

 A. Is always affiliated with a real estate board

 B. Always uses its own listing agreements, which contain its rules and regulations

 C. Specifies how the commission will be split between brokers and sales associates

 D. None of the above

12.10 An installment land contract (contract for deed, land contract, bond for deed, or installment contract) is most commonly used when financing is coming from:

 A. The FHA

 B. The VA

 C. Freddie Mac or Fannie Mae

 D. None of the above

12.11 An installment land contract (contract for deed, land contract, bond for deed, installment contract) transfers title to:

A. The lender at the closing or settlement

B. The buyer at the closing or settlement

C. The FHA or VA at the closing or settlement

D. None of the above

12.12 When a borrower using an installment land contract (contract for deed, land contract, bond for deed, installment contract) defaults, it may be necessary to take legal action to:

A. Force a quitclaim deed

B. Quiet title

C. Transfer title

D. None of the above

12.13 An option binds:

A. The property owner

B. The optionee

C. Both of the above

D. None of the above

12.14 A lease with option to buy (lease option) usually is an option that permits the tenant to:

A. Extend the lease if the property is sold during the term of the lease

B. Buy the property at a preset price during the term of the lease

C. Both of the above

D. None of the above

12.15 A right of first refusal differs from an option in that:

A. In an option, the purchase price is specified

B. In a first refusal, the purchase price is specified

C. Both of the above

D. None of the above

12.16 Property exchanges take advantage of:

A. Lower commission rates

B. Tax regulations

C. Elimination of taxes

D. None of the above

12.17 A buyer agency agreement in most states:

A. Is prohibited

B. Must be in writing

C. Is permitted only when the buyer is represented by an attorney

D. None of the above

ANSWERS

The answer to each question is indicated by the letters A, B, C, or D. The explanation of the answer is indicated by the page number and an arrow that points to the appropriate paragraph on the page.

Q 12.1 C Page 182	Q 12.5 D Page 184	Q 12.9 D Page 191	Q 12.13 A Page 201	Q 12.17 B Page 194
Q 12.2 D Page 183	Q 12.6 C Page 185	Q 12.10 D Page 200	Q 12.14 B Page 201	
Q 12.3 D Page 183	Q 12.7 D Page 190	Q 12.11 D Page 200	Q 12.15 A Page 201	
Q 12.4 D Page 184	Q 12.8 C Page 193	Q 12.12 B Page 200	Q 12.16 B Page 202	

CHAPTER 13

Estimating How Much a Property Is Worth

When asked what a house is worth, some people answer, "Whatever someone will pay for it." That certainly is true as far as it goes. The problem with this simplistic answer is that it does not address some questions, such as: How long will the house have to be on the market in order to obtain this price? How must the house be marketed in order to obtain this price? Should the house be listed at this price or higher in order to allow for the bargaining that is traditional in real estate transactions? Is this price the same as what the owner would be legally entitled to receive if it was condemned for public use? Is it the same as what the owner would expect to receive if the house was destroyed by fire or some other natural disaster?

These are only a few of the questions that need to be addressed in order to estimate how much a property is worth?" Appraisers will tell you that in order to obtain an accurate estimate of the value of a property, you should use a licensed or certified appraiser who has been trained to take all the steps necessary to produce the estimate.

RESPs know that most people who list their properties for sale will not pay for an appraisal. They want a value to be estimated for free. There are two ways they can obtain a free estimate of value.

ONLINE APPRAISALS

To find out what is available you need to go to an online search engine such as Google and type in "free real estate appraisal." The result of the search should **13.2→** be a list of current Web sites that will produce what is called a free *online appraisal* of any house address you type into the program. As this book was being written, there were pending court cases challenging the use of the word *appraisal* in conjunction with the estimates that are produced by these Web sites.

What these programs do is call upon their vast databases that have information on millions of homes and millions of home sales. There are about 100 million homes in the United States and about 6 million sell each year. The program compares the description of the house and the value be asked for with the data about recent sales in the same area.

When the house being valued is a simple house in average condition for its age and there are many comparable sales of similar houses in the same market area, the programs can give a reasonable accurate value estimate. When the house being valued is atypical or not in average condition, the program is more likely to make an error in the value it estimates. This is also true when the comparable sales are not similar to the house being valued.

Probably the best thing about these programs is the information about comparable sales in the same market as the house being valued. With this information, homeowners can often make better estimates than the online source, as they have information about their own house that is not in the database.

COMPARATIVE MARKET ANALYSIS (CMA)

13.3→ RESPs use a tool called a *comparative market analysis* to estimate the value of houses they are trying to list for sale or convince potential buyers to make offers on. Most RESPs are trained in how to perform a CMA in their market area. Often there is a computer program available as part of the local MLS system that can help RESPs prepare the CMA.

CMAs are about facts that can be qualified and quantified. There is very little room for judgment. Usually the only judgment that the preparer of the CMA must make is estimating the value of the identifiable differences between the house being valued and comparable houses sold in the area. The CMA is designed to give a quick capsule of information such as the number of bedrooms and baths, the approximate square footage, the size of the major rooms, amenities such as fireplaces and pools, the age of the home, property taxes, and listing agent contact information. For example, a comparable sale might have two full baths, while the house being valued has two and a half baths. The preparer of the CMA is asked to input an adjustment that reflects the difference between houses with two baths and houses with two and a half baths.

CMAs can include homes that are currently for sale and those that have recently sold. They can go back in time as long as a year, a month, or a week.

CMAs can cover areas as narrow as one or two streets surrounding a home or as broad as an entire subdivision.

Not covered by the CMA are those factors that affect the buyer's perception of the house. This includes such features as the design, view, noise levels, and orientation on the lot. These perceptions explain why one home will ultimately command a higher or lower price than another home with similar features. Much of a home's value is ultimately determined by the emotional impact it has on buyers.

For privacy reasons, the CMA that is offered for public consumption does not list every piece of information that has been obtained by the seller's agent. It will give the what, when, and where, but it won't give the who (the seller's identity) and the why (the reason the home is being put up for sale). The justification for this is twofold: to protect the seller's privacy and to keep from inadvertently giving the buyer an advantage in a distress situation.

AUTOMATIC VALUATION MODELS (AVMS)

An *automatic valuation model* (AVM) is a computer model that computes the estimated market value (sale price) of a house, based on the selling price of computer-selected comparable sales and adjustments made by the software for the differences between the comparables and the house being appraised. They have been around since the early 1990s, but many real estate professionals still consider them to be experimental. AVMs are being used by Fannie Mae, Freddie Mac, and a variety of others who wish to obtain the value of a home using computer software. Comparable sales are obtained from whatever data sources are available to the operator of the AVM.

`13.4➤`

The system works in two different ways. In the first method, the computer is programmed to select the comparable sales based on an algorithm. In the other method, a computer operator selects the best comparable sales based on information provided by the computer or based on other sources known to the operator.

Some people think that an AVM can be used as part of an appraisal but should probably not be used as an appraisal by itself because there haven't been any on-site inspections. They claim that AVMs deal only with data. AVMs cannot tell you such things as interior or exterior remodeling that has been completed, the condition of the interior, any interior design deficiencies, and what the landscaping is like. This is information an appraiser must know. Others claim that where there are a sufficient number of appropriate comparable sales, the AVM's estimated value of a house, made without information about the interior of the property, is good enough for the user's purposes.

It seems likely that the role of AVMs will continue to grow within the arenas of online valuations, lending, and portfolio management. Ongoing model testing within many markets indicates there is sometimes a close parallel between AVM results and the results of traditional appraisal analyses.

Real estate professionals should keep abreast of this fast-developing AVM technology to determine whether it can be useful to them in their real estate practices. However, they should be careful when considering its use not to be misled by claims that overestimate the accuracy of the values being estimated by AVMs.

APPRAISALS BY LICENSED OR CERTIFIED APPRAISERS

What constitutes a real estate appraisal and who can make one depends on state laws. RESPs should be familiar with their respective state's laws.

Millions of real estate appraisals are made every year by licensed and certified real estate appraisers. The most common type of appraisal is of a single-family residence for the purpose of obtaining a mortgage. The second most common type is when homeowners refinance their homes or obtain home equity loans. There are approximately 100,000 licensed and certified appraisers in the United States.

THE IMPORTANCE OF THE APPRAISER

The role of professional appraisers is to provide opinions on value to help their clients make decisions. For example, an appraisal helps a lender decide whether a given property constitutes adequate security for a proposed loan. Some appraisals help buyers and sellers decide how much to buy or sell a property for, determine how much to insure a property for, or estimate the value of a property for estate or tax purposes. Appraisers play an important part in the process of government acquisition of real property by eminent domain by helping to set a fair price for the property acquired. These are just a few of the many reasons appraisers estimate property value.

Appraisers provide clients with five qualities (represented by the mnemonic A-E-I-O-U):

13.7→

> 1. **A**dequate knowledge
> 2. **E**xperience
> 3. **I**ntegrity
> 4. **O**bjectivity
> 5. **U**ncompromised willingness to do the work on a timely basis for a mutually agreed-on fee

Types of Appraisal Assignments

Real estate appraisals are generally made by fee appraisers, who are independent contractors or employees of independent contractors. Appraisals are also

13.8→ made by the staffs of lending institutions and other companies and government agencies that require appraisals. Trainees who are supervised by licensed or certified appraisers may also make appraisals, but they must be cosigned by a supervising appraiser who accepts full responsibility for the appraisal. As of January 1, 2008, only certified appraisers are able to be supervising appraisers.

Here is a partial list of those who use the services of a real estate appraiser:

- Buyers and sellers of homes
- Lending institutions
- Investors
- Architects
- Builders and developers
- Lawyers
- Tenants
- Insurers and the insured
- Accountants
- Business corporations
- Nonprofit organizations
- Government agencies at federal, state, and local levels
- Public utility companies

The list of users of appraisals is seemingly endless, and the need for appraisers appears to be growing and continues to change with the role of the computer becoming increasingly important.

Definition of a Real Estate Appraisal

There is no one standard accepted definition of the terms *appraisal* and *real estate appraisal*. However, most of the accepted definitions incorporate the following seven principles:

13.1→

1. An appraisal is an opinion of value.
2. The opinion must be appropriately supported with general and specific data.
3. It must be as of a specific date.
4. The value estimated must be defined.
5. The property being appraised must be adequately and accurately described.
6. The person making the appraisal must be qualified by reason of adequate education and experience.
7. The person making the appraisal must be unbiased and have no undisclosed interest in the property.

Thus, an appraisal is an appropriately supported, objective, and unbiased opinion of the value, as of a specific date, of an adequately and accurately described property, made by a qualified person who has no undisclosed interest in the property.

13.6➤ An appraisal may include such complicated considerations as various interests, equities, retrospective and prospective values, and other conditions. It may be based on hypothetical conditions as long as the requirements stated in the Uniform Standards of Professional Appraisal Practice (USPAP) for including hypothetical conditions are followed.

Purpose and Intended Use of Appraisals

13.5➤ The purpose and intended use of every appraisal must be known to the appraiser and stated in the appraisal. The fundamental purpose of most appraisals is to estimate some kind of value. The need for an appraisal of market value may arise from many situations, including:

- Transfer of ownership
- Financing and credit
- Just compensation in condemnation (eminent domain) proceedings
- As a basis for taxation
- To establish rental schedules and lease provisions
- Feasibility analysis

In addition to the need for estimating market value, appraisals are also made to estimate:

- Insurable value
- Going-concern value
- Liquidation value
- Assessed value (which may be a percentage of market value)

Although the list does not include all the needs for appraisals, it does indicate the broad scope of the professional appraiser's typical activities.

Regulation of Real Property Appraisers

In response to the failure of a large number of savings and loan institutions in the 1980s, Congress conducted several hearings to determine the root cause of the crisis and took steps to ensure that a similar crisis would not occur in the future. During the course of their investigation, Congress was surprised to learn that appraisers, the individuals estimating the value of the underlying collateral of loans, were generally unregulated. While professional licensing issues generally fall into the domain of state governments, Congress was concerned about protecting the future integrity of deposit insurance funds.

Accordingly, when passing legislation in 1989 to address the financial institution crisis (known as the Financial Institutions Reform, Recovery and Enforcement Act, or FIRREA), Congress included a provision known as Title XI mandating the regulation of real estate appraisers by the states. The regulatory program contained three components:

13.9→

> 1. Each state government is to establish an appraiser regulatory body to issue licenses and certificates and to address enforcement of disciplinary issues.
>
> 2. The Appraisal Foundation provides private-sector expertise regarding appraisal standards and appraiser qualification.
>
> 3. A small federal government agency, the Appraisal Subcommittee was created to oversee the program to ensure it remained consistent with the original intent of Congress.

THE VALUATION PROCESS

For over 60 years, the appraisal profession has been working to perfect a process for estimating the value of real estate. The process is not stagnant—it improves as time goes on. Appraisers who feel they have an improvement to the process are invited to write an article for one of the appraisal journals published by the professional organizations. The Appraisal Foundation, through its Appraisal Standards Board, also is changing the valuation process each time it changes the *Uniform Standards of Appraisal Practice* (USPAP). The valuation process that follows incorporates the latest changes that were made by the 2006 USPAP that become effective January 1, 2008.

13.10→

- Definition of the problem
- Determine the scope of work
- Data collection and property description
  - Market data
  - Subject property data
  - Comparable property data

- Data analysis
  - Market analysis
  - Highest and best use analysis
- Land (site) value opinion
- Application of the approaches to value
  - Cost approach
  - Sales comparison approach
  - Income approach
- Reconciliation of value indications and final value opinion
- Report of final opinion of value and conclusions

Definition of the Problem

The first step in an appraisal is to define the problem to be solved. There are seven major steps in the definition of the problem:

13.11 →

> 1. Identification of the client and other intended users
> 2. Identification of the intended use of the appraiser's opinions and conclusions
> 3. Identification of the type and definition of value
> 4. Identification of the effective date of the appraiser's opinions and conclusions
> 5. Identification of the characteristics of the property (including location and property rights to be valued)
> 6. Identification of any extraordinary assumptions necessary in the assignment
> 7. Identification of any hypothetical conditions necessary in the assignment

Identification of Client and Other Intended Users

The identification of the client and other *intended users* is important, as it affects the appropriate level of reporting and who has status in a professional liability suit against the appraiser. USPAP requires that the intended user(s) of the appraisal be identified in the appraisal report. *Freddie Mac* and *Fannie Mae* limit the definition of the intended user to the lender/client.

Identification of the Intended Use of the Appraiser's Opinions and Conclusions

USPAP requires that the intended use be reported in every appraisal. It is helpful for the appraiser to know the purpose of the appraisal so that the report will provide the reader with all the information required to make a decision. The objective of most appraisals is to estimate the value of a property as of a specific date.

Identification of the Type and Definition of Value

The type of value must be identified. Typically market value is the type of value, but often other types of value are possible. Examples of other types of value include investment value, insurable value, and auction value.

Once the type of value has been identified, the appraiser is obligated to determine which definition for the type of value is being relied on for assignment. It is required that appraisals that are made for loan purposes base their opinion of value on market value. The current accepted definition of market value is usually attached to each appraisal or a copy is filed by the appraiser with the client and is referred to in the appraisal. Implicit in this definition is the consummation of a sale as of the specified date and the passing of title from seller to buyer.

Identification of the Effective Date of the Appraiser's Opinions and Conclusions

An appraisal must be an opinion of value as of a *specific date.* The value of a property may change from day to day. For example, the sudden announcement of some event that affects the subject market will have a significant effect on the value of property. Typical announcements that affect the value of property are the expansion or contraction of business activities that are major sources of employment in the area. Other announcements that may suddenly affect value are the addition or relocation of roads and highways or anything else changing in close proximity to the *subject property.*

Sudden changes in the physical condition of the property by fire, the environment, or human-made additions, demolitions, or alterations may affect the property value. It is also acceptable for an appraisal to be as of some date in the past. The appraiser then makes *assumptions* about the condition of the property and the *site* as of that date and uses data that reflects values as of the date of the appraisal.

When the *effective date of the appraisal* is the same as the date of the last inspection of the subject property, no assumptions about the future or the past are required. When the effective date of the appraisal is either before or after the date of last inspection, the appraisal must contain the assumptions the appraiser has made about the property and the market as of the effective date of the appraisal.

Identification of the Characteristics of the Property (Including Location and Property Rights to Be Valued)

Every appraisal must contain an accurate description of the *real estate* (site and *improvements*) and any personal property included in the value estimate. A more precise identification, such as that provided by a legal description that can be copied from the deed or mortgage, is also required. When available, a survey helps to precisely identify a property, and may be included or cited in an appraisal report.

An appraisal of *real property* is not directly a valuation of the physical land and improvements; it is a valuation of the *rights of ownership*. A specific appraisal may require a value estimate of all *property rights*, while another will analyze only limited rights in property. Ownership of property may be held by an individual, a partnership, a corporation, or a group of people. When ownership is vested in more than one interest, each may hold an equal or an unequal share.

The property rights or interests to be appraised may be *fractional interests* such as air rights over a specified property, subsurface rights, an easement, a right-of-way, or fee simple (subject to an easement). Because the value of real property is not limited to its physical components, the appraisers cannot define the problem precisely until they are fully aware of which property rights are to be included in the analysis, as defined by the client. Without this knowledge, the appraisers may produce an estimate of value that is irrelevant to the problem. A clear understanding of the rights being appraised will also help the appraisers evaluate the complexity of the problem and plan appropriately for the amount of work the appraisal will require.

Identification of Any Extraordinary Assumptions Necessary in the Assignment

It is important to include all *extraordinary assumptions* in every appraisal report. This precaution reduces the potential for successful professional liability suits against the appraiser because it discloses to the users what the appraiser did and did not factually support in the process of making the appraisal.

Identification of Any Hypothetical Conditions Necessary in the Assignment

13.12→ *Hypothetical conditions* are assumptions that are known not to exist but are assumed for purposes of analysis. Before you make an appraisal with a hypothetical condition, it is necessary to be familiar with all the current USPAP requirements pertaining to hypothetical conditions. Keep in mind that the 2006 USPAP states:

> Comment: A hypothetical condition may be used in an assignment only if:
> - it is required to properly develop credible opinions and conclusions;
> - the appraiser has a reasonable basis for the extraordinary assumption;
> - use of the extraordinary assumption results in a credible analysis; and
> - the appraiser complies with the disclosure requirements set forth in the USPAP for extraordinary assumptions.

Scope of Work Determination and Planning the Appraisal

The second step of the valuation process is determination with the client what the scope of work will be, and making an appraisal plan. This will vary with the assignment. The following six steps are useful in planning:

---

1. Decide which data is needed

2. Identify the sources of the needed data

3. Determine what personnel are needed

4. Make a time schedule

5. Make a flowchart

6. Present a fee proposal, agree on a fee, and sign a contract

---

Data Needed

The type of data required for an appraisal consists of *general data* about the market and location and specific data about the subject property and the comparable properties.

GENERAL DATA

A collection is divided into the broad categories of social, economic, governmental, and environmental factors that affect the value of the property. There are a variety of ways to organize the general data. The most common way is to break the data down into regional, state, community, and neighborhood sections.

An advantage of this system is that once the data is assembled and organized, it can be used for other appraisals in the same region, state, community, or neighborhood. In some areas, two of the classifications may be combined.

For example, the state and regional data are often the same. When a community is small, it may contain only one neighborhood.

SPECIFIC DATA

Specific data collection is probably the most difficult aspect of performing an appraisal. This is especially true when the property is located in a territory that is unfamiliar to the appraiser.

DATA SOURCES

An appraiser should maintain a reliable data collection and storage system. A large bank of market data should be accumulated in the appraiser's own files and should be organized to serve the appraiser's needs most effectively. Only some of the data will be immediately pertinent; the remainder is collected, filed, and cross-indexed for future use. Sales information is usually collected and recorded on standardized sheets or cards. Many appraisers are now using computers for data storage, retrieval, and analysis.

PERSONNEL NEEDED

The most common configuration of an appraisal company consists of the designated appraiser, who is usually the owner or manager, and an assistant who helps gather data and/or completes on his or her own, with supervision, the less complex assignments. A clerical support person is usually available to staff the office, answer the phone, and do most of the typing, computer entry, filing, and billing. Whether an office is a typical small appraisal company or a larger facility, a decision must be made for each assignment about how the work will be divided among the available personnel.

A simple appraisal made in a one-person shop requires only one individual. An appraiser in solo practice may have to recruit outside help for a complex assignment.

TIME SCHEDULE AND FLOWCHART

Time schedule: The timely production of appraisals is essential to the successful management of an appraisal practice. In many areas, the competition for single-family appraisal work requires delivery of the finished report within a few days of receiving the assignment. A schedule of how the work will be performed is a good management tool. This helps the staff begin with a clear understanding of the exact nature of the work to be done by each person, which will go a long way toward the efficient completion of an assignment.

Flowchart: A flowchart is commonly used to keep track of the work in an appraisal office. This can be as simple as a calendar on which the dates are marked when portions of the appraisal are due. Another common type of flowchart is a metal board on which magnetic holders are displayed indicating the steps of the appraisal and when they are due. Many offices also have computerized flowcharts that help them keep track of the status of each job in progress. Many computerized offices now use e-mail notification programs to update clients about the progress on their appraisal assignments.

FEE PROPOSAL AND CONTRACT

Some lenders and their management companies determine how much they will pay for an appraisal, and the appraisers must only decide if they are willing to do the work for the fee being offered. Many other clients require the appraisers to quote a fee or a fee range in advance of a commitment to proceed with an appraisal assignment.

The relationship some appraisers have with select regular clients is so well established that these clients permit the appraiser to proceed with an assignment without having previously agreed on a fee. The fee an appraiser may charge for the services performed depends on the reputation of the appraiser. Appraisers who, in the view of their clients, have an established reputation for experience and sound judgment command higher fees than those appraisers who do not. This is especially true for more complex assignments.

Since appraisers are professionals, competent work is required regardless of the fee charged. An inadequate fee is not a valid excuse for inadequate work, since a professional is obliged to perform competent work regardless of the fee received. Therefore, the appraiser should be careful to correctly estimate the scope of work an assignment will require, so that a reasonable fee can be quoted. When an appraisal is performed for a regular client, such as a lending institution, mortgage broker, mortgage banker, or relocation company, the appraiser often elects to work without a contract. However, even in these situations, a contract or a letter of authorization is desirable if it can be obtained. Personnel in large institutions often change jobs; what is authorized by one employee may be objectionable to the replacement employee. When making appraisals for the public or their representative, it is very desirable to have an appraisal contract that reflects the scope of work, time frame, and how and when the appraiser will be paid. It is also customary in many areas for the appraiser to receive a retainer.

Data Collection and Property Description

Market Area Data

13.13➤

The *market area* is a geographic area in which the subject property is located and which includes the area from which a majority of demand and competition is drawn. For residential properties, it is that area in which the majority of potential buyers of the subject property would consider an alternative choice acceptable. The market area may be as small as a part of a neighborhood, a whole neighborhood, or more than one neighborhood. It can be a part of a community or a whole community. Sometimes, it is as large as a part of a region or a whole region, and in some instances market area includes more than one state.

Appraisers describe the market area and identifies its boundaries. They consider all the significant social, economic, governmental, and environmental influences that affect property values in their region.

Highest and Best Use Data

Subject property data: Specific data pertaining to the subject property includes title and record data, the relationship of the site to general land patterns, a description and analysis of the physical characteristics of the property, and *highest and best use* analysis.

Specific Characteristics of the Land and Improvements, Personal Property, and Business Assets

Title and record data: Pertinent title data may include the identity of the owners, type of ownership, zoning, existing easements and encroachments, zoning regulations affecting the property, assessed value and taxation, and deed or other restrictions.

Relationship of site to land pattern: Descriptive data includes a complete evaluation of the site. Site features such as size, shape, topography, site and building orientation, utilities, and relationship to the existing land-use patterns are also analyzed here.

Characteristics of the Site

Legal description: A parcel of *land* consists of any parcel that can be identified by a common description and is in one ownership. A special characteristic of real estate is that every parcel is unique. The best identification of a parcel is a legal description and a survey, which eliminates all confusion because it specifically identifies and locates a unique piece of real estate. The three methods used in the United States to legally describe land are *metes and bounds,* the *rectangular (government) survey system,* and the *lot and block system.*

Other descriptive information: The description of the site should also include information about the type of ownership. The property may be in fee simple ownership, *planned unit development* (PUD), de minimis PUD, condominium, cooperative, or some unique form of fractional ownership. (Fannie Mae and Freddie Mac permit use of the Uniform Residential Appraisal Report (URAR) form for single-family residences in fee simple ownership, on leased land, or when there is a PUD. It may not be used for multifamily residences or cooperative or condominium ownership.) The appraiser should check for any apparent rights that may affect the value such as surface or subsurface rights, easements, restrictions, air rights, water rights, beach rights mineral rights, obligations for unique lateral support, easements for common walls, etc.

The appraiser is not responsible for reporting rights that are not apparent. The appraiser is responsible for researching these issues to a level that is necessary to develop a credible appraisal result. This standard has two components: (1) the expectations of the intended users for similar assignments and (2) the amount of research an appraiser's peers would conduct for a similar assignment.

The description of the property also includes information about the applicable zoning regulations and other environmental regulations that affect the use of the property. It is the responsibility of the appraiser to determine and report if the improvements are a nonconforming (legal or illegal) use based on the local ordinances.

Comparable Property Data

Sales, listings, offerings, and vacancies: Sufficient specific data must be collected in the market to apply the sales comparison approach.

Cost and depreciation: To develop the *cost approach,* the appraiser collects information on what it would cost to reproduce the subject property, as of the effective date of the appraisal.

Income and expenses, capitalization rates, and so on: To develop both the *income capitalization approach* and the *gross monthly rent multiplier (GMRM) approach,* it is necessary to obtain information about rentals in the subject market area. This data is used to estimate a market rent for the subject property and to develop an appropriate GMRM and capitalization rates.

Data Analysis

Data analysis has two components: market analysis and highest and best use analysis. Every appraisal assignment, including single-family house appraisals, must be based on an understanding of the market conditions that

13.14→ affect the subject property and must include a highest and best use analysis of the property.

Market Analysis

The type of market analysis performed by an appraiser depends on the type of subject property. This six-step process can serve as the foundation for all market analysis.

> **1.** Property productivity analysis
>
> **2.** Market delineation
>
> **3.** Demand analysis and forecast
>
> **4.** Competitive supply analysis and forecast
>
> **5.** Supply and demand study
>
> **6.** Capture estimation

Property productivity analysis: First, the appraiser identifies which features of the subject property shape productive capabilities and potential uses of the property. Those attributes can be physical, legal, or locational, and are the basis for the selection of comparables.

Market delineation: Given the potential uses of the subject property, the appraiser identifies a market for the defined use (or more than one market, if the property has alternative uses).

Demand analysis and forecast: Economic base analysis considers existing and anticipated market demand. An appraiser studies population and employment data to analyze and forecast demand. The scope of work required by the assignment (as well as time and budgetary constraints) will dictate to what extent demand side variables must be investigated.

Competitive supply analysis and forecast: Marginal demand is established through analysis of existing and anticipated supply of the subject property type.

Supply and demand study: The appraiser investigates the interaction of supply and demand to determine if marginal demand exists and if the market is out of equilibrium. The purpose of the study is to determine if there is adequate demand relative to the existing supply plus supply that is in the process of being developed to generate an acceptable return. These studies are also referred to as *feasibility studies.*

Capture estimation: By comparing the productive attributes of the subject property to those of competitive properties, the appraiser can judge the market share the subject is likely to capture, given market conditions, demand, and competitive supply.

The data and conclusions generated through market analysis are essential components in other portions of the valuation process. Market analysis yields information needed for each of the three approaches to value.

Highest and Best Use

Two separate highest and best use analyses are made: highest and best use as though vacant, and highest and best use as improved. Some appraisers think this is the most important part of the appraisal process.

Elements in Highest and Best Use Analysis

13.15➤ To estimate the highest and best use of a site, the appraiser utilizes four tests. The projected use must meet all four of these tests:

---

1. Physically possible
2. Legally permissible
3. Financially feasible
4. Maximally productive

Each potential use of a property is considered and tested by the appraiser. If a proposed use fails to meet any of the tests, it is discarded and another use is reviewed. The highest and best use meets all four tests.

PHYSICALLY POSSIBLE (SUITABLE)

The use of a site must be physically possible. Uses might be limited by the physical characteristics of a site, such as size, frontage, topography, soil and subsoil conditions, and climate conditions. Despite the need for single-family residential housing, an area of severe terrain with poor subsoil characteristics cannot be considered appropriate for residential development.

LEGALLY PERMITTED

Each use must be tested first to see if it is legally permitted on the site. Public legal restrictions consist of zoning regulations, building codes, environmental regulations, and other applicable ordinances. Private restrictions are limitations that run with the land and are passed from owner to owner. Generally, they are imposed by the developer of the tract who attempts to preserve the value of the entire development by restricting what may be done with individual sites. Easements, encroachments, party-wall agreements, and the like, also restrict the development of a site.

FINANCIALLY FEASIBLE

A realistic assessment of market demand for a proposed use is a critical factor. For example, acreage may be available that is zoned for single-family residential use of a certain concentration, served by all utilities, and with good proximity and access; however, similar subdivisions already in the market have remained unsold for some time. There is no need for the additional sites, so although the property meets the first two tests, it fails the test of economic feasibility. Thus, market demand acts to create highest and best use. In reviewing alternative uses, the appraiser must consider the demand for each use and the other available competitive land suitable for that use, which constitutes the supply. These factors must be weighed in the economic analysis. All physically possible and legal uses that fail to meet the test of economic feasibility are discarded. The remaining uses produce some net return to the property.

MAXIMALLY PRODUCTIVE

The fourth test is essentially a test for maximum return. The appraiser is seeking the most profitable among all of the legally permitted, physically suitable, and financially feasible uses.

Highest and Best Use As Though Vacant

Analyzing the highest and best use of the site as though vacant serves two functions. First, it helps the appraiser identify comparable properties. The comparable properties' highest and best use should be similar to that of the subject property.

The second reason to analyze the property's highest and best use as though vacant is to identify the use that would produce maximum income to the site, after income is allocated to the improvements. In the cost approach and some income capitalization techniques, a separate value estimate of the site is required. Estimating the highest and best use of the site as though vacant is a necessary part of deriving a site value estimate.

Because change is constantly occurring, the existing use of land is often no longer the highest and best use. If the land alone has a higher value under an alternate physically suitable, legally permitted use than the whole property as currently improved and utilized, the proposed use becomes the highest and best use. The existing improvement is at the end of its economic life but it will still be the highest and best use during the transition period.

It is not sufficient to simply state the type of improvement that is the highest and best use. The ideal improvement must be described. The answer that it is a single-family residence is not sufficient. The residence should be described in some detail and, at a minimum, include its size and room configuration.

Highest and Best Use As Improved

There are two reasons to analyze the highest and best use of the property as improved. The first is to help identify comparable properties. Comparable improved properties should have the same or similar highest and best uses as the subject property.

The second reason to analyze the highest and best use of the property as improved is to decide whether the improvements should be demolished, renovated, or retained in their present condition. They should be retained as long as they have some contributory value and the return from the property exceeds the return that would be realized by a new use, after deducting the costs of demolishing the old building and constructing a new one. Identification of the most profitable use is crucial to this determination.

Land (Site) Value Opinion

Purpose of Separate Land (Site) Valuation

Even after a property has been improved, it is necessary and possible to make a separate estimate of the value of the site. Separate site valuations are required by statute in most states for ad valorem (real estate) tax purposes. The assessed value is almost universally split between the land (or site) and the improvements. Special assessments for public improvements, such as streets, water lines, and sewers, are often based on their estimated effect on land or site values. Income tax preparation also requires that the cost of a property be split between the improvements and the site. The first step of the cost approach is to estimate a separate market value of the site. Separate site value estimates are also commonly used for establishing condemnation awards, adjusting casualty losses, deciding whether to raze existing improvements to free the site for a new use, or establishing site rentals.

Application of the Three Approaches to Value

The sixth step of the valuation process is the application of the three approaches traditionally used by appraisers to estimate the value of a property. USPAP requires that the appraiser consider the use of all three approaches to estimate the value of each property appraised.

However, it is recognized that all three approaches may not be necessary to arrive at a credible opinion of value. When an appraiser elects not to use one or two of the three approaches to value, the reasons for their elimination must be detailed in the appraisal report.

The three traditional approaches to value are:

> **1.** Cost approach
>
> **2.** Sales comparison approach
>
> **3.** Income approach

Using two or three approaches to value instead of just the sales comparison approach provides the appraisers with an opportunity to corroborate their estimate of the value of the property.

Cost Approach

The cost approach starts with an estimate of the value of the site and site improvements. This first step is required by Freddie Mac and Fannie Mae, even
when the cost approach is not used to estimate the value of the improvements.

Historically, the cost approach was the only approach used by appraisers for
many appraisals. After World War II, it fell out of favor. Today, some states prohibit it for condemnation cases. Many relocation companies also discourage appraisers from using it. Freddie Mac and Fannie Mae do not require the use of the
cost approach. However, many lenders/clients require it for insurance purposes.

Experienced appraisers know that when correctly used the cost approach
is a valuable technique. They feel more confident when they are able to make
two or three independent estimates that tend to confirm each other than
when their value estimate is based solely on the sales comparison approach.

The cost approach is most appropriate when the site value is well substantiated, when the improvements are new or nearly new, when they are the
highest and best use, and when they do not suffer from substantial amounts
of depreciation. To estimate the value of a property using the cost approach,
the appraiser identifies the information that will be required from the data
gathered when the property was inspected.

STEPS IN THE COST APPROACH
The data is processed following these five steps:

---

1. Estimate the value of the site and site improvements.
2. Estimate the *reproduction cost* of the improvements. Some appraisers use *replacement cost* instead. When replacement cost is used, this should be noted
   in the comments section of the appraisal report.
3. Estimate the amount of depreciation from all causes and categorize it into the
   three major types of depreciation: physical deterioration, functional obsolescence, and external obsolescence.
4. Deduct the total estimated depreciation from the reproduction or replacement
   cost of the improvements to derive the amount of value the improvements contribute to the property.
5. Add together the value of the site, the value contributed by the site improvements and landscaping, and the cost of all the improvements, less the applicable depreciation.

COST APPROACH SUMMARY
When used correctly, the cost approach provides the appraiser with an excellent
way to support the values estimated via the other approaches to value. To be

useful, it must include a supported site value estimate, an accurate estimate of the reproduction cost of the improvements, plus a complete and accurate estimate of all forms of depreciation that affect the property. Only in rare instances can the cost approach be used alone to estimate the value of a residential property. There are usually comparable sales available even for unique residences. On the other hand, the cost approach often is the only applicable approach for the valuation of special-purpose, governmental, and institutional properties.

Sales Comparison Approach

The sales comparison approach involves making a direct comparison between the subject property and other properties that have been sold (or listed for sale) in the same market area.

When carefully collected, analyzed, verified, and reconciled, market data usually provides the best indication of *market value* of a property. The price that a typical buyer pays is often the result of a shopping process, in which many properties being offered for sale have been examined and evaluated. Buyers often base their value conclusions primarily on properties that are being offered for sale. Appraisers use this information, in addition to information about properties that have sold and were rented, to reach their value estimate.

Individual sales often deviate from the market norm because of individual motivations, knowledge, and/or conditions of sale. In sufficient numbers, however, they tend to reflect market patterns. When information is available on a sufficient number of comparable sales, offerings, and listings in the current market, the resulting pattern is the best indication of market value.

STEPS IN THE SALES COMPARISON APPROACH
The appraiser follows these five steps:

1. The appraiser finds *comparable sales,* listings, and offerings.
2. The appraiser verifies each sale including selling price, terms, motivation, and its bona fide nature.
3. The appraiser analyzes each comparable property and compares it to the subject property in terms of time of sale, location, physical characteristics, and conditions of sale.
4. The appraiser makes the necessary adjustments to compensate for any dissimilarities noted between the comparables and the subject property. The adjustments are derived by comparing comparables with each other whenever possible.
5. The appraiser derives an indicated value for the subject property by comparison with the adjusted selling prices of the comparables.

SALES COMPARISON APPROACH SUMMARY

The sales comparison approach is generally considered the most applicable

13.17→ approach in residential appraising, since it reflects most directly the actions of buyers and sellers in the market. In order to obtain all the information needed to use a comparable sale, the appraiser should inspect each comparable property and verify the nature of the sale with the buyer, seller, or broker. These are the people who can tell the appraiser about the conditions of sale and the actual physical condition of the property at the time of sale.

New techniques using more sales are available as alternatives to these techniques. They do not depend on adjustments based on limited market information, but rather on statistical treatment of many comparable sales. Regression analysis and other statistical techniques are the basis of automated valuation models (AVMs). When the sales comparison approach is based on a sufficient number of carefully chosen sales similar to or adjustable to the subject property, the value indication is usually persuasive.

Income Capitalization Approach

Many people buy property for the income it will produce and the increase in value that they hope will take place over the period of time that they hold the property. The income a property produces flows to the owner in a variety of ways:

- Current cash flow
- Current tax savings
- Deferred income from rents
- Capital gains from the sale or gift of the property in the future
- Tax savings from the gift or trade of the property in the future

In the income capitalization approach, appraisers measure the present value of the future benefits of property ownership. Income streams and values of property on resale (reversion) are capitalized (converted) into a present, lump-sum value. Basic to this approach are these formulas:

$$\text{Income} \div \text{Rate} = \text{Value}$$

$$\text{Income} \times \text{Factor} = \text{Value}$$

The income capitalization approach, like the cost and sales comparison approaches, requires extensive market research. Specific areas that an appraiser investigates for this approach are the property's gross income expectancy, the expected reduction in gross income from lack of full occupancy and collection loss, the expected annual operating expenses, the pattern and duration of the property's income stream, and the anticipated value of the resale or other real property interest reversions. When accurate income and expense estimates are established, the income streams are converted into present value by the process of capitalization. The rates or factors used for capitalization are derived by the investigation of acceptable rates of return for similar properties.

Research and analysis of data for the income capitalization approach are conducted against a background of supply and demand relationships. This background provides information on trends and market anticipation that must be verified for data analysis by the income capitalization approach.

The investor in an apartment building, for example, anticipates an acceptable return on the investment in addition to return of the invested funds. The level of return necessary to attract investment capital fluctuates with changes in the money market and with the levels of return available from alternative investments. The appraiser must be alert to changing investor requirements as revealed by demand in the current market for investment properties and to changes in the more volatile money markets that may indicate a forthcoming trend.

ESTIMATED NET OPERATING INCOME (NOI)

The first step in the income approach is to estimate the net operating income (NOI) of the property. This appraisal technique is accomplished by making a reconstructed operating statement for the property. This statement uses information gathered by the appraiser from the owner, management, accountant, tax person, and a variety of other sources. It usually cannot be obtained from a single source in the format that is required.

The potential gross income (PGI) is estimated using market data and the rental history of the property being appraised. A vacancy and collection allowance is deduced from this figure. Any other income is added, and the result is a projection of what the effective gross income (EGI) of the property would be if it were vacant on the date of the appraisal, and were then rented to a typical tenant in the market at current rental rates.

Next, the typical expenses are projected for the coming year after being divided for clarity into fixed expenses, operating expenses, and reserves. Other expenses such as interest, amortization, depreciation, and expenses, not directly related to the running of the property, are not included.

All of the fixed expenses, operating expenses, and reserves are subtracted from the EGI to produce the NOI. See Figure 13.1.

Figure 13.1 Example of a reconstructed operating statement (12-unit apartment house).

INCOME ANALYSIS	
Potential gross income:	
6 two-bedroom units w/o air conditioning @$750/mo. =	$ 54,000
(750 x 12 = 9,000 x 6 = 54,000)	
2 two bedroom units w/air conditioning @$800/mo. =	19,200
(800 x 12 = 9,600 x 2 = 19,200)	
2 three-bedroom units w/o air conditioning @$1,000/mo. =	24,000
(1,000 x 12 = 12,000 x 2 = 24,000)	
2 three-bedroom units w/air conditioning @$1,100/mo. =	26,400
(1,100 x 12 = 13,200 x 2 = 26,400)	
Total:	$ 123,600
Other Income	
Laundry machines (concession)	2,400
Vending machines	1,250
Vacancy and collection loss (6%)	(7,416)
EFFECTIVE GROSS INCOME	$ 119,834
OPERATING EXPENSES	
Fixed Expenses	
Insurance (apartment package including rents)	$ 5,600
Flood insurance	600
Property tax	14,846
School district tax	8,480
Total Fixed Expenses:	$ 29,526
Variable (Operating) Expenses	
Management fees	$ 8,080
Utilities	
Electricity (halls only)	$ 1,646
Gas	16,600
Telephone	250
Water	3,200
Sewer charge	320
Rubbish removal	770
Employee payroll:	
Part-time janitor	$ 8,000
Payroll taxes	240
Employee benefits	690
Worker's compensation insurance	240
Lawn care	690
Maintenance supplies	500
Maintenance & repairs	2,400
Painting & decorating	1,200
Snow removal	240
Extermination services	480
Legal fees	300
Accounting	600
Bank charges	160
Total Operating Expenses:	$ 46,606

Figure 13.1 *(Continued)*

Reserves	
Kitchen appliances	$ 1,200
Lobby furniture	200
Carpeting	2,000
Air conditioning	600
Roof	1,000
Total Reserves:	**$ 5,000**
TOTAL EXPENSES:	**($ 81,132)**
NET OPERATING INCOME PROJECTION:	**$ 38,702**

Note: Some appraisers do not use a reconstructed operating statement that is as detailed as this example. They reduce the size (often to one page) by combining some of the items.

CAPITALIZATION

The second step in the income capitalization approach is to convert the NOI projection into an estimate of the value of the property on the date of the appraisal. This process is called *capitalization* and is usually done by dividing the NOI by the capitalization rate.

$$\frac{NOI}{Capitalization\ Rate} = Value\ of\ Property$$

Direct capitalization: There are a variety of ways to develop a direct capitalization rate directly from the market using data collected in the market. If the preceding formula converts NOI into value, then the following formula would convert value into a direct capitalization rate (assuming the NOI is also known).

$$\frac{NOI}{Value\ of\ Property} = Overall\ Capitalization\ Rate$$

The type of rate developed in this way is called an *overall capitalization rate.* For example, assume there is information available about a property similar to the one being appraised. It shows that the comparable property sold for $370,000 and that it had an NOI of $37,000. Using the preceding formula, the overall capitalization rate is taken from this data as follows:

$$\frac{\$37,000\ (NOI)}{\$370,000\ (Sale\ Price)} = .10\ (Overall\ Capitalization\ Rate)$$

Like any other data being used in the appraisal process, the more similar the data source is to the property being appraised, the better it is. Also, it is not good practice to develop a rate from just one set of data.

ADVANCED CAPITALIZATION TECHNIQUES

Some appraisers have become serious students of band of investment, mortgage equity components, the built-up method, "Ellwood," and other capitalization techniques. However, some feel that even the more complex theories are needed to produce the best results in all instances.

Reconciliation of Value Indications and Final Opinion of Value

The seventh step in the valuation process is the *reconciliation* of the value indications obtained in each of the three approaches to derive a *final estimate of value* for the subject residence as of the effective date of the appraisal. Under no circumstances are these value indications merely averaged. This would be analogous to asking three people for the right time and then averaging their replies. Rather, the appraiser considers the relative applicability of each of the three approaches to the final estimate of value and reviews the reliability of the data used in each approach.

In the reconciliation, the appraiser brings together all of the data and indicated values resulting from the three approaches and evaluates them in a logical cause-and-effect analysis, which leads to a supportable value conclusion. In this process, the appraiser must evaluate the quality and quantity of data, choose the approach or approaches that are most applicable to the specific appraisal problem, and select from among alternative conclusions or indications of value those that best represent the value of the subject property.

The final estimate should be rounded to indicate the degree of accuracy. By rounding to the nearest $100, the appraiser indicates the belief that the estimate is accurate to the nearest $100. With the data available for most appraisals, it would be difficult to estimate value to $100 accuracy. Therefore, appraisers often round their estimates to the nearest $1,000.

Report of Final Value Opinion and Conclusions

The final step of the valuation process is to produce an appraisal report. The report may be verbal, a letter, on a form, or a short- or long-form narrative report. USPAP requires that every written appraisal report contain, at a minimum, the following:

13.18➤

- Identity of the client
- Intended user(s)
- Intended use(s) of the appraisal
- Identification of the real estate
- Interest in the property appraised
- Type of value estimated
- Effective date of the value opinion
- Date of the report
- Scope of work
- Data analyzed
- Techniques employed
- All extraordinary assumptions
- All hypothetical conditions
- Signed certificate

Form Reports

Most single-family appraisals are made on forms. Many single-family appraisals are now being made on the *Uniform Residential Appraisal Report* (URAR) form. Freddie Mac and Fannie Mae also have forms that are widely used for small income properties and condominiums, PUDs, and cooperatives. The Appraisal Institute, software vendors, and others also develop new forms from time to time.

Narrative Reports

It is the responsibility of the appraisers to determine with the clients what type of report will best satisfy the clients' need. This is usually done as part of determining the scope of work. The appraisers are afforded the best opportunity to support opinions and conclusions and to convince the clients of the soundness of their value estimate in a *narrative appraisal report.*

The Appraisal Institute and other appraisal organizations require the production of narrative appraisal reports as part of their requirements to obtain a designation.

Oral Reports

There are situations in which an oral report is required because of the circumstances of the assignment. When an oral report is made, the appraisers must preserve the notes and factual records used in the appraisal process as well as complete memoranda of each analysis, conclusion, and opinion contained in the oral report. All of the USPAP requirements for making an appraisal also apply to appraisals that are the basis of an oral report.

SUMMARY

The valuation process is the orderly step-by-step procedure an appraiser follows to produce a credible appraisal. It begins with the definition of the problem to be solved and concludes with a report of the solution in the form of an estimate of the defined value. The purpose of the appraisal process is to provide the outline for making a thorough, credible appraisal in an efficient and professional manner.

Most appraisers would agree that making appraisals is an art, not a science. They would further explain that the profession is constantly trying to make appraising more scientific. A big step toward this goal has been the development of the valuation process. Within this theoretical framework, a concise, logical, and clearly supported value conclusion can be presented that meets the needs of clients as well as the standards of the appraisal profession. New techniques using statistical methods to abstract information from the market, such as automatic valuation models, using multiple regression analysis, and other statistical techniques, are making the appraisal process more scientific.

REVIEW QUESTIONS

13.1 The definition of the word *appraisal* usually includes the following concepts:

A. An appraisal is an opinion of value.

B. An appraisal must be as of a specific date.

C. The appraiser is unbiased.

D. All of the above.

13.2 An online appraisal:

A. Uses the computer to help the appraiser fill out the URAR

B. Usually estimates a value without interior inspections

C. Complies with the USPAP because it is unbiased

D. All of the above

13.3 A comparative market analysis:

A. Uses the computer to help the appraiser fill out the URAR

B. Is used by real estate salespeople as part of the listing process

C. Complies with USPAP because it is not made by an appraiser

D. All of the above

13.4 Automatic valuation models (AVMs) are:

A. Often used to appraise complex houses

B. Predicted to soon replace traditional appraisals

C. Used by Freddie Mac and Fannie Mae

D. All of the above

13.5 The purpose of an appraisal is usually to estimate:

A. Some kind of value

B. The highest price a property will sell for in the open market

C. Both of the above

D. None of the above

13.6 Each written appraisal report must do all of the following except:

A. Identify and describe the real estate being appraised

B. Define the value to be estimated

C. State the purpose of the appraisal

D. Include a copy of the mortgage

13.7 Appraising is, by definition, a vocation that primarily involves intellectual activities and requires:

A. Knowledge

B. Objectivity

C. Personal integrity

D. All of the above

13.8 The supervising appraiser who cosigns a trainee's report must:

A. Inspect the interior of the property being appraised

B. Have a designation from a major appraisal organization

C. Accept full responsibility for the contents of the report

D. All of the above

13.9 Real estate appraiser licenses are issued by:

A. The state in which the appraiser does business

B. The Appraisal Foundation

C. The Appraisal Subcommittee

D. None of the above

13.10 The Uniform Standards of Professional Appraisal Practice can be changed by:

A. The state in which the appraiser does business

B. The Appraisal Foundation

C. The Appraisal Subcommittee

D. None of the above

13.11 USPAP requires that every written appraisal report must identify:

A. The intended use of the appraisal

B. The intended user of the appraisal

C. The effective date of the appraisal

D. All of the above

13.12 Hypothetical conditions are assumptions that:

A. Do not exist on the date of the appraisal

B. May exist on the date of the appraisal

C. Both of the above

D. None of the above

13.13 The market area:

A. Is never bigger than the neighborhood

B. Usually includes where people do their shopping

C. Both of the above

D. None of the above

13.14 Every appraisal assignment must include:

A. A highest and best use analysis

B. The street address of the property being appraised

C. Both of the above

D. None of the above

13.15 The four tests for highest and best use are:

A. Physically possible, legally permitted, financially feasible, and maximally productive

B. Physically possible, legally prohibited, financially feasible, and maximally productive

C. Generally possible, legally permitted, financially feasible, and maximally productive

D. None of the above

13.16 The first step of the cost approach is to estimate the:

A. Value of the site

B. Value of the site improvements

C. Reproduction cost of the improvements

D. Sources of all forms of depreciation

13.17 The sales comparison approach is the best indication of value when:

A. There is not enough data to use the cost approach

B. Used for single-family property appraisals

C. There is not enough data to use the income approach

D. None of the above

13.18 The best way to reconcile the different values developed from the three approaches is to:

A. Pick the highest of the three

B. Pick the average of the three

C. Calculate the mean of the three

D. None of the above

ANSWERS

The answer to each question is indicated by the letters A, B, C, or D. The explanation of the answer is indicated by the page number and an arrow that points to the appropriate paragraph on the page.

Q 13.1 D Page 211	Q 13.5 A Page 212	Q 13.9 A Page 213	Q 13.13 D Page 219	Q 13.17 B Page 228
Q 13.2 B Page 208	Q 13.6 D Page 212	Q 13.10 B Page 213	Q 13.14 A Page 221	Q 13.18 D Page 232
Q 13.3 B Page 208	Q 13.7 D Page 210	Q 13.11 D Page 214	Q 13.15 A Page 223	
Q 13.4 C Page 209	Q 13.8 C Page 211	Q 13.12 A Page 216	Q 13.16 A Page 226	

CHAPTER 14

Ins and Outs of Getting a Mortgage

14.1 ➤ **W**hen Realtors and lenders run home-buying seminars for the public they often discover that the topic the attendees are most interested in learning about is how to finance their contemplated purchases. Commercial brokers know that providing acceptable financing is often the difference between making a sale and losing one. Most sales contracts contain a mortgage clause that allows buyers to cancel the contract if they are not able to obtain acceptable financing.

Interest rates and the availability of mortgage money have a direct effect on the value of real estate. There is a complex relationship between financing and the valuation of property that is difficult to recognize, explain, and understand. Experts agree that the market reflects this relationship, but acknowledge it is difficult to pin down. Many publications and Internet sources publish the prevailing interest rates for the wide variety of mortgages that are available in each community at any given time.

Buyers and sellers are affected by changes in interest rates and the availability of mortgage money, which play a major role in buying decisions. Because every parcel of real estate is fixed in location and has a relatively long life, it makes excellent security for a loan. Because it is high in cost compared to the assets of a typical buyer, real estate is almost always financed. A long-term loan secured by a lien on the property is called a mortgage, from the French word *mortgage,* or "death grip."

This chapter covers the documentation of financing arrangements, which includes mortgages and notes, deeds of trust, contracts for deed, and security deeds. Types of foreclosure and its alternatives, together with the special federal legislation that protects borrowers, are explained in detail. Mortgage points and discounts and mortgage assumption continue the discussion.

MORTGAGE MONEY SOURCES

Mortgage money is supplied by the primary mortgage market and the secondary mortgage market. The government has an important role in keeping funds available at interest rates that are affordable.

Primary Mortgage Market

The primary mortgage market is made up of lenders who originate mortgage loans and people and companies that originate loans and sell them to primary lenders. They may use their own funds or funds derived by selling the mortgages into the secondary mortgage market. Primary lenders make their money from the interest they receive on the loans, points, servicing fees, and profits from selling the mortgages for more than their acquisition costs.

Savings and Loan Associations

The primary purpose of savings and loan associations (S&Ls) was and still is to provide a place for the public to save their money and earn interest, and to make mortgage loans. Originally, these institutions specialized in residential loans. Now they make all types of loans and mortgages.

All savings and loan associations are either federally or state chartered. Federally chartered S&Ls have their depositors' savings insured by the Bank Insurance Fund (BIF) and the Savings Association Insurance Fund (SAIF), both of which are managed by the FDIC. State-chartered S&Ls have their deposits insured by state deposit insurance companies.

Mutual Savings Banks

Mutual savings banks are found primarily in the eastern states. They are very similar to S&Ls, and are either federally or state chartered. They tend to specialize in residential mortgages and are especially active in FHA- and VA-insured mortgages.

Commercial Banks

Commercial banks are an important source of all types of mortgage funds. They range from small state-chartered banks to giant international organizations.

Insurance Companies

Insurance companies accumulate billions of dollars of their customers' money, which they hold in reserve for the payment of future policy benefits. Because a substantial portion of these funds is from life insurance and pension policies, the insurance company holds the funds for many years and looks for safe long-term investments. A substantial amount of this money is invested in mortgages.

Insurance companies usually do not originate their own loan portfolios. They buy blocks of residential mortgages from other loan originators and institutions. They also obtain their large commercial and industrial loans from mortgage brokers and other loan originators.

Credit Unions

Credit unions accumulate money from their members and loan it back to their members in the form of both short-term loans and mortgages. They also act as loan originators and servicers.

Pension Funds

Pension funds operate very similarly to life insurance companies. They collect premiums and invest them. They use them mostly in the future for retirement benefits for their policyholders.

Partnerships, REITs, and Other Investment Groups

There are a variety of business organizations and corporations that collect money from investors and invest in real estate and real estate loans. These include limited and general partnerships, real estate investment trusts (REITs), and corporations.

Secondary Mortgage Market

The *secondary mortgage market* is where mortgages are bought and sold after they have been originated and funded. The lender or other loan originator sells their loans to raise additional capital and to maintain required levels of liquidity. The buyers of the loans either use their own capital or (more often) package the loans together and issue debentures and other financing instruments that are sold to investors.

14.12 ➤ Often the new owner of the loans will contract with the loan originator or a service company to provide services such as payment collection and foreclosure if needed. The three major buyers of mortgages are:

> 1. *Fannie Mae* (formerly called the Federal National Mortgage Association, or FNMA)
>
> 2. *Freddie Mac* (formerly called the Federal Home Loan Mortgage Corporation)
>
> 3. *Ginnie Mae* (Government National Mortgage Association, or GNMA)

Fannie Mae

The Federal National Mortgage Association now known as *Fannie Mae* is a quasi-governmental corporation. It is privately owned and its stock is traded on the New York and other stock exchanges. However, it was started in 1938 as a federal government agency, primarily for the purchase of FHA-insured mortgages. It was privatized in several stages, ending in 1968 when 100 percent of its stock was sold to the public.

Now Fannie Mae can buy and sell any kind of mortgage. In return for being able to borrow money directly from the U.S. Treasury at favorable interest rates, it is required to participate in many different kinds of lending programs and abide by a variety of government directives. The president of the United States appoints one-third of Fannie Mae's board of directors. The rest are elected by the stockholders.

Freddie Mac

The Federal Home Loan Mortgage Corporation now known as *Freddie Mac* was created in 1970 by the federal government to provide additional mortgage money to the S&Ls, which were running out of money to loan. Depositors took their money out of the S&Ls and invested it elsewhere in order to receive higher rates of interest. When money flows out of a lending institution faster than it comes in from loan payoffs and new deposits, it is called *disintermediation*. In 1989, FHLMC became a private corporation, and it now competes directly with Fannie Mae.

Freddie Mac borrows money for the U.S. Treasury and also raises money by selling its debentures in the general securities markets. It is no longer limited to buying S&L mortgages. Its stockholders elect some of its directors, and some are appointed by the president of the United States.

Ginnie Mae

The *Government National Mortgage Association* (GNMA or Ginnie Mae) was created by the federal government in 1968 and is still 100 percent owned by the government. It is under the direction of the Department of Housing and Urban Development (HUD).

Ginnie Mae is responsible for some old FHA mortgages and a variety of special assistance programs. It is also a major factor in the secondary mortgage market, especially in packaging FHA, VA, and FmHA (Farmers Home Administration) mortgages for investment.

FINANCING AND RISK

Lending institutions, mortgage brokers, and others who make and buy mortgage loans analyze the risk in making real estate loans very much as they would any other investment. The security of the real estate in the mortgage loan gives added incentive to many institutions and individuals to make mortgage loans versus some other type of investment. However, mortgage loans have risks, such as delinquencies, which may result in the need to foreclose. Another risk is that at some point in the future, the loan will be greater than the liquidation value of the real estate—the amount for which the real estate can be sold under pressure—thereby resulting in a loss to the financial institution. The high risk of commercial mortgage loans has received a substantial amount of publicity. Defaulted commercial mortgages were and continue to be one of the major causes of the failure of thrift institutions during the late 1980s.

When analyzing the relationship of financing to real estate values, it is necessary to consider the risks involved. The quoted interest rate for a mortgage loan is the cost of the money. Rates of interest tend to be commensurate with the risk involved in a specific investment: the lower the risk, the lower the interest rate.

Interest Rates versus Yield

The amount of interest that the borrower is charged for a mortgage loan is made up of several components. The first component is known as the safe interest rate. The safe interest rate is the interest rate of federal bonds of the same duration as the mortgage loan. Additional interest is added to reflect the difference in risk between lending to the government and lending to a property owner. To this is added the cost of acquiring and servicing the loan plus a profit for the lender. Not all of these components are reflected in the interest rate. Some are obtained from points and discounts, loan origination fees, and loan servicing fees.

An interest rate may be different from the actual yield on an investment. Loans are bought and sold in the secondary mortgage market for amounts above or below their face value. For example, a 10 percent interest rate on a $50,000 loan pays $5,000 on an annual basis. If an individual or institution acquires the loan at a discounted price of $45,000, the yield per year would be $5,000 on a $45,000 investment. This is a rate of return of 11.11 percent ($5,000 divided by $45,000), rather than the contract rate of 10 percent. Conversely, if the investor paid $55,000, the yield is reduced to 9.09 percent ($5,000 divided by $55,000).

Points and Discounts

To compete in the market, it is necessary at times for the lender to charge *points*. For example, if a loan were to be made in the amount of $100,000 at the going interest rate of 9 percent, the lender, believing that rate to be inadequate, may make one of the following adjustments.

14.11 ➤ The borrower may be asked to pay points. A point is 1 percent of the face value of a loan. If the charge was four points on a $100,000 loan, the fee would be $4,000.

Another technique is to use a discount rate. By discounting the loan 3 percent, the amount of money actually advanced at the time of closing is 3 percent less than the original $100,000; however, the borrower still pays 9 percent interest on $100,000. In other words, a 9 percent return would be earned by the lender on $100,000, even though only $97,000 was loaned. This increases the yield to the lender, providing compensation for what the lender perceives to be a higher risk or to match yields in other types of investment opportunities.

14.3 ➤ To compare mortgages offered with various point charges, it is necessary to compare their effective rate of interest. Lenders are required by the truth-in-lending laws to tell the borrower the *annual percentage rate* (APR) on all loans they make. The APR allows consumers to compare several loan offers with ease.

Loan Origination Fees

Another way lenders can earn extra money on loans is for them to charge a loan origination fee. These fees are technically different from interest or points. They are an expense to the borrower that is paid directly to the lender or loan originator. Typical loan origination fees range from ½ percent to 2 percent of the face amount of the loan.

Assumption

An important distinguishing characteristic between many conventional mortgages and VA-, FHA-, and FmHA-insured mortgages are their assumption provisions.

A mortgage or *deed of trust* is assumed when the property is sold and the existing mortgage or deed of trust is taken over by the buyer. When the mortgage or deed of trust is at or below current interest rates, the ability to assume the mortgage or deed of trust may add value to the property or make it easier to sell.

There are two different ways a buyer may take over an existing mortgage or deed of trust. The buyer may take title to the property subject to a mortgage or deed of trust, or the buyer may assume it. There is an important technical difference between "taking over" and "assuming."

When a mortgage or deed of trust is assumed by the new buyer, the buyer assumes the entire unpaid debt evidenced by the note. In the event that the new buyer defaults and the property is foreclosed, the new buyer is personally responsible for the entire unpaid balance on the assumed note. In the event that the proceeds of the foreclosure sale are insufficient to pay the note, the new buyer must personally make up the deficit.

When a mortgage or deed of trust is taken over rather than assumed, the new buyer is *not* personally responsible for the payment of the note. When the note is in default, the property may be sold to pay off the note. If there are insufficient funds from the sale to pay off the note, the new buyer is not personally responsible. The lender may only try to collect the deficit from the original signer of the note.

THE MONEY MARKET: WHERE THE MONEY COMES FROM

Money is defined as all currency, plus all deposits in personal checking accounts and "near monies," which include time and savings deposits, savings and loan shares, mutual savings bank deposits, and short-term U.S. government securities. All of these assets are cash or the equivalent of cash because they are available for expenditure without delay. To understand the competition for investment funds, it is necessary to comprehend to a certain extent the nature of the whole money market.

The amount of money available for borrowing is regulated by the U.S. Treasury Department and the Federal Reserve System (the FED). It is their obligation to assist the economy by making sure adequate money is available. The Fed's original purpose, as expressed by its founders, was to give the country a lasting currency, to provide facilities for discounting commercial paper, and to improve the supervision of banking. As the economy changed, broader objectives were outlined—namely, to help counteract inflationary and deflationary movements and to share in creating conditions favorable to a high level of employment, a stable dollar, growth of the country, and a rising level of consumption.

The mortgage market, which provides the basic supply of funds for making mortgages, is in direct competition for investment dollars. At times, the mortgage market is not competitive with other markets. Then the supply of funds for mortgages goes down, the cost of money goes up, or both occur. At other times, a slow decline in the cost of money takes place without a corresponding reduction in the supply of money.

Types of First Mortgages

14.12→ Prior to the Great Depression of the 1930s, most first mortgages were straight loans. Payment on them consisted of interest only. At the end of the mortgage term, the entire *principal* became due. Such loans were also called *term loans.*

For example, the borrower took out a $50,000 mortgage loan for five years, a typical mortgage term before 1930, at 10 percent interest. The borrower would pay $5,000 interest per year in annual, semiannual, quarterly, or monthly payments. At the end of the term, the entire $50,000 had to be paid off, either in cash or from the proceeds of a new mortgage, often from the same lender.

After the crash of 1929, most mortgages required regular periodic payments of principal, called *amortization,* in addition to the interest payments. A mortgage where the payments of interest and amortization reduce the loan balance to zero at the end of the loan is called a *direct reduction loan.*

In an effort to solve the problems of a wide variety of buyers in financing the purchase of a home, second home, or investment property, and the changing needs of the commercial and industrial loan markets, government agencies, as well as the lending and real estate industries, continue to create new alternative mortgage instruments and financing techniques.

The following are the most common types of first mortgages being offered in the 2000s.

Fixed-Rate Mortgage (FRM)

A *fixed-rate mortgage* (FRM), which is the typical loan made by most lending institutions, provides for repayment of the principal amount (the unpaid balance of a loan) over a specified number of years, in equal monthly payments. These payments include some principal reduction plus interest. Interest is computed on the remaining principal balance at the end of each month (or other payment period). As the principal of the loan is reduced, the interest portion of the monthly payment becomes less, while the principal payment increases each month. Unless there is a loan payment called for at the end of the term, the amount of principal paid off is sufficient to liquidate the mortgage loan over its term.

Adjustable-Rate Mortgage (ARM)

In the past 20 years, interest rates have changed much more rapidly than in the past. Lending institutions in the years since the Depression, with large portfolios of low-interest mortgages, found themselves in serious financial trouble when the rates of interest they were forced to pay to keep and attract depositors exceeded the yield on their mortgage portfolios.

14.13➤   To prevent a recurrence of this problem, an *adjustable-rate mortgage* (ARM) was developed as an alternative mortgage instrument, carrying an interest rate that varies with changes in market rates. Since 1985, the majority of home buyers have financed the purchase of their homes with ARMs. ARMs now account for about 60 percent of home mortgages being written.

The interest rate on an ARM is indexed to some other rate. This means that when the interest rate changes on the indexing instrument or scale, the interest rate also changes on the mortgage.

There is an endless variety of ARMs being offered. They have a few common characteristics:

- The interest rate on the mortgage changes only once or twice a year (or less often)—not every time the interest rate on the index instrument changes.
- There is a maximum amount that the interest may be increased in any one year (often 2 percent).
- There is a total maximum increase in the interest rate (often 6 percent) over the life of the mortgage.

The concept of variable-rate financing calls for the borrower to share with the lender the risks of fluctuating interest rates. Although the terms of one ARM may vary widely from another, there are several characteristics common to nearly any adjustable rate financing plan.

- The index is an indicator of current economic conditions and interest rates, and specific requirements apply when a lender selects an index.
- The index must be beyond the control of the lender.
- The index must be readily available to and verifiable by the public. In most ARM mortgages, rate increases are at the option of the lender, while rate decreases are mandatory.

The following are some of the most popular ARM mortgages.

Convertible ARM (CARM)

Convertible ARMs (CARMs) allow the borrower to convert to a fixed-rate mortgage, usually anytime from the thirteenth through the sixtieth month. When a borrower converts, the new interest rate will usually be ⅝ percent over Fannie Mae's 60-day posted yield for fixed-rate mortgages. The borrower is sometimes charged a conversion fee of about 1 percent of the original principal balance, plus a processing fee. A borrower's cost to convert may be substantially less than the cost of refinancing, but this is not always true.

Growing Equity Mortgage (GEM)

The purpose of the *growing equity mortgage* (GEM) is to allow the borrower to make increased payments, with the increases going directly to the reduction of the mortgage principal. The amount of the mortgage payment typically doubles over the term of the mortgage so that the mortgage is paid off in substantially less time than with level payments.

Graduated Payment Mortgage (GPM)

The interest rate remains fixed throughout the term of the loan, but the monthly payments start out at a low level and gradually increase until they rise above the level at which a standard fixed-rate mortgage would have been written. Since the amount of mortgage payment a family can carry depends upon its current income, the *graduated payment mortgage* (GPM) is particularly attractive to the young family buying a first home, because the income requirements to qualify for a GPM are significantly less than those for a fixed-rate mortgage. A GPM enables a buyer to buy a more expensive home now in anticipation of higher income in the future. Some GPMs involve negative amortization in their early years. Their major drawback is that they may induce people to buy houses they really can't afford.

Graduated Payment Adjustable-Rate Mortgage (GPARM)

The *graduated payment adjustable-rate mortgage* (GPARM) is a blend of the GPM and ARM. Buyers can take advantage of the initial low payments of a GPM, while lenders get the flexible rate advantage of the ARM. The GPARM is not accepted by Fannie Mae.

Rate Improvement Mortgage (RIM)

A *rate improvement mortgage* (RIM) is usually a 20- to 30-year fixed-rate mortgage with a one-time interest rate improvement option. Some lenders charge a conversion fee and a processing fee at the time the rate improvement option is exercised.

Reverse Annuity Mortgage (RAM)

14.14→ The *reverse annuity mortgage* (RAM) is designed for retired or semiretired homeowners with incomes that are relatively low, who own their homes free and clear or with small mortgage balances. They often face the choice of moving or turning some of their equity into cash to make their mortgage payments. Under a RAM, the lender pays the borrower a fixed annuity, based on a percentage of the value of the property. The homeowners are not required to repay the loan until their demise, at which time the loan is paid through probate. In effect, a RAM enables a retired couple to draw on the equity of their home by increasing their loan balance each month. This is actually negative amortization. No cash payment of interest would be involved, as the increase in the loan balance each month would represent the cash advanced, plus interest on the outstanding balance.

Shared Equity Mortgage (SEM)

The *shared equity mortgage* (SEM) is an arrangement usually made between parents and their children, whereby the parents sell the property to their children and through a sale-leaseback arrangement lease it back for the remainder of their lives. Sales proceeds are invested in a life annuity on behalf of the parents. These payments are used to pay the rent. If there is anything left over after the rent is paid, it goes to the parents to help them with their living expenses.

Shared Appreciation Mortgage (SAM)

At the height of the real estate boom, lenders wanted to share the profits that developers were making. They felt that their mortgages were a significant contribution to those profits and they wanted a share. Under a *shared appreciation mortgage* (SAM) the lender offered a below-market interest rate in return for a percentage of the appreciation of the property.

Other Types of Loans

Second Mortgages

In addition to a first mortgage, a *second mortgage* or junior mortgage may be used to facilitate the purchase of a residential property. As its name implies, a second mortgage is secondary to the rights of the first mortgagee. It is used in circumstances where the buyer is unable to arrange for adequate financing based on one mortgage and requires a second mortgage. This technique provides additional funds and facilitates the purchase of the property when the buyer may not be able to do so otherwise.

Home Equity Loans

The use of *home equity loans* increased substantially during the 1980s as a result of the effective advertising of lenders. They were able to convince the public that second mortgages, which is what a home equity loan really is, were an acceptable way to borrow money. The Tax Reform Act of 1986 (TRA '86) further increased the popularity of home equity loans by preserving their tax deductibility, while making personal loan interest nondeductible.

Many home equity loans are open-ended junior loans against which the homeowner can draw and pay back money as needed. When the property is sold or the first mortgage is refinanced the home equity loan has to be paid off.

When property owners need to borrow funds, they should explore their options and then decide based on their personal needs and tax situation whether it is better for them to take out a home equity loan, refinance their home with a new first mortgage, or seek other types of financing. Reasons for home equity loans range from college tuition for children to paying for luxury vacations.

MORTGAGE LAW

In the United States, a mortgage is a voluntary lien that property owners put on their property to use the property as security or collateral to borrow money. The property owners, who are the borrowers, become the mortgagors. The lender, who loans the money, is the mortgagee.

The type of documentation used to record this transaction varies from state to state and is described next in this chapter. In states with title theory, the mortgagor actually gives legal title to the mortgagee and retains only equitable title as long as the loan remains unpaid. In states with lien theory, the mortgagor does not give up title to the property. Instead, the mortgagor gives the mortgagee a lien on the property. Some states use the intermediate theory, based on the principles used in the title theory states. An extra step is added, which requires the mortgagee to foreclose in order to effectively get legal title to the property.

These legal and technical differences have little effect, in reality, on the actual rights of mortgagees and mortgagors. In all 50 states, when the mortgagor defaults, the mortgagee has the right to foreclose the property used as security.

DOCUMENTATION OF FINANCING ARRANGEMENTS

When real estate is pledged as collateral for a loan, it is necessary for the protection of the lenders to create documents that establish their claim against the real estate and contain all the agreements between the borrowers (*mortgagors*) and the lenders (*mortgagees*). *Hypothecation* is the technical term used to describe the pledging of property as security for a loan, without surrendering the property to the lender.

There are four basic ways by which the details of a real estate financing arrangement are recorded:

> **1.** Mortgage and note
> **2.** Deed of trust and note
> **3.** Contract for deed
> **4.** Security deed

The use of security instruments has been commonplace in this country for many decades. The requirements of the secondary mortgage market have helped standardize these forms. However, every state has its own special variation of one or more of these four combinations.

It is a mistake to learn only about those forms used in your own state. Many customers come from other states. It enhances the credibility of real estate professionals when they can explain not only how mortgage documents work in their state but also how they differ from the documents used in the customer's state.

Because long-term financing arrangements are necessary in most cases when a property is purchased, loan security instruments have been developed to fit these needs. These legal documents comprise two parts: the lien and the note.

The traditional first mortgage loan is categorized as a *conventional mortgage*. Nonconventional mortgages are those that are insured or guaranteed by an agency of the federal government, such as the Federal Housing Administration (FHA) or Veterans Administration (VA) or a private insurance company. Since the 1930s, the FHA has been insuring loans to persons who require assistance because of their lack of financial capacity. The VA provides VA loan guaranties—a similar service for veterans. Both FHA loans and VA loans have interest rates that tend to be lower than those for conventional loans. They usually also have longer terms and a higher loan-to-value ratio.

Other types of financing include deeds of trust, privately insured and guaranteed loans, cash, second mortgages, and contract purchases.

Legal restrictions and requirements applying to a mortgage vary from state to state. Such legal considerations have an impact on the loan security instrument and are two-sided. On one side, the homeowner and other property owners are given as much protection and encouragement as possible. On the other side, the risk to the lender must be considered.

The best examples are the foreclosure laws of the various states. A state having foreclosure legislation excessively favorable to the borrower may attract few funds from outside the state. Those states that give the greatest protection to the mortgagee, with short time periods for foreclosure, tend to attract more funds with lower interest rates from around the country and overseas.

Mortgage and Note

A *mortgage* is a *security instrument* whereby property owners make a pledge of their real estate as collateral for the payment of the debt described in a note that is an integral part of the mortgage instrument. In some states, a mortgage is a conditional transfer of the property to the lender.

The *note* is a financing instrument acknowledging a debt and spelling out how it is to be repaid. Not all notes are secured by a mortgage. However, all mortgages contain a note with the specifics of the collateralized loan.

Note Provisions

A typical note used for loans secured by real estate contains the following provisions.

NAME AND ADDRESS OF THE LENDER
The note states who loaned the money and to whom it must be repaid. It often contains the address of the lender. Most notes are assignable by the lender, who may change the payment arrangements by notifying the borrower.

AMOUNT OF THE LOAN TO BE REPAID
Traditionally, the amount of the loan to be repaid is written out in words, such as "Twenty Two Thousand Five Hundred Dollars and Twenty Five Cents," and in numerals, such as "$22,500.25."

PROMISE TO PAY
The exact words "promise to pay" clearly establish the obligation of the borrower, also known as the maker of the note, to repay the loan.

INTEREST RATE
Most notes require the borrower to pay interest in addition to the repayment of the borrowed money. The note may contain a statement that each payment is first applied to any unpaid interest and the remainder is applied toward the repayment of the principal.

The note should state whether the interest is due in advance or in arrears, and the payment period.

Some states have usury laws to protect consumers. These laws set the maximum amount of interest that can be charged for various types of loans. Loans made at higher than permitted rates of interest may become uncollectible.

PAYMENT DUE DATES

The note must contain a schedule of payments. It must clearly indicate when each payment is due and the amount of the payment. When a periodic payment, such as monthly, quarterly, semiannually, or annually, is specified as due, the note must state when the first payment is due and when the payments stop.

AMOUNT OF EACH PAYMENT

What the parties agree on determines how the principal of the note will be repaid. The most common way for a residential mortgage loan to be repaid is with equal monthly payments calculated to pay off 100 percent of the principal during the term of the loan.

Another popular term payment plan is to calculate the monthly payments based on a term other than the loan. For example, the payments for a 10-year loan may be calculated on a 20-year repayment schedule. The note then requires that the unpaid balance be paid off in a lump sum at the end of the loan, after 10 years. This lump sum is called a *balloon payment*.

Balloon payments are also used with notes that specify that the periodic payments made during the term of the loan are for interest only. The principal is paid off in lump sums according to the terms of the note, usually at the end of the loan term.

NAME OF THE BORROWER

The note states who the borrower is. When there is more than one borrower, their relationship to each other is often stated. The borrower is also called the *maker of the note*.

SIGNATURE OF THE BORROWER

Often at a closing there will be more than one copy of the note. The borrower should be careful to sign only one copy. Notes are usually negotiable instruments, which means that the lender may assign the note to someone else. This assignment is accomplished by the lender signing the back of the note. Whoever has possession of the assigned note has evidence that the debt is owed to them.

When a note is paid in full, the borrower is entitled to the return of the note, marked "paid in full" by whoever owned the note last.

SECURITY (IF ANY)

When something is offered to the lender to secure the payment of the note, such as a mortgage on some real estate, it is often mentioned in the note. A note is a stand-alone instrument that is evidence of the personal obligation of the borrower to make specified payments on specified dates.

14.4➤ A mortgage is a lien document, which establishes a lien only during the period of time when any principal or interest, as spelled out in the note, remains unpaid.

When a payment specified by the note is not paid as scheduled, the lender may seek to collect the unpaid payments from the borrower of the note, without taking any action to foreclose the property being offered as security.

14.5➤ It is not customary for the lender to sign the note.

DATE SIGNED

A note should contain the date it was signed by the borrower. This may become important in establishing the order of claims against the borrower at some future date.

NOTICE

Some notes require that the lenders give the borrowers notice that they are in default before the lenders can require the borrowers to pay the note in full, as required in an acceleration clause. The notification clause may also specify how change of address notification is made.

ACCELERATION

The acceleration clause is a provision of most notes that makes the entire balance due when a payment is not made as promised and the loan is in default.

LATE CHARGES

Some notes have a provision that charges the maker of the note a specified late charge if a payment is made after its due date or after the grace period specified in the note.

COLLECTION COSTS AND EXPENSES

Many notes contain a provision that requires the maker of the note to pay any collection costs and expenses that the lender incurs when the maker of the note is in default.

SIGNATURE OF COSIGNERS

Lenders may require someone other than the person to whom the money was loaned to guarantee that the payments will be made as promised. This person is called a *cosigner*. The cosigner guarantees payment of the note by signing the note. Cosigners are liable for full payment of the note in the event the maker fails to make the promised payments. The most common cosigner is the spouse of the maker of the note.

Mortgage Provisions

The mortgage for a typical single-family house contains the following provisions.

RECORDING INFORMATION

A mortgage is recorded to give notice to the world of its existence and to establish the priority of the lien it creates against the property being used as security for promised repayment of the note, which is part of the mortgage.

The date and time the mortgage is received by the government official in charge of recording establishes its lien priority. The date and time are usually stamped on the mortgage, often in a place provided at the top of the form for this purpose.

The mortgage is then copied or microfilmed, and a copy is retained by the recording official in the official's office, where it is available for public inspection. The original mortgage is returned to the lender, who holds it until the note is paid off and then returns it to the borrower, together with a release of mortgage, to be filed wherever the original mortgage was filed.

BORROWER'S NAME

The borrower is the mortgagor who pledges his or her property as security for the repayment of the note. To more positively identify the mortgagor, the person's name is often followed by his or her address. Traditionally, only the city and state of the borrower's address is shown.

LOAN AMOUNT

Traditionally, the amount of the loan to be repaid is written out in words, such as "Twenty Two Thousand Five Hundred Dollars and Twenty Five Cents," and in numerals, such as "$22,500.25."

GRANTING CLAUSE

The granting clause is a statement by the mortgagor acknowledging receipt of the loan and granting to the lenders and their successors, heirs, and assigns the mortgage on the property described in the mortgage document.

DESCRIPTION OF THE PROPERTY (LEGAL DESCRIPTION)

The mortgage document must contain a description of the property, in whatever form is customary in the area where the mortgaged property is located. This is usually a legal description.

HABENDUM CLAUSE

The habendum clause begins "to have and to hold" and clarifies the ownership that is stated in the granting clause, which will become the mortgagee's in the event of default.

COVENANT OF SEISIN

The covenant of seisin clause warrants that the mortgagor has title to the property described in the description clause and that it is free and clear of any liens or encumbrances that would interfere with the property being used as collateral, other than those disclosed in the mortgage.

PROPERTY TAX, CHARGES, CLAIMS, AND ASSESSMENT CLAUSE

A mortgage obligates the mortgagor to take steps to protect the mortgagee's interest in the collateral property. Financial erosion can take place if property taxes, special assessments, adverse claims, and any other charges and liens, which have priority over the mortgage, are left unpaid.

Taxes, liens, special assessment liens, mechanic's liens, and environmental liens are all examples of liens that may jump in front of a first mortgage. In some states, unpaid utility bills and irrigation fees also have a priority claim against a property.

A prudent mortgagee will establish a mechanism to be certain that the mortgagor pays such charges and assessments that they do not become liens against the property.

INSURANCE CLAUSE

The value of the collateral property can be diminished if the property is damaged or destroyed. The mortgagee is protected against some types of damage or destruction by the insurance clause. The no waste and mainte-nance clause, which is described later in this chapter, provides additional protection.

The insurance clause often gives the mortgagee broad authority to specify the type and amount of insurance required to be kept in force by the mort-gagor to protect the property. The insurance clause may also require that the insurance policies contain provisions that require notification to the mort-gagee if the policy is being canceled, and approval of any payment of claims for losses to the mortgagor. The mortgagee does not have to approve claim payments to the mortgagor unless the mortgagor restores the property in a manner satisfactory to the mortgagee.

Other insurance clauses spell out exactly what type and level of insurance policies are required to be maintained on the property during the life of the mortgage.

The most common type of insurance required is fire and related perils in-surance. Title insurance is now almost always required, except in a few states where it still is not used on all residential mortgages.

TAX AND INSURANCE RESERVE CLAUSE

The tax and insurance reserve clause requires the mortgagor to make regular payments, in advance to the lender, of sufficient funds to pay the property taxes and insurance premiums on the property when they become due. These payments are held in an impound account or escrow account by the lender, who makes the insurance and tax payments when they are due.

ACCELERATION CLAUSE

The acceleration clause in the mortgage is more comprehensive than the acceleration clause in the note, which is a way to accelerate a debt when the note payments are not made as promised.

The mortgage acceleration clause makes all unpaid payments immediately due when any single payment is not made as promised. They all also become due if and when the mortgagor fails to pay the property taxes, special assessments or claims, and charges as required by the property tax, charges, claims, and assessment clause.

Acceleration also occurs when the insurance clause or the maintenance clause is violated.

Acceleration is a very important protection for the mortgagee. Without it, each time the mortgagor fails to carry out one of the provisions of the mortgage, including making payments when they are due, the mortgagee would have to sue to make the mortgagor comply with the specific mortgage requirement or to collect a single skipped payment.

The acceleration clause makes the whole mortgage due when the mortgagor fails to live up to any of the promises made in the mortgage, and it is a very powerful inducement by the mortgagee to force the mortgagor to perform as promised.

PREPAYMENT CLAUSE

If a note, mortgage, deed of trust, or other loan document does not have a prepayment clause or a lock-in clause, the mortgagor may prepay the loan without any penalty.

The prepayment clause states what penalty will be charged when and if there is a prepayment. It may also stipulate when prepayments are permitted. A typical prepayment requirement is that prepayments can be made only on the annual anniversary of the loan.

LOCK-IN CLAUSE

Some loan documents contain a lock-in provision that prohibits the borrower from prepaying the loan. The intention of the lock-in is to prevent the borrower from prepaying the loan when interest rates are lower than they were when the loan was originated.

WATER RIGHTS PROTECTION CLAUSE

In states where water is scarce, the state appropriates water for irrigation purposes on specific parcels of land. These water appropriations are valuable and, if lost or transferred, decrease the value of the property.

The water rights protection clause requires the mortgagor to maintain whatever water appropriation rights are assigned to the mortgaged property and prevents the mortgagor from transferring the rights without permission from the mortgagee.

NO WASTE AND MAINTENANCE CLAUSE

Most mortgages are for long periods of time, during which the property will lose value if it is not well maintained.

The no waste and maintenance clause prohibits the mortgagor from committing or permitting any waste of the property and requires the mortgagor to preserve and repair the property as needed.

It also provides that, in the event of a foreclosure, the mortgagee—without permission of the mortgagor—may ask the court to appoint a receiver to take care of the property. The receiver's duties will include collecting the rents, paying expenses, maintaining irrigation and crops, and making any repairs that are needed to preserve the value of the property.

COLLECTION COST CLAUSE

The collection cost clause provides that, in the event of a foreclosure, the cost of the foreclosure proceeding, including the receiver's fee, attorney's fee, court costs, appraisers, and so on, will be added to the unpaid interest and principal and paid for out of the proceeds of the foreclosure sale or the payment made to redeem the mortgage.

DEFEASANCE CLAUSE

The defeasance clause says that the mortgagor will regain full and clear title to the property when all of the note payments are made as promised. It implies that the mortgagee will take whatever steps are necessary to clear title, including returning the note and signing whatever releases, receipts, or quitclaim deeds may be required.

DATE OF MORTGAGE

The date on which the mortgage was signed by the mortgagor is usually indicated near the signature.

ALIENATION CLAUSE

The alienation clause prevents a new buyer of a property used as security on a note from assuming the mortgage, deed of trust, and so on, without the permission of the lender. Most lenders will not give the needed permission unless they are satisfied with the creditworthiness of the new buyer and the interest rate being received on the old loan. Some lenders also charge additional fees to permit the assumption of a loan.

SIGNATURE OF PROPERTY OWNER

The property owners become the mortgagors when the mortgage is signed, indicating that they agree to comply with all of the mortgage provisions.

ACKNOWLEDGMENT OF SIGNATURES

Many states have statutes that require the signers of a mortgage to take an oath in the presence of a notary public or other state-approved official, saying that the signing of the mortgage was their free act and deed. The person who verifies the oath is responsible for determining that the people who sign the mortgage are who their signatures represent them to be.

The recording official in many states will not accept a mortgage for recording unless it is acknowledged.

WITNESS OF SIGNATURES

In addition to the signatures being acknowledged, they may be witnessed. The witnesses also provide evidence that the signatures are genuine. They can be called on to identify the person who signed the mortgage. In addition, they can be required to provide evidence at some future time as to the apparent condition of the signer at the time of the mortgage signing.

COPY OF NOTE

For a mortgage to be valid, it must contain a copy of the note it securitizes, which specifies the schedule of payments to be made.

Deed of Trust

A deed of trust, also known as a trust deed and note, is primarily used instead of a mortgage in California and about 20 other states to secure first mortgages made by government-insured lending institutions.

The intended purpose of the deed of trust is to make the foreclosure process easier in the event that the borrowers do not fulfill all their promises. In reality, the ease of foreclosure is more often determined by the statutes that control the foreclosure process than by whether a mortgage deed or trust deed is used.

The use of a trust deed introduces a third party, called a *trustee,* into the lending process. The parties to the loan transaction have different names

`14.7 ➤` when a deed of trust is used. The borrower is called the *trustor,* the lender is called the *beneficiary,* and an independent person or company, usually selected by the lender, is the *trustee.*

To establish a real estate trust, the borrower executes a trust deed that transfers legal ownership of the property being used as collateral to the trustee, who holds it for the benefit of the lender. Like the mortgage and note form of collateral, the trust deed also includes the note that contains the repayment promises made by the borrower.

When the loan is paid in full, the trustee issues and records a release deed.

Note Provisions of Deed of Trust

The note used with a deed of trust is similar to the note used with a mortgage. It states the amount of money to be repaid, the interest rate applicable, and a schedule containing the amount of each payment and when it is due. It also contains the other miscellaneous provisions similar to those in a note used with a mortgage.

One difference is that a note used with a mortgage refers to a specific mortgagee that services the note. The note used with a deed of trust refers to a specific deed of trust that services the note. This facilitates the intended purpose of a deed of trust and a note, which is to make it easier for the loan to be transferred from one lender to another, usually by the sale of the loan in the secondary mortgage market.

Another intent of the deed of trust and note is to make it easier for the lender to secure title in the event that the borrower defaults, especially if the borrower abandons the property and moves out of state or out of the country and disappears. However, as further explained in the foreclosure section of this chapter, all states have a series of statutory requirements controlling what the lender or trustee must do to foreclose a property. It is these procedures rather than the form of financing instrument that primarily controls and affects how a property is foreclosed.

Lien and Intermediate Theory States

In lien and intermediate theory states, title does not actually transfer to the mortgagee or trustee until the borrower fails to make the payments called for in the note or fails to comply with the provisions of the mortgage or deed of trust.

Contract for Deed

The contract for deed is also called a real estate contract, land contract, contract for sale, or bond for deed. This instrument is less standardized than mortgage and deed of trust forms because it is often used by individuals rather than regulated lenders. Also, unlike the mortgage and deed of trust instruments, it usually does not contain a note. The entire financial arrangement between the parties is spelled out in a single document.

14.2→

A contract for deed is often used when a buyer is unable to obtain financing from a lending institution, either because of the unique characteristics of the property or more often because the buyer cannot meet the credit requirements of any lending institution.

These contracts allow the buyer to take possession of the property and to immediately use the property. They are intended to provide the seller the maximum possible protection against default by making it as easy as possible for the seller to redeem the property in the event of default.

When the buyer defaults, the original owner-seller usually is allowed to keep all of the payments that have been made. The seller may also elect to bring an action against the buyer to force the buyer to make the rest of the payments and comply with the other contract provisions.

When a contract for deed is used, the buyer-borrower is called the *vendee* and the seller-lender is called the *vendor*. A unique feature of the contract for deed method of financing is that title remains with the original owner until the buyer has made all the payments as promised. This provides the original owner with the added protection of not having to foreclose the property in the event of default, because the owner has not yet transferred the title to the buyer. However, the recorded land contract produces a cloud on the title that the original owner has to have removed if the buyer defaults on the payments or any other provisions of the contract.

Many of the contract provisions are similar to those found in a mortgage or deed of trust, such as the insurance clause, no waste or maintenance clause, acceleration clause, and collection clause.

When all the payments have been made as promised, the original seller is obligated to deliver a deed to the buyer. In areas where escrow is used, the deed is prepared and held in escrow until the payments are completed.

Because a contract for deed is both a sale and a financing agreement, both the seller and the buyer are required to sign the contract and have their signatures witnessed and acknowledged according to the customs of their state.

Security Deed

In Georgia, the primary instrument used is a security deed. This is a warranty deed with a reconveyance clause. The security deed transfers title to the lender when the loan is made. When all the payments have been made as called for in the accompanying note, the lender is required to execute the reconveyance clause, which is a cancellation clause that is part of the security deed document. When it is recorded, title reverts to the borrower.

If the borrower defaults, a special clause in the security deed called the *power of sale clause* allows the lender to sell the property without going through a judicial foreclosure.

FORECLOSURE

When borrowers are unable or unwilling to make their mortgage payments or when they fail to comply with other provisions of the security instruments described here, they are in default. The lenders or whoever is servicing the mortgage may elect to institute the foreclosure process as a way to recover the unpaid balance on the loan, plus any unpaid interest. They will also try to recover any costs they incur when implementing the foreclosure process.

14.8➤

When there is an acceleration clause, the whole loan becomes due if any provision of the loan documents are in default.

The lender, in addition to foreclosing on the property, can seek a *deficiency judgment* in the courts against the signer and cosigner of the note, forcing them to pay the difference between what is received from the sale of the property and the total of the unpaid note, unpaid interest, and collection costs.

Alternatives to Foreclosure

Foreclosures are expensive, cause hardships, and are bad for the public relations image of a lending institution. Responsible lenders try to avoid foreclosure proceedings whenever possible. The federal government, through its agencies such as the FHA, VA, and FmHA, and by special legislation, also tries to reduce the number of foreclosures. Foreclosures can also be prevented by renegotiation of the loan or by obtaining the deed to the property from the mortgagor.

Soldiers and Sailors Civil Relief Act of 1940

14.9 ➤ The Soldiers and Sailors Civil Relief Act of 1940 came back into prominence during the recent American military conflicts. It gives the courts broad power to stop lenders from foreclosing on property during the period when the owner is in military service. The act generally overrides the provisions of a mortgage, deed of trust, or land contract. In order to enforce any of these contracts' foreclosure provisions, a court order is needed if the owner is in the military service, even when the documents say that no court action is needed. This has made it necessary, as a regular part of any foreclosure action, to supply the court with a military affidavit, proving that the property owner is not in the military service. The courts are mandated by the act to protect military personnel from actions by creditors where their ability to keep their financial promises and obligations has been affected by being in military service.

The Housing Act of 1964

One of the advantages of an FHA- or VA-insured mortgage is the provision
14.10 ➤ in the Housing Act of 1964 that requires lenders to help mortgagors in situations where they default on their mortgages for reasons that are beyond their control, such as losing their job, sickness, or death.

Both these agencies have the authority to make interest payments on behalf of the mortgagor. Theoretically, they can collect these payments from the mortgagor at some time in the future, but in actuality this is not frequently done.

Loan Payment Renegotiation

When mortgagors become unable to make their promised payments or comply with the other agreements they made in the financing instruments, they have the possible alternative of renegotiating their loan with the lender.

Many lenders recognize that foreclosures should be avoided and will therefore try to work out payment schedules that borrowers can meet. They may even postpone payments until some future time. Lenders may agree to all new loan terms. This is called *recasting a loan*. The more equity the borrower has in the property, the more concessions the lender is likely to make. Lenders also take into consideration the current state of the real estate market. Lenders do not like to foreclose when it is going to be difficult to resell the property.

Deed in Lieu of Foreclosure

When lenders come to the conclusion that there is little or no equity in the property and that the probability of the borrowers ever being able to keep the payment commitments and other agreements made in the loan documents is small or nonexistent, they still should try to avoid a foreclosure. One way to do this is to convince the borrowers to convey to the lenders a quitclaim deed to the property. To induce the mortgagors to deed the property to the lenders, the lenders may agree to give the mortgagors a release of their personal liability.

Types of Foreclosures

In spite of their efforts to avoid foreclosure proceedings, the time may come when the lender decides that it is necessary to foreclose on a property used as security for a note that is in default.

There are basically three different types of foreclosure, and each state has statutes that determine exactly how and when they are used:

> **1.** Strict foreclosure
>
> **2.** Judicial foreclosure
>
> **3.** Nonjudicial foreclosure

Strict Foreclosure

In some states, it is possible for a mortgagee to take title to the property used as collateral in a mortgage or deed of trust, without offering it for sale. The mortgagee usually must convince the court that the property owner has no equity in the property, that the high cost of the public sale of the property is wasteful, and that none of the proceeds will go to the property owner.

In a *strict foreclosure* the court sets a series of dates called *law days* in some areas. The first date is the deadline for the owners of the property to redeem it by paying off the liens. When property owners fail to redeem the property, they lose all claim to it. Since no value has been established, the lenders usually lose their right to collect any deficiency from the borrowers.

The next law day is the date the property is offered to the most *junior lien* holders who have the right to claim the property by paying off any liens that were on record prior to theirs. A typical example is when a home equity loan lien has been recorded after a first mortgage lien. The home equity loan is junior to the first mortgage, because it was recorded after the first mortgage. If the junior lien holders fail to redeem, they lose all their interest in the property and their lien becomes valueless.

Each lien holder has a date on which to either redeem the property or lose his or her interest in the property forever. When none of the junior lien holders redeems the property, the title passes to the senior lien holder, who is usually the first mortgagee or holder of the first deed of trust or contract for sale. At this time, all the interests of the property owners and junior lien holders are extinguished.

Judicial Foreclosure

A *judicial foreclosure* is also known as a foreclosure by sale. The first thing the court does in the foreclosure proceedings is to set a *redemption date* by which time the property owners may redeem the property by paying off the debt and the court costs.

The number of days allowed to the property owners to redeem their property is called the *statutory right of redemption* in some states because it is set by a state statute. It is sometimes called the *equitable right of redemption,* when it is based on historic common law.

When the property owners fail to redeem their property, the court appoints someone, often the sheriff or a trustee, to advertise and sell the property at a public auction. The proceeds are used to pay the cost of the sale and the court costs first. Whatever remains is distributed to the lien holders in the order of their liens. When there are not sufficient proceeds from the sale to pay off all the lien holders, the unpaid creditors can ask the court for a deficiency judgment against the signers and cosigners of the note. This requires them to pay the differences between the sale proceeds and the total debt.

When a property is sold by foreclosure, the mortgagors are entitled to a *satisfaction of judgment* in some states showing that their debt has been paid in full.

Nonjudicial Foreclosure

A nonjudicial foreclosure is also known as the power of sale method of collateral property recovery. The lender or trustee has the right to sell the property when the mortgage or deed of trust is in default, without going to the court to get permission. One of the problems with this method is the responsibility it places on the lender or trustee to comply with the federal and state statutes, such as the Soldiers and Sailors Civil Relief Act of 1940. Another problem is that some state statutes prohibit the mortgagee from bidding on the property when this method of foreclosure is used. Other states prohibit or limit deficiency judgments with this type of foreclosure. Because of these and other technical problems, this method of foreclosure is not widely used.

ALTERNATIVE METHODS FOR FINANCING PROPERTY

Contract for Deed

Another means of financing property is with a conditional sales contract or contract for deed (buying on contract). This device requires the seller to finance the sale of the property to the new buyer. Title does not pass from the seller to the buyer until the buyer has satisfied the contract by paying it off. This method was previously discussed in this chapter in the "Security Deed" section.

Purchase Money Mortgages

In order to make a sale or for their own personal investment objectives some sellers elect to finance the sale of their property with a purchase money mortgage. Instead of mortgage payments being made to a lending institution, the payments are made to the seller. The note can be secured with any of the instruments described earlier in this chapter.

Package Loans

A package loan is a loan whereby the borrower offers the lender as security not only the real estate, but also some personal property and fixtures. This type of loan is popular in some areas for purchasing condominiums. Package loans are standard for financing motels, hotels, nursing homes, and other commercial loans, where the value of the equipment is significant.

Blanket Loans

A blanket loan is when the borrower offers the lender more than one piece of property as security. A common provision of a blanket loan is a release clause that permits the borrower to unmortgage one or more of the secured pieces of property on repayment of a specific amount of the blanket loan.

Wraparound Loans

A wraparound loan is when the borrower offers the lender a property that is already being used as security for another loan. When there is sufficient equity in the property, above the amount of the first mortgage, a lender will take a mortgage that is subject to the first mortgage and leave it in place. In the event that the borrower defaults, the first mortgage lien holder has a claim that precedes that of the holder of the wraparound mortgage.

Open-End Loans

Open-end loans are built around open-end notes, which permit the borrowers to add to the amount of money they initially borrowed under prescribed conditions spelled out in the note. An open-end mortgage or deed of trust usually contains a maximum amount of money that can be borrowed without the creation of a new mortgage and note or deed of trust and note.

Bridge Loans

Bridge loans, sometimes also called *swing loans,* are usually made for short terms. Their purpose is to finance the transition from one property to another. The equity in one property is used as security for a loan that is used to buy another. The bridge loan is paid off either when long-term financing is obtained for the property being purchased or when the property used as bridge loan security is sold. These loans provide interim financing until the borrower can make the needed sale and/or secure permanent financing.

Construction Loans

Construction loans are often open-end loans. Their purpose is to finance property that is under construction or being improved. The money is paid out to the borrower as the construction or improvement proceeds. When construction reaches preagreed-on steps, the mortgagor applies to the lender for additional advances of money based on the amount of work that has been finished. Construction loans are either replaced by permanent financing, which is called take-out loans, when the construction project is complete, or they automatically turn into permanent loans after the last advance has been made and the project is completed.

Sale and Leaseback

One of the ways property owners can raise money and still have control of the property they occupy is to sell the property to a third party and then lease it back. This is called a *sale and leaseback*. It is common in the case of larger commercial or industrial properties.

MORTGAGE INSURANCE

Private Mortgage Insurance (PMI)

A variation of FHA-insured loans has been developed by private mortgage insurance companies for conventional mortgages and is called *private mortgage insurance* (PMI). Such companies typically insure the risk to the lender on the top 10 percent above the amount traditionally loaned as a conventional mortgage. If an 80 percent loan-to-value ratio were available, the next 10 percent (increasing the loan to 90 percent of value) is insured by the private mortgage company.

FHA, VA, and FmHA-Insured Mortgages

FHA-insured, VA-guaranteed, and FmHA-insured loans tend to be in a market by themselves. The length of the term may be greater and the original loan-to-value ratio may be very high when compared with conventional mortgages.

FHA-Insured Loans

The *Federal Housing Administration* (FHA) is part of the Department of Housing and Urban Development. Its primary purpose is to provide mortgage insurance to encourage lenders:

- To make loans on property in amounts that they would be unwilling to loan without the protection of the government-guaranteed insurance that pays off the loan in the event the borrower is unable or unwilling to do so.

- To make mortgages at lower than market interest rates.
- To make mortgages to people who do not have an adequate credit rating to obtain conventional financing.
- To make mortgages in rundown or declining areas.
- To make mortgages on types of property that would be difficult to finance, such as housing for the elderly, low-income housing, home improvements, condominiums, or nursing homes.

The FHA does not ordinarily loan money. The frequently used term *FHA loan* refers to a loan insured by the FHA rather than one made by them.

When a loan is insured by the FHA, the borrowers pay an insurance premium for the FHA insurance in addition to their regular mortgage payment.

In addition to the insurance premium, to obtain an FHA-insured mortgage the property must meet FHA construction requirements and must be appraised by an FHA-approved appraiser.

VA-Guaranteed Loans

The Department of Veterans Affairs (VA) was originally authorized to guarantee loans made to veterans by the Servicemen's Readjustment Act of 1944, which was intended to help World War II veterans. The act has been extended to apply to Korean and Vietnam veterans and to other veterans who have completed at least six years of Reserve or National Guard service.

Veterans using a VA-insured mortgage can purchase houses and mobile homes with little or no down payment, and at below-market interest rates.

Similar to the FHA loan, the term *VA loan* does not mean that the VA made the loan, but rather that the loan is insured by the VA.

The amount of the mortgage that the VA will guarantee is determined by a certificate of reasonable value (CRV), which is issued based on the value estimated by a VA-approved appraiser and current VA eligibility regulations.

Many VA mortgages are assumable by new buyers. However, the original mortgagors remain liable for payment in the event the new buyers default. If the new buyers have good credit, the original owners may get a substitution of entitlement, which makes them eligible for another VA loan and may relieve them of responsibility for the original loan.

Farmers Home Administration (FmHa)

The *Farmers Home Administration* (FmHA) both insures and makes loans to farmers and ranchers who are unable to secure credit from conventional sources at reasonable interest rates.

FmHA loans are available for a wide range of purposes including rural housing; purchasing and improving farms and ranches; buying equipment, seed, and fertilizer; and rural community rehabilitation programs. FmHA is also involved in many other types of rural development programs.

NEW TYPES OF MORTGAGES (GIMMICKS?)

Recently other types of mortgages have been advertised by lenders as being superior to more traditional mortgages.

Biweekly Mortgage

A biweekly mortgage is one in which payments are made every two weeks rather than the more typical payment made once a month. Payments are calculated initially according to the terms of the contract on a monthly basis and then halved. Payments made on a biweekly basis in this manner result in the equivalent of 13 monthly payments per year.

In order to be sure that the payments are made on a timely basis, many lenders require that the payment be transferred directly from the borrower's bank account, which must be maintained in the lender's institution.

There is no doubt that the total amount of interest paid over the course of such a loan is substantially less than on a similar monthly payment loan, as shown in Figure 14.1.

	Regular Monthly Payments	Bimonthly Payments	Additional ¹⁄₁₂ of Monthly Payments	True Biweekly
Monthly payment:	$665.30		$665.30	
Biweekly payment:				$332.65
Bimonthly payment:		$332.65		
Monthly prepayment:			$55.44	
Annual prepayment:				
Total interest paid:	$139,508.90	$139,146.09	$105,367.50	$105,046.26
Total interest saved:		$362.81	$34,141.39	$34,462.64
Loan will be paid off:	in 360 months	in 359 months	in 285 months	in 284 months

Figure 14.1   Payment Plans Comparison Chart
Loan Term: 30 Years | Loan Amount: $100,000.00 | Interest Rate: 7.000%

Teaser Rate Mortgages

14.15➤ "Teaser rate" is the nickname given to mortgages whereby the first six-month initial interest rate or first-year interest rate is substantially below market rate. *Teaser rate loans* are offered by lenders as an enticement to potential borrowers to apply for their ARM mortgage versus that of a competitor.

Of course, it is poor underwriting practice to qualify the borrower based on the reduced first-year payments!

When selecting an ARM, buyers should be cautious about these incentive teaser rates. These below-market initial interest rates are in effect for a limited period of time, typically 6 or 12 months. At the end of that period, the interest rate is automatically increased to the contract rate. The increase in monthly payments could be a shocking experience. Although a periodic interest cap may be in effect, the increase in excess of the cap may be carried over to the next adjustment date. Full disclosure must be provided by the lender, and an APR that varies drastically from the market should be suspect.

SUBPRIME MORTGAGES

Subprime lending, also called *B-paper, near-prime,* or *second chance* lending, is a general term that refers to the practice of making loans to borrowers who do not qualify for market interest rates because of problems with their credit history. A subprime loan is one that is offered at a rate higher than that for A-paper loans, due to the increased risk.

Subprime lending is typically defined by the status of borrowers. A subprime loan is, by definition, a loan made to someone who could not qualify for a more favorable rate. Subprime borrowers typically have low credit scores and histories of payment delinquencies, charge-offs, or bankruptcies. Because subprime borrowers are considered at higher risk to default, subprime loans typically have less favorable terms than their traditional counterparts. These terms may include higher interest rates, regular fees, or an up-front charge.

Proponents of subprime lending in the United States have championed the role it plays in extending credit to consumers who would otherwise not have access to the credit market. Opponents have criticized the subprime lending industry for predatory practices such as targeting borrowers who did not have the resources to meet the terms of their loans over the long term. These criticisms have increased since 2006 in response to the growing crisis in the U.S. subprime mortgage industry, wherein hundreds of thousands of borrowers have been forced to default and several major subprime lenders have filed for bankruptcy. By the middle of 2007, the large number of subprime loans in foreclosure was becoming a threat to the whole economy.

Subprime Lenders

A subprime lender is one who lends to borrowers who do not qualify for loans from mainstream lenders. Some are independent, but many are affiliates of mainstream lenders operating under different names.

Subprime lenders seldom if ever identify themselves as such. The only clear giveaway is their prices, which are uniformly higher than those quoted by mainstream lenders.

Subprime Borrowers

A subprime borrower is one who cannot qualify for prime financing terms but can qualify for subprime financing terms. The failure to qualify for prime financing is due primarily to low credit scores.

Subprime Lending Terms

Subprime lenders base their rates and fees on the same factors as prime lenders. For example, rates are higher the lower the credit score and the smaller the down payment. However, the entire structure of rates and fees is higher at subprime lenders.

A substantially higher percentage of subprime than of prime loans go into default. Observers of this meltdown have cast blame widely. Some have highlighted the predatory practices of subprime lenders and the lack of effective government oversight. Others have charged mortgage brokers with steering lenders to unaffordable loans, appraisers with inflating housing values, and Wall Street investors with backing subprime mortgage securities without verifying the strength of the portfolios. Borrowers have also been criticized for entering into loan agreements they could not meet.

Subprime loans are loans to borrowers displaying one or more of these characteristics at the time of origination or purchase. Such loans have a higher risk of default than loans to prime borrowers. Generally, subprime borrowers will display a range of credit risk characteristics that may include one or more of the following:

- Two or more 30-day delinquencies in the last 12 months or one or more 60-day delinquencies in the last 24 months
- Judgment, foreclosure, repossession, or charge-off in the prior 24 months
- Bankruptcy in the last five years
- Debt service–to–income ratio of 50 percent or greater
- Otherwise limited ability to cover family living expenses after deducting total monthly debt service requirements from monthly income

Subprime mortgages are proliferating in the early part of the twenty-first century. About 21 percent of all mortgage originations from 2004 through 2006 were subprime, up from 9 percent from 1996 through 2004. Subprime mortgages totaled $600 billion in 2006, accounting for about one-fifth of the U.S. home loan market.

In early 2007, many subprime mortgage lenders filed for voluntary bankruptcy protection, ceased originating mortgage loans, and/or ceased conducting business altogether. Furthermore, many of these companies also face criminal investigations into their accounting and business practices.

ALL-CASH PURCHASES

A few buyers provide all cash for the purchase of a property. Through the sale of other property or the accumulation of funds in some other manner, they are able to purchase property with a lump-sum cash payment. Such financial arrangements quite often expedite the purchase and affect the negotiating ability of the buyer, who may receive a discount from the seller for being able to close at once.

SUMMARY

Residences have traditionally been financed with long-term mortgages categorized as conventional mortgages and nonconventional mortgages that are insured or guaranteed. Ownership of most commercial and industrial property is also financed with some type of mortgage.

The government, through the Federal Reserve Banking System, attempts to control the economy by controlling the interest rates through the reserve requirements affecting federal banks.

Risk is an important factor in setting mortgage interest rates. Lenders can make small adjustments to interest rates by charging borrowers points or other fees at the inception of the loan.

Adjustable-rate mortgages (ARMs) are an alternative to fixed-rate mortgages. Their interest rates are tied to some other financial instrument. Usually, the amount they can change in a year is limited, as is their total potential interest change.

Other types of purchase financing include second mortgages, deeds of trust, conditional sales contracts, private mortgages, purchase money mortgages, and FHA/VA-insured mortgages.

Several new types of mortgages have been introduced by lenders in an attempt to increase their share of the mortgage market. Biweekly mortgages, mortgages with low initial "teaser" rates, and mortgages with reverse amortization are now being offered.

Mortgage interest rates are affected by many things including the national money policies, creditworthiness of the borrower, and the quality of the property being offered as security.

There are many different types of mortgages being offered by many different types of lenders.

The real estate license exam has questions on mortgage law, documentation, and the common provisions of mortgage notes and deeds. Foreclosure and the alternatives to foreclosure including the federal laws that protect our servicemen and -women are explained. This section also covers the many different kinds of foreclosures and how they operate.

There are a variety of organizations including the VA, FHA, and FmHa that guarantee lenders that the borrower will pay back the loan. Private mortgage insurance is also available.

Other types of mortgages have been advertised by lenders as being superior to more traditional mortgages. They are based on gimmicks that rarely work to the advantage of the borrower.

Subprime mortgages are made to borrowers who have poor credit ratings. It is not surprising that they have a large rate of foreclosure, and this has the potential to become a major national economic problem.

Finally, it should be mentioned that some real estate is purchased for all cash without any financing.

REVIEW QUESTIONS

14.1 What is the most popular subject of consumer home buying seminars?

A. House construction

B. Environmental hazards

C. Financing

D. All of the above

14.2 Which of the following usually *does not* contain a note?

A. Mortgage

B. Deed of trust

C. Contract for deed

D. All of the above

14.3 A conventional mortgage is one that is:

A. FHA insured

B. VA insured

C. FmHA insured

D. None of the above

14.4 A mortgage establishes a lien on a property:

A. For a period not to exceed 30 years

B. Only during the period a loan remains unpaid

C. Only during the life of the lender

D. All of the above

14.5 A note is customarily signed by:

A. The borrower

B. The notary public

C. The lender

D. All of the above

14.6 By recording a mortgage and note, notice is given to:

A. All the creditors

B. All abutting property owners

C. The world

D. All of the above

14.7 In a deed of trust:

A. The borrower is called the trustor

B. The lender is called the beneficiary

C. An independent party is named as trustee

D. All of the above

14.8 When a lender forecloses on a property, they try to recover:

A. All unpaid interest

B. All unpaid principal

C. Collection costs

D. All of the above

14.9 The Soldiers and Sailors Civil Relief Act of 1940 gives mortgage foreclosure protection to military personnel who served in the Iraq war or:

A. World War II

B. Korean War

C. Vietnam War

D. All of the above

14.10 The Housing Act of 1964 helps defaulting FHA and VA mortgagors who:

A. Have a death of a wage earner in their family

B. Have lost income caused by sickness

C. Have lost income caused by job layoffs

D. All of the above

14.11 A mortgage point is:

A. 1 percent of the face value of the mortgage

B. $1,000

C. $10,000

D. None of the above

14.12 Prior to the Depression of the 1930s, the most popular type of mortgage loan was a:

A. Straight loan

B. Amortizing loan

C. Level payment loan

D. None of the above

14.13 An adjustable-rate mortgage (ARM) is a mortgage with:

A. Interest rates that are adjusted according to a schedule

B. Payments that are adjusted according to a schedule

C. Interest rates that go up and down according to a schedule

D. None of the above

14.14 Which of these mortgages is designed for retired people?

A. Reverse annuity mortgage (RAM)

B. Shared equity mortgage (SEM)

C. Both of the above

D. None of the above

14.15 Teaser rate mortgages have:

A. High interest rates for the first few payments and then lower interest rates for the balance of the mortgage

B. Low interest rates for the first few payments and higher interest rates for the balance of the mortgage

C. Low interest rates for the first few payments and lower interest rates for the balance of the mortgage

D. None of the above

ANSWERS

The answer to each question is indicated by the letters A, B, C, or D. The explanation of the answer is indicated by the page number and an arrow that points to the appropriate paragraph on the page.

Q 14.1 C Page 239	Q 14.4 B Page 253	Q 14.7 D Page 259	Q 14.10 D Page 262	Q 14.13 D Page 247
Q 14.2 C Page 260	Q 14.5 A Page 254	Q 14.8 D Page 261	Q 14.11 D Page 244	Q 14.14 C Page 248
Q 14.3 D Page 244	Q 14.6 D Page 255	Q 14.9 D Page 262	Q 14.12 A Page 246	Q 14.15 B Page 270

CHAPTER 15

Property Transfers and Closings

The big day in the life of an RESP is the day the closing takes place. No matter how many times this happens in your life it is always an important event. Here is tangible proof that what you have been doing to make a sale has been successful. Unlike many other successful things you do in your life, when you have a successful closing you get rewarded both with praise and with money.

BEFORE THE CLOSING

A real estate closing is the culmination of a series of events that must take place before the title of the property transfers from the seller(s) to the buyer(s). How this happens varies throughout the country and may also vary depending on the type of property involved. In all cases, a time comes when real estate sales are finalized, and ownership passes from the seller(s) to the buyer(s). The secret of a good closing is for the RESP to be certain that all the required documents are delivered to whomever is running the closing, preferably before the closing or at the time of the closing, by the parties that are responsible for delivering the needed papers.

Typical Buyer Requirements at the Closing

Here is a list of the most common things the buyers or their representatives will be looking for at the closing:

- An executed deed to the property
- Evidence of good title (best evidence is title insurance)
- Evidence that all liens and encumbrances have been removed
- A survey (the buyer should inspect the survey prior to the closing to be certain that it represents accurately their understanding of what property they are buying [size, shape, encroachments, easements, and so on])
- Results of any inspections (buyer should be satisfied with the results of the inspections prior to the closing and how any problems indicated that need to be corrected will be corrected)
- Any existing leases or other agreements affecting the property
- Evidence that all work done on the property, or contracted for, has been paid in full

Typical Seller Requirement at the Closing

- The money to pay for the property is available at the closing in a form acceptable to the seller.
- If the buyer is obtaining a mortgage, all arrangements are complete and the proceeds of the mortgage will be available at the closing.
- It is to the seller's best interest to determine if everything the buyer expects the seller to do before the closing has been done to the buyer's satisfaction.

Inspection Immediately Prior to the Closing

It is a good practice to have the buyer(s) inspect the property immediately prior to the closing. In many areas this inspection is know as a walk-through. The buyer(s) should make sure the premises have been vacated (unless there are carry-over tenants) and that all the seller(s) and tenant's personal property has been removed. The buyer(s) should also determine that none of the real estate has been removed.

For example, an expensive chandelier may be removed and replaced with a standard light fixture. The property should be in substantially the same condition as it was when the sales contract was signed. The buyer(s) should check that the mechanical systems and equipment are in good working order and that no damage was done to the property as a result of the seller(s) or their tenants moving out. If agreements were made to repair or improve the property, this work should be checked.

It is to the best interest of the RESP to be certain that, when any problems are discovered by the buyer(s), they should be resolved prior to the closing or escrow date. It is common for money to be held in escrow to guarantee the problem resolution rather than delay the closing.

TYPES OF CLOSINGS

15.1→ There are two basic types of closings:

- Face-to-face closing
- Escrow closings

Face-to-Face Closings

In the East, and part of the Midwest, South, and Mountain States, title passes at a meeting of the parties, which often includes the buyer(s), seller(s), attorney(s), broker(s), title insurance company representatives, and representatives of the lender. This meeting is variously called a real estate *closing, closing meeting,* or *settlement.* Sometimes there are separate closings for the processing of the loan and the transfer of title. The closing is conducted by a person who may be the buyer's or seller's attorney, an *escrow agent (officer),* a broker, or a representative of the title company or of the lender.

The people who often attend a face to face closing are:

- The buyer(s) and their attorneys
- The seller(s) and their attorneys

It is common in some areas for one attorney, often the one who is conducting the closing, to represent both the buyer(s) and the seller(s). The RESP should be cautioned not to recommend this procedure, as there is always the potential of conflict of interest. When attorneys represent both parties to a transaction, they are required to explain to both parties about the possibility of a conflict of interest arising. The attorney is required to obtain signed permission from both parties that includes a statement that they have been advised about the possibility of a conflict of interest and understand what that means.

The following is only a partial list of the most common people who attend a face-to-face closing:

- The RESPs involved in the transaction together with their brokers
- The representatives of the lending institutions
- The representatives of the title insurance company

This list does not imply that there is any requirement that these people attend the closing.

Escrow Closings

In most states the first step in completing a real estate sale is the execution of a sales contract that spells out all the terms and conditions of the sale. In some states a binder is completed prior to the preparation of a sales contract. When the stipulations and conditions of the sales contract have been met, the contract (and often the deposit) are turned over to whomever is going to conduct the closing.

In many parts of the country, including most of the West and parts of the Midwest, South, Mountain States, and even parts of the East, title is transferred by a process known as an *escrow closing*. As part of their negotiations the buyer(s) and seller(s) select a neutral third party who acts as the escrow agent (in some places called an escrow holder or escrow officer). Technically, the escrow agents can be anyone the parties agree to in their negotiations. In most cases they are an attorney; a representative of the title company, a trust company, or an escrow company; or a representative of a lending institution. In some areas brokers act as escrow agents. Some states have laws that specify who can act as an escrow agent in that state. For example, in California escrow agents must have a license unless they are a lending institution, title insurance company, attorney, or broker. All California escrow agents must comply with the provisions of the California Escrow Law.

Creating a Valid Escrow

Three basic requirements must be met to create a valid escrow.

There must be a binding contract between the buyer(s) and the seller(s). The most common form is a sales contract signed by the buyer(s) and seller(s). It can also be a receipt for deposit, agreement of sale, option, exchange agreement, or a variety of other legally binding documents.

When there is a new mortgage involved, there should be a loan commitment from the new lender and arrangements made for the proceeds of the new mortgage to be delivered to the escrow agent before the closing.

There must be an agreement as to who the escrow agent will be and arrangements for all the necessary documents and funds to be delivered to the escrow agent in time for the agreed-on closing date.

Seller's Deposits with the Escrow Agent

This is a list of the most common things the seller usually deposits with the escrow agent:

- An executed deed to the property
- Any insurance policies that will be transferred to the buyer
- Documentation from the existing mortgage lender as to what must be done to pay off or assign the current mortgage
- If applicable, a release of mortgage
- Any other documents needed to deliver clear title

Buyer's Deposits with the Escrow Agent

This is a list of the most common things the buyer usually deposits with the escrow agent:

- All the funds needed to complete the sale (unless otherwise agreed on, a certified check is required)
- All the documents needed to release and mortgages or liens
- Any inspection reports to be supplied by the seller
- Any other documents needed to deliver clear title

Real Estate Broker's Role

When there is one or more brokers involved in a sale, they have a role in the closing that ranges from just collecting their commission to actually conducting the closing.

As a matter of practicality many brokers follow the progress of the sale from the time of the signing of the sales contract to the closing. They make sure everything is moving along as scheduled and that everyone is satisfied. They often are required to help in the negotiations that are required as a result of the title search, inspections, appraisal, and the walk-through. These problems are often resolved by credits to the buyer(s) or seller(s), which are negotiated by the broker(s) after the signing of the sales contract.

15.2➤ Sometimes a dispute arises between the buyer(s) and seller(s) that cannot be resolved by the parties. An escrow agent has no power to resolve a disagreement. To resolve an otherwise unresolvable conflict the escrow agent can seek the help of the courts. The escrow agent files an interpleader asking the court to resolve the dispute. The RESP people involved in the sale should do everything possible to prevent this from happening.

REAL ESTATE SETTLEMENT PROCEDURES ACT OF 1974 (RESPA)

When the property being sold is the type that is covered by the Real Estate Settlement Procedures Act of 1974 (RESPA), the transfer of title must be done exactly as required by this law. Closing for other types of property must comply with any applicable state laws.

15.3→ RESPA applies to many residential properties. Specifically it covers one- to four-family properties such as a house, a condominium or cooperative apartment unit, a lot with a manufactured house, or a lot on which a house will be built or placed immediately following settlement when any of these are financed with a federally related first mortgage loan. When the transaction is regulated by RESPA the following specific requirements must be complied with.

Settlement Costs—a HUD Guide

At the time when a mortgage loan application is made for a federally related mortgage, the applicant(s) must be given a copy of the HUD Guide—Settlement Costs. Part One of this booklet describes the settlement process and the nature of charges and suggests questions the applicant might ask of lenders, attorneys, and others to clarify what services they will provide the applicant for the charges they quote. It also contains information about the rights and remedies of the applicant available to them under the provisions of RESPA. It alerts the applicant to unfair and illegal practices.

Part Two of the booklet is an item-by-item explanation of settlement services and costs, with sample forms and worksheets that help the applicant in making cost comparisons.

It is pointed out in the booklet that terminology varies by locality so that the terminology used in the booklet may not exactly match the local terminology used in the applicants specific area of the country.

Good-Faith Estimates

At the time of the loan application the lender must provide the applicant(s) a good-faith estimate of the settlement service charges the applicant(s) will **15.4→** likely incur. It is preferred that this *good-faith estimate* be provided on the same day the loan application is received. However, the lender is required to mail it or deliver it to the applicant within three business days of the date the application is filed with the lender.

The good-faith estimate must include the lender's estimate of the charge for each item payable in connection with the loan as listed in section L "Settlement Charges" on HUD-1 settlement statement. This estimate is based on the lender's experience in the locality in which the property is located. The lender is not required to estimate paid-in-advance hazard insurance or other reserves deposited with the lender.

Some lending institutions follow the practice of designating specific settlement service providers to be used for legal services, title examination services, title insurance, or the conduct of settlement. Where this occurs, the good-faith estimate must clearly state that use of the particular provided is required and the estimate is based on charges of the particular provider, giving the name, address, and telephone number of each designated provider, and describing the nature of any relationship between the provider and the lender.

RESPA permits the lender to designate providers of these services as long as the lender and the provider are not part of a controlled business arrangement.

The applicant is advised in the booklet to compare the costs of the designated provider with the costs of similar services from other providers and to use this comparison as a factor in the selection of which lender to use.

Uniform Settlement Statement (HUD-1)

15.5→ All transactions covered by RESPA must use the Uniform Settlement Statement (HUD-1) as the closing statement. This form is designed to itemize all the financial details of the transaction. The form provides an orderly way for the lender to itemize all the charges they make in conjunction with their loan. One day prior to the closing the buyer(s) are permitted to see the closing statement, which must at that time contain all the information that is then available (some information may not be available until the actual settlement date).

Kickbacks

15.6→ Kickbacks and referrals of business for gain are often tied together. RESPA prohibits anyone from giving or taking a fee, kickback, or anything of value under an agreement that business will be referred to a specific person or organization. It is also illegal to charge or accept a fee or part of a fee where no service has actually been performed.

This requirement does not prevent title companies, attorneys, or others actually performing a service in connection with the mortgage loan or settlement transaction, from receiving compensation for their work. It also does not prohibit payment pursuant to cooperative brokerage, such as multiple listing service and referral arrangements, or arrangements between real estate agents or brokers.

REQUIREMENTS TO COMPLETE A REAL ESTATE TRANSACTION

To complete any real estate transaction, whether it be residential, commercial, industrial, and so on, and whether it is or is not covered by RESPA, requires that a series of events must take place. However, not every sale requires all these events to take place and some sales require items to occur which are not on this list. The order that these events occur varies from sale to sale. Often they consist of the following:

- Sales contract is executed by buyer(s), seller(s) and broker(s).
- Closing or escrow agent is selected.
- Buyer(s) make loan application(s).
- Needed reports, inspections, and documents are ordered and obtained (appraisal, credit report, survey, soil report, termite inspection, property structural inspection, environmental inspection, geologic hazard report, and so on).
- The RESPA loan applicant is given a HUD Booklet and a good-faith estimate.
- Title is searched and title evidence secured (abstract, title insurance policy, Torrens certificate).
- Title insurance policy is issued.
- Lender orders an appraisal and credit report.
- Deed is prepared and executed.
- Mortgage deed and note are prepared and executed.
- Buyer(s) make a final inspection of the property called a walk-through.
- New hazard insurance policies are secured, or existing policies are assigned to buyer(s).
- A closing statement is prepared.
- Income and expenses are prorated between buyer(s) and seller(s).
- Buyer(s) pay the balance due from them.
- Seller(s) receive funds due to them.
- Unpaid taxes are paid.
- Existing mortgage is paid off and release or estopple certificate obtained from lender.
- Other liens and encumbrances are removed or disclosed.
- Real estate commissions are paid (if applicable).
- Loan charges are paid (origination fees, points, inspection reports, credit reports, and so on).

- Attorney fees, escrow fees, and other fees are paid.
- Conveyance taxes are paid.
- IRS report 1099 is filed.
- Documents are recorded.
- Possession of property is transferred to buyer(s).

The HUD-1 Settlement Statement provides a good outline of settlement services that apply to all federally related transactions and many other real estate closings, too.

Broker(s) Commission

15.7→ The commission is calculated based on the existing agreements between the buyer(s), seller(s), and broker(s). In many states a disclosure statement is required that clearly acknowledges that all parties know who was represented by the broker(s) and how, when, what, and by whom the broker(s) will be paid.

Items Payable in Connection with Loan

Many of the charges incurred for the obtaining of a loan, which are listed below, are paid by the seller. However, different arrangements may be negotiated and spelled out in the sales contract. When the buyer(s) finance the property with a VA-insured loan, the seller(s) may be required to pay the points. The seller(s) may also have to pay a prepayment penalty to pay off their existing loans. The most common loan charges are:

- Loan origination fee
- Loan discount
- Appraisal fee
- Credit report
- Lender's inspection fee
- Mortgage insurance application fee
- Assumption fee
- Survey
- Inspection reports
  - Termite and infestation report
  - Structural inspection
  - Environmental report
  - Soil report
  - Geologic hazard report

The Real Estate Settlement Procedures Act (RESPA) requires that the lender supply a copy of the HUD information booklet *Settlement Costs and You* to every mortgage borrower (except those refinancing) of a one- to four-family property. The following material is quoted directly from this booklet.

Loan Origination

"This fee covers the lender's administrative costs in processing the loan. Often expressed as a percentage of the loan, the fee will vary among lenders and from locality to locality. Generally the buyer pays the fee unless another arrangement has been made with the seller and written into the sales contract."

Loan Discount

15.8→

"Often called 'points,' a loan discount is a one-time charge used as the yield on the loan to what market conditions demand. It is used to offset constraints placed on the yield by State or Federal regulations. Each point is equal to one percent of the mortgage amount. For example, if a lender charges four points on a $60,000 loan, it amounts to a charge of $2,400."

Appraisal Fee

"This charge, which may vary significantly from transaction to transaction, pays for a statement of property value for the lender, made by an independent appraiser or by a member of the lender's staff. The lender needs to know if the value of the property is sufficient to secure the loan if you fail to repay the loan according to the provisions of your mortgage contract, and the lender must foreclose and take title to the house. The appraiser inspects the house and the neighborhood, and considers sales prices of comparable houses and other factors in determining the value. The appraisal report may contain photos and other information of value to you. It will provide the factual data upon which the appraiser based the appraised value. The appraisal does not, however, give rights to the purchaser nor necessarily detect or discuss defects in the property or title to the property." *Current banking regulations require that a copy of the appraisal be given to the borrower.*

"The appraisal fee may be paid either by the buyer or the seller, as agreed in the sales contract. In some cases this fee is included in the Mortgage Insurance Application Fee."

Credit Report

"This fee covers the cost of the credit report, which shows how you have handled other credit transactions. The lender uses this report in conjunction with information you submitted with the application regarding your income, outstanding bills, and employment, to determine whether you are an acceptable credit risk and to help determine how much money to lend you."

Lender's Inspection Fee

"This charge covers inspections, often of newly constructed housing, made by personnel of the lending institution or an outside inspector."

15.9➤

Mortgage Insurance Application Fee

"This mortgage insurance application fee covers processing the application for private mortgage insurance which may be required on certain loans. It may cover both the appraisal and application fee."

Assumption Fee

"This fee is charged for processing papers for cases in which the buyer takes over the payments on the prior loan of the seller."

Survey

"The lender or the title insurance company may require that a surveyor conduct a property survey to determine the exact location of the home and the lot lines, as well as easements and rights of way. This is a protection to the buyer as well. Usually the buyer pays for the surveyor's fees, but sometimes this may be handled by the seller."

Pest and Other Inspection Reports

15.10➤ Some of the other inspection reports that lenders require are a termite and infestation report, structural inspection, environmental report, soil report, and a geological hazard report.

"This fee is to cover inspections for termite or other pest infestation of the home. This may be important if the sales contract included a promise by the seller to transfer the property free from pests or pest-caused damage. Be sure that the inspection shows that the property complies with the sales contract before you complete the settlement. If it does not, you may wish to require a bond or other financial assurance that the work will be completed. This fee can be paid either by the borrower or seller depending upon the terms of the sales contract. Lenders vary in their requirements as to such an inspection."

Items Required by the Lender to be Paid in Advance

Many lenders require the following items to be paid in advance at the closing:

- Interest
- Mortgage insurance premiums
- Hazard insurance premiums
- One-time FHA and VA fees

15.11➤

Interest

15.12➤ Lenders usually require that borrowers pay at settlement the interest that accrues on the mortgage from the date of the settlement to the beginning of the
15.13➤ period covered by the first monthly payment.

Mortgage Insurance Premium

15.14➤ Mortgage insurance protects the lender from loss due to payment default by the Borrow(s). The lender may require the payment of the first monthly premium or a lump-sum premium payment at the time of the settlement.

Hazard Insurance Premiums

15.15➤ Hazard insurance protects both the owner and lender from loss by fire and other hazards. The coverage is often included as part of a package policy. Flood insurance is required for federally related loans when the property is in a FEMA-designated flood area. This is usually covered by a separate policy. The lender may require a month's premium or a year's premium be paid in advance.

One-Time VA and FHA Fees

When the property is financed with an FHA or VA mortgage, there may be insurance charges and funding fees that are required to be paid in advance.

Reserves and Deposits with Lenders

Reserves (sometimes called *escrow* or *impound* accounts) are funds held in an account by the lender to ensure future payment for such recurring items as real estate taxes and hazard insurance.

15.16➤ For loans that are covered by RESPA the maximum amount that the lender can require borrowers or prospective borrowers to deposit into a reserve account at settlement is a total gross amount not to exceed the sum of

(1) an amount that would have been sufficient to pay taxes, insurance premiums, or other charges that would have been paid under normal lending practices and ending on the due date of the first full monthly mortgage installment payment plus (2) an additional amount not in excess of one-sixth (two months) of the estimated total amount of taxes, insurance premiums, and other charges to be paid on the dates indicated above during any 12-month period to follow.

Once the borrowers begin their monthly payments they cannot be required to pay more than one-twelfth of the annual taxes and other charges each month, unless a larger payment is necessary to make up for a deficit in the borrower's account or to maintain the cushion of the one-sixth of annual charges mentioned in (2) above. A deficit can be caused if your taxes or hazard insurance premiums go up.

Title Charges

Title charges may cover a variety of services performed by title companies and others and may include fees directly related to the transfer of title, and settlement or closing fees:

- Title examination fee
- Title search fee
- Document preparation fee
- Title insurance binder
- Settlement or closing fee
- Fee for title insurance
- Legal charges, which include fees for lender's, buyer's, and seller's attorney or the attorney preparing the title work
- Fees for settlement agents and notaries

These are the most common fees. However, in some areas, there are additional charges customary to that area.

Government Recording and Transfer Charges

Recording and the charges for recording different types of documents vary widely from area to area. These charges are established by law and are often based on the number of pages recorded.

The most common arrangement is for the seller to pay the *recording charges* or filing fees needed to clear all defects and furnish the buyer with a clear title. These may include any releases needed to clear title, satisfaction of mortgage documents, quitclaim deeds, affidavits, releases of mechanic's liens, and so on. The buyer often pays for the recording of the deed that conveys the title, and the new mortgage or deed of trust.

There are no laws that govern who pays which charges. It is usually determined by custom in an area. However, as part of the negotiation, the charges can be shifted from the customary party to whomever the buyer and seller agree on.

Additional Settlement Charges

Some additional settlement charges that often occur are appraisal fees, survey costs, and fees for various others inspections.

SECURING GOOD TITLE

The many different types of titles and estates are covered in a separate chapter in this text. Most sales result in the buyer(s) obtaining a warranty or quitclaim deed and title insurance or a certificate of title to guarantee that the title they receive is good. This insures that the buyer(s) will be able to refinance and/or sell the property in the future.

The *transfer of title* by a deed during a person's lifetime is called voluntary alienation. A deed is a written instrument by which owners of real estate intentionally convey their rights and interests. The original owner(s) [seller(s)] are called the *Grantor(s)* and the new owner(s) [buyer(s)] are the *Grantee(s)*.

When a property is being sold in most areas it is the obligation of the seller(s) to deliver *marketable title*. To be marketable the title must be free from any significant liens and encumbrances. Someone must be hired to search the title records and prepare an *abstract of title* which is a brief history of the documents that appear on the public record that pertain to the property being transferred.

Title Insurance

15.17➤ The most common method for the buyer(s) to be sure they have good marketable title is to purchase *title insurance* from a company licensed in their state to issue title insurance. It then becomes the obligation of the title insurance company to examine the abstract or title and determine if the title is marketable. If it is, they will issue a *preliminary title report,* commitment, or binder. If sometime in the future you discover that you did not get good title to your property when you purchased it, you can make a claim with the title insurance company. If your claim is valid, the title insurance company will have to pay whatever it costs to correct the title deficiency. The most common times that title defects are discovered are when the property is refinanced or sold.

Common Title Insurance Exclusions

Usually at the time of the closing the title insurance company issues a title insurance policy. This policy can be written for the benefit of either the lender or the property owner (or both). The standard title insurance policy has a variety of exclusions that often can be eliminated by negotiation with the title insurance company, usually by paying an extra premium. Some of the standard exclusions are the following:

- Rights and claims of persons in actual physical possession of the property (even though they have no recorded lease)
- Easements and liens that are not recorded
- Unrecorded rights of eminent domain
- Rights or claims that would have been revealed by a survey
- Mining claims
- Reservation
- Water rights
- Zoning and governmental restrictions
- Environmental restrictions

Abstract or Title Search

15.18➤ The purpose of the title search and abstract is to determine whether the seller(s) can convey clear title to the property and to disclose any matters on record that could adversely affect the buyer(s) or the lender.

Clearing Title

When a title problem is discovered, it is reported to whomever is conducting the closing. Often it can be removed by arrangement for payment at the time of the closing. Prior mortgages, liens, and judgments are often handled in this way.

Title Charges

Title charges may cover a variety of services performed by title companies and others and include fees directly related to the transfer of title and settlement or closing fees. Some typical fees that are charged are:

- Title examination
- Title search
- Document preparation

- Title insurance binder
- Settlement or closing fee
- Fee for title insurance
- Legal charges, which include fees for lenders, buyer's and seller's attorneys, or the attorney preparing the title work
- Fees for settlement agents and notaries

These are the most common fees. However, in some areas, there are additional charges customary to that area.

Survey

15.19 ➤ The lender, title insurance company, or buyer(s) may require that a surveyor conduct a property survey to determine the exact location of the boundary lines and the location of the improvements on the site. The survey will also show the location of rights-of-way, easements, and encroachments. In many areas it is customary for the buyer(s) to pay to update or obtain a new survey. However, other payment arrangements can be negotiated in the sales contract.

Inspections

It is very common for a sales contract to contain provisions stating that the sale is contingent upon inspections being made and the results of these inspections being satisfactory to the buyer(s). When the inspections disclose problems that are curable, the sales contract may contain provisions for how they will be cured. Sometimes they must be cured before the closing takes place. When the work to cure the problem is to take place after the closing, a bond or other financial assurance that the work will be completed is arranged for. Some of the most common inspections are:

- Termite and infestation reports
- Structural inspection
- Environmental report
- Soil report
- Geologic hazard report

Recording

In all 50 states and U.S. territories, place(s) are maintained to record deeds, mortgages, liens, and other documents that affect the ownership of real estate. These records are always open for public inspection. There is always a government official who is in charge of the recording of these documents. Each state and territory has a *recording act* that requires that these documents be recorded in the area where the property is located. Therefore, for any specific piece of real estate, there is only one specific place where its documents are recorded. Throughout America there is a great variety of names for these places, buildings where they are located, and people who are in charge. There are also many statutes that regulate the form of the documents to be recorded and the recording process.

Torrens System

A few states still use the Torrens System to register titles. In these states an application is made with the clerk of the court in the county in which the real estate is located. The applicants must prove that they are the owner(s) of the property. If the court is satisfied, it enters an order to register the real estate, and the register of titles is further directed to issue a certificate of title. The records of the register's office in a Torrens state show the owner of the property and all mortgages, judgments, and liens. It does not record tax liens and some other items that are normally recorded on the land records.

INCOME AND EXPENSE PRORATION

Most real estate sales contracts contain a provision that the income and expenses of the property being transferred be divided between the buyer(s) and seller(s). The general rule is that the buyer(s) receive a credit from the seller(s) for any income they have received that is for the use of the property after the date of the closing. The seller(s) receive a credit for some expenses they have paid that cover the period after the closing. The opposite is also true. If tenants are behind in their rent, whatever rent is later collected belongs to the seller(s). The sales contract may call for an adjustment at the closing, and the delinquent rent then is kept by the buyer(s) when it is collected or the sales contract may require the delinquent rent be turned over to the seller(s) if and when it is collected. The opposite is sometimes also true for some expenses. Items that are prorated are spelled out in the sales contract and/or by the customs of the area in which the property is located.

Basis of Proration

In many areas it is the custom, when prorating, to use a 30-day month because it simplifies the proration calculations. This produces a small inaccuracy when the month is not 30 days. Another way is to divide by 365 to determine a daily rate. Some states have a requirement that all prorations be made on a daily basis.

The date of proration is also not nationally uniform. A common method is to use the closing date. Some state laws use the day before the closing. The proration date can also be agreed on in the sales contract.

Items Commonly Prorated

15.20➤ The following is a list of income and expenses that are commonly prorated. This list can be altered by the sales contract and varies from area to area:

- Rents
- City/town taxes
- County taxes
- Other property taxes
- School district taxes
- Fire district taxes
- Hazard insurance premiums
- Flood insurance premiums
- Interest on assumed loans
- Utilities
  - Water
  - Electricity
  - Sewer
  - Telephone
  - Cable
- Association Dues

Proration of Property Taxes

Almost every real estate sale requires proration of real estate taxes. There are a variety of different kinds of property taxes. The most common are city/town taxes, county taxes, school district taxes, and fire district taxes.

To calculate a tax proration it is necessary to determine when the tax was due, what portion has been paid by the seller(s), and what period of time is covered by the payment. The opposite is true if there are unpaid taxes that are due or if taxes are levied in arrears.

Another complication in the proration of taxes is that they may not be billed on the date they are due. It is common in some areas to set the tax rate many months after the due date and to further complicate the calculation by allowing semiannual payments.

Chapter 19 contains examples of simple and complicated tax prorations.

Figure 15.1 Settlement Statement HUD-1—front of the form.

A. **Settlement Statement**	U.S. Department of Housing and Urban Development	OMB Approval No. 2502-0265 (expires 11/30/2009)

B. Type of Loan

1. ☐ FHA	2. ☐ FmHA	3. ☐ Conv. Unins.	6. File Number:	7. Loan Number:	8. Mortgage Insurance Case Number:
4. ☐ VA	5. ☐ Conv. Ins.				

C. Note: This form is furnished to give you a statement of actual settlement costs. Amounts paid to and by the settlement agent are shown. Items marked "(p.o.c.)" were paid outside the closing; they are shown here for informational purposes and are not included in the totals.

D. Name & Address of Borrower:	E. Name & Address of Seller:	F. Name & Address of Lender:

G. Property Location:	H. Settlement Agent:	
	Place of Settlement:	I. Settlement Date:

J. Summary of Borrower's Transaction		**K. Summary of Seller's Transaction**	
100. Gross Amount Due From Borrower		**400. Gross Amount Due To Seller**	
101. Contract sales price		401. Contract sales price	
102. Personal property		402. Personal property	
103. Settlement charges to borrower (line 1400)		403.	
104.		404.	
105.		405.	
Adjustments for items paid by seller in advance		**Adjustments for items paid by seller in advance**	
106. City/town taxes to		406. City/town taxes to	
107. County taxes to		407. County taxes to	
108. Assessments to		408. Assessments to	
109.		409.	
110.		410.	
111.		411.	
112.		412.	
120. Gross Amount Due From Borrower		**420. Gross Amount Due To Seller**	
200. Amounts Paid By Or In Behalf Of Borrower		**500. Reductions In Amount Due To Seller**	
201. Deposit or earnest money		501. Excess deposit (see instructions)	
202. Principal amount of new loan(s)		502. Settlement charges to seller (line 1400)	
203. Existing loan(s) taken subject to		503. Existing loan(s) taken subject to	
204.		504. Payoff of first mortgage loan	
205.		505. Payoff of second mortgage loan	
206.		506.	
207.		507.	
208.		508.	
209.		509.	
Adjustments for items unpaid by seller		**Adjustments for items unpaid by seller**	
210. City/town taxes to		510. City/town taxes to	
211. County taxes to		511. County taxes to	
212. Assessments to		512. Assessments to	
213.		513.	
214.		514.	
215.		515.	
216.		516.	
217.		517.	
218.		518.	
219.		519.	
220. Total Paid By/For Borrower		**520. Total Reduction Amount Due Seller**	
300. Cash At Settlement From/To Borrower		**600. Cash At Settlement To/From Seller**	
301. Gross Amount due from borrower (line 120)		601. Gross amount due to seller (line 420)	
302. Less amounts paid by/for borrower (line 220)	( )	602. Less reductions in amt. due seller (line 520)	( )
303. Cash ☐ From ☐ To Borrower		**603. Cash** ☐ To ☐ From Seller	

Section 5 of the Real Estate Settlement Procedures Act (RESPA) requires the following: • HUD must develop a Special Information Booklet to help persons borrowing money to finance the purchase of residential real estate to better understand the nature and costs of real estate settlement services; • Each lender must provide the booklet to all applicants from whom it receives or for whom it prepares a written application to borrow money to finance the purchase of residential real estate; • Lenders must prepare and distribute with the Booklet a Good Faith Estimate of the settlement costs that the borrower is likely to incur in connection with the settlement. These disclosures are manadatory.

Section 4(a) of RESPA mandates that HUD develop and prescribe this standard form to be used at the time of loan settlement to provide full disclosure of all charges imposed upon the borrower and seller. These are third party disclosures that are designed to provide the borrower with pertinent information during the settlement process in order to be a better shopper.

The Public Reporting Burden for this collection of information is estimated to average one hour per response, including the time for reviewing instructions, searching existing data sources, gathering and maintaining the data needed, and completing and reviewing the collection of information.

This agency may not collect this information, and you are not required to complete this form, unless it displays a currently valid OMB control number.

The information requested does not lend itself to confidentiality.

Previous editions are obsolete	Page 1 of 2	form **HUD-1** (3/86) ref Handbook 4305.2

Figure 15.2 Settlement Statement HUD-1—back of the form.

L. Settlement Charges

	Paid From Borrowers Funds at Settlement	Paid From Seller's Funds at Settlement
700. Total Sales/Broker's Commission based on price $ @ % =		
Division of Commission (line 700) as follows:		
701. $ to		
702. $ to		
703. Commission paid at Settlement		
704.		
800. Items Payable In Connection With Loan		
801. Loan Origination Fee %		
802. Loan Discount %		
803. Appraisal Fee to		
804. Credit Report to		
805. Lender's Inspection Fee		
806. Mortgage Insurance Application Fee to		
807. Assumption Fee		
808.		
809.		
810.		
811.		
900. Items Required By Lender To Be Paid In Advance		
901. Interest from to @$ /day		
902. Mortgage Insurance Premium for months to		
903. Hazard Insurance Premium for years to		
904. years to		
905.		
1000. Reserves Deposited With Lender		
1001. Hazard insurance months @ $ per month		
1002. Mortgage insurance months @ $ per month		
1003. City property taxes months @ $ per month		
1004. County property taxes months @ $ per month		
1005. Annual assessments months @ $ per month		
1006. months @ $ per month		
1007. months @ $ per month		
1008. months @ $ per month		
1100. Title Charges		
1101. Settlement or closing fee to		
1102. Abstract or title search to		
1103. Title examination to		
1104. Title insurance binder to		
1105. Document preparation to		
1106. Notary fees to		
1107. Attorney's fees to		
(includes above items numbers:)		
1108. Title insurance to		
(includes above items numbers:)		
1109. Lender's coverage $		
1110. Owner's coverage $		
1111.		
1112.		
1113.		
1200. Government Recording and Transfer Charges		
1201. Recording fees: Deed $; Mortgage $; Releases $		
1202. City/county tax/stamps: Deed $; Mortgage $		
1203. State tax/stamps: Deed $; Mortgage $		
1204.		
1205.		
1300. Additional Settlement Charges		
1301. Survey to		
1302. Pest inspection to		
1303.		
1304.		
1305.		
1400. Total Settlement Charges (enter on lines 103, Section J and 502, Section K)		

Proration of Rents and Security Deposits

When the property being transferred is rented, it is customary to prorate the rents. To calculate a rent proration it is necessary to determine what rents and security deposits have been collected by the seller and what period of time the collected rents and security deposits cover. Most states require that interest be paid on security deposits to the tenant when they are returned. The buyer is entitled to a credit for the accrued interest they will have to pay the tenant when the security deposit is returned.

Dry Closings

Sometimes a face-to-face closing takes place in stages. In some areas this is known as a *dry closing*. This is usually required because the transaction is very complicated and whoever is conducting the closing feels a rehearsal is needed to be certain everything is in order. It is also caused when some item needed for the closing cannot be obtained in time for the closing. At a dry closing, some or all of the papers are signed and the money is turned over to the person in charge of the closing. When everything is in order the money is released to the seller(s) and the documents are delivered and recorded.

Conveyance Taxes

15.21→ On January 1, 1968, the federal government ended its tax of $1.10 per $1,000 of equity involved in a real estate sale. Since before World War II, deeds had attached to the federal document stamps that were proof that the federal tax had been paid. No tax was levied on the amount of an assumed mortgage. Therefore, if a property sold for $400,000 with a $350,000 assumed mortgage, the tax would apply only to the $50,000 additional capital. However, if a new mortgage was obtained, the tax would be due on the full $400,000. A fringe benefit to brokers and appraisers was that it was possible to determine the sale price of any property with a recorded deed by looking at the attached document stamps.

When the federal tax ended, many states instituted a *conveyance tax* of their own. These taxes vary from those that are the same as the old federal tax to some that are close to .05 percent of the sale price. These taxes are usually paid at the time the new deed and mortgage are recorded.

IRS Reporting Requirements

15.22→ Federal tax law now requires that IRS Form 1099 be filed for each real estate sale. The IRS code provides a list that determines who is responsible for filing the 1099. The person who conducts the closing is primarily responsible; next comes the lender, then the seller(s), and last the buyer(s). It is the responsibility of everyone on this list to determine that someone ahead of them has filed the 1099. If the 1099 is not filed, everyone on the list is subject to IRS penalties.

Failure to Close on Time

The sales contract usually establishes a time to close the sale. This is a date that has been agreed on by the buyer(s) and seller(s). They often have taken into consideration such things as when the buyer(s) need use of the property, when the seller(s) can vacate the property, and how long it will take for the buyer(s) to accumulate the cash they need to obtain a satisfactory loan commitment. Time also must be allowed for the completion of the appraisal and any other inspections that are part of the agreement.

Short delays caused by a variety of reasons are quite common. When one or both parties want to reduce the chance of there being a delay in the closing, they often add to the sales contract wording to the effect that "time is of the essence." As long as both parties want to close it is usually possible to work out fair financial compensation to make the parties whole from the results of the delayed closing.

When the delays are excessive, it may be necessary to terminate the sale and refund the buyer's deposit. As long as this is mutually agreeable it presents no problem. When one party has been damaged by the failure to close, it may be necessary to work out some financial compensation. It is always best to obtain mutual releases when a transaction is terminated without the transfer of the property. Otherwise the buyer(s) have some undetermined obligation to buy and the seller(s) some obligation to sell. This may present a problem when it comes to the future transfer of title of the property.

A more difficult problem to deal with is when one of the parties wants to get out of the deal and uses the delay as an excuse to terminate the contract. Common causes for this situation are when the buyers find a less expensive or more desirable property and when they have trouble raising the needed capital. Sellers may discover other potential buyers who are willing to pay a higher price, or they are unable to obtain a suitable substitute property.

In general the courts will not allow the buyers or sellers to cancel a contract based solely on delayed closings. This is true even when the sales contract contains the provision "time is of the essence." The courts are much more inclined to award monetary damages to the party that demonstrates that they have been damaged by the delay.

When one party refuses to close, the other party in most areas has three choices. They can work out some kind of a financial settlement or they can institute a court action either to force the reluctant party to close or to pay damages.

SUMMARY

When the buyer(s) and seller(s) reach an agreement to transfer title to a property, the agreement should be reduced to writing. The most common document created is a real estate sales contract.

The actual transfer of title takes place at either a face-to-face closing or an escrow closing. When an escrow closing is used, someone is appointed as the escrow agent who is a natural party that acts in compliance with escrow instructions provided by the buyer(s) and seller(s).

All of the applicable documents and funds are delivered to the escrow agent who, after checking them over, disburses the funds and records and distributes the documents. As part of the process the escrow agent prepares a closing statement that prorates the property income and expenses and shows all the costs of the buyer(s) and seller(s). Many residential property closings are regulated by the Real Estate Settlement Procedures Act of 1974 (RESPA). Closing for other types of property must comply with any applicable state laws.

For properties covered by RESPA, at the time when a mortgage loan application is made, the applicants must be given a copy of the HUD Guide—Settlement Costs. The lender must also supply the applicants with a good-faith estimate of their closing costs. For an RESPA-regulated closing, a Uniform Settlement Statement (HUD-1) must be used.

The sellers must provide the buyers a marketable title that is free from any significant liens and encumbrances. Someone is hired to search the title records and prepare an abstract of title. The most common method for the buyers to be sure they have good marketable title is to purchase title insurance.

Many sales contracts contain provisions stating that the sale is contingent upon inspections. When the inspections disclose problems that are curable, the sales contract may contain provisions for how they will be cured. Some of the most common inspections are termite and infestation; structural inspections; and environmental, soil, and geologic hazard reports.

Buyers should inspect the property immediately prior to the closing. They should make sure the premises have been vacated, that all the seller's and tenant's personal property has been removed, and that none of the real estate has been removed. The property should be in substantially the same condition as it was when the sales contract was signed. When problems are discovered they should be resolved prior to the closing or escrow date.

The income and expenses of the property are prorated between the buyers and sellers. Prorated items are spelled out in the sales contract and/or by the customs of the area in which the property is located.

Short closing delays are caused by a variety of reasons. As long as both parties want to close, it is usually possible to work out fair financial compensation to make the parties whole from the results of the delayed closing. When the delays are excessive, it may be necessary to terminate the sale and refund the buyer's deposit. A more difficult problem to deal with is when one of the parties wants to get out of the deal and uses the delay as an excuse to terminate the contract. In general, the courts will not allow the buyers or sellers to cancel a contract based solely on delayed closings. This is even true when the sales contract contains the provision "time is of the essence." When one party refuses to close, the other party in most areas has three choices. They can work out some kind of a financial settlement or they can institute a court action either to force the reluctant party to close or to pay damages.

REVIEW QUESTIONS

15.1 The basic types of closings are:

   A. Face-to-face and escrow closings

   B. Back-to-back and escrow closing

   C. Face-to-face and back-to-back closing

   D. None of the above

15.2 When there is a dispute between the buyer and the seller that cannot be resolved by the parties, the escrow agent seeks the help of the court by filing:

   A. An action in intercession

   B. An intervention action

   C. An interpleader action

   D. None of the above

15.3 The Real Estate Settlement Procedures Act of 1974 (RESPA) applies to the closing of:

   A. All types of real estate

   B. All residential real estate

   C. Single family residences

   D. One- to four-family residences

15.4 RESPA requires that a Good Faith Estimate of the settlement services charges to the applicants be mailed or delivered to the loan applicant no later than:

   A. 3 days before the loan application is accepted

   B. the same day the loan application is accepted

   C. 3 days after the loan application is accepted

   D. when the loan application is approved

15.5 RESPA requires that, for all real estate closing covered by RESPA, the settlement statement use be a:

   A. FHA approved form

   B. FNMA approved form

   C. HUD-1 Settlement Statement

   D. State approved form

15.6 RESPA prohibits:

   A. Referral fees from one broker to another broker

   B. Referral fees which are kickbacks from a vendor

   C. Referral fees from a salesperson to a broker

   D. All of the above

15.7 A broker's commission for sales regulated by RESPA is always:

A. 6 percent

B. Set by state law

C. Set by Federal law

D. None of the above

15.8 Loan discounts are often called:

A. Credits

B. Debits

C. Points

D. None of the above

15.9 A lender's inspection fee most often is for the inspection of:

A. Newly constructed houses

B. Historic houses

C. Contemporary style houses

D. Inner city houses.

15.10 A common inspection report required by lenders is:

A. A termite inspection

B. A structural inspection

C. An environmental inspection

D. All of the above

15.11 Which of the following sometimes requires the seller to pay the points to the lender?

A. FHA regulations

B. VA regulations

C. RESPA regulations

D. None of the above

15.12 Many lenders require the following item to be paid in advance at the closing:

A. Mortgage interest

B. Mortgage insurance premiums

C. Hazard insurance premiums

D. All of the above

15.13 Many lenders require that mortgage interest be collected at the closing from the date of the closing to:

A. The end of the year

B. The end of the mortgage

C. The date of the first payment

D. One month after the date of the first payment

15.14 Mortgage insurance protects:

A. The lender from loss due to payment default of the borrower

B. The borrower from loss due to lending institution failure

C. Both of the above

D. Neither of the above

15.15 Most homeowner insurance policies provide coverage for:

A. Loss from fire

B. Loss from flood

C. Both of the above

D. Neither of the above

15.16 RESPA limits the amount of reserves a lender may require to the amount of taxes, insurance, and other charges currently due, plus a reserve of:

A. One month's charges

B. Two months' charges

C. Six months' charges

D. One year's charges

15.17 The best method for a buyer to be sure they have good title is:

A. Have their own attorney do the title search

B. Buy a title insurance policy

C. Get a certificate of title

D. None of the above

15.18 The purpose of an abstract of title is to:

A. Determine the amount of any unpaid loan

B. Discover any unrecorded liens or encumbrances

C. Verify the survey

D. None of the above

15.19 Most surveys show:

A. Rights of way

B. Easements

C. Encroachments

D. All of the above

15.20 Which of the following are commonly prorated at a closing?

A. Rents

B. Taxes

C. Hazard insurance premiums

D. All of the above

15.21 The federal conveyance tax of $1.10 per $1,000:

A. Applies to all types of real estate

B. Applies only to commercial and industrial property

C. Applies only in states that do not have their own conveyance tax

D. Ended in 1968

15.22 Who is primarily responsible for filing the IRS form 1099 for each real estate sale?

A. The person who conducts the closing

B. The seller

C. The lender

D. The buyer

ANSWERS

The answer to each question is indicated by the letters A, B, C, or D. The explanation of the answer is indicated by the page number and an arrow that points to the appropriate paragraph on the page.

Q 15.1 A Page 279	Q 15.6 B Page 283	Q 15.11 B Page 288	Q 15.16 B Page 288	Q 15.21 D Page 297
Q 15.2 C Page 281	Q 15.7 D Page 285	Q 15.12 D Page 288	Q 15.17 B Page 290	Q 15.22 A Page 297
Q 15.3 D Page 282	Q 15.8 C Page 286	Q 15.13 C Page 288	Q 15.18 D Page 291	
Q 15.4 C Page 282	Q 15.9 A Page 287	Q 15.14 A Page 288	Q 15.19 D Page 292	
Q 15.5 C Page 283	Q 15.10 D Page 287	Q 15.15 A Page 288	Q 15.20 D Page 294	

CHAPTER 16

Environmental Hazards

Millions of houses and other properties are affected by hazardous substances and detrimental environmental conditions. They range from elevated radon levels that can be corrected for a few thousand dollars to PCB contamination so severe that the property is not habitable, usable or transferable. One of the keys to success as a real estate salesperson is to have the reputation of being knowledgeable about real estate.

For many years being knowledgeable about financing was what impressed your friends and other potential customers. Now everyone is thinking "green." Environmental questions are beginning to appear on the license and broker exams.

This chapter is an overview of the environmental problems that affect real estate, especially residential property. This basic environmental knowledge will help you both in your professional and personal life.

ENVIRONMENTAL PROBLEMS

The following is a list of the major environmental problems that affect real estate in the United States:

Unsafe drinking water
Unsafe liquid waste disposal

Soil contaminants
Nearby hazardous waste sites
Asbestos
PCBs
Radon
Underground storage tanks (USTs)
UREA formaldehyde (UFFI) insulation
Lead paint
Indoor air pollution
Outdoor air pollution
Wetlands
Mold
Excess noise (Noise pollution)
Electromagnetic radiation
Light pollution
Waste heat
Acid mine drainage
Agricultural pollution
Geological hazards
Infectious medical waste
Pesticides and termiticides
Chemical storage and storage drums
Pipelines

Unsafe Drinking Water

Every property needs an adequate supply of safe drinking water, as recognized by Congress through the enactment of the Safe Drinking Water Act (SDWA) in 1974. This law and its 1986 and 1996 amendments empower the *Environmental Protection Agency* (EPA) to protect public health by regulating the nation's public drinking water supply. The law was amended in 1986 and 1996 and requires many actions to protect drinking water and its sources: rivers, lakes, reservoirs, springs, and groundwater wells. (SDWA does not regulate private wells which serve fewer than 25 individuals.)

Public Water Systems

16.3 ➤

Public water comes from either surface or ground sources. There are about 15,000 public systems in the United States that obtain their water from surface sources. These surface water systems serve an estimated 150 million people. There are about 175,000 public systems that obtain their water from ground water sources. These groundwater systems serve about 100 million people. These numbers indicate that the majority of Americans receive their drinking water from public systems.

Most of us take it for granted that the public drinking water we drink is clean and safe. Unfortunately, waterborne diseases are still a problem in the United States. Most of the waterborne disease outbreaks occur in small public water systems, which usually serve less than 3,300 persons.

About 30 million Americans get their drinking water from these small public water supply systems. The most frequently reported waterborne disease in the United States is acute gastrointestinal illness (AGI) also called gastroenteritis.

Obtaining safe drinking water starts with watershed management to protect the sources of the water from contamination. The second step requires filtration to remove existing contaminants and, finally, disinfection to kill pathogens remaining in the water.

Chlorine is the most frequently used disinfectant. It can be added to the water both before and after the filtration process. Chlorine has an unpleasant taste and smell and some possible other undesirable side effects. Public health officials believe the benefits of chlorine far outweigh its presently known risks, so it is widely used.

In most parts of the country, public water companies are able to supply ample drinking water. However, there are often shortages of water for washing, sanitation, irrigation, and industrial purposes.

Private Water Supplies and Wells

Many properties receive their water from small private water companies or from wells on or off the property. The possibility of water from these sources being unsafe is substantially higher than when it is supplied by a public water company.

The safety of water from wells and small private water supplies is often below acceptable standards. Users of water from these sources should be made aware of this fact and cautioned to take necessary steps to protect themselves against using unsafe water.

Lead in Water

16.1➤ Lead is one of the most dangerous substances humans can ingest. Children are especially susceptible to its harmful effects, which include serious damage to many organs including the brain, kidneys, nervous system, and red blood cells. Infants are at the highest risk since they can be harmed by even small amounts of lead in their drinking water or the water used to make their formula.

Since 1987, all public water systems have been required to notify the public about any lead in the water they supply. Most public water systems supply lead-free water. You can contact your public water company to provide you with lead information.

Much of the lead that is found in drinking water comes from the lead in pipes and plumbing fixtures through which the water travels. Currently, 20 ppb (parts per billion) of lead or less is considered to be safe.

The authors believe that lead is so dangerous to babies in their first six months of life that they should be fed only bottled water.

16.2➤ Drinking water can also be contaminated by radon, PCBs, dioxins, and many other hazardous chemicals.

Unsafe Liquid Waste Disposal

Sewers

16.4➤ The liquid waste produced by the typical community comes from homes, commercial establishments, and industries. It is carried by sewer pipes to treatment plants and then is discharged, usually into natural waterways. To avoid pollution, all wastewater should pass through treatment plants.

16.5➤ Sewers have been around for thousands of years. Most sewers in the ancient world were used to remove storm water. Some sewers in United States communities are combined systems, which remove storm water as well as domestic, commercial, and industrial liquid waste. Separate storm water and waste disposal systems are much better suited to modern metropolitan conditions. It is uneconomical to build plants large enough to accept the enormously enlarged inflow from rainstorms and to treat sewage at the same time. In addition, a combined system must be made so large that it may not be able to provide adequate velocity for the dry-weather flow of the wastewater alone.

The arrangement of a sewer system is governed by topography and the relation of points in the system to the point of treatment and disposal. In flat terrain, gravity flow must often be augmented by a pumping system. Pipe sizes and slopes must be able to give adequate scouring velocities at minimum flows. Pipes are usually made of vitrified clay or concrete. Concrete, usually reinforced, is used for the larger mains.

If municipal wastes produced by industry contain toxic substances, pollution is combated by setting standards limiting the maximum concentrations of toxic effluent that may leave the plant. To comply with such standards, an industrial plant must either clean the effluent water before discharge or redesign the industrial process so that certain highly toxic substances are not discharged into the municipal system.

Municipal water pollution is combated by one of three levels of treatment.

Primary treatment involves the separation of solid materials by screens or by settling in still tanks, sometimes aided by chemical precipitation. Removal of grits and solids is accomplished by screening, grinding, flocculation (causing small particles to combine to form larger respirable particles), and sedimentation. In primary treatment, most of the settleable solid materials are removed.

Secondary treatment entails oxidizing and dissolving colloidal organic material by the action of bacteria and other organisms with oxygen. This stage is accomplished by trickling filters, aeration, and passage through sludge activated with bacteria.

Advanced or tertiary treatment refers to all treatments beyond the secondary stage, to the point of water purification where it is once again potable.

After sewage is treated, the remaining sludge is digested with the help of bacteria and concentrated by drying in beds, in centrifuges, or by heat. The final sludge may be incinerated, discharged in the sea, or used for landfill or to condition soil.

Septic Systems

16.6 → Health experts estimate that 50 percent of the septic systems now in use are not working properly. Yet, almost 50 million people in 15 million homes, especially in the suburbs and rural areas, depend upon a septic system for their waste disposal and 25 percent of the new houses being constructed do not connect to municipal systems.

A typical septic system consists of a large concrete tank with a capacity of 900 gallons (about 8 feet by 4 feet by 4 feet) buried in the ground. One end accepts the waste material from the house drain line. Once inside the tank, the waste tends to separate into three parts. The solid waste materials (only about 1 percent of the total volume) sink to the bottom. The grease (also less than 1 percent of the total volume) rises to the top. The rest is liquid. Bacteria in the tank decompose the solid wastes and grease and a relatively clear liquid flows from the opposite end through the drain line. It flows into a distribution box that directs the liquid into a network of buried perforated pipes called a leaching field or into a seepage pit. From here, the liquid runs off into the ground to be absorbed.

The required capacity of the tank depends on the size of the house and usage. The size of the leaching field depends on the soil's capacity to absorb water. The rate at which the soil will absorb water can be measured by making a percolation test. A hole at least 12 inches deep is dug in the ground and filled with water. Each hour the depth of the water is measured. Anything less than an inch decrease in depth each 30 minutes is substandard. This test should be carried out in the wettest season of the year and preferably by an expert. Usually the local health department will make the test at no cost or for a nominal charge. Also, it is likely that the local health authorities will have previous knowledge of the individual system.

Septic tanks must be checked frequently to make sure they are not clogged and that the bacterial action is working properly. Chemicals must be used with care since they can kill the bacteria. Often the tank must be pumped out and the cycle started anew.

Cesspools

A cesspool is similar to a septic system except that it consists of a covered cistern of stone, brick, or concrete instead of a tank. The liquid seeps out through the walls directly into the ground rather than into a leaching field or seepage pit. It is important to learn about a home's particular system, including the location of the clean-out main (often buried in an unmarked spot), so that inspections and repairs can be made as required. A properly working system should produce no odor. Odor in a septic system is one of the first signs of trouble.

New owners should find out how often the system has to be pumped out. In many towns, the local health officer is knowledgeable about many systems and about problems in general in a particular neighborhood. Learning the location of the clean-out main from the current owner saves a lot of digging and searching if it is buried. Septic system problems may sometimes be corrected by simply pumping out the tank. Sometimes new leaching fields are required. Unfortunately, there are situations when the soil absorption rate is poor or the water table is close to the surface and little can be done to make the system function properly.

Soil Contaminants

Soil is perhaps the single most important natural resource on Earth. Without high-quality soil, agriculture and therefore human civilization would be impossible.

The soil provides a home for many benign species of bacteria and other small organisms that play a crucial role in recycling organic material and wastes. It filters rainwater to keep groundwater supplies clean. Modern industrial society, however, assaults this precious resource with a variety of contaminants and threatens to overwhelm nature's ability to cope with wastes. The result is damage to human health and to the overall environment.

Toxic chemicals that get into the soil are spread through runoff and leaching. Runoff occurs when water sweeps contaminants on the ground into wells, rivers, lakes, or adjacent land. Leaching is the process by which contaminants are flushed by water through permeable soil.

Nearby Hazardous Waste Sites

The dimensions of the hazardous waste problem and its impact on human life, the value of real estate, lending policies, and business in general are so enormous they are almost impossible to comprehend. We now produce over 1 ton of waste annually for each person in the USA. This does not include the more than 6 billion tons of industrial waste that are also produced each year.

Add to this even larger amounts of waste produced by the agriculture and mining industries. Although the hazardous waste situation is not new, it was not until the 1970s that the general public became aware of the problem.

The first toxic waste story which appeared in the headlines in 1978 was Love Canal in Niagara Falls, New York. Dozens of homes had to be evacuated because they were so badly contaminated by wastes buried over 25 years before on or near the sites on which their homes were built. Investigators found toxic waste pollution in foundations, walls, floors and even in the air and drinking water in peoples' homes. Toxic wastes were also found in a nearby recreational bathing area. Exposure to them caused skin rashes, blisters, and other medical problems. These toxins were also suspected to be the source of more serious long-term illnesses.

The next big environmental waste story in the media, which appeared in 1981, was the Valley of the Drums in Kentucky, a massive, noxious deposit of leaking storage drums. The third but far from the last of these horror stories took place in the little community of Times Beach in Missouri in 1982. Oil contaminated with highly toxic dioxin had tainted the soil and the water of this eastern Missouri town.

Besides the millions of dollars of destroyed real estate values and millions spent to clean up costs, lives were disrupted and people became aware that their health had been endangered. Citizen groups and environmentalists began lobbying Congress for legislation to protect people against the dangers posed by hazardous waste abandoned at sites throughout the country. They demanded action to clean up the mess.

16.7→ As a result, Congress passed the *Comprehensive Environmental Response, Compensation and Liability Act* (CERCLA) in 1980.

This law established several key objectives. It provided for the development of comprehensive programs to set priorities for cleaning up the worst existing hazardous waste sites. It established tough provisions requiring responsible parties to pay for toxic waste cleanups, even if they no longer owned or operated the site(s) identified. It created a $1.6 billion Hazardous Waste Trust Fund, popularly known as the Superfund.

This fund had three specific goals:

1. To respond immediately to emergency situations involving hazardous substances

2. To perform remedial cleanups in cases where responsible parties could not be made to clean up the site

3. To advance scientific and technological capabilities in all aspects of hazardous waste management, treatment, and disposal

Rather than directly use taxpayers' dollars for cleanups, the Superfund received its money from a special added tax on crude oil and 42 commercial chemicals.

How Hazardous Sites Are Identified

EPA created a computerized data base containing reports of sites in each state identified as having potential environmental problems. Information identifying sites can be sent to the EPA from the general public, real estate professionals, or government employees. Almost 35,000 sites suspected of containing hazardous wastes have been entered into the CERCLA list.

Once the EPA is informed of a possible hazardous site, it collects all available information from its own files, state and local records, and the U.S. Geological Survey maps. This together with any other available information is used to identify the area and the parties most likely to have disposed hazardous waste on the site.

Next, a preliminary assessment is made of potential hazards. The EPA tries to determine the size of the contamination, the identity of the parties involved, and the types and quantities of wastes disposed of on the site. If a preliminary assessment turns up evidence that the site may pose a threat to human health or the environment, inspectors go to the site to collect sufficient evidence to rank its toxicity.

EPA site inspectors look for the obvious signs of danger such as leaking storage drums, dead or discolored vegetation, and so on; take soil and water samples; and evaluate how the hazardous materials on the site could harm people, animals, vegetation, air, water, and property on or near the site. Special attention is paid to the possible access of children to the site.

CERCLA also allows states or territories to designate one top-priority site. On September 16, 1985, the EPA adopted an amendment to the National Contingency Plan (NCP), the Federal regulation by which CERCLA is implemented. Under Section 300.66(b)(4) of the NCP, a site can be included in the *National Properties List* (NPL) if it meets these three requirements: the Agency for Toxic Substances and Disease Registry (ATSDR) of the U.S. Centers for Disease Control has issued a health advisory that recommends removing people from the site; the EPA determines the site poses a significant threat to public health; and the EPA anticipates it will be more cost-effective to use its remedial authority than to use its emergency removal authority to respond to the site.

CERCLA restricts the EPA's authority to respond to certain sites by expressly excluding some substances—petroleum, for example—from the definition of "release." In addition, the EPA may choose not to use CERCLA because the federal government can undertake or enforce cleanup under other laws, thus preserving the Superfund for sites where no other law is available. However, if the EPA later determines that sites not listed are not being properly responded to, it may consider placing them on the National Priorities List.

Property that is near a hazardous waste site has a high probability of becoming contaminated from the hazardous substances that travel from the waste site to the subject property. Hazardous waste can travel underground in the groundwater, on the surface by surface water, by winds, or by being carried from the hazardous waste site to the subject property. Hazardous waste can also be carried in the air by the wind, rain, birds, insects, and so on.

The following indicators can help to identify soil contamination:

1. Nearby observed or known sources of present or past soil contamination.
2. Information disclosed about problems with soil contamination by owners, occupants, and others knowledgeable about the property.
3. The method used for the disposal of sanitary waste is not a municipal sewer system. It is a septic system, cesspool, or other method.
4. Ground areas are observed with stains or excessively stressed vegetation.
5. Sizable areas of debris, trash, or junk are observed on the property.
6. Seeping or unusual standing fluids are observed.
7. Unusual odors.
8. Dead wildlife is found on the premises.
9. The property now or in the past was used for commercial, industrial, or agricultural purposes.

Asbestos

Asbestos is a naturally occurring mineral that was used extensively in the manufacture of fireproof materials prior to 1979. The presence of asbestos in a building does not necessarily mean that the health of the occupants is endangered, as long as the asbestos-containing material (ACM) is in good condition and is intact. When ACM becomes friable asbestos, deteriorated or disturbed due to building maintenance or renovation, asbestos fibers can be released into the air and create a serious health hazard. Exposure to asbestos particles can lead to such diseases as cancer and asbestosis.

Any material containing at least 1 percent asbestos is considered to be an ACM. ACM is often found in pipe insulation, boiler or furnace insulation, and floor or roofing tile. ACM can also be found sprayed or troweled on materials on ceilings, walls, or other surfaces. It is impossible to tell for certain from observation alone whether a material contains asbestos.

16.8➤

OSHA governs worker exposure to asbestos. There are no federal regulations requiring the removal of asbestos from a residence. However, if asbestos abatement is undertaken, federal regulations under the Clean Air Act apply to asbestos removal. State regulations may also apply to the disposal and removal of asbestos.

Construction materials containing asbestos have been used extensively in schools and other buildings. The concern about exposure to asbestos in these buildings is based on evidence linking various respiratory diseases with occupational exposure in the shipbuilding, mining, milling, and fabricating industries. The presence of asbestos in a building does not mean that the health of building occupants is endangered.

If ACM remains in good condition and is unlikely to be disturbed, exposure will be negligible. However, when ACM is damaged or disturbed—for example, by maintenance or repairs conducted without proper controls—asbestos fibers are released. These fibers can create a potential hazard for building occupants.

Asbestos-Related Disease

Most people with asbestos-related diseases (asbestosis, lung cancer, and mesothelioma) were exposed to high levels of asbestos while working in asbestos industries prior to 1972. Extrapolation of the relationship between exposure level and disease indicates that only a small proportion of people exposed to low levels of asbestos will develop asbestos-related diseases. Smokers, children, and young adults are at somewhat greater risk.

Federal Regulations Regarding Asbestos in Buildings

Current regulations restrict the use of most asbestos products in new buildings.

PCBs

Polychlorinated biphenyls, or PCBs, belong to the family of chemicals called chlorinated hydrocarbons. First produced in 1929 and used over the years in a variety of different products, PCBs were banned by the EPA in 1976. The law was not made retroactive to ban materials containing PCBs produced before that date.

PCBs are very chemically stable and fire resistant. As a result, their most popular use was in making the fire retardant dielectric fluid in electrical transformers and capacitors. They were also used to make protective wood coating and inks. PCBs can also be found in older fluorescent lightbulbs.

PCBs are ordinarily safe. Problems arise only when the integrity of the equipment containing them is damaged, creating a leak. If ingested through contaminated soil or groundwater, PCBs can have serious adverse affects on health. PCBs have been known to damage skin and the reproductive system. They are also suspected carcinogens.

Property that is near a hazardous waste site has a high probability of becoming contaminated from PCBs that travel from the waste site to the subject property. PCBs can travel underground in the groundwater, on the surface by surface water, by winds, or by being carried from the hazardous waste site to the subject property.

Residential Properties

PCB contamination of residential properties is usually not a problem, with the exception of contamination that comes from leaking fluorescent light ballasts, capacitors, and leaking transformers. These are more commonly found in larger residential properties than they are in single-family residences.

PCBs make their way onto residential properties through the groundwater and by being dumped or left on the property by former users. When the drinking water is supplied from a well, the appraiser should recommend that the water be tested to determine if the water is free from PCBs and other contaminants.

Commercial, Industrial, Institutional, and Special-Purpose Properties

PCBs present a significant problem for commercial, industrial, institutional, and special-purpose properties. They may have been improperly stored by the current or former owners and/or occupants; leaked from fluorescent light ballasts, capacitors, and transformers; or dumped on or channeled to the site through the groundwater.

Agricultural Properties

PCBs in the groundwater are an especially significant potential problem for agricultural properties. The sources of the PCBs are similar to those of the other types of properties described earlier. Because agricultural properties often use wells as a water source for drinking water as well as for irrigation, the appraiser should always recommend that the groundwater be tested for PCBs and other contamination.

Radon

16.11▶
16.10▶ Radon-222 is a radioactive gas. Humans cannot see, smell, or taste it, but it turns up almost everywhere. Every state in the U.S.A. has at least one hot spot where there is a dangerous level of radon.

16.9▶ Radon occurs naturally in rocks and soil. Radon atoms are uranium's direct descendants. When atoms of uranium-238 decay, they produce several generations of other radioactive elements. The fifth generation is radium which, in turn, decays into radon.

The evolution of radon is the single critical event in the chain of events leading to its formation. Unlike its solid ancestors, radon is a gas and is mobile. The slightest fissure in surrounding rock is enough to spring radon gas from its centuries-old prison in the earth. Though great concentrations of uranium are rare, traces of it are common in ordinary rock and soil. Concentrations vary but, on average, about six atoms of radon emerge each second from every square inch of soil. A typical concentration of radon in soil is between 500 and 1,000 picocuries per liter of air (pCi/L).

There has to be a fairly rich concentration of uranium in the soil to find very high radon concentrations in the home.

How to Test for Radon

The most popular commercially available radon detectors are the charcoal canister and the alpha track detector. However, a variety of different measurement methods are available for determining radon concentrations. Charcoal canisters usually are used for making short-term measurements of two to seven days. Results are reported either in working levels of radon (WL), or picocuries per liter (pCi/L) of radon gas. Only EPA-listed detectors should be used.

Because no level of radon is considered absolutely safe, a person should try to reduce radon levels in his or her home as much as is possible and practical. A person should definitely take action to reduce radon if the average annual level is higher than 4 (pCi/L).

Actions to Reduce Radon Exposure

Reducing the rate of radon entering the house can be accomplished either by blocking off or sealing the places through which it enters or by reversing the direction of the flow of these pathways so the indoor air and radon is pushed out rather than brought into the house. The best way to force radon out of the house is to increase ventilation.

A contractor who specializes in ridding homes of radon should be hired for the more complex remedies.

Underground Storage Tanks (USTs)

There are approximately 4 million *underground storage tanks* (USTs) in the United States. The ones that are leaking are called *leaking underground storage tanks* (LUSTs).

In September 1988, the EPA issued its technical requirements rule (53 FR 37082-37212), which was mandated under the Resource Conservation and Recovery Act (RCRA) legislation–Subtitle I, passed in 1984. These rules cover about half of the estimated 4 million USTs. Not covered by these regulations are several million domestic heating oil tanks (HOTs), farm tanks, flow-through process tanks, and storage tanks situated on or above the floor of underground areas.

All USTs that have been installed since December 1988 fall under federal regulation and older tanks now have to meet these standards within the next 10 years. Tanks must be equipped with devices that prevent spills and overfills, be corrosion-protected, and be equipped with an EPA leak detection system.

Apparent Indications of Possible USTs

It is impossible to determine just from observation whether there are or have been USTs on or nearby the subject property. This can be determined only by testing for USTs by a qualified UST or an environmental inspector.

UREA Formaldehyde Insulation

16.13 → According to the EPA, *urea formaldehyde foam insulation* (UFFI) is a thermal insulation material that is no longer used because of formaldehyde gas emission. UFFI is a thermal insulation material that is no longer used because of formaldehyde gas emission.

16.12 →
16.14 → After the Korean War, UFFI was blown into the walls of older homes to improve insulation qualities. Because of the problems, UFFI has not been used since 1980. Since formaldehyde gas emissions from UFFI decrease with time, most houses insulated with UFFI no longer have significant source of formaldehyde gas.

The debate as to potential health effects resulting from living in UFFI homes continues. A March 3, 1986 report by the National Cancer Institute (NCI) added fuel to this debate when it found little evidence that formaldehyde causes cancer among the more than 1.3 million workers who are regularly exposed to it in more than 50,000 factories. Many scientists feel that three to four years after UFFI is installed, formaldehyde emissions become minimal and pose little human health risk.

Lead and Lead Paint

Lead was a common material used in paints made prior to World War II. Since then, the use of lead house paint was significantly reduced, but the use of lead in paint did not stop completely until 1978. Even after that date, lead paint often was sold or used. Lead paint commonly exists in low income housing, but it exists in private housing as well. According to a study by the Federal Department of Housing, 75 percent of the privately owned homes built before 1980 contain lead-based paint. Harmful amounts of lead can get into the air from lead paint when it flakes or chips or is scraped, sanded, or heated with an open flame as part of a paint removal process.

The lead paint does not need to be obviously chipping to cause a hazard, but may be rubbed off from friction surfaces such as window casings or doorjambs. Once lead dust gets into the air, it can be inhaled into the body. Ingesting lead paint chips or breathing lead dust is especially hazardous for children. As lead dust settles on the floor, it is reintroduced into the air each time the carpets or rugs are swept or vacuumed. Particles of lead are so fine they can pass through a vacuum cleaner filter and return into the house air. Lead-contaminated soils, found near buildings that were frequently painted and scraped, are also a health hazard. Lead-contaminated soils can harm children who play in the dirt or the people who consume vegetables grown in contaminated soils.

16.15➤

How Health Is Affected by Lead

An elevated level of lead in the blood stream is a serious health hazard. Lead poisoning, even at low levels, can cause detrimental health effects such as mental retardation, learning disabilities, and behavioral problems. In response to this danger, which many believe to be the most serious environmental hazard of our time, Congress passed the Residential Lead-Based Paint Hazard Reduction Act in 1992. The act requires owners or renters of target housing (built before 1978) to disclose the presence of lead-based paint, provide a lead hazard information pamphlet to prospective purchasers and renters, and permit a purchaser a 10-day period to conduct a risk assessment or inspection for the presence of lead-based hazards.

The regulations define lead-based paint as paint that contains lead in excess of 1.0 milligrams by centimeter squared or 0.5 percent by dry weight. Further, any contract for the sale or lease of housing affected by the act must contain a lead warning statement.

Detection of Lead

There are two ways to measure the lead content of paint. The first is to physically remove paint chips or dust and send the samples to a laboratory for analysis. Lab analysis is the only method available for testing soil. The other increasingly popular testing method is to measure the lead content of paint still in place by using an X-ray fluorescence gun.

Abatement of Lead

Many states already have laws requiring the abatement of lead paint. Merely repainting the surfaces with a lead-free paint is insufficient; the lead paint must be encapsulated or removed. Abatement can be a costly procedure, requiring the replacement of woodwork and windows. To safely remove lead paint from a dwelling, workers must wear protective clothing and respirator masks. It is standard procedure to vacuum all surfaces with a HEPA vacuum cleaner, wash the lead-covered surfaces with detergent after the paint has been removed by scraping or sanding, and then vacuum the surfaces a second time.

Disposal of lead-based paint wastes must be done according to local and federal lead disposal requirements. Lead paint waste may be considered a hazardous waste.

Indoor Air Pollution

Surveys indicate that the pollutant levels within the average U.S. home are higher than those in the air outside the home. These surveys also suggest that the level of pollutants is often potentially harmful to the occupants.

Most people spend approximately 90 percent of their time indoors. There-fore, the quality of the indoor air they breathe has a potentially significant ef-fect on their health. Ironically, people who are most exposed to indoor air pollutants are, because of their older age and poorer health, the people who are most susceptible to the adverse effects of indoor air pollutants.

Outdoor air enters and leaves a building in three ways:

16.19→

> 1. Infiltration: where the air flows through construction joints and cracks around windows and doors, in the foundation, or from crawl spaces or other areas under the building
>
> 2. Natural ventilation: where air enters through open windows and doors
>
> 3. Mechanical ventilation: where a variety of mechanical de-vices ranging from small window fans to complex computer controlled heating and air conditioning systems are used

The rate at which outside air replaces indoor air is called the air exchange rate. When there is little infiltration, natural ventilation, or mechanical ven-tilation, the air exchange rate is low and the amount of indoor air pollution can increase.

The harmful effects of indoor air pollutants fall into two categories: those experienced immediately after exposure and those that do not show up for a long period of time after exposure to the pollutants.

Some of the immediate symptoms people experience after either a single or repeated exposure to air pollutants are irritation of the eyes, irritation of the nose, irritation of the throat, headaches, dizziness, fatigue, and nausea.

These symptoms are often of short duration and may be alleviated by eliminating exposure to the source of the pollutant. The likelihood of developing any of these symptoms varies from person to person and is often related to age and health.

There is evidence that people can become sensitized to biological pollutants after repeated exposure. This also appears to be true for exposure to chemical pollutants. More serious health problems connected with exposure to indoor air pollutants show up only after repeated exposure over a long period of time. These long-term effects include emphysema and other respiratory diseases, heart disease, and cancer.

The most common way to identify the presence of indoor air pollutants is by the immediate effect they have on people who become exposed to them. Symptoms often appear after a person moves into a new home or workplace, after remodeling, after refurnishing, or after a building has been treated with pesticides.

Tobacco Smoke

16.16 ➤ Tobacco smoke comes from cigarettes, pipes, and cigars. Stop people from smoking in the building. Nonsmokers' exposure to environmental tobacco smoke is called passive smoking, secondhand smoking, or involuntary smoking. More and more people refuse to be in buildings where smoking is permitted.

Biological Contaminants

Biological contaminants include bacteria, mold and mildew, viruses, animal dander, cat saliva, mites, cockroaches, and pollen.

Be careful when using cool mist or ultrasonic humidifiers. Keep basements dry through the use of a dehumidifier. Clean and disinfect basement floor drains regularly. These can become the breeding ground for biological contaminants. They should be cleaned frequently and filled with fresh clean water daily.

Thoroughly dry and clean water-damaged carpets and other building materials as soon as possible after they become wet and damaged. Keep the building clean. Dust mites, pollens, animal dander, and other allergy-causing agents can be reduced although not completely eliminated by regular, thorough cleaning. Unfortunately, vacuuming can stir up some airborne biological contaminants. People who are allergic to these pollutants should avoid vacuuming and leave the building when a vacuum cleaner is being used.

Carbon Monoxide

Carbon monoxide is a gas produced by combustion from unvented kerosene and gas heaters, leaking chimneys and furnaces, down drafting from wood stoves and fireplaces, gas stoves, automobile exhaust from attached garages, and tobacco smoke.

Take special precautions when operating fuel-burning, unvented space heaters. If they are used, follow the manufacturer's instructions, use the appropriate fuel, and keep the heater properly adjusted.

Install and use exhaust fans over cooking stoves and ranges and keep the burners properly adjusted. Never use a gas stove to heat a home.

Be sure the flue is fully opened when you use a fireplace (especially a gas fireplace). Keep wood stove emission to a minimum by using stoves which are certified to meet EPA standards.

Have central air-handling systems, which include furnaces, flues, and chimneys, inspected annually. Repair any cracks or other damaged parts and change furnace filters monthly.

Organic gases come from paint, paint strippers, solvents, wood preservatives, aerosol sprays, cleaners and disinfectants, moth repellents, air fresheners, stored fuels, automotive products, hobby supplies, and dry-cleaned clothing.

Products that emit organic gases should be used sparingly in well-vented areas following the manufacturer's instructions. Store them in well-ventilated areas, safely out of the reach of children. Because they can leak, it is advisable to dispose of partially full containers of old or unneeded chemicals.

Keep exposure to paint strippers, adhesive removers, aerosol spray paints, and pesticide spray "bombs" to a minimum. They contain methylene chloride and other harmful chemicals. Keep exposure to newly dry-cleaned clothes to a minimum as they are cleaned with perchloroethylene, a suspected carcinogen.

Radon, urea formaldehyde foam insulation (UFFI), asbestos, and pesticides are covered separately in this chapter.

Outside Air Pollution

Outdoor air pollution ranges from things that smell bad like low tide and salt marshes, piles of rotting garbage, and many wastes from manufacturing operations to air pollutants like carbon monoxide, which is both odorless and deadly.

Some areas of the country are known for their severe air pollution conditions. One well-known example is the Los Angeles, California, basin. Studies made by the American Lung Association demonstrate that, in Los Angeles, there is a direct connection between air pollution and acute upper respiratory infections, influenza, bronchitis and other lung diseases, allergic disorders, and heart and vascular disease. Another large study by the American Lung Association indicated a substantial rise in the number of children hospitalized for asthma and eczema as a result of air pollution.

Air pollutants occur in the form of either particulate matter or gases. Many air pollutants of both forms are harmful to humans. Some air pollutants such as sulfur oxides eat away at bridges, building facades, and sculptures. Even crops can be damaged by polluted air.

According to the EPA, wood smoke is waste. Any smoke that escapes from your woodstove or fireplace unburned is wasted fuel that will stick in your chimney as creosote or be released as air pollution. An old or poorly installed woodstove can result in higher maintenance costs, greater risk of smoke in your home, and more environmental pollution. It could cause a house fire.

Properly installed EPA-certified woodstove and fireplace inserts offer many benefits. They burn wood efficiently and more safely, and heat your home effectively with much less smoke. With EPA-certified woodstoves and fireplace inserts, you should see only a thin wisp of steam coming from your chimney.

16.17 → Another major air polluter is automobiles. According to an EPA pamphlet entitled *Do You Own a Car?*, "Motor vehicles contribute more than one half of the total man-made air pollution in this country. They emit nearly three-quarters of the total amount of the poisonous gas carbon monoxide. They also emit over one third of the hydrocarbons and one third of the oxides of nitrogen, two major causes of the unhealthy smog that hangs over a great many of our cities."

According to EPA, the Northeast has the most problems caused by acid rain. Prevailing wind patterns subject the Northeast to transported air pollutants year round. Granite bedrock geology and related soils leave large sections of the Northeast with little natural defense against acid precipitation. Lakes, streams, and drinking water supplies naturally low in alkalinity have little ability to neutralize the acid and buffer its effects.

Wetlands

16.18 → Wetlands are lands where saturation with water is the dominant factor determining the nature of soil development and the types of plant and animal communities living in the soil and on its surface.

Historically, wetlands have been subject to dumping, filling, and draining, with little thought given to the consequences caused by these activities. Only relatively recently has the role of wetlands, bogs, floodplains, and swamps become more fully understood in maintaining and improving environmental quality.

Agriculture accounts for the majority of wetlands destruction, being responsible for 87 percent during the last century. Today, it is estimated that wetlands are disappearing across the United States at a rate of 100,000 to 125,000 acres yearly.

The major piece of federal wetland legislation is Section 404 of the Clean

Water Act (33 U.S.F. 1251 et seq.), which stipulates that a permit must be obtained from the U.S. Army Corps of Engineers by individuals or businesses interested in altering wetlands through dredging or filling. This includes most ditching, land clearing, and land leveling activities; and construction of levees, dikes, dams, and most roads along waterways.

Coastal Wetlands

The ecology of the wetlands that lie along the coasts of the United States is strongly affected by the adjoining seas. The salt content of the water and the rise and fall of the tides influence the types of plants that grow here in salt marshes and the creatures that live among their roots and stalks.

A special value of coastal wetlands is their ability to soften the force of hurricanes and help protect people and their homes from winter storms. Both environmentally and economically, wetlands may do a better job of damage control than man-made sea walls.

Wetland Regulation

Activities within wetland and watercourse boundaries need to be prudently regulated. These regulations ensure an orderly and fair process to balance the need for the economic growth and the use of land with the need to protect its environment and ecology. Wetland regulation occurs under a variety of federal laws in addition to the Clean Water Act.

Mold

Mold is the latest in a series of environmental hazards that have caught the attention of the public and has affected the value of real estate. The most authoritative source of information about mold is the Centers for Disease Control and Prevention (CDC), which is the U.S. federal agency mandated to protect the health of the population by providing credible information to enhance health decisions.

Molds are microscopic fungi that live on plant or animal matter. No one knows how many species of fungi exist, but estimates range from tens of thousands to perhaps three hundred thousand or more. Most are filamentous organisms and the production of spores is characteristic of fungi in general. These spores can be air-, water-, or insect-borne. Some common indoor molds are cladosprium, penicillium, alternaria, aspergillus, and mucor.

Some people are sensitive to molds. For these people, exposure to molds can cause symptoms such as nasal stuffiness, eye irritation, or wheezing. Some people, such as those with serious allergies to molds, may have more severe reactions. Severe reactions may include fever and shortness of breath.

People with chronic illnesses, such as obstructive lung disease, may develop mold infections in their lungs.

Molds are found in virtually every environment and can be detected both indoors and outdoors year round. Mold growth is encouraged by warm and humid conditions. Indoors they can be found where humidity levels are high, such as basements or showers. Sensitive individuals should avoid areas that are likely to have mold. Inside homes, mold growth can be slowed by keeping humidity levels below 50 percent and ventilating showers and cooking areas. Mold growth can be removed with commercial products or a weak bleach solution (1 cup of bleach in 1 gallon of water). In situations where mold exposure is unavoidable, sensitive people should wear a tight-fitting face mask.

Generally, it is not necessary to identify the species of mold growing in a residence, and the CDC does not recommend routine sampling for molds. Current evidence indicates that allergies are the types of diseases most often associated with molds. Since the susceptibility of individuals can vary greatly because of either the amount or the type of mold, sampling and culturing are not reliable in determining health risk. No matter what type of mold is present, you should arrange for its removal. Furthermore, reliable sampling for mold can be expensive, and standards for judging what is and what is not an acceptable or tolerable quantity of mold have not been established.

A commonsense approach should be used for any mold contamination existing inside buildings and homes.

Excess Noise (Noise Pollution)

Excess noise is unpleasant and can even cause physical damage to the body. A brief exposure to sound at the level of 140 to 150 decibels can rupture the eardrums. Steady exposure to ninety decibels of sound, the level of traffic noise in the city, can cause permanent hearing loss. Properties that are subject to excess noise often suffer a loss in value.

There are many sources of excess noise. Airplanes, trains, and automobiles create large amounts of excess noise. Industries, mining, construction, military bases, sports complexes, entertainment facilities, and shopping centers are other common causes of excess noise.

The federal government now regulates noise. This began with the control of aircraft noise with the Federal Aviation Act of 1958. Occupational noise was regulated by the Occupational Safety and Health Act of 1970 and, most recently, the Noise Control Act of 1972 regulated noise levels of manufactured products.

Various individual states and communities also have noise pollution control laws. Some communities have secured noise-measuring devices and are issuing summons to those who exceed the local limits.

Electromagnetic Radiation

"Health issues that affect our living environment often become important to relocation professionals as home purchasers seek redress for real or perceived harm they have suffered due to characteristics in their homes."

This is the opening sentence from an article "Electromagnetic Radiation, A New Hazardous Substance Issue for Relocation?" which appeared in the November, 1990 issue of *Mobility,* the magazine of the Employee Relocation Council. The author, Ronald J. Passaro, is President of Res-I-Tec., a home inspection company and the founder of the American Society of Home Inspectors.

16.20 ➤ This article points out that newspapers are carrying stories about the growing concern over the perceived hazards of radiation, high-voltage power lines, emissions from radio and television station transmitters, video display terminals (VDTs), microwave ovens, television sets, and the dangers to health from all sources of electromagnetic radiation. Passaro also says that as long as a significant number of people think electromagnetic radiation is harmful, it may affect the value of any property that is exposed to what is perceived to be excess amounts.

Recently there has been much media attention about the growing concern over the perceived hazards of high-voltage power lines, emissions from radio and television station transmitters, electric blankets, computer terminals, microwave ovens, television sets, and the general danger from electromagnetic radiation.

Electromagnetic fields are a natural phenomenon and are generated in large amounts by the geomagnetic field of the earth. They also come to the earth from the sun and the stars. Field strength varies from place to place depending on a variety of factors—some natural such as the iron ore content found in the soil and some man-made such as the iron and steel in buildings, bridges, etc.

16.21 ➤ The unit of measurement of electromagnetic radiation is called a *gauss* after a German mathematician, Carl Friedrich Gauss.

There are three broad categories of electromagnetic radiation. High-frequency waves include those known as ultraviolet and X-rays. Visible light, infrared light, and microwaves are middle-frequency waves. Radio and television transmitters emit low-frequency waves. Extremely low-frequency waves (ELFs) come from high-voltage power lines, any other type of wiring including household wiring, and all electrical appliances.

The evidence that weak electromagnetic radiation is harmful to humans is controversial. One exception is the high-frequency waves that are suspected to be a possible cause of cancer. On the other hand, some scientists believe that there is a good possibility that all electromagnetic waves are harmful and that it is just a matter of time before this will be scientifically proven. In the meantime, many recommend the prudent avoidance of electromagnetic fields—that is, one should not needlessly expose oneself until more is known. In his article Passaro points out that, as long as a significant number of people think that electromagnetic radiation is harmful, it may affect the value of any property with what is perceived to be excess amounts.

Light Pollution

16.22➤ Light shining onto a property from a nearby source is a form of light pollution. It ranges from occasional headlights of passing automobiles to large amounts of light from sports complexes, shopping centers and malls, parking lots, and so on. Often it is possible to screen a property for some of these objectionable sources of light.

Waste Heat

Power plants, nuclear plants of all types, steel mills, chemical plants, refineries, and a variety of other industrial and commercial properties produce waste heat. This heat is discharged into the air or into bodies of water. So far there is little evidence that waste heat is harmful to humans. However, fish and other wildlife may be adversely affected. There is a possibility that a property would suffer some environmental harm if it were near a source of excess waste heat discharge.

Acid Mine Drainage

Acid mine drainage is a significant source of pollution in the United States, but it is relatively unknown because it usually occurs in isolated areas of the country, where mining operations are carried out.

Agricultural Pollution

There are millions of people in the United States who consider themselves farmers. Regulating farm policies is primarily the responsibility of the U.S. Department of Agriculture (USDA). A new national farm policy is written every five years by Congress. The ostensible purpose is to ensure abundant and cheap food for the nation.

Environmental experts believe that the national farm policy forces many farmers to farm in a way that is environmentally unsafe. The reality is that many farms are major sources of agricultural pollution. They pollute not only their own land but also surrounding properties.

Major sources of pollution on farms are the many pesticides used for bug and weed control, fertilizers, animal waste, and fuels. When these chemicals get into the groundwater, they can travel many miles, spreading the pollution wherever they go.

For real estate professionals, agricultural pollution presents two basic problems: how it affects any agricultural property and how it affects the nonagricultural properties that may be subject to agricultural pollution emanating from nearby agricultural properties.

Geological Hazards

16.23→ Every parcel of real estate is an integral part of the surface of the earth, which is constantly changing. These changes are evidenced by erosion of the coastlines, erosion of our farmlands, landslides, earthquakes, and volcanic activity. They create geological hazards, which threaten property and human life.

Erosion

The movement of the land surface from one place to another by water or wind is called *erosion*. Some of its causes are fanning, mining, construction activities, and a wide variety of other activities of mankind. It is also a natural process caused by flooding, breaking up of cliffs, and the washing away of dunes and beaches.

Volcanic Eruption

Some of the most devastating natural disasters have been the result of volcanic eruption. Currently, lava flows in Hawaii are destroying properties as their owners stand by watching helplessly. The eruption of Mount St. Helen's a few years ago damaged properties for miles around. Volcanic eruptions can occur suddenly without warning almost anywhere, but they usually occur in areas known to have a history of volcanic activity. Volcanic eruptions may consist of lava, ash, cinder, and mud flows.

Earthquakes

Serious life-threatening earthquakes have occurred at least a half dozen times in California this century. (San Francisco in 1906 and 1990, Long Beach in 1933, San Fernando in 1971, and Whittier in 1987). Lesser earthquakes have occurred all over the country. About 70 percent of California land area is in or relatively adjacent to a fault zone.

Fault Creep

16.24➤ Not all fault movement results in violent earthquakes. *Fault creep* is the gradual displacement of the rocks along a fault line. The forces they create cannot be halted by any means known at this time. A typical fault creeps about a half-inch per year. This is enough to substantially damage concrete foundations, street paving, sidewalks, tennis courts, pools, and so on.

Tsunami

16.25➤ When an earthquake takes place under the ocean, it can produce a tidal wave also called a *tsunami* in the parts of the world where they are common. Some of these waves are very high and have caused tremendous loss of life and damage to property.

Subsidence

16.26➤ The surface of land (called *subsidence*) may drop away for a variety of reasons. Many of these drops are caused by human activities such as the withdrawal of groundwater for irrigation and drinking purposes or taking of gas, oil, coal, and other mined ores out of the earth and not replacing it with something else to hold up the ground. Natural causes are hydrocompaction and the oxidation of peat.

Landslides

16.27➤ Landslides are caused when rocks, soil, fill, and vegetation work loose from the side of a hill as a result of an earthquake, rain, snow, or any other reason, and tumble down the mountain or hillside. Properties on the sides of hills and in the valleys below them are also in some degree of danger. Even an occasional loose rock can do considerable damage and a major slide can wipe out property and endanger human and animal life. Not all landslides are rapid. Some move only a few inches per year.

Nearby Hazardous Property

Anytime there is a nearby hazardous property, there is a possibility that whatever is making the nearby property hazardous will be carried through the groundwater or by other means to adjacent properties.

Infectious Medical Waste

Infectious medical waste describes waste generated through the provision of health care. Every year, over 500,000 tons of medical waste are generated by hospitals and other health care facilities, such as nursing homes.

Currently, however, the EPA issues guidelines and regulations on infectious waste transportation, storage, and disposal. Compliance is optional. Most states have stepped into this regulatory void by passing specific laws controlling infectious wastes, usually by designating them as another category of controlled wastes.

Pesticides

16.28► *Pesticide* is a generic term for any chemical used to control or destroy pests such as insects, rodents, and weeds. The use of pesticides since World War II has had a profound impact on human life. Pesticides helped launch the Green Revolution, which led to record crop production in the industrialized world. In some third-world areas, they played a critical role in fighting the spread of insect-borne diseases such as malaria.

Unfortunately, the advances achieved through pesticide use have been bought at a cost. Pesticides can be harmful when consumed or absorbed by living creatures. The use of chemicals such as DDT and chlordane has been identified as the cause of substantial damage to human health and to the surrounding environment. In reality, nearly every pesticide can have deleterious effects.

By 1972, the EPA gained the sole authority to register pesticides for use in the United States through the *Federal Insecticide, Fungicide, and Rodenticide Act* (FIFRA). Under FIFRA, the EPA conducts tests of submitted pesticides to determine the toxicity and environmental effects of the chemical(s) involved. In making the decision whether or not to grant registration, the risks of each pesticide tested are balanced against the benefits of its use if made available. As of this date, about 30,000 pesticide products have been registered by the EPA under FIFRA.

The purpose of the federal regulation of pesticides is to prevent any serious health damage from occurring. Nevertheless, even the legal use of pesticides can be damaging to health and the integrity of the environment. Fortunately, many approaches can be taken to reduce pesticide use and exposure.

Termiticides

Termiticides are part of a pesticide group whose purpose is to eliminate termites and protect the wood products on which they feed. Termiticides protect the wood in buildings, fences, and porches from the ravages of insects. Without protection, termite infestations would seriously reduce the effective lives of many wood structures and require great expenditures for maintenance and repair.

Termiticides are used by injection into soil and crawl space, filling a protective trench outside the house and/or injecting into hollow-block walls and creating a chemical barrier between building wood and the termite.

Chemical control of termites began after World War II with the marketing of chlordane, heptachlor, aldrin, and dieldrin, all from the family of organic chemicals known as cyclodienes. As of 1983, all of these chemicals were banned from further use in the United States by the EPA.

Chemical Storage and Storage Drums

16.29➤ Whenever chemicals are stored anywhere on or nearby a property, there is a potential for environmental pollution by the chemicals. Not all steel drums and drums made of other materials contain chemicals or other hazardous substances. Unfortunately many users use 55-gallon steel storage drums for illegal chemical storage because they do not want to pay for legal removal of the chemicals. Large storage areas filled with drums are suspect at any manufacturing or processing facility. The risk is that over time the drums will begin to leach toxic materials into the ground and groundwater.

Pipelines

Natural gas and gasoline pipelines have been known to explode and kill those nearby. Oil pipelines can leak and cause environmental damage. There are enough people who are concerned about living near pipelines to cause a negative impact on the value of some properties that are located near them.

Phases of Environmental Inspection

Anyone who purchases a property without an environmental inspection is taking what many people think is an unnecessary financial risk.

For a single-family residence the best thing to do is to have an appraisal, home inspection, and some environmental inspections. One good reason for RESPs to carry professional liability insurance is that, should they not be able to prove they gave this advice to the buyer and environmental problems are discovered on a property they sold, they may be subject to a lawsuit for damages.

At an absolute minimum every home buyer should be encouraged to have the water tested (especially if it is not from a public water company). If there is a well and septic system, they should be tested. Houses built before 1979 should be tested for lead. The safest thing any home buyer can do is have a Phase I environmental inspection. Reality is they rarely do.

When it comes to investment, commercial, and industrial property, the agents should secure written proof that they have recommended a Phase I environmental inspection.

A *Phase I environmental inspection* is designed to evaluate the present condition of the property and determine the likelihood of a release having occurred. The major sources of Phase I information include site contacts, historical information, published information, regulatory information about the site and surrounding areas, and a site walk-over survey with a particular emphasis on likely contaminant sources. If Phase I information suggests the possibility that a release of hazardous material has occurred or other environmental problems exist, a Phase II investigation should be executed.

A *Phase II environmental inspection* is designed to determine if there has been an on-site release and should assist the parties in a transfer in evaluating their respective risks. A Phase II inspection includes on-site environmental sampling and laboratory analysis. It also may require extensive sampling, and may be conducted in several stages to more effectively obtain the required information. It is extremely important that Phase II be designed to explore the likely sources of contamination defined in Phase I.

A *Phase III environmental inspection* should be designed to define the degree, extent, and rate of migration of any on-site release, and to evaluate the potential impact on human safety of the environment. Phase III investigations may require extensive field activities and sampling at the site and may be conducted in several stages to more effectively obtain the required information.

SUMMARY

Millions of properties are affected by hazardous substances and detrimental environmental conditions. The government has established the EPA to regulate potential sources of future pollution, clean up existing pollution, and educate the public about hot environmental hazards that affect their health and safety.

This chapter summarized what the major hazards are, how they affect people, and how they can be identified and abated or avoided. Many real estate professionals are finding that a good understanding of environmental issues is essential to working in this field.

Buyers and sellers have responsibilities regarding environmental exposure and disclosure, and the laws regarding both are changing rapidly. Keeping current in this rapidly changing area of real estate is a challenge, but it is also necessary to protect everyone involved in real estate transactions.

REVIEW QUESTIONS

16.1 One of the most dangerous substances humans can ingest that is found in drinking water is:

A. Fluorides

B. Iron

C. Copper

D. Lead

16.2 Drinking water can be contaminated by:

A. Radon

B. PCBs

C. Dioxins

D. All of the above

16.3 Most people in the United States get their drinking water from:

A. Large regulated public water companies

B. Small public water companies

C. Wells

D. Private water supplies

16.4 The term *liquid waste* is used by environmentalists to describe:

A. Waste from chemical plants

B. Waste from power plants

C. Waste from farm runoff

D. None of the above

16.5 The most satisfactory way to dispose of liquid waste is in:

A. A cesspool

B. A septic system

C. A municipal sewer system

D. All of the above

16.6 What percentage of American septic systems are estimated by health experts to have a major malfunction at least once a year?

A. 25 percent

B. 50 percent

C. 75 percent

D. Almost 100 percent

16.7 The National Properties List (NPL) has listed:

A. All of the identified suspected hazardous waste sites in the United States

B. Over 10,000 suspected hazardous waste sites in the United States

C. Over 35,000 suspected hazardous waste sites in the United States

D. None of the above

16.8 The kind of asbestos that is dangerous to human health is:
A. Friable asbestos
B. Non-friable asbestos
C. Both of above
D. None of the above

16.9 The EPA's danger level for radon in the home is:
A. 1 picocurie per liter
B. 4 picocuries per liter
C. 10 picocuries per liter
D. 40 picocuries per liter

16.10 Which of these states have not reported high levels of radon?
A. Arizona, Utah, and Mississippi
B. Arizona, North Dakota, and Utah
C. The New England states
D. None of the above

16.11 Radon is:
A. Animal
B. Vegetable
C. Radioactive gas
D. None of the above

16.12 Urea formaldehyde foam insulation (UFFI) was first used as a building material:
A. Right after the Civil War
B. Between World War I and World War II
C. Between World War II and the Korean War
D. After the Korean War

16.13 UFFI stands for:
A. Uniform friable foam insulation
B. Urea formaldehyde foam insulation
C. Urea friable foam insulation
D. None of the above

16.14 UFFI is usually installed by:
A. Nailing it between the studs
B. Laying it down over the ceiling studs
C. Blowing it in between the wall studs
D. None of the above

16.15 Lead paint is most harmful when:
A. Eaten by farm animals who are sold later for their meat
B. Eaten by small children
C. Gotten on the skin and left unwashed
D. Eaten by elderly people who touch it and don't wash their hands

16.16 Which of these are common indoor air pollutants?
A. Tobacco smoke
B. Biological contaminants
C. Carbon monoxide
D. All of the above

16.17 Which of these are common outdoor air pollutants?

A. Tobacco smoke

B. Biological contaminants

C. Carbon monoxide

D. All of the above

16.18 Wetlands are defined as areas where:

A. cattails are the primary growth

B. skunk cabbage is the primary growth

C. saturation with water is the dominant factor

D. None of the above

16.19 Outdoor air enters a building by:

A. Positive pressure

B. Infiltration

C. Dispersal

D. Discharge

16.20 Electromagnetic radiation is emitted from:

A. All electrical appliances

B. High-voltage power lines

C. Television sets

D. All of the above

16.21 The measurement of electromagnetic radiation is:

A. A picocurie

B. A gauss

C. A microwatt

D. None of the above

16.22 Common sources of light pollution are:

A. The headlights of oncoming cars

B. Sports complexes

C. Shopping centers

D. All of the above

16.23 Which of the following are considered to be geological hazards?

A. Erosion

B. Volcanic eruption

C. Earthquakes

D. All of the above

16.24 Fault creeps are gradual displacements:

A. Of rocks along a fault line

B. That don't cause property damage

C. That can be halted with fault proof construction

D. Are always a result of a violent earthquake

16.25 Tsunamis start from earthquakes under the sea, and:

A. Their waves rarely cause much damage

B. Their waves have caused a great deal of damage

C. Are unknown on the west coast

D. None of the above

16.26 Sinking of the surface of the land is:
- A. Sufferance
- B. Subsidence
- C. Severalty
- D. None of the above

16.27 Landslides:
- A. Can occur very quickly
- B. Can occur very slowly
- C. Can be caused by an earthquake
- D. All of the above

16.28 *Pesticide* is a generic term for any chemical used to control or destroy:
- A. Insects
- B. Rodents
- C. Weeds
- D. All of the above

16.29 A common means of storing hazardous chemicals until they can be disposed of is:
- A. Special chemical-proof fiberglass tanks
- B. 25-gallon EPA plastic containers
- C. 55-gallon steel storage drums
- D. All of the above

ANSWERS

The answer to each question is indicated by the letters A, B, C, or D. The explanation of the answer is indicated by the page number and an arrow that points to the appropriate paragraph on the page.

Q 16.1 D Page 307	Q 16.7 D Page 311	Q 16.13 B Page 317	Q 16.19 B Page 319	Q 16.25 B Page 328
Q 16.2 D Page 308	Q 16.8 A Page 313	Q 16.14 C Page 317	Q 16.20 D Page 325	Q 16.26 B Page 328
Q 16.3 A Page 306	Q 16.9 B Page 315	Q 16.15 B Page 318	Q 16.21 B Page 325	Q 16.27 D Page 328
Q 16.4 D Page 308	Q 16.10 D Page 315	Q 16.16 D Page 320	Q 16.22 C Page 326	Q 16.28 D Page 329
Q 16.5 C Page 308	Q 16.11 C Page 315	Q 16.17 C Page 322	Q 16.23 D Page 327	Q 16.29 D Page 330
Q 16.6 B Page 309	Q 16.12 D Page 317	Q 16.18 C Page 322	Q 16.24 A Page 328	

CHAPTER 17

Landlord and Tenant Relationships

HISTORY OF LANDLORD AND TENANT RELATIONSHIPS

The relationship today between those who own property and those who rent property goes back to the relationship that existed in England before the United States was founded. The monarchs owned everything and granted the use of their land to lords and other favored people. The lords leased the land (hence the term *landlord*) to the tenants who farmed the land and paid rent to the landlord.

Today a substantial amount of the property in the United States is not owner occupied. It is rented (with or without a written lease) to those who occupy the property. Most of them in turn pay rent to the owner (landlord).

Generally there are three different positions to consider. There are owners, managers, and tenants. There are also agents who negotiate the arrangements between these parties.

This chapter will cover the vocabulary used in landlord, manager, and tenant relationships and the legal papers used to reflect the relationship between landlord and tenant as these are the subjects that are tested on the real estate agent license exams. Because over 35 million people rent the premises in which they live, this chapter will stress the documentation used for residential leasing. However, it will also include information about other types of leases.

Pay careful attention to the terms that are used in this chapter as many of the questions on the exam will test your knowledge of this specialized vocabulary, which may be unfamiliar to you.

LEASEHOLD ESTATES

17.1 ➤ A lease divides the interests in the property between the property for a specific period of time. In broad terms, during this period the owner(s) or landlord(s) or lessor(s) have the right to receive rent and have an obligation to 17.2 ➤ maintain the property and pay agreed-upon expenses. At the end of the lease the landlord gets back all the rights including the right to occupy the property. This is called the *reversion*. The tenant(s) or lessee(s) have the right to occupy the property and not to be interfered with. This is known as their *right of quiet enjoyment*. They are obligated to pay rent and whatever ex- 17.3 ➤ penses are specified in the lease. At the end of the lease they return possession of the property to the landlord(s).

17.4 ➤ The tenant's right to occupy the property is called a *leasehold estate*. The two most common types of leasehold estates are *periodic estates* and *estates* 17.5 ➤ *for years*. A month-to-month lease is an example of a periodic estate. It continually renews itself for like periods until either party decides to terminate it. An example of an estate for years is a lease with a specific starting time and a specific conclusion. It does not automatically renew itself. However, it may contain options that provide for renewals under stated conditions.

Two other leasehold categories are *estates at will* and *tenancy at sufferance*. An estate at will can be terminated at any time by the landlord or the tenant. They are not very common. This arrangement is sometimes entered into when a landlord is trying to sell a condominium unit. It is hard to find tenants who are willing to move out whenever the unit is sold, unless the landlord gives them the same right to terminate should they find substitute accommodations.

TYPES OF LEASES AND RENTS

There are a wide variety of leases and no standard way to classify them. One major distinction is the way in which the rent is paid. The other is the type of property being rented. There is a traditional relationship between the type of property and the type of rent a tenant pays. For example, most apartments are rented, with the tenant paying a gross rent. Most shopping center stores are rented on percentage rents. Most land is leased with a net rent payment.

Gross Rent Leases

17.6 ➤ Most residential leases and many other leases are *gross rent leases,* which call for payment of gross rent. The tenant is required to pay a fixed amount of rent each month. The landlord usually pays all the taxes, property hazard and liability insurance, and repairs. Often, the landlord pays for water and sewerage, and the tenant pays for the other utilities. However, alternate arrangements are also common.

Net Rent Leases

17.7 ➤ *Net leases, double net leases, triple net leases,* and *absolute net leases* are all terms used to describe leases where most or all of the expenses of running the property are paid by the lessee or renter. Since these terms are not universal and have different meanings in various areas, it is important that the lease set out exactly which expenses are paid by the lessor and the lessee.

Graduated (Step-up) Leases

17.8 ➤ A *graduated lease,* also known as a *step-up lease,* is one in which the rental amount changes from period to period over the term of the lease. The lease contract specifies that change in the rental amount due. This type of lease is often utilized for new tenants who bargain for rent concessions in the early term of their lease to help them get started at the new location.

Escalated Leases

17.9 ➤ An *escalated lease* is usually a gross lease that provides for rental changes in proportion to changes in the lessor's costs to maintain the property. The escalation is often tied to increases in taxes or other operating expenses.

Indexed Leases

17.10 ➤ An *indexed lease* is one where the rent changes directly in relationship to a published index. For example, if the index increases 4 percent, the rent increases 4 percent. Often, this type of adjustment is made annually. A common index used is the *consumer price index* (CPI) published by the U.S. Department of Labor.

Reappraisal Leases

Reappraisal leases call for the property to be appraised at agreed-upon intervals and the rent adjusted based on the value estimated in the appraisal. Sometimes the lease calls for the appraiser to directly estimate a new rental amount. Other times, the appraiser is asked to estimate the market value of the property, and the lease calls for the rent to be a percentage of estimated market value.

Percentage Leases

Another type of lease is a *percentage lease*, which provides that, in addition to a basic rent, the landlord receives a percentage of the gross sales of the tenant, derived from the operation of the tenant's business on the premises. Some percentage leases give the tenant a credit for the basic rent against the rent calculated from the sales. Others collect the percentage on top of the basic rent. Percentage leases are almost always used for shopping centers and malls. They are very common in rental of retail stores. The amount paid ranges from a few percent paid by anchor stores in shopping malls to 20 percent or more paid by small specialty shops and concessions.

Ground Lease

A lease for land only is called a *ground lease* and the rent paid is *ground rent*. These are typically long-term leases. Often they run from 25 to 99 years. They used to run longer, but many states have laws that say the leases of 100 years or more are actually sales, and the lessor and their estate lose the right of reversion.

Ground leases for residential land are very common in Hawaii, where they have been used for many years. More recently, they have increased in popularity in parts of California and other isolated places in the country. The typical residential ground lease calls for the lessee to pay all the expenses of the property, including the cost to construct the improvements. In Hawaii it is traditional for ground leases to be renewed even when the lease does not call for a renewal. Because of the length of many residential ground leases, some of them contain provisions for rent increases from time to time. Nonresidential ground leases tend to be for shorter periods of time. Their rental arrangement tends to be more complex. They are often indexed or tied to the sales of the lessee's business. One reason they are popular is that land does not depreciate. Investors transferred the ownership of the land to institutions that did not need the tax write-off from depreciation.

Agricultural Leases

Agricultural land is leased using a special agricultural lease, usually on a percentage basis to tenant farmers who pay a percentage of the crop as rent. When the owner of agricultural land is paid by the tenant in cash in advance, it is called *cash rent*. When the rent is a percentage of the crop or a percentage of the profits made on the sale of crops, it is called *sharecropping*.

Oil and Gas Leases

An *oil and gas lease* is a unique form of lease whereby the property owners, in effect, are forming a partnership with someone who will explore for oil and gas on their property. Traditionally, the land owners receive a one-time payment as an inducement to sign the lease. The exploration company then receives the right to drill and explore for oil and gas for a specified period of time. When the exploration is successful, the property owners share in the income received for the oil and gas that is taken off the property.

Sale and Leaseback

A *sale and leaseback* is the result of a transaction wherein property owners sell their property to an investor and immediately lease the property back from the investor so they can continue to use the property. This type of transaction is usually made by business owners who own the property they occupy and use for their business. The owners wish to retain use of the premises, but by selling the real estate they obtain capital they need for their business. There are also potential tax advantages to this type of arrangement. It also can be used to create a retirement device for the owners of the business, who shift the ownership of the real estate from the business to their own personal names.

Sandwich Lease

A *sandwich lease* is a lease agreement created when an original tenant subleases to another tenant, who occupies and uses the premises. The original tenant, in addition to being the lessee, also becomes the sublessor and the new tenant becomes the sublessee. The original tenant is the "sandwich" between the property owner and the sublessee.

Mobile Home Lease

California and other states where there are large numbers of mobile homes have passed special laws that govern the rental of mobile homes and mobile home sites. In the absence of a special statute, the general leasing statutes also apply to mobile homes.

Mobile home parks are subject to the same provisions against discrimination as other residential landlords. Controlling the type and size of the mobile homes in a park is not considered to be discrimination as defined in the fair housing laws.

17.18→   A unique feature of the mobile home law in California is that it limits the reasons a mobile home park owner can terminate a mobile home lease.

Vertical Lease (Mineral Lease)

A property owner usually owns not only the surface of the land but also what is under the land and over the land. In areas where there are valuable

17.19→ minerals under the land, the owner may lease the subsurface mineral rights separately from the surface rights. This is known as a *vertical lease* or *mineral lease*. The rent can be a fixed amount or a percentage of the value of the minerals that are extracted from the land.

Air Rights Lease

Another type of vertical lease is an *air rights lease*. In densely populated areas, the air rights over the land are leased for use separately from the surface rights. The government and railroads are also leasing the air rights over highways and railroad tracks for separate development. The three large apartment complexes on the New York side of the Hudson River entrance to the George Washington Bridge are examples of the leasing and development of air rights over a highway.

CREATING A VALID LEASE

A lease is a written or oral agreement between the landlord and the tenant. Every state has a law called the Statute of Frauds. Most of these statutes require that all leases for one year or more be in writing. Therefore an oral lease for two years is usually not a valid contract. An oral lease for less than a year is a valid contract if the oral agreement contains the required elements to make a valid contract. To eliminate misunderstanding and have a clear understanding of all the parties' obligations to each other, it is a good idea to have all leases in writing.

To be a valid contract, the lease should contain the following elements required in a contract:

- Identification and address of the lessor and lessee
- Description of the property being leased (when the lease is for less than the whole premises, it must clearly describe what part is covered by the lease)
- An offer by the lessor to let the property and an acceptance by the lessee to accept possession and pay rent and agreed upon expenses
- A starting and ending date
- Signatures of the parties who must have the legal capacity to enter into a lease
- As with all contracts, a legal purpose for the lease

TYPICAL LEASE PROVISIONS

Identification of the Parties

It is customary to state the names and addresses (in some areas just the state) of the parties to the lease.

Terms

This is often stated first in number of months and years, and then by stating the commencing and ending dates.

Rents

The total rent, annual rent, and monthly rent are spelled out and also written in figures in many leases. Some rental arrangements are very complex. They are based on a percentage of business done by the tenant. Rents may also be subject to adjustment based on various cost of living indexes.

Late Charges

Some leases call for late charges when the rent is not paid on time. This clause spells out when a late charge is due and how much it will be. This clause often states that the payment of late charges does not preclude the lessor from exercising other rights they have under the lease.

Security Deposit

The amount of the deposit is stated, as well as when it will be returned, who gets the interest it earned, and what the tenant has to do to get the deposit back. Generally the tenant is required to have paid all the rent on time, vacated when required, and surrendered the premises in good condition. There is a difference between a security deposit that is usually returned to the tenant after the premises are vacated and advance rent, which may be used as payment of the final month's rent. Some states have laws that spell out how deposits are handled, especially residential deposits.

Use of Premises

The tenant is restricted to use the premises only for specific purposes. In residential leases, the number of people who may occupy the premises is often stated. For commercial and retail leases, there are often clearly specified uses, such as what products can be sold, processed, manufactured, and so on. Shopping center leases often go into great detail as to how the premises may be used, including the hours of operation, how merchandise may be displayed, and other features.

Pets

Many residential leases try to control the tenant's right to have pets. Some prohibit them completely. Others limit the type, size, and number of pets. Some leases permit pets only when an additional security deposit is given by the lessee.

Keys

This clause spells out how many sets of keys are provided to the tenants, their right to make duplicates, the requirement not to change the locks, the landlord's and management company's right to have keys to the premises, the prohibition of the installation of additional locks to the premises doors, and who will pay for the replacement of lost keys.

Insurance

Many leases require the tenant to carry various kinds of insurance. Some require that the landlord be added to the policy as an additional insured. Some leases require that in addition to the tenant's own property the insurance also cover the property of the landlord.

Repairs

Repair responsibility is usually divided between the landlord and the tenant. Who is responsible for which repairs is spelled out in the lease.

Alterations and Improvements

This provision should spell out what alterations are going to be made by the landlord at the landlord's expense, and what alterations, if any, the tenant will be permitted to make at their own expense.

Services

Typical services provided by the landlord are snow removal, cleaning services, guard services, and so on.

Utilities

The lease should clearly spell out who pays for each of the utilities. When separate metering is not available in multiple tenant buildings, the lease should state on what basis the utility costs will be divided.

Assignment and Subletting

When all of a lessee's right are transferred to another party it is called an *as-*
17.21➤ *signment.* When only part of the lessee's rights are transferred, it is called a *sublet.* The landlord becomes the sublessor, and the new tenant becomes the sublessee. In most cases the assignment or subletting of a lease does not re-
17.20➤ lieve the original tenants of their responsibilities. Most leases prohibit assignment or subletting without the lessor's permission.

Injury or Loss

This clause limits the lessor's responsibility to the tenant for payment of damages caused by loss or damage to the tenant's property or injury of the tenant or any other person injured on the premises. In some states, the lease includes an indemnification clause which states that if the lessor has to pay any damages because of the loss of property or personal injury, the tenant will reimburse the lessor. There is a general principal of law that prohibits anyone from not being liable for their negligence no matter what a contract says. Therefore, the ability to enforce this clause varies from state to state.

Entry of Landlord

The essence of a lease is that the landlord transfers to the tenant the right to use the premises. It is the responsibility of the landlord to make sure that the tenant can use the premises as specified in the lease. Many leases give the landlord the right to enter the premises under certain conditions to make repairs and to show the premises to prospective purchasers of the property or prospective future tenants.

Renewal

Some leases state that they are not renewable. Others provide for renewal only if the tenant gives the landlord notice before some specified time. Others provide automatic renewal unless one or both parties give notice that the lease is terminated. Many leases provide for renewals at adjusted rents.

Option to Purchase

This clause gives the lessee the right to purchase the premises at some time in the future for an established price or a price that is determined by appraisal or some other method. A typical purchase option clause or lease purchase clause contains specific dates during which the option may be exercised by giving notice (and sometimes making a deposit) to the landlord.

Breach

Most of these clauses first state that the failure of the landlord or tenant to comply with the other provisions of the lease constitutes a breach of the lease. Breach clauses also spell out what the lessor may do when the lessee breaches the lease. It often provides that either party must notify the other party of a breach and give them some specified period of time to correct the breach before any further action can be taken. Another common clause is that the party who causes the breach is responsible for the attorney's fees of the other party.

Unless the lease has been drawn or reviewed by an attorney who is familiar with the specific laws in the applicable state, there is a good possibility that the rights spelled out in this clause may conflict with the state laws.

Destruction of the Premises

This clause spells out what happens if the property is destroyed by fire or some other hazard. The clause may state how long the landlord has to repair the property, when the tenant can terminate the lease if the property is not repaired, and whether the landlord has the option of not repairing the property. There are special precedents that apply to agricultural land. In general, the tenant is responsible for rent payments no matter what happens to the land.

Surrender of Premises

This restates the tenant's obligation to surrender the premises in good condition. It often contains the wording that damage caused by normal wear and tear is not the responsibility of the tenant. Other clauses state that the tenant must surrender the premises in the same condition as when they took possession.

Signs, Decals and Posters

This clause controls what signs, decals, posters, and other advertising material may be placed on the premises. It may also require approval by the lessor. The clause may also prohibit or permit the lessor to put a "for sale" or "for rent" sign on the premises during the period when the lessee occupies the premises.

Savings Clause

This is a technical clause that states that if and when some other clause in the lease is found by a court to be invalid, this will not void the rest of the lease.

Notices

This section provides instructions as to where notices required in the lease should be sent and how they must be transmitted. Sometimes certified mail, registered mail, or ordinary mail are required.

Figure 17.1 Typical residential lease.

Residential Lease

Providence, RHODE ISLAND, January 3, 200_

Henry Harrison & Ruth Lambert   , LESSOR, and Diane Becker & Mark Steinhoff, LESSEE, agree as follows:

1. LESSOR leases to LESSEE and LESSEE leases from LESSOR the following premises: Unit # 2115 at Corliss Landing, 555 South Main Street, Providence, R.I. 02903 together with the following furniture and fixtures: _____ washer/dryer

2. The term of this lease shall be   years), __ months commencing February 1, 200_ and terminating January 31, 200_.

3. LESSEE is to pay rent as follows: $ 900.00 payable on the first day of every month in advance. The rent shall be paid at Corliss Landing, 555 So. Main St., Providence, R.I. 02903 or at any other address designated by the LESSOR in writing.

4. LESSEE has deposited with LESSOR $ 1550.00 as security for the full and faithful performance of each and every term, provision, covenant, and condition of this lease. This security deposit will be held by the LESSOR in accordance with the terms and conditions set forth by Rhode Island law. If LESSEE defaults in respect to any of the terms, provisions, covenants, and conditions of this lease, including but not limited to, the payment of rent, to repair damages to the premises caused by the LESSEE, or to clean such premises upon termination of the tenancy, LESSOR may use, apply or return the whole or any part of this security for payment of any or all of the above-mentioned specific purposes. At the expiration of the term of this lease or any extension thereof, the said security deposit or portion thereon shall be returned to the LESSEE in accordance with the tern's and conditions for return of security deposits as set forth by Rhode Island law. It is expressly understood that in no event shall the deposit be used or applied by the LESSEE as a payment of rent.

5. LESSEE agrees to pay for all utilities except water, sewer fees, and ____, which shall be paid for by LESSOR.

6. LESSEE has examined the premises and all furniture and fixtures contained herein, and accepts the same as being clean and in good order, condition and repair, with the following exceptions only: _____.

7. The premises are rented for use only as a residence for a single family and not for more than ____ adults and ____ children. No animal or pet except ____ shall be kept on the premises without LESSOR'S prior written consent.

8. LESSEE shall not disturb, annoy, endanger, or inconvenience other tenants of the building or neighbors, nor use the premises for any immoral or unlawful purposes, nor violate any law or ordinance, nor commit waste or nuisance upon or about the premises.

9. LESSEE acknowledges the receipt of a copy of the LESSOR'S rules and regulations for the property, a copy of which is attached hereto, and by reference incorporated here. LESSEE further acknowledges that he/she has read the same, understands them, and shall observe said rules and regulations.

Figure 17.1 *(Continued)*

10. LESSEE, agrees that during the term of this lease and such further time as he/she occupies the premises, LESSEE will keep the leased premises and all pipes, wires, glass, plumbing, and other equipment and fixtures repaired, and of the same kind, quality, and description, and in such good repair, order and condition as the same are at the beginning of, or may be put in during the term, reasonable wear and tear and damage by unavoidable fire or casualty only excepted.

11. LESSEE agrees to indemnify and save. LESSOR harmless from all liability, loss or damage arising from any nuisance or harm made or suffered on the leased premises by the LESSEE, his/her family, guests, agents or servants or from any carelessness, neglect or improper conduct of any of such persons, including damage to the building or its contents from the leakage of water in or from the leased premises caused or permitted by LESSEE.

12. LESSEE shall not paint nor make alterations of the property without LESSOR'S prior written consent, which shall not be unreasonably withheld.

13. In the event the premises become uninhabitable during the term of this lease, either party may terminate the same upon 30 days written notice.

14. Upon not less than 24 hours advance notice, LESSEE shall make the demised premises available to LESSOR or his authorized agent or representative, for the purpose of entering to make necessary or convenient repairs, and to show the premises to prospective tenants, purchasers, or encumbrancers. In an emergency, LESSOR, his agent or authorized representative may enter the premises at any time without securing prior permission from LESSEE for the purpose of making corrections or repairs to alleviate such emergency. LESSOR shall give LESSEE notice of any entry made to the premises during LESSEE'S absence.

15. LESSEE shall not let or sublet all or any part of the premises nor assign this lease or any interest in it without the prior written consent of LESSOR.

16. If LESSEE abandons or vacates the premises, LESSOR may at his option terminate this lease, re-enter the premises, and remove all property.

17. In the event that any action shall be commenced by either party hereto arising out of, or concerning this lease or any right or obligation derived therefrom, then in addition to all other relief at law or equity, the prevailing party shall be entitled to recover attorney's fees as fixed by the Court.

18. Either party may terminate this lease in the event of a violation of any provision of this lease by the other party in the manner of and as provided by law.

19. The waiver by LESSOR of any breach shall not be construed to be a continuing waiver of any subsequent breach.

20. The LESSOR agrees to allow the LESSEE to give thirty (30) days notice of terminating the lease in the case of change of employment

_____   _____

LESSOR   LESSEE

Henry S Harrison/Ruth Lambert   Diane Becker/Mark Steinhoff

Management

When the property is professionally managed, this clause notifies the tenant that the management company is acting as the representative of the landlord.

Other Conditions

Some leases are many pages long. Often residential leases contain a whole set of rules and regulations about the use of the premises. Shopping center leases go into great detail about how the tenants are expected to run their business and participate with the other tenants and landlord to promote the overall welfare.

Signatures and Acknowledgments

Space is provided for the signatures of all the parties to the lease, witnesses, and notarization where it is used. The use of witnesses and notarization of signatures is based on local law and local custom. Often they are used even when they are not required by law.

Figure 17.1 represents a typical residential lease.

LANDLORD/TENANT LAWS

There are federal and state laws that prohibit discrimination and require special access for the handicapped. They are covered in Chapter 5 in this book.

In many states the legislatures have passed special landlord/tenant laws that apply mostly to residential real estate. These laws generally limit the amount of security deposit that may be required and spell out who will hold the deposit, where it will be held, and what happens to interest that is earned on the deposit.

The laws often require the landlord to maintain the premises in a fit condition for living and require the tenant to keep the unit clean and not damage it beyond normal wear and tear. Some state laws regulate how and when the landlord may enter the premises to make needed repairs and inspections. Some states have separate court divisions to handle disputes between tenants and landlords.

There tends to be less legislation about commercial leases. Traditionally, the court interprets these leases strictly, so it is important for the parties to understand what they are agreeing to when they sign multipage commercial leases.

Contract and Economic Rent

All real estate professionals should be familiar with the difference between contract rent and economic rent. The term *economic rent* is frequently used by appraisers. It is the rent a property will bring in the current market, assuming that the property is vacant and available to be rented. It is the *economic rent* that appraisers primarily use to estimate the value of an income producing property.

17.22 → Contract rent is the amount of rent that is actually being paid by the lessee to the lessor. When a lease is first signed, the contract rent called for by the lease tends to be the economic rent. As time passes, there tends to be a difference between the economic rent and the contract rent. One of the purposes of graduated leases, indexed leases, and percentage leases is to try to eliminate the difference between the contract rent and the economic rent over a period of time. Unfortunately, there is no perfect method of doing this. One of the best ways is to have the rents adjusted periodically based on current appraisals.

Tenant's Breach and Eviction

The most common serious lease breach is the failure of the tenant to pay the agreed-upon rent in a timely manner. Other common causes of breach by the tenant are failure of the tenant to use the property for agreed-upon purposes, interfering with another tenant's use of the property, failure to pay expenses as required by the lease, damaging the property, and failure to maintain the property as called for by the lease. Failure to move out at the end of the lease is also a breach of the lease.

When tenants breach the lease and do not move out, the landlord must initiate a lawsuit to recover any unpaid rent, be reimbursed for any damages suffered because of the tenants' breach, and have the court remove the tenants from the premises. When tenants fail to vacate the premises, they become holdover tenants. The landlord then has a choice of allowing them to remain on a month-to-month basis without a lease, enter into a new lease, or evict the tenants. In many areas, the lawsuit to remove the tenants is called a *suit for possession* (actual eviction). It is also known as an *eviction*. Most states require that the landlord give the tenants notice when they start an eviction lawsuit (often by actual service by a sheriff).

When the landlord obtains an eviction order from the court, the tenants have to vacate the premises. If they fail to do so, the court will take steps to physically remove them from the premises. This is usually accomplished by a bailiff, sheriff, or another court officer.

In some areas, it takes many months to obtain an eviction judgment and even a longer time to get the court to enforce the eviction order. Often, during this time period, the tenants are paying no rent and continue to do whatever act was the cause of the original eviction lawsuit. Some landlords at this point take matters illegally into their own hands. They may shut off utilities, block entrances and exits to the premises, actually go on to the premises that are still occupied by the tenant, or do a variety of other things to harass the tenants. These illegal actions can subject the landlord to criminal punishment.

Landlord's Breach and Constructive Eviction

17.23→ When the landlord fails to keep the property fit for occupancy as required by the lease, and the tenants are forced to move out, this action is called a *constructive eviction.*

Eminent Domain

The government's power to take private property for public use is clearly established in law. When a property that is taken is leased, the tenants may have a right to some of the just compensation from the taking. Normally the government pays for the entire fee simple. Lessees have a leasehold interest called a *leasehold estate,* when their contract rent is less than the economic rent for the property that is taken.

Some leases contain a clause that eliminates the tenants' claim for any compensation from taking. Other leases spell out how the tenants' claim will be determined. When a lease does not contain an eminent domain clause, the tenants usually have a claim for compensation if they can prove that they have a leasehold interest.

Recording Leases

In most areas, leases can be recorded at the same place where deeds and other real estate documents are recorded. Many tenants and their attorneys feel it is not necessary to record a lease, because possession of the property by the lessee serves as notice to the world that the property is occupied by someone other than the owner. A buyer would have to assume there may be a lease and would have to take this into consideration.

In some areas, a *memorandum of lease* is filed instead of a long lease. In a memorandum of lease, the terms of the lease are not disclosed to the public, which is one of the major reasons leases are not filed. Retail stores are an example of tenants who do not like to disclose their leases, which often call for a percentage of sales as rent. They do not want other landlords to know what they are paying, as this information could be used against them in negotiations for alternate space.

RENT CONTROL

Rent control was first instituted during World War I for the stated purpose of discouraging the construction of new housing, because material and labor were scarce, and setting rent ceilings so landlords would not receive excess profits caused by the housing shortage.

During World War II, the federal government and some large cities established rent controls. Most of these World War II rent controls were eliminated after the war. The biggest exception is New York City, where rent control still regulates a substantial portion of the multifamily housing market.

Since the 1970s isolated cities around the country have adopted various forms of rent control in an effort to continue to make city housing available to moderate and low income families. It is hard, except for political reasons, to justify rent control. Most real estate professionals in New York think it fails to serve its stated purpose and leads to unjust enrichment of selected tenants. They also feel it produces a situation when normal building maintenance is often neglected due to low revenues.

SUMMARY

A lease is a contract between a property owner, known as the lessor or landlord, and someone who uses the property, known as the lessee or tenant. The owner has the right to receive rent, and at the end of the lease, gets back all of the rights including the right to occupy the property, called the reversion. The tenant or lessee has the right to occupy the property. This is known as the right of quiet enjoyment. At the end of the lease, the tenant returns possession of the property to the landlord who pays expenses and performs other responsibilities as specified in the lease.

The tenant's right to occupy the property is called a leasehold estate. The two most common types of leasehold estates are periodic estates and estates for years. There are two other leasehold categories called estates at will and tenancy at sufferance.

Each state has laws called the Statute of Frauds, which require that leases of over one year in duration be in writing. A valid lease must contain the same basic elements as any other contract.

There are federal and state laws that prohibit discrimination and require special access for the handicapped. In many states there are special landlord/tenant laws that apply mostly to residential real estate, which limit the amount of security deposit that may be required, spell out who will hold the deposit, where it will be held, and what happens to interest that is earned on the deposit.

The laws often require the landlord to maintain the premises in a fit condition for living and require the tenant to keep the unit clean and not to damage it beyond normal wear and tear. There tends to be less legislation about commercial leases.

There are a variety of different types of rents including gross rents where the landlord pays most of the expenses, step-up and graduated rents, which change over the term of the lease, and indexed rents, which change based on some published index. There are a variety of net leases that call for the tenant to pay all or most of the expenses.

Other less common types of leases are ground leases, where the tenant usually makes and pays for the improvements, and vertical leases for subsurface or air rights.

The rent the tenant pays is called contract rent. What the property would rent for if it were currently available for rent is called economic rent.

When tenants breach a lease either by not paying the rent or not complying with some other lease provision, the landlord must give the tenants notice to cure their default. If they do not, the landlord must bring a court action called an eviction, which asks the court to remove the tenants from the premises and pay damages. A holdover tenant is one who does not leave the premises at the end of the lease. A constructive eviction is when the landlord fails to keep the property fit for occupancy and the tenant is forced to move out.

When a property is taken by eminent domain, the tenant may have a right to some of the just compensation from the taking. Some leases contain a clause that eliminates the tenant's claim for any compensation from an eminent domain taking. Other leases spell out how the tenant's claim will be determined. When a lease does not contain an eminent domain clause, the tenants usually have a claim for compensation if they can prove that they have a leasehold interest.

REVIEW QUESTIONS

17.1 Which of the following is the property owner?
   A. Lessor
   B. Lessee
   C. Sublessee
   D. Sublessor

17.2 Getting the property back at the end of the lease is called the:
   A. Holdover
   B. Reversion
   C. Both of the above
   D. None of the above

17.3 The right of quiet enjoyment means:
   A. No noisy traffic
   B. No noisy airplane traffic overhead
   C. Both of the above
   D. None of the above

17.4 A leasehold estate:
   A. Is the property owner's interest in the property
   B. An ownership estate created by the reversion
   C. Both of the above
   D. None of the above

17.5 A month-to-month lease:
   A. Terminates after the twelfth month of occupancy
   B. Can never go for more than a year
   C. Terminates only by mutual consent of both parties
   D. None of the above

17.6 Most residential apartment leases are:
   A. Net leases
   B. Constructive leases
   C. Gross leases
   D. None of the above

17.7 In which of these net leases does the tenant pay the fewest expenses?
   A. Net
   B. Double net
   C. Triple net
   D. Absolute net

17.8 A graduated lease (also known as a step-up lease) has stepped payments that:
   A. Usually go up during the lease
   B. Usually go down during the lease
   C. Both of the above
   D. None of the above

17.9 An escalated lease:

A. Automatically renews at the end of the first period

B. Usually is a net lease

C. Usually is a gross lease

D. None of the above

17.10 An index lease provides for:

A. Regular payments at regular index periods

B. Payments that vary according to the items included in the national index

C. Rent changes based on an agreed upon index

D. None of the above

17.11 A percentage lease calls for:

A. Rent rebates based on the CPI index if it goes down

B. Rent adjustments based on the nation average mortgage percentage rate

C. Additional rent based on the percentage of the building that is vacant

D. None of the above

17.12 A lease for only the land is called a:

A. Ground lease

B. Limited ground lease

C. Restricted ground lease

D. None of the above

17.13 An agriculture lease usually calls for the tenant to pay:

A. A flat annual ground rent charge

B. A percentage of the crop as rent

C. Both of the above

D. None of the above

17.14 A typical oil and gas lease calls for the tenant to pay:

A. A flat amount upon signing the lease

B. The property owner a percentage of the oil or gas that is sold

C. Both of the above

D. None of the above

17.15 A common reason property owners enter into sale and leaseback arrangements is to:

A. Raise capital for their businesses

B. Transfer the ownership of the property from the business to the business owners

C. Both of the above

D. None of the above

17.16 Which type of lease is associated with the terms *cash rent* and *sharecropping*?

A. Oil and gas leases

B. Sandwich leases

C. Agricultural leases

D. None of the above

17.17 A sandwich lease usually includes which of the following parties?

A. Property owner, lessor, sublessee

B. Lessor, lessee, sublessor

C. Property owner, lessee, sublessee

D. None of the above

17.18 One of the unique provisions of some mobile home leases (including those written in California) is:

A. No restrictions on the size of the mobile home are allowed

B. The reasons the lease can be terminated are limited

C. Both of the above

D. None of the above

17.19 A vertical lease is very similar to:

A. A net lease

B. A mobile home lease

C. An oil and gas lease

D. None of the above

17.20 The process of subletting gives the parties to a lease special names. Which is true?

A. The landlord becomes the sublessor.

B. The new tenant become the sublessee.

C. Both of the above.

D. None of the above.

17.21 When all of a lessor's rights are transferred to another party, it is:

A. An assignment

B. A transfer

C. A transformation

D. A sandwich

17.22 All real estate professionals should know the meaning of the appraisal terms economic rent and contract rent. In fact:

A. Economic rent and contract rent are the same

B. Contract rent is the same as actual rent

C. Economic rent is the same as actual rent

D. None of the above

17.23 Constructive eviction is:

A. When the tenants fail to pay their rent and are evicted

B. When the tenants violate the use provision of the lease and are evicted

C. When the landlord fails to repair the premises and the tenants must move

D. None of the above

ANSWER

The answer to each question is indicated by the letters A, B, C, or D. The explanation of the answer is indicated by the page number and an arrow that points to the appropriate paragraph on the page.

Q 17.1	A	Page 338	Q 17.6	C	Page 339	Q 17.11 D	Page 340	Q 17.16 C	Page 341	Q 17.21 A	Page 345
Q 17.2	B	Page 338	Q 17.7	A	Page 339	Q 17.12 A	Page 340	Q 17.17 C	Page 341	Q 17.22 B	Page 351
Q 17.3	D	Page 338	Q 17.8	A	Page 339	Q 17.13 B	Page 341	Q 17.18 B	Page 342	Q 17.23 C	Page 352
Q 17.4	D	Page 338	Q 17.9	C	Page 339	Q 17.14 C	Page 341	Q 17.19 C	Page 342		
Q 17.5	D	Page 338	Q 16.10 C	Page 339	Q 17.15 C	Page 341	Q 17.20 C	Page 345		

CHAPTER 18

Assessments and Property Taxes

I t is important for brokers and sales associates to understand property taxation for two reasons:

18.1 ➤ 1. The amount of property tax that must be paid on a property affects the decisions people make about buying and selling the property. When lenders qualify buyers to determine the size of mortgage they can carry, they deduct property tax payments from the buyers' income stream. The higher the taxes, the smaller the mortgage a buyer will qualify for.

2. At the closing of a real estate transaction, the taxes are prorated so that the seller and the buyer each pay their correct portion, based on the part of the year that they owned the property. This is called *proration*. It affects the amount of cash the buyer will have to pay at the closing.

There are two basic types of property taxes. The first is the general property tax, which is based on the value of the property. The other type is special assessments levied to cover the cost of special improvements such as streets, sidewalks, storm and sanitary sewers, lighting, and so on.

GENERAL PROPERTY TAXES

Traditionally, a substantial portion of the funds needed by a community to provide services to its citizens is raised by general taxes levied on real estate, based on the value of the property. Hence the term *ad valorem* (Latin for "according to value") taxation.

These taxes support local governments, schools, police and fire services, libraries, local street maintenance, parks, public hospitals, welfare programs, and other public services. The power to tax real estate is vested in the legislative branch of the government. Taxes pay for services that tend to make ownership more desirable, but net benefit is obviously decreased when taxes are out of proportion to those benefits.

18.3→

STEPS LOCAL GOVERNMENTS TAKE

There are four steps a local government takes to determine the amount of real estate taxes due from each property owner:

> **1.** Budgets are prepared and approved by each taxing body.
>
> **2.** Each property is appraised.
>
> **3.** The amount of taxes to be collected from each property is determined.
>
> **4.** The taxes are billed and collected.

Budgets Are Prepared and Approved by Each Taxing Body

Budgets are prepared, approved, and enacted into law for the coming tax year by the legislative body that has lawmaking authority for each taxing district. Taxing authorities vary from state to state and within states. Typical taxing bodies include counties, cities, boroughs, towns, villages, school districts, fire districts, sanitation districts, and county road departments.

From the total expenses in each budget, all sources of revenue are deducted except property taxes. These include federal and state aid, revenue sharing, sales tax income, business licenses, permit fees, income tax revenue, and so on. Whatever is left in the budget must come from property taxes.

Each Property Is Appraised

Depending on the state, assessors who work for the state, county, or community appraise each property in their territory. This is a big job. Often, the community hires an outside firm specializing in mass property valuations to help the assessor and his or her staff. How often this process takes place depends on the laws of the state. The most common time period is every 10 years, or when a property is sold or improved.

18.4→ Usually the assessed value is intended to represent some percentage of market value. This is set by state or local law. In communities with efficient assessors and frequent revaluations, there is a good relationship between assessed values and market values. In communities where the assessor is unqualified, understaffed, or not motivated, or where revaluations are infrequent, there may be little relationship between assessments and market values.

A real estate assessment is often divided between the land and the improvements. Sometimes the site improvements are assessed separately.

In some communities, the assessed value of land for tax purposes bears a reasonable relationship to market value, particularly when a recent revaluation has been made. In other communities, the assessed value does not have a realistic relationship to value. Part of the problem is caused by assessors' predilections for using standard tables.

Assessors' Standard Tables

Unit-foot depth and corner premium tables are often used by assessors to establish uniformity between assessments in valuations made for tax purposes. The purpose of such tables is to express equivalent values for one foot of frontage, applicable to sites of varying depth. For a lot of any stated type or location, a standard depth is established (originally fixed at 100 feet in most localities). For example, if the adopted standard depth is 100 feet, a lot 50 by 100 feet worth $2,175 would have unit-front-foot value of $43.50. Another lot, 50 feet wide and 150 feet deep, might be worth $2,500, or $50 per front foot, using the same unit-front-foot value of $43.50 multiplied by a *depth factor* of 115 percent. The percentages are designed to provide a uniform system of measuring the additional value due to added depth in a lot.

18.5→ One of the first depth rules was the 4-3-2-1 rule, which described a system where the front quarter of a lot contributed 40 percent of the value; the second quarter, 30 percent; the third quarter, 20 percent; and the fourth quarter, 10 percent. Because this left too wide a margin of variation for assessment purposes, the deficiency usually has been overcome by the establishment of more specific depth tables expressed in percentages for every foot, or at least for every 10 feet of depth, to reflect the conditions applicable in a certain locality or for certain types of property (residential, business, industrial, commercial).

Similarly, corner influence (premium) tables have been developed for ad valorem tax purposes, to establish the amount by which the market value per unit-foot of an inside lot varies when compared with a lot with a corner location. Such tables are also related to the localities and types of land for which they are prepared.

Property Tax Appeals

When property owners do not agree with the assessed value of their properties, they have the right to appeal the assessment. The appeal process varies from state to state and within states. However, they tend to follow a general pattern. The first step is usually an informal meeting with the assessor or the assessor's staff. Here property owners explain the basis for their dissatisfaction and the assessor explains how the assessed value was calculated. Sometimes mistakes are discovered and, as a result of these meetings, an assessment is changed and the matter is resolved at this level.

$\boxed{\text{18.6} \blacktriangleright}$

If the disputed assessment is not resolved, the next step is an appeal to an assessment appeals board. This is a more formal proceeding where each side tells why they feel their idea of the assessed value is correct. These boards usually have the power to change the assessment based on the evidence they are presented. Finally, if the dispute is not resolved, it is referred to whichever court has jurisdiction, and a formal hearing is held by a judge or referees appointed by the court. The court makes a finding, which, like any other court decision, can be appealed.

$\boxed{\text{18.13} \blacktriangleright}$

The Amount of Taxes to Be Collected from Each Property Is Determined

There may be a single tax rate or a series of separate tax rates to provide segregated funding for education, utilities, and so on.

Two long-standing traditions exist in the assessment and taxation process. One is that assessments are often a percentage of market value, as discussed earlier; the second is that the tax rate in many places is expressed in mills rather than as a percentage of assessment. Gradually this practice is being discontinued and some taxing authorities are using the unit of taxes per hundred dollars of value.

Mill Rates

$\boxed{\text{18.7} \blacktriangleright}$

A *mill* is a tenth of a cent. The *mill rate* is the number of dollars per thousand dollars of assessed value.

Example #1

Assessment	$1.00
Mill Rate	100 ($1.00 × .100)
Taxes	$ .10

Example #2

Assessment	$1,000
Mill Rate	90
Taxes	$90

Example #3

Assessment	$200,000
Mill Rate	35
Taxes	$7,000

This system is confusing to the public because it is difficult to readily compare the taxes in one community with those in another. For example, a lot that has a value of $80,000 might be assessed at 70 percent in one community with a tax rate of 40 mills. Taxes would be calculated as follows:

Market value	$80,000
Assessment ratio 70% (.70 × $80,000 = $56,000)	
Assessment	$56,000
Tax rate	40 Mills
Taxes	$2,240 (.040 × $56,000)

A similar lot also valued at $80,000 in another community might be assessed at 35 percent with a tax rate of 80 mills.

Market value	$80,000
Assessment ratio 35% (.35 × $8,000 = $28,000)	
Assessment	$28,000
Tax rate	80 Mills
Taxes	$2,240 (.080 × $28,000)

In those states where tax rates are expressed in terms of dollars per $100 of assessed value, here is how the preceding example is calculated:

Assessment	$28,000
Tax rate	$8.00
Taxes	$224 (280 × $8)

Widely varying assessment ratios and mill rates can produce the same tax burden on a property, depending on their combined influence. However, far too often a community's supposed assessment ratio (for example, 60 percent of market value) is actually not in effect. Although legally set at 60 percent, the actual relationship of the assessed value to market value may be markedly different among similar properties or among different classifications of property.

EFFECTIVE TAX RATE

Sometimes it is necessary to compare the tax burden on the property being marketed to that of competitive properties, both in the same community and in competing communities. One way to accomplish this is to compare the dollars of taxes directly with the market value. This is done by dividing the actual dollar amount of the tax burden on a property by the market value of the property, to give an *effective tax rate*.

18.8➤

Market value	$80,000
Taxes	$2,240
Tax rate	.028 or 2.8% ($2,240 ÷ $80,000)

By using this direct comparison method, it is easy to determine how consistent the taxes are within a community and also how taxation in one community compares with that of competitive communities.

Taxes are billed and collected. Different states and communities have a variety of methods for billing and collecting taxes. They also differ as to when the tax payments are due. Typically, property taxes can be paid in quarterly or semiannual installments. Usually all the taxes from the various taxing authorities are billed and collected by one tax collector. How to prorate taxes at the time of a closing is explained in Chapter 19.

SPECIAL ASSESSMENTS

18.9➤ *Special assessments* are taxes levied by a specific district taxing authority for a definite period of time, usually for a public improvement such as sewers, street paving, or sidewalk construction. Usually the assessment is based on the benefits derived by the property from the improvement rather than the cost of providing the improvement to a specific property. For example, it might cost $3,000 to provide sewers for one lot and $1,000 to provide sewers for another lot in the same project area. The amount of the special assessment, however, may well be equal, based on the assumption that the lots would be equally enhanced in value.

TAX EXEMPTIONS

18.10➤ Most states have laws that exempt the payment of property taxes for two main groups:

> 1. Types of properties
> 2. People who are eligible for property tax exemptions

Tax-Exempt Properties

Tax-exempt properties often include properties used for tax-exempt purposes, such as schools, public hospitals, and real estate owned and used by religious organizations. The government (federal, state, and local) does not pay
18.2➤ taxes on its property.

Some properties are tax exempt because the taxing authority granted them tax-exempt status as an inducement to locate in the area or not to leave the area. Some states have tax exemptions for agricultural land and historic properties.

Personal Tax Exemptions

Most personal exemptions are for specific amounts rather than for a complete exemption from tax. Some classes of people who receive tax exemptions are veterans, senior citizens, handicapped persons, and low-income earners.

EQUALIZATION

18.11➤ *Equalization* is used in some jurisdictions where there is a provision in the state law to correct general inequalities in statewide tax assessments by the use of an *equalization factor*. Such a factor may be provided for use in portions of the state where the assessments need to be raised or lowered to make them equal to average statewide assessment to value ratios.

18.12→ The assessed value of each property in the area to be equalized is multiplied by the equalization factor. This produces an equalized assessment, which is multiplied by the tax rate to calculate the amount of taxes due.

PROPERTY TRANSFER TAXES AND SALE PRICE RECORDING

Some states have property transfer taxes, recording fees, and other taxes, which are collected at the time of the sale or when the transfer of a property is recorded.

SUMMARY

It is important for brokers and sales associates to understand property taxation for two reasons. First, the amount of property tax that must be paid on a property affects the decisions people make about buying and selling the property. Second, at the closing of a real estate transaction, the taxes are prorated so that the seller and the buyer each pay their correct portions.

There are four steps a local government takes regarding real estate taxes. Budgets are prepared and approved by each taxing body, each property is appraised, the amount of taxes to be collected from each property is determined, and the taxes are billed and collected.

Two long-standing traditions exist in the assessment and taxation process. One is that assessments are often a percentage of market value; the second is that the tax rate in many places is expressed in mills rather than as a percentage of assessment. A mill is a tenth of a cent. The mill rate is the number of dollars of tax due per thousand dollars of assessed value.

Special assessments are taxes levied by a specific district taxing authority for a definite period of time, usually for a public improvement such as sewers, street paving, or sidewalk construction. Most states have laws that exempt the payment of property taxes by many types of properties and by certain groups of people, such as veterans, the elderly, or disabled people.

Equalization is used in some jurisdictions where there is a provision in the state law to correct general inequalities in statewide tax assessments. The assessed value of each property in the area is multiplied by an equalization factor.

Some states have property transfer taxes, recording fees, and other taxes, which are collected at the time of the sale or when the transfer of a property is recorded.

REVIEW QUESTIONS

18.1   The amount of a property's tax:

A. May help determine the amount of mortgage a buyer can qualify for

B. Is subject to renegotiation at the time of the sale

C. Both of the above

D. None of the above

18.2   Which of the following is not true about ad valorem taxes?

A. They are primarily used to pay for schools.

B. They are based on the value of the property.

C. They are levied against all types of property.

D. They are classified as general taxes.

18.3   In most states, what branch of government has the final say on a community's budget?

A. The tax collector

B. The legislature

C. The assessor

D. None of the above

18.4   Assessed value:

A. Can be any percent of market value

B. Is never a percent of market value

C. Is a percentage of the most recent sales price

D. None of the above

18.5   When using the old 4-3-2-1 depth table, what percent of the value of the total piece of land was allocated to the front 25 percent of the land?

A. 25 percent

B. 30 percent

C. 40 percent

D. None of the above

18.6   Which has the final say about property assessments?

A. The assessor's office

B. The board of tax appeals

C. The courts

D. None of the above

18.7   A mill is:

A. A tenth of a dollar

B. 1 percent of a dollar

C. A tenth of a cent

D. None of the above

18.8   The effective tax rate is:

A. A percentage of market value

B. A percentage of assessed value

C. Declared annually by the state for equalization purposes

D. None of the above

18.9 Special assessments are often levied for:

A. Sewers

B. Airports

C. New government buildings

D. None of the above

18.10 Tax exemptions are sometimes granted to:

A. Certain classes of property

B. Certain classes of people

C. Both of the above

D. None of the above

18.11 Equalization tries to ensure that:

A. Different classes of property pay equal amounts of taxes

B. Different states in a region pay equal taxes

C. Property is uniformly assessed throughout a state

D. All of the above

18.12 To equalize assessments, an equalization factor is multiplied by:

A. The annual mill rate

B. The property's market value

C. The property's assessed value

D. None of the above

18.13 Which has the final say about a property's assessment?

A. The assessor

B. The board of tax appeals

C. The courts

D. None of the above

ANSWERS

The answer to each question is indicated by the letters A, B, C, or D. The explanation of the answer is indicated by the page number and an arrow that points to the appropriate paragraph on the page.

Q 18.1	A	Page 359	Q 18.4	A	Page 361	Q 18.7	C	Page 362	Q 18.10	C	Page 365	Q 18.13	C	Page 362
Q 18.2	C	Page 365	Q 18.5	C	Page 361	Q 18.8	A	Page 364	Q 18.11	C	Page 365			
Q 18.3	B	Page 360	Q 18.6	C	Page 362	Q 18.9	A	Page 365	Q 18.12	C	Page 366			

CHAPTER 19

Don't Let the Mathematics Scare You

Currently no more than 10 percent of the questions on any real estate license exam that we are aware of require mathematical calculations. There are questions about closing and how to make adjustments for items such as property taxes that must be prorated between the buyer and the seller. However, the license exams *do not require* that the applicant know how to fill out a HUD Form 1 closing statement.

The questions on most of the examinations can be answered without the use of a calculator. When you check your state's current examination requirements and rules, they will instruct you as to exactly what will be required and whether you need to bring or use a calculator. Complete information about how to contact your state's Real Estate Commission is provided in the Introduction of this book.

In this chapter we start with a review of adding, subtracting, multiplying, and dividing that can be done with a pencil and paper or a simple calculator. You must also be able to apply these techniques to the calculation of the day-to-day transactions that are part of an RESP's activities including understanding what takes place at a closing and how prepaid expenses are between the buyer and the seller (*prorated*), a process called *proration*.

We will cover the different types of mathematical problems that you may expect to find on the examination. The questions at the end of this chapter and on the practice examinations provide you additional opportunities to practice what you have learned in this chapter.

Finally, keep in mind that, at most, 10 percent of the questions on the examination are mathematical questions. Many of them are quite simple, so even if you miss a few of the harder ones, it will not substantially affect your exam results.

Among real estate professionals and bankers, the Hewlett-Packard HP 12c and the TI BA II Plus calculators are popular. The HP 12c was introduced in 1981 and has become a classic. Throughout this chapter we have illustrated how the problems in the chapter can be solved using one of these two calculators. Of course, there are many other financial calculators that will do the same calculations.

BASIC ARITHMETIC

There are four basic arithmetic operations known as addition, subtraction, multiplication, and division.

Addition

Addition is the process of adding two or more numbers together to produce the *sum* of the numbers. The symbol for addition is a plus sign (+).

EXAMPLE

$$\$120 + \$135 + \$130 = \$385$$

PROBLEM #1
What is the total of these four rents: $765.00, $895.00, $1,467.50, and $3398.22? The reason that they are such odd numbers is that they are based on a percentage of the sales of the tenant's retail store.

ANSWER

$$\$765.00 + \$895.000 + \$1,467.50 + \$3,398.22 = \$6,525.72$$

The steps needed to solve this problem on the HP 12c and the TI BA II Plus calculators are shown in Figure 19.1.

Figure 19.1 Solutions to problem #1.

19.1→

What is the total of these rents: $765.00, 895.00, $1,467.50, $3,398.22?

SOLUTION TO PROBLEM #1 (USING HP 12C CALCULATOR)

HP 12C KEY STROKES					
Key/#	**Key/#**	**Key/#**	**Key/#**	**Display**	**Explanation**
ON	f	REG		0.00 (shows last settings)	Turns on calculator and clears the screen
f	2			0.00	Sets display to 2 decimal places
765.00	ENTER			765.00	Enters first number
895.00	+			1,660.00	Adds number to previous total
1467.50	+			3,127.50	Adds number to previous total
3398.22	+			6,525.72	Adds number to previous total

The total of the rents is **$6,525.72**

SOLUTION TO PROBLEM #1 (USING TI BA II PLUS CALCULATOR)

TI BA PLUS KEY STROKES					
Key/#	**Key/#**	**Key/#**	**Key/#**	**Display**	**Explanation**
ON/OFF	CE/C			0.00	Turns on calculator and clears display
765.00	+			765.00	Enters first number
895.00	+			1,660.00	Adds number to previous total
1467.50	+			3,127.50	Adds number to previous total
3398.22	+			6,525.72	Adds number to previous total

The total of the rents is **$6,525.72**

Subtraction

Subtraction is the process of deducting one number from another to produce the *difference* between the numbers. The symbol for subtraction is a minus sign (−).

EXAMPLE

93 inches − 10 inches = 83 inches

PROBLEM #2
What is left when $34,692.27 is subtracted from $56,495.22?

ANSWER

$$\$56,495.22 - \$34,692.27 = \$21,802.95$$

The steps needed to solve this problem on the HP 12c and the TI BA II Plus are shown in Figure 19.2.

Figure 19.2 Solutions to problem #2.

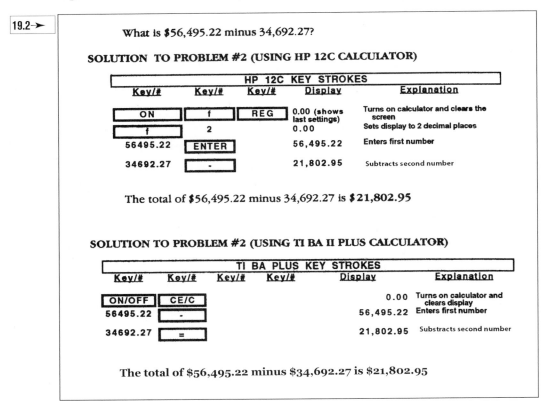

The total of $56,495.22 minus $34,692.27 is $21,802.95

Multiplication

Multiplication is the process of multiplying one number, the *multiplicand*, by another number, the *multiplier*, to produce a result, which is called the product. The multiplier is also sometimes known as a *coefficient*. The symbols for multiplication are a times sign (×) or a period (·). In algebra it is also a sign to multiply when one number is inside a bracket and the other is outside the bracket.

EXAMPLE

$$4 \times 5 = 20$$

$$6 \cdot 7 = 42$$

$$8(9) = 72$$

PROBLEM #3
What is $78,076.23 multiplied by .06?

ANSWER

$$\$78,076.23 \times .06 = \$4,684.57$$

The steps needed to solve this problem on the HP 12c and the TI BA II Plus calculators are shown in Figure 19.3.

Figure 19.3   Solutions to problem #3.

19.3→

What is $78,076.23 multiplied by .06?

SOLUTION TO PROBLEM #3 (USING HP 12C CALCULATOR)

HP 12C KEY STROKES				
Key/#	**Key/#**	**Key/#**	**Display**	**Explanation**
ON	f	REG	0.00 (shows last settings)	Turns on calculator and clears the screen
f	2		0.00	Sets display to 2 decimal places
78076.23	ENTER		78,076.23	Enters first number
.06	X		4,684.57	Multiplies first number by this number

The total of $78,076.23 multiplied by .06 is $4,684.57

SOLUTION TO PROBLEM #3 (USING TI BA II PLUS CALCULATOR)

TI BA PLUS KEY STROKES					
Key/#	**Key/#**	**Key/#**	**Key/#**	**Display**	**Explanation**
ON/OFF	CE/C			0.00	Turns on calculator and clears display
78076.23	X			78,076.23	Enters first number
.06	=			4,684.57	Multiplies first number by this number

The total of $78,076.23 multiplied by .06 is $4,684.57

Division

Division is the process of dividing one number, the *dividend,* by another number, the *divisor,* to produce a result, which is called a *quotient.* The symbol for division is (÷) or a line placed under the dividend and over the divisor.

EXAMPLE

$$18 \div 9 = 2$$

$$\frac{20}{5} = 4$$

In the preceding examples, 18 and 20 are the dividends and 9 and 5 are the divisors; 2 and 4 are the quotients. The number 20 is also known as the *numerator* and 5 the *denominator,* when the numbers are shown as fractions. Therefore, the value of a fraction is found by dividing the numerator by the denominator.

PROBLEM #4
What is $23,578.85 divided by 50?

ANSWER

$$\$23,578.85 \div 50 = \$471.58$$

The steps needed to solve this problem on the HP 12c and the TI BA II Plus calculators are shown in Figure 19.4.

Figure 19.4   Solutions to problem #4.

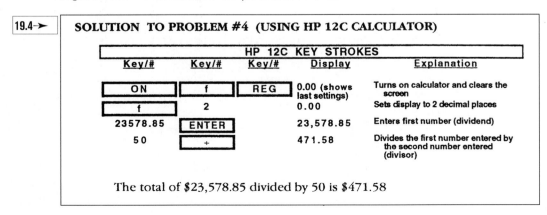

19.4→

SOLUTION TO PROBLEM #4 (USING HP 12C CALCULATOR)

HP 12C KEY STROKES				
Key/#	**Key/#**	**Key/#**	**Display**	**Explanation**
ON	f	REG	0.00 (shows last settings)	Turns on calculator and clears the screen
f	2		0.00	Sets display to 2 decimal places
23578.85	ENTER		23,578.85	Enters first number (dividend)
50	÷		471.58	Divides the first number entered by the second number entered (divisor)

The total of $23,578.85 divided by 50 is $471.58

Figure 19.4 *(Continued)*

19.4➤

SOLUTION TO PROBLEM #4 (USING TI BA II PLUS CALCULATOR)

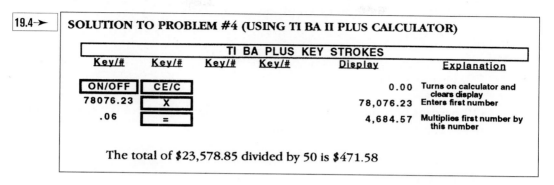

The total of $23,578.85 divided by 50 is $471.58

PERCENTAGES

Problems that require the use of percentages are frequently encountered by real estate professionals. Most of these problems can be solved by using the same simple method and formula.

To solve the problem you have to know two of the three components. Whenever you know any two components it is easy to calculate the third unknown component.

Here are the three components:

Part = P

Rate = R

Whole = W (sometimes called B for base)

Commissions

It goes without saying that, if you are in real estate, you have to know about commissions. You can be certain that there will be at least one commission calculation problem on the real estate license exam.

Here are the components of a commission problem:

Part (P) is the commission.
Rate (R) is the commission percentage.
Whole (W) is the sales price.

There is one more thing to remember. When you use a percentage in any calculation, you first have to convert it to a decimal. You do this by dropping the percentage sign, adding a zero to the left of the percentage number, and moving the decimal point two places to the left.

3% becomes .03
4.5% becomes .045
.7% becomes .007

320 percent becomes 3.20. (This was tricky because there is a invisible decimal at the right of any whole number.)

320 is really 320.
1 is really 1.
22 is really 22.

Following are examples of how to solve the three different kinds of commission problems.

EXAMPLE #1

19.5➤ How is the commission calculated when you know the sale price and the commission percentage? The formula for calculating the commission is

P (commission) = W (sale price) × R (commission percentage)

In this example, the sale price is $170,000 and the commission percentage is 6.5 percent.

SOLUTION

$170,000 × .065 (6.5% converted to a decimal) = $11,050

EXAMPLE #2

19.6➤ How is the commission percentage calculated when you know the sale price and the commission? The formula for calculating the commission percentage is

R (commission percentage) = P (commission) ÷ W (sale price)

In this example, the sale price is $180,000 and the commission is $7,200.

Solution: $180,000 ÷ $7,200 = .04 or 4%
(.04 converted to a percentage)

EXAMPLE #3

19.7➤ How is the sale price of a home calculated when you know the commission percentage and the commission? The formula for calculating the sale price is

W (sale price) = P (commission) ÷ R (commission percentage)

In this example, the commission percentage is 5 percent and the commission is $6,500.

SOLUTION

Sale Price = $6,500 ÷ .05 (5% converted to a decimal) = $130,000

PRORATION

One of the major differences between the agents' license exam and the brokers' exam are the many questions about closings and closing statements. Some of the license exams have one or two questions on proration. For single-family houses it is the procedure that expenses that have been paid by the sale, covering a period of time beyond the closing date, are split between the buyer and the seller. Since the expenses have been paid by the seller, it is necessary for the buyer to give the seller a credit on the closing statement for the seller's share of these prepaid expenses.

The most common expenses that are prorated are property insurance premiums when the buyer assumes the seller's insurance, property taxes, interest on any assumed loan, fuel oil left in the tank, and utility bills when the service is not switched on the date of the closing.

There are some local customs that have to be known when proration is done in real life. For examination purposes you will be told whether to use the actual number of days in a month or assume that all months have 30 days. You will be told whether to use 365 days for a year or just 360 days.

For income producing, the process may include income that has been collected by the seller that covers a period of time beyond the closing date. Questions covering this subject rarely appear on a license exam.

The following are examples and problems showing proration of insurance premiums, property taxes, interest on an assumed loan, fuel oil in the tank, and utilities bills.

Proration to Property Taxes

Prorated property taxes are common to many real estate transactions. The key issues are when the taxes are due, what portion has already been paid, and what period of time is covered by the taxes that have been paid. It is also necessary to know if months will be considered to have 30 days or the actual number of days, how the number of days in the year will be counted (365 or 360), and how the day of the closing will be counted.

EXAMPLE

In the market of this sale, taxes are paid in arrears. The tax year runs from October 1 to September 30. In this market the actual number of days in the month and year are used for proration. The day of the closing is considered to be owed by the seller.

The annual taxes are $5,472.00.
The property was purchased on February 22 of the following year.
Number of days the seller owned the house:
    October 31 days
    November 30
    December 31
    January 31
    February 22
    Total 145
Annual Taxes $5,472 ÷ 365 = 12.53 per day
145 days × 12.53 = $1,816.85 taxes owed by the seller to the buyer

Proration of Insurance

Prorated insurance occurs when the buyer takes over an insurance policy that is already paid for. The key issues are when the policy started, what portion has already been paid, and what period of time the insurance has been paid for. It is also necessary to know if months will be considered to have 30 days or the actual number of days, how the number of days in the year will be counted (365 or 360), and how the day of the closing will be counted.

EXAMPLE

In the market of this sale, insurance is paid in advance. The insurance policy started March 1 and was paid for through February 28 the following year. In this market 30 days were used to count a month and 360 days for a year. The day of the closing is considered to be owned by the buyer.

The annual insurance premium was $959.85.
The property was closed on May 20.
Number of days the seller owned the house:
    March 30 days
    April 30
    May 19
    Total 79 days
Annual insurance premium $959.85 ÷ 360 = $2.67 per day
Number of days the insurance prepaid by the seller 360 − 79 = 281 days
281 days × $2.67 = $750.27 for prepaid insurance owed by the buyer to the seller

Proration of Interest on Assumed Loan

The seller has a second mortgage that is being assumed by the buyer. As of the day of the closing, the balance due is $37,528.00. Interest on the loan is 12 percent per year paid in arrears. Interest was paid through the last day of the month before the closing. The buyer in this market is considered to own the house on the day of the closing. The closing was on the 17th of the month. A year is considered to be 360 days.

The number of days the seller owned the house since the end of last month was 16 days.
The annual interest was $37,528. $\times$ .12 = $4,503.36
The interest per day is $4,503.36. $\div$ 360 = $12.50 per day
The number of days the seller owned the house since the last interest payment was 16 days.
16 days $\times$ $12.50 interest per day equals $200.00 owed by the seller to the buyer.
Mortgage assumption payment owed by the buyer to the seller: Unpaid Interest is −$200.00 from a balance of $37,528.00 = a total of $37.328.16.

Proration of Fuel Oil Left in Tank

The seller filled the 275-gallon oil tank on the morning of the closing and paid for the oil upon delivery. Oil costs $3.25 per gallon.
The buyer owes the seller $275.00 $\times$ $3.25 = $893.75

Proration of Utility Bills

The electric service was not going to be transferred to the buyer until seven days after the closing. In this market the buyer is considered to own the property on the day of the closing. The estimated monthly bill is $150. Thirty-day months are used for adjustment purposes. The closing was on the 16th of the month.

Estimated daily electric bill $150.00 $\div$ 30 = $5.00 per day.
The seller owes the buyer for 15 days: $5.00 $\times$ 15 = $105.

PERIMETER, AREA, AND VOLUME

A real estate professional needs to know how to calculate the *area, perimeter,* and *volume* of buildings, sites, and equipment with the gross living area used by appraisers. This requires the knowledge of how to calculate the perimeter of an irregular-shaped house.

Perimeter

House Perimeter

The perimeter is the outer boundary of an area. It is the total of all the exterior dimensions.

PROBLEM #5
What is the perimeter of the house in Figure 19.5?

Figure 19.5　House perimeter.

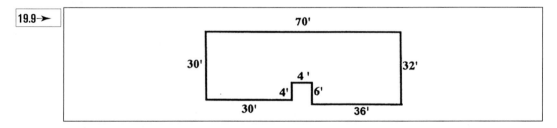

SOLUTION
The perimeter of this house = 30′ + 30′ + 70′ + 32′ + 36′ + 6′ + 4′ + 4′ = 212′.

Site Perimeter

PROBLEM #6
What is the perimeter of the site in Figure 19.6?

Figure 19.6　Site perimeter #32.

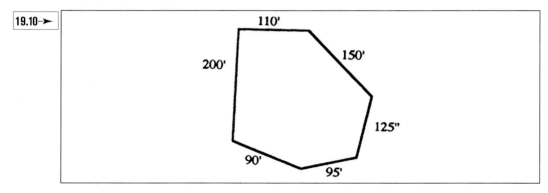

SOLUTION
The perimeter of the site = 90′ + 95′ + 125′ + 150′ + 110′ + 200′ = 770′.

Area

Most real estate area calculations are of a flat plane or surface. It may be the area of a room, office, house, commercial building, industrial plant, and so on. Most American real estate areas are expressed in square feet (sq. ft.). Most other countries use the metric system, which expresses area in square meters. A square foot contains 144 square inches. Occasionally, a unit of square yards is used. A square yard is nine square feet. Most of these surfaces have *right angle* (90-degree) corners. Their area can be calculated by breaking them up into a group of squares and rectangles.

Site and land areas are often more complex in shape. In order to calculate these areas, it is necessary to break it up into smaller shapes with known formulas and then calculate the smaller areas. The smaller areas are added together to produce the total area of the complex shape. Sites are often measured in *acres*. An acre is 43,560 square feet. Some buildings and sites have curved surfaces. Their areas can only be approximated by using straight lines. Their exact area can be calculated by an architect, engineer, surveyor, or someone else with special training.

Squares

A *square* is a flat surface with four straight sides of the same size and with opposite sides parallel to each other. To calculate the area of a square, you multiply one side by the other side.

Area of a square = side × side

PROBLEM #7
What is the area of the square in Figure 19.7?

Figure 19.7 Square.

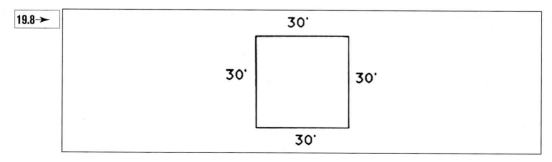

SOLUTION

$$\text{Area} = 30' \times 30' = 900 \text{ sq. ft.}$$

Rectangles

Any flat surface with four straight sides is called a *quadrilateral*. A *rectangle* is a flat surface with four straight sides. The opposite sides are the same size and opposite sides are parallel to each other. All of a rectangle's corners are 90 degrees. To calculate the area of a rectangle you multiply one side by any other side that is *perpendicular* (a line going at 90 degrees from another line) to it.

PROBLEM #8

What is the area of the rectangle in Figure 19.8?

Figure 19.8   Rectangle.

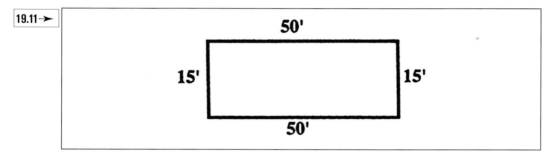

SOLUTION

$$\text{Area} = 15' \times 50' = 750 \text{ sq. ft.}$$

Parallelograms

A *parallelogram* is a flat four-sided surface with both pairs of opposite sides parallel. The area of a parallelogram is equal to the product of its base and height.

PROBLEM #9

What is the area of the parallelogram in Figure 19.9?

SOLUTION

$$\text{Area} = 400' \times 150' = 60,000 \text{ sq. ft.}$$

Figure 19.9 Parallelogram.

19.12➤

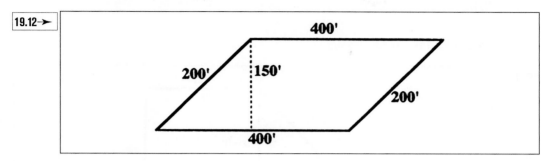

Volume

Cube

A cube is a solid object bounded with six square faces. Its volume is its length × width × height.

PROBLEM #10

What is the volume of the cube in Figure 19.10?

Figure 19.10 Cube.

19.13➤

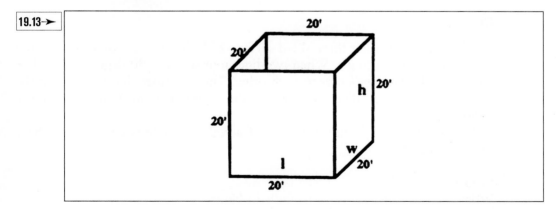

SOLUTION

Area = 20′ × 20′ × 20′ = 8,000 cubic feet

Trapezoids

A *trapezoid* is a flat four-sided surface with only one pair of opposite sides parallel. The parallel sides are called the bases and the nonparallel sides are called the legs. The area of a trapezoid is equal to one-half the sum of its bases times its height.

PROBLEM #11

What is the area of the trapezoid in Figure 19.11?

Figure 19.11 Trapezoid.

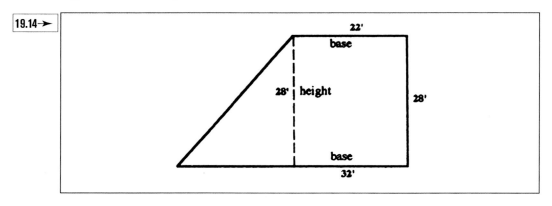

SOLUTION

$$Area = \frac{1}{2}(22' + 32') = 27'$$

$$27' \times 28' = 756 \text{ sq. ft.}$$

Right Triangles

A *right triangle* is a flat three-sided surface with the intersection of two of the sides at a 90-degree angle. When two lines intersect at a 90-degree angle, they are said to be *perpendicular* to each other. The two sides that intersect at the 90-degree angle are called the base and the height. The third line is called the *hypotenuse.*

The formula for finding the area of a right triangle is one-half the base times the height.

PROBLEM #12

What is the area of the right triangle in Figure 19.12?

Figure 19.12 Right triangle.

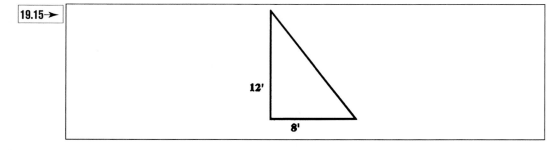

SOLUTION

Area = ½(base × height) = ½(8′ × 12′) = ½(96) = 48 sq. ft.

Circles

A circle is a round flat surface. The perimeter of a circle is called the *circumference*. A straight line drawn from any point on the circumference through the center of the circle to the opposite side of the circumference is called the *diameter*. A straight line from the center of the circle to the circumference is the *radius*. The radius is one-half the diameter. The ratio of the circumference of a circle to its diameter is called *pi*.

Pi (π) = 3.1415926536 rounded to 3.14.

Area = π × radius²

PROBLEM #13

What is the area of the circle in Figure 19.13?

Figure 19.13 Circle.

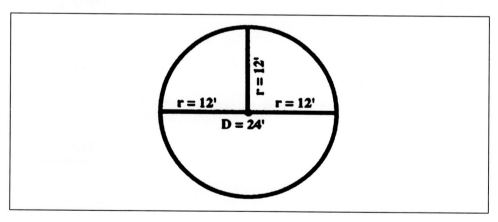

SOLUTION

Area = π × radius² = 3.14 × 12² = 3.14 × 144 = 452.16 sq. ft.

REVIEW QUESTIONS

19.1 What is the total of these rents: $2,765.00, $3,895.00, $8,467.00, $16,398.92?
   A. $31,552.92
   B. $31,525.92
   C. $31,516.92
   D. $35,116.92

19.2 What is $5,135,356.89 minus $54,678.43?
   A. $5,880,678.46
   B. $5,088,678.46
   C. $5,080,687.46
   D. $5,080,678.46

19.3 What is $34,672.31 multiplied by .05?
   A. $173.36
   B. $1,733.62
   C. $17,336.20
   D. $173,361.55

19.4 What is $173,361.55 divided by 50?
   A. $28,841.46
   B. $34,673.10
   C. $3,467.23
   D. $54,765.21

19.5 Calculate the commission due on the sale of a piece of real estate. The sale price is $290,000 and the commission percentage is 7 percent.
   A. $20,300
   B. $17,400
   C. $2,030
   D. $1

19.6 Calculate the commission percentage a broker received for selling a piece of property when the commission was $31,750 and the property sold for $635,000.
   A. 5 percent
   B. 5.5 percent
   C. 5.75 percent
   D. 6 percent

19.7 Calculate the sale price of a piece of property when you know that the commission percentage was 6 percent and that the commission received by the broker was $8,400.
   A. $14,000
   B. $140,000
   C. $5,040
   D. $50,040

19.8 What is the area of the following square?

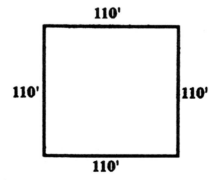

   A. 1,210 sq. ft.
   B. 440 sq. ft.
   C. 12,100 sq. ft.
   D. 4,400 sq. ft.

19.9 What is the perimeter of the following house?

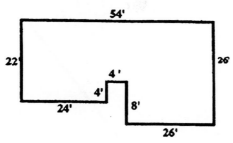

A. 160′
B. 164′
C. 172′
D. 168′

19.10 What is the perimeter of the following site?

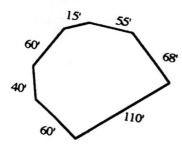

A. 408′
B. 458′
C. 400′
D. 393′

19.11 What is the area of the following rectangle?

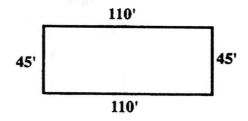

A. 12,000 sq. ft.
B. 1,210 sq. ft.
C. 4,950 sq. ft.
D. 49,500 sq. ft.

19.12 What is the area of the following parallelogram?

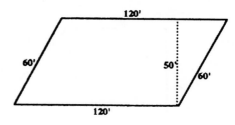

A. 3,000 sq. ft.
B. 6,000 sq. ft.
C. 7,000 sq. ft.
D. 7,200 sq. ft.

19.13 What is the volume of the following cube?

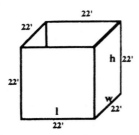

A. 1,064 cu. ft.
<u>B.</u> 10,648 cu. ft.
C. 4,400 cu. ft.
D. 44,000 cu. ft.

19.14 What is the area of the following trapezoid?

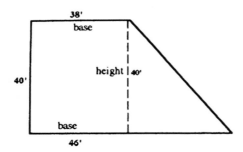

A. 1,600 sq. ft.
B. 1,546 sq. ft.
<u>C.</u> 1,680 sq. ft.
D. 1,840 sq. ft.

19.15 What is the area of the following right triangle?

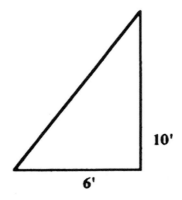

A. 27 sq. ft.
B. 28 sq. ft.
C. 29 sq. ft.
<u>D.</u> 30 sq. ft.

CHAPTER 20

How to Make Money Investing in Real Estate

Sooner or later almost everyone who has chosen real estate as a career considers making an investment in real estate. Here are some of the many real estate investments you can buy:

Single-family houses
Cooperative apartments (co-ops)
Condominium units (condos)
Timeshares
Small income properties (two- to four-family)
Apartment buildings
Office buildings
Shopping centers
Farms and ranches
Miscellaneous commercial and industrial property
Vacant land
Syndications
Partnerships
Real estate investment trusts (REITs)
Corporations

Different real estate investors have differing investment goals. The type of real estate investment they make should be based on these goals, and, in an ideal world, this would be the case. However, many real estate investments are based on emotional appeal and a variety of other reasons unrelated to investment goals.

Almost all real estate investors expect their investment property to appreciate in value over the time they hold the investment. Historically, with a few exceptions, this has been true, especially since World War II, assuming that the investment is held for a long period of time.

ADVANTAGES OF INVESTING IN REAL ESTATE

One of the best-kept secrets in the United States is that there are more millionaires who made their money primarily by investing in real estate than from any other type of investment. This was even true before the recent real estate boom and the bust that followed it.

By far the most common real estate investment is the owner-occupied house. It is a great investment because you have a place to live and all the other advantages of owning your own home besides the investment advantage.

Leverage

When you buy 500 shares of Apple stock for $100 per share you will pay $50,000 for the stock. If you hold the stock for five years and it goes up 25 percent, you can sell it for $62,500 and make a profit of $12,500.

You can buy a $250,000 house with the same $50,000 down and finance the balance with a mortgage of $200,000. If at the end of the same five-year period the value of the house has increased 25 percent it would now be worth $312,500. You could sell the house, and your profit would be $62,500. In addition, you would recover your mortgage amortization and be subject to favorable tax treatment during the ownership period.

That is the magic of leverage. Of course, if the value of the house goes down, your loss would be greater, too.

Leverage is a characteristic of most real estate investments. It is also available for other types of investments. However, many other types of investments are bought without leverage.

Inflation

One of the best protections against inflation is to own real estate. Since World War II the cost of living has gone up each year (with a few short-term exceptions). This is called *inflation*. Because the amount of a mortgage does not increase with inflation, real estate owners are paying off their mortgages with dollars that have less value than when they took out the mortgage.

Income properties tend to become more profitable because the rents and expenses increase with the inflation but the mortgage payments remain constant, unless you have an adjustable-rate mortgage (ARM). This is why most real estate investors insist on fixed-rate mortgages.

Cash Flow

Another of the goals of owning property besides living in it and selling it for a profit is to hold the property and rent it to tenants for sufficient rent to pay all the expenses (including the mortgage payments, but not including depreciation) and have some money left over. This is known as having an income property with a *positive cash flow*. If it is necessary to add additional capital to pay the expenses, it is called *negative cash flow*.

Equity Buildup

Another advantage of owning an income property is that part of each mortgage payment is amortization (repayment of the mortgage principle). The reduced mortgage debt is added to the profit from the sale. This is called *equity buildup*. This same principle reduction applies to owner-occupied real estate as well as investment property.

Other Advantages of Real Estate as an Investment

Historically, real estate has provided an above-average rate of return. In addition to the advantage of leverage, it also takes advantage of inflation, population increases, and the relative scarcity of good development land. Because real estate is a physical entity, many investors feel they have more direct control over a real estate investment than various alternatives. Real estate enjoys tax benefits not available to other type of investments. Real estate taxes and mortgage interest are tax deductible. For investment properties, depreciation is a deductible expense that can be very substantial in certain types of properties.

DISADVANTAGES OF REAL ESTATE AS AN INVESTMENT

- The amount of cash needed is often greater than other types of available investments.
- Unexpected damage to the property may not be covered by insurance. (See Chapter 22, "What You Need to Know about Insurance.")

- Lack of liquidity is a historical disadvantage of owning real estate. It is hard to quickly sell when you need your investment capital for other purposes. An increasingly popular alternative to selling is to refinance the first mortgage or obtain a home equity loan.

  One way owners obtain needed money from a real estate investment is to borrow the money and secure the loan with a second mortgage. Until the 1970s, there was a social stigma attached to borrowing money in this manner. Then the Money Store came along and they hired the popular baseball player Phil Rizzuto. Using a series of humorous TV ads, they convinced the pubic that a home equity loan (which is often secured by a second mortgage) was socially acceptable. Instead of the home being a nonliquid asset, it is now a money machine that can quickly and easily be tapped whenever money is needed for education, health care, or vacations. Proceeds from a second mortgage can even be used to purchase a second home or another type of investment.

  Nonliquidity is still a disadvantage of most other types of real estate investment when they are compared with competitive investment opportunities.

- Almost all real estate requires active management, either by the owner, family members, or hired property managers.

  The owner-occupied single-family home is no exception. Any one of the over 100 million homeowners will confirm that it takes work to manage their home.

  An exception is housing for the elderly. If it is a condominium, then the unit owners are responsible only for the maintenance of the interior of their unit. Everything else is taken care of by the homeowners' association. When the house is in a planned unit development (PUD), most management and maintenance problems are handled by the homeowners' association. In many PUDs, the unit owners are responsible only for the maintenance of their own small lot, while all the common elements are maintained by the homeowners' association.

  Some housing for the elderly is a modified form of PUD. By agreement, the homeowners' association assumes responsibility for the maintenance of more than would be included in a normal PUD, such as all the land and the exteriors of the homes.

TYPES OF REAL ESTATE INVESTMENTS

Single-Family Houses

Most home buyers want to believe that the house they are buying is a good investment as well as a good place to live. A knowledgeable RESP must be able to explain the reasons why a house is a good investment:

- Historically houses have always gone up in value over any long period of time. Even when there has been a severe dip in prices, the market recovers and the prices go on to new heights.
- Desirable land continues to increase in price as it becomes scarcer. This makes new houses more expensive to build.
- The population of the United States continues to increase, and homeownership is increasing as a percentage of the population.
- When you buy a house and obtain a mortgage, you take advantage of leverage.
- There are special tax deductions available to homeowners.

The majority of single-family houses are freestanding units on their own sites, and owned in fee simple. Party wall units and townhouses are also popular. Single-family dwellings can also be in PUDs or on leased land. They can be owner-occupied primary residences or second homes. All of these types of single-family homes can also be bought and rented, thereby becoming income properties.

Cooperative Apartments (Co-ops)

Cooperative apartments or "co-ops" are popular in only a few American cities. Because many co-operative projects require the owner to be an occupant, their investment value is similar to an owner-occupied single-family house. Their more complex ownership configuration is described in Chapter 7, "Types and Forms of Ownership."

Condominium Units (Condos)

The biggest change in American homeownership since World War II is the condominium, which did not exist prior to that time.

The advantages of living in a condominium are similar to those of single-family ownership. Additional advantages are that many condominium developments include an amenity package that ranges from open spaces to elaborate recreational facilities such as beach access, pool clubs, tennis courts, and so on. Most of the management is handled by the homeowners' association.

Types of Condominiums

- In-town residences with few amenities
- Suburban residences with few amenities
- Suburban residences with recreational facilities

- Resort and vacation homes
- Retirement housing
- Student housing
- Large projects and new towns

Condominiums can be new units or units in existing buildings that have been converted to condominium ownership. Either new or old, they can take the form of a high-rise, a townhouse, small groupings of party wall units, or free-standing units.

Investing in Condominiums

Condominiums are probably the easiest type of real estate investment to make. They are one of the few types of real estate investments that do not require the owner to be active in the management of the investment. Most condominium projects have a management company that will perform almost all the management. This is appealing to owners who occupy the units as well as those who have no intention of ever living in them. These owners can hopefully profit by renting the units or selling them at a higher price than they paid. They also have the advantage of requiring a modest investment as compared with most other real estate investments with the exception of time-share units. They are also easy to mortgage and therefore the investor can take advantage of leverage.

During the early 2000s, real estate values in many parts of the United States rose rapidly. Many people who were interested in investing in real estate at this time discovered that a condominium unit was just what they needed. Investors would buy units before they were constructed and "flip" them before they even took title to the property. Others held on for a longer period of time and sold the unit at a profit. Because of leverage, they made large returns on their investments.

When the market slowed down in 2006, it became harder to flip the units. When it became necessary to hold the unit, the owner had to pay the common charges, taxes, and insurance, which were rarely covered by any rents they received.

Investors soon learned that leverage works in both directions and, when they were finally able to sell at a small loss, it turned out to be a larger loss because of leverage.

Timeshares

A timeshare is an ownership form where a single unit is divided among a group of owners, each of whom owns a different period of time. The most common arrangement is where each owner owns a designated week each year. There are also floating time, rotating time, and complex points pro-grams. Ownership can be deeded or by means of a right-to-use contract.

Most timeshares are in resorts or highly desirable destination areas, such as Orlando or Las Vegas. Trading a timeshare week for a different week in another resort is facilitated by companies such as Resort Condominiums International (RCI) and Interval International. Units are usually sold by the initial developer and then resold by independent agents. Owners of a timeshare unit must decide each year whether they will use their unit, rent it, or exchange it for a unit in another resort and/or at another time.

One of the advantages of timeshare ownership is that the owner does none of the management. You arrive on the day of the week when your timeshare starts, pick up the keys, and go to a clean unit, usually stocked with clean linens, kitchenware, furniture, appliances, and so on. You live there for the week and, at the end of the week, you leave the keys on the kitchen table with a tip for the maid. If there is a problem, such as a leaking sink or burnt-out porch light, usually a phone call to the management company is all that is required to solve it.

The bad news is that timeshares are often initially sold using very high-pressure tactics, including projections of substantial increases in value, which rarely occur. With few exceptions, however, most timeshare resales are at the same price or lower prices than the initial acquisition cost. Most timeshare owners buy to facilitate taking regular vacations in a preferred area without the effort of preplanning.

Timeshares are big business. There are over 1,500 timeshare developments in the United States, which include over 150,000 units. Multiply 150,000 by 52 weeks and you see that there are over 7.5 million individually owned weeks. Many real estate agents located near a timeshare unit develop a sup-plemental business of renting and selling these units.

Small Income Properties (Two- to Four-Family Dwellings)

An advantage of a small income property is that the investor has the choice of being an owner-occupant with the other units rented to tenants, or the owner can choose to live elsewhere. In addition to the advantages of lever-age, there is the additional tax advantage of depreciation, which is not de-ductible for most owner-occupied dwellings.

LARGER REAL ESTATE PROPERTIES

There are many different types of investment properties, ranging from vacant land to skyscrapers. One typical classification system describes six major categories: residential, office building, retail, commercial, industrial, and special-purpose buildings. Other classification systems recognize many variations and different categories.

Apartment Buildings

Millions of Americans live in apartment houses. There seems to be no end in sight for the expansion of population in most of the United States. Rental apartments provide housing for many people who (for a wide variety of reasons) do not want to own their own dwelling. One advantage of an apartment house is that it does not depend on one or just a few tenants. When a unit becomes vacant, it usually can be rented within a reasonable period of time. Leases tend to be relatively short so that as the value of the property increases, the rents can also be increased.

Apartments come in all shapes, sizes, and styles. One common way to classify them is to divide them into garden-style, townhouse, and high-rise apartments.

Garden Apartments

Today, in many areas, the garden apartment will provide the most housing for the money. It also usually provides parking, which is critical where commuting to work is necessary.

Apartment buildings require a high level of management. Fewer and fewer owners are willing to do the work themselves and most hire professional management companies to be responsible for day-to-day upkeep. Apartments are owned in almost all types of ownerships ranging from a single owner, who also occupies one of the units, to international corporations that own apartment buildings throughout the world.

High-Rise Apartments

All other things being equal, the least expensive way to build an apartment building is to construct a high-rise building. Depending on where you are, the most economical building height is usually three or four stories. However, in the larger cities like New York and Chicago there are quite a few six-story buildings (without elevators) that lead one to the conclusion that a six-story walk-up was the most economical apartment type to build at some point in the past.

Townhouses

Another economical type of construction is the townhouse configuration that features common exterior side walls. This style is found in most of the large East Coast and West Coast cities. There are hundreds of townhouses in Chicago, Philadelphia, Baltimore, and many other cities.

Office Buildings

Owner-Occupied Office Buildings

There is much to be said for the operators of a business to own the building where they have their main operations. The building can be freestanding, with a single owner-occupant. Many of the benefits are the same as owning a single-family home. In addition, there is an advertising and prestige value to owning a commercial building. The tax advantages are better than those for a single-family home, because depreciation is tax deductible and so is the rent. If the owner's business is profitable, it is unnecessary to worry about getting a tenant or collecting rent. Such ownership makes an ideal vehicle to accumulate money for the owner's future retirement needs.

An alternative is an owner-occupied building with additional tenants. However, this makes the owner a landlord and increases the management tasks. Some owner-occupants, who have other tenants as well, hire a manager to take the burden of the day-to-day operation off their hands.

Non-Owner-Occupied Office Buildings

There are a variety of other types of office buildings, which range from small suburban buildings to large central city offices. Almost every city in the United States has one or more office buildings that are over 20 stories. Many of these buildings are owned by financial institutions such as banks and insurance companies. Others are corporate headquarters. They are owned by almost every type of real estate ownership form there is. Office buildings are generally ranked as being Class A through Class D. The best is Class A.

Shopping Centers

Shopping Centers are often subdivided into four categories: neighborhood, community, regional, and superregional.

Neighborhood or Strip Shopping Centers

These small shopping centers are usually less than 100,000 square feet. Many are less than half that size. Their primary market area is their immediate neighborhood, often within a radius of 1.5 miles or five to ten minutes driving time. Typically they consist of a supermarket and a variety of small retail stores and service facilities. It is not uncommon for them to be owned by an individual or a small group of local owners.

Community Shopping Centers

These medium-size shopping centers range from 100,000 to 300,000 square feet. Their primary business comes from an area within three to five miles or 10 to 20 minutes' driving time. Typically they include a junior department store, a discount or variety store, a supermarket, some small retail operations, a service business, and recreational facilities. Ownership may be local investors or larger shopping center groups.

Regional Shopping Centers

Their size ranges from 300,000 to 900,000 square feet. To be successful, they must include one or more well-known department stores, usually at least 100,000 square feet in size. They will include many smaller stores, most of which will be part of a national chain, restaurants, offices, banks, movie theaters, and other recreational facilities. Their business comes from a large radius, often 8 to 10 miles in size. These centers are commonly owned by syndicates, large national shopping center developers, REITs, and public corporations. They are also owned by pension funds and insurance companies.

Superregional Shopping Centers

Most of them are enclosed multistory malls with large parking lots and garages. Small ones run 500,000 square feet, the larger ones well over a million. Some, like the Mall of America, attract customers from all over the world. Most are owned by large corporations and REITs. They can have hundreds of stores, elaborate food facilities, theaters, recreation facilities, and so on.

Farms and Ranches

This is a unique type of real estate that requires special skills on the part of a RESP, broker, or investor. Farms range in size from small family operations, many of which are now converting to organic farming, to giant 25,000-acre or larger farms owned by agribusiness corporations. It is beyond the scope of this book to do more than recognize this large and important segment of American real estate.

Miscellaneous Commercial and Industrial Property

Commercial/industrial brokers specialize in the income-producing properties described earlier in this chapter plus a variety of miscellaneous properties such as retail stores, warehouses, fast-food buildings, other franchise properties, gasoline service stations, and so on. They also sell buildings that can be used for a variety of industrial purposes.

Vacant Land

Investments in vacant land range from individual building lots ready to be built on to large tracts of land. These tracts of land are in various stages of development ranging from wilderness with no passable access to subdivided land that has been developed to land where all the needed utilities are in place and the roads are completed.

The investment in land can be speculative and is not for beginners. Congress has passed the Federal Interstate Land Sales Full Disclosure Act, which regulates interstate land sales of unimproved lots. It is intended to regulate land speculators who subdivide large tracts of land, often in the Sunbelt states, and sell them to prospective retirees, who buy them sight unseen.

MULTI-INVESTOR OWNERSHIP FORMS

Syndications

Syndication is a broad term used to describe a group of people who band together to invest in some real estate that is too large or expensive for them to own as individuals. It is not a form of ownership, but rather an investment strategy. The ownership can take the form of a partnership corporation or a real estate investment trust (REIT).

Partnerships

A partnership can be as simple as two people joining together to own some real estate. The ownership form can be a simple tenancy in partnership.

Alternatively, a partnership may be a group of hundreds of partners. Large properties are often owned by a general partnership. In this form of ownership each partner is responsible for all of the liabilities of the partnership.

Another type of partnership is a limited partnership consisting of both general partners and limited partners. The general partners organize and operate the partnership, contribute some of the capital, and agree to personally accept the financial liability of the partnership. Limited partners provide the bulk of the needed capital, but are not involved in the day-to-day management of the partnership and have no personal liability for the debts of the partnership. Their risk is limited to their investment in the partnership. Partnerships do not pay income or capital gains taxes. Each partner pays a share of the taxes based on his or her own individual tax rate.

Real Estate Investment Trusts (REITs)

In 1961, a law was passed by the U.S. Congress that created a special type of trust that is permitted to own real estate called a real estate investment trust (REIT). The intention was to make it possible for small investors to invest in a portfolio of large properties or mortgages that formerly were available only to investors such as rich individuals, large corporations, and pension funds.

There are three different kinds of REITs:

- *Equity trust REITs* invest in a number of different kinds of real estate and sell their shares to investors.
- *Mortgage trust REITs* use the shareholders' money to buy and sell real estate mortgage loans.
- *Combination trust REITs* invest the shareholders' money in both real estate properties and mortgages.

In the past, this type of investment participation could also be accomplished by a corporation owning real estate and selling its shares to small investors. The problem was that both the corporation and the individual investor were taxed on the profits (double taxation).

The REIT Act provided that if an investment trust followed a strict set of rules—for example, they must have at least 100 owners technically called beneficiaries and distribute at least 95 percent of their income to the beneficiaries each year—they avoid double taxation. The REIT does not pay any taxes, and the owners are taxed at their individual tax rates. Other advantages of REITs are that they utilize professional management teams and the individual owners have no management responsibilities. The limit of an investor's risk is his or her investment. They have no personal liability for the REIT's debts. Many REITs are quite large, and their shares are traded nationally. Thus, it is easy for an individual investor to buy and sell shares.

Corporations

Every state has laws that create corporations that are owned by their shareholders and can do most things individuals can do, including owning real estate. For tax purposes, there are two types of corporations. Corporations that pay income and capital gains taxes are called *C corporations* and corporations that are taxed like partnerships are called *S corporations*. Recently, limited liability corporations (LLCs) have become another way to hold title to investment real estate. Both of these types of corporations sell stock to shareholders, whose liability is limited to their total investment.

PYRAMIDING

Pyramiding is the method used by many of the real estate investors who became millionaires by investing in real estate. The investor buys a property and then improves the property and sells it at a profit. Some of these investors improve their chances of making a profit by doing some or all of the improvement work themselves. This is called investing their *sweat equity*. With the proceeds from the first sale, the investor buys one or more other properties and repeats the process.

An alternative pyramiding method is to retain the original property and refinance it based on its increased value as the result of the improvements. The original property is retained and additional property is purchased with the additional borrowed money.

Many of these millionaires have used a combination of these two techniques.

HOW TO GET STARTED AS AN INVESTOR

There are hundreds of books, courses, seminars, and so on, being offered on how to get started as a real estate investor. Many of them claim that they will teach you foolproof "get rich quick" schemes. I have been looking for over 40 years and I have yet to find one that I would recommend. Don't be fooled by the pictures of the promoters riding around in fancy cars and the testimonies shown of people who swear by their systems.

My advice is first to buy your own home and then to buy an office building for your business when it becomes successful.

My first successful investment was a run-down single-family house in an area that was being redeveloped by the City of New Haven. With help from the redevelopment agency, my investment partner and I converted it into a four-family house, kept it for a while as a rental property, and later sold it at a reasonable profit.

What I learned from this experience is that buying in a neighborhood that is improving (gentrifying) increases your chances of success. There is a very good possibility that neighborhoods that are being redeveloped will improve in value in the short term. The help that you can get from the city is amazing. I don't understand why more people do not take advantage of all the free help that is available in most communities. It was astonishing how much I learned just by renovating one building.

We also learned a lot about being landlords. One of our tenants, who was a drama student at Yale and who went on to become a famous movie star, painted the inside of his entire apartment black—including the bathroom tile, sink, and tub. Had we exercised our right to occasionally inspect the apartment, he would not have been able to leave without paying for the damage, which greatly exceeded his security deposit.

Notice that I didn't say that the success story just described was my first investment. It wasn't. My first investment was in a small apartment house 60 miles from my home, which I went into with a group of close friends. We believed the sad story of the old man who was selling, didn't know the neighborhood, and didn't get any of the help that was available. We were lucky that, after holding the building for quite a few years, we managed to get most of our money back. We certainly did not make a profit!

With 20-20 hindsight, I am glad we bought this first loser because it got us started in what turned out to be a successful investment partnership, and taught us a lot about what not to do! I have always liked having investment partners for a variety of reasons. The most important thing for me was that when I was not available to solve a problem, one of my partners usually was.

Getting started in investing in real estate is like getting the first olive out of the jar: after that, the rest are easy.

SUMMARY

Almost every real estate professional seriously considers investing in real estate. They discover that real estate is an excellent investment and they want to join the millions of successful real estate investors.

The single-family owner-occupied house is the most popular real estate investment. It is the foundation of successful investment planning. It is a prime example of the magic of leveraging and historically has been a successful way to protect an investment against inflation. Owning a building for your own business is also very desirable.

Real estate enjoys unique tax benefits. Real estate taxes and mortgage interest are tax deductible. For investment properties, depreciation is also a deductible expense.

Some of the disadvantages of real estate are risk, nonliquidity, large minimum investments, and the need for active and experienced management.

Investment property can often produce a positive cash flow that is not taxable because of depreciation, which is tax deductible even though it does not come out of cash flow. This is often called the "magic of real estate."

There are many different types of real estate investments. Each has its own characteristics, advantages, and disadvantages.

Almost anyone can buy a few shares of a real estate investment trust and become a real estate investor. REIT mutual funds make the process very easy.

Corporations are large owners of real estate. Those that pay taxes are called C corporations, and those that elect to be taxed as a partnership are called S corporations. Recently, limited liability corporations (LLCs) have become a popular way to hold title to real estate.

Pyramiding is how most real estate millionaires make their money. One safe way to start is to buy a property, fix it up using your own "sweat equity," and either sell it and invest the proceeds in another property or hold it and use the proceeds of a new mortgage to buy another property.

Investing in real estate is not for everyone. However, it has special appeal to real estate professionals who can use their general knowledge about real estate to help them make a successful real estate investment more likely. Also, ownership of even a single-family home is a great learning experience for the new RESP. All of the headaches and advantages of real estate ownership will be theirs to enjoy.

CHAPTER 21

Other Real Estate Career Opportunities

The first thing that comes to mind when most people think of working in real estate is to become a salesperson or broker in a real estate agency. This is because the agency branch of real estate is the largest, and employs the most people. However, there are many other career opportunities in real estate, which are briefly described in this chapter.

Real estate careers fall into various categories. This breakdown is quite arbitrary. Many real estate professionals engage in more than one of the following activities:

- Residential sales
- Commercial and income property sales
- Farm brokerage
- Industrial brokerage
- Real estate education
- Real estate counseling
- Property management
- Residential rental agents
- Appraising
- Property inspection

- Insurance
- Government service
- Development and construction
- Investment

Most of the activities can be conducted with a real estate agent license or a brokers license. Appraising and insurance definitely require separate licenses. Real estate investment sales may require a securities license. There is legislation pending in a few states to require home inspectors to be licensed.

RESIDENTIAL SALES

Every community in the United States has one, and probably many, real estate sales agencies that handle residential sales. Almost everyone knows someone who is in this business. At any one time, there are about 2 million people who sell houses full- or part-time. In a typical year, they sell over 5 million new and used houses. This business is not evenly divided. Some part-time salespeople sell none or only a few houses per year. Many successful career salespeople and brokers sell millions of dollars worth of houses annually. Residential sales is the starting career for many people who change to one of the many other real estate career opportunities.

To be a successful real estate salesperson requires a variety of skills and interests. Many different types of people with a wide variety of likes, dislikes, interests, and skills become successful real estate salespeople.

Generally, to be successful, one must be willing to work hours at times that are convenient to clients, rather than themselves, including evenings and weekends. Successful salespeople like to sell and feel rewarded when they make a sale. Probably more important, they do not become discouraged when they show a property and do not make a sale.

Successful residential salespeople acquire broad knowledge about their territory and understand the unique characteristics of the many different neighborhoods within it. They also acquire a good working knowledge about the fundamentals of real estate and about the product (houses) they are selling.

Besides these characteristics, successful salespeople are instinctively adept at interpersonal relationships. They instill confidence in their clients. They are able to identify a client's true buying motives and find properties that fit these needs. They are not afraid to ask for a deposit and can focus on closing sales.

COMMERCIAL AND INCOME PROPERTY SALES

There are far fewer successful salespeople who specialize in selling properties other than single- and multiple-family residences. These people differ widely in what they do. Some are residential brokers who occasionally list, show, and sell a nonresidential property as the occasion arises. These mixed careers are more common in smaller cities and towns than they are in bigger cities, where specialization is more common. Many people who identify themselves as commercial-industrial brokers sell almost everything but single-family residences. Others specialize in just commercial, retail, office buildings, industrial, or other groups of properties. A few brokers develop very specific specialties, such as motels and hotels, health care facilities, fast-food operations, and so on. Many years ago, I met a broker who sold only breweries. He wore a black stovepipe hat in which he kept all his listing information. He said he kept all his information "on" his head. He was very successful.

Typical characteristics of successful nonresidential brokers are competency in mathematics (which is needed to put together the complex financing that is often required), knowledge about current laws, and the ability to understand and explain why properties are good investments or meet other needs of their clients.

These brokers tend to make fewer sales than residential brokers, but the commissions from the sales are usually larger than in the typical residential sale. Such brokers should have the type of personality that resists becoming discouraged during long periods between sales. Generally it takes longer to become established as a nonresidential broker than it does for residential sales.

FARM BROKERAGE

This is a specialty that requires a unique set of skills. Just a rural background may not be enough. Today's successful rural brokers often are graduates of colleges with agricultural programs. Good on-the-job training is also helpful.

INDUSTRIAL BROKERAGE

A growing number of people are specializing in selling and leasing industrial property. The Society of Industrial Realtors® (SIR) offers excellent education programs and awards the SIR designation to those members who meet their stringent education, experience, and reputation requirements.

The buyers and lessors of industrial property tend to be sophisticated and look to do business with brokers who are knowledgeable and have established successful reputations. This is one of the most difficult real estate specialties to break into. People wishing to enter this specialty should seek out successful brokers with whom they can affiliate.

REAL ESTATE EDUCATION

Real estate traditionally has been taught by real estate professionals, for the most part on a part-time basis, plus a relatively small group of full-time real estate instructors and professors.

Once you have obtained some experience, it is relatively easy to obtain a part-time position teaching real estate principles and practices and other real estate courses. Many instructors start their teaching careers at adult education courses given at local high schools, community colleges, real estate boards, and proprietary schools.

Most universities and many colleges have real estate departments that offer a wide variety of courses. These programs provide real estate education as part of a general business education program, as well as for students who want to make real estate a career. They are often led by professional real estate educators with PhDs and other advanced degrees. There are currently several hundred real estate professors and many more full-time real estate instructors at these facilities.

REAL ESTATE COUNSELING

Real estate counselors are people who sell advice for a fee. They are highly trained and often have years of experience. Real estate counseling differs from real estate appraising. Appraisers are primarily interested in estimating the value of a property. They try to be objective. Real estate counselors are hired to help clients solve a real estate problem. They look at the problem through the eyes of the client. Typical problems they are hired to help solve are where a client should locate a facility (store, office, factory, warehouse, etc.), what type of property they need, and how to best utilize a property they already own.

PROPERTY MANAGEMENT

It takes a different type of person and different skills to be a property manager than it does to be a salesperson. Property management is a growing field. A substantial part of its expansion resulted from the growth of condominiums, which often use professional property managers.

Property managers can be independent operators who work for many different property owners or they can be employees of corporations, institutions, the government (federal, state, local), or individual property owners. All of these entities own property and often need professional help to manage them.

The independent manager was historically paid a percentage of the collected rent to manage a typical income-producing property. Many such management arrangements still exist. The trend is for property managers to work for a fixed fee or salary, and many become the employee of the property owner, and are paid a salary and benefits as well.

A typical property manager is responsible for the property's rental, establishing an ongoing relationship with the tenants, the property's maintenance and repair, bookkeeping, and the supervision of maintenance and security personnel.

Successful property managers are good at public relations, knowledgeable about how properties operate, know about mechanical systems and how to maintain them, and keep current on laws concerning rentals, zoning, and the environment.

RESIDENTIAL RENTAL AGENTS

In many cities there are companies and agents who specialize in renting apartments, condominium units, and houses. They seek out units that are for rent and tenants who are looking for rentals. Some charge the landlord a fee or commission for renting and others charge the tenant for their services.

APPRAISING

There are now over 70,000 licensed and certified real estate appraisers listed in the Federal Registry. As a result of federal legislation, all 50 states and U.S. territories now offer separate appraisal licenses and certifications. While an appraisal license or residential certification permit only the appraisal of residential properties, a General Certification permits the appraisal of all types of property. The Uniform Standards of Professional Appraisal Practice (USPAP) limit all appraisers to appraising only properties they are qualified to appraise by reason of their education and experience. Some states require that all appraisers be licensed or certified. Other states require a licensed or certified appraiser only when the appraisal is made for federally related purposes (which includes most mortgage loans).

Appraisers generally are people who do not like sales and contingent commission payments. They like to do their work and not have to worry about being paid. Historically, appraisers tend to be people who started in other branches of real estate. Today many appraisers come straight from college or other non–real estate careers.

The appraisal profession is very well organized. The Appraisal Foundation represents many of the appraisal organizations in their dealings with the government. They have a contract with the federal government to establish appraisal standards and appraiser qualifications, which the states then incorporate into their license and certification laws. Most appraisers belong to one or more of over 30 national appraisal organizations, which award designations to indicate the level of education and experience that the appraiser has obtained. There is a large variation in the requirements to obtain one particular designation versus another.

Some appraisers operate as independent contractors or work for independent contractors who do work for many clients. Many lenders employ staff appraisers. The government is also a large employer of appraisers who work as assessors in state highway departments, property acquisition departments, and for the federal government in many agencies including the Post Office, Department of Defense, and the IRS.

PROPERTY INSPECTION

There are a variety of property inspectors. Some do general inspections; others make special inspections such as structural, termite, environmental, and so on.

It takes special training and experience to make property inspections. In some states, special licenses are required.

INSURANCE

The insurance industry is closely connected to real estate in many ways. A large percentage of the insurance sold protects property from fire, windstorm, liability, earthquake, flood, and many other perils. Property owners buy insurance to protect themselves from potential liability that may occur as a result of property ownership and use.

Title insurance is directly connected to real estate. It protects lenders and property owners from defects in the title to their property that may make it impossible to finance or sell when the defects are discovered.

Because of the close association between real estate and insurance, many real estate brokers also sell insurance. It requires separate training and different licenses to sell insurance.

GOVERNMENT SERVICE

The government at the federal, state, and local level owns and operates a vast amount of real estate. For example, about one-third of all the land in the United States is owned by the government. The government owns and maintains most of the roads and highways. The government owns office buildings, courthouses, airports, subways, hospitals, post office facilities, and museums. This list is just a small part of the real estate that is government owned and operated.

The list of government agencies that employ people to operate and manage their real estate is also very large. A few of the large government agencies involved are the Department of Defense, Bureau of Land Management, Federal Housing Administration (FHA), Veterans Administration (VA), and the Forest and Park Service.

DEVELOPMENT AND CONSTRUCTION

It is not uncommon for real estate brokers to try their hand at subdividing and construction. However, many people in the development and construction branch of real estate have never been directly involved in any other real estate activities.

Developers and builders acquire land, and then improve the land and construct buildings on it in the hope of making a profit. Their activities range from the acquisition and improvement of a single residential lot into a home they sell to developing large subdivisions in planned communities. Commercial and industrial developers also range from small independent operators to large multinational development corporations. They also convert and remodel existing buildings. Many developers do their own marketing, hiring salespeople to sell the property they create.

There are many career opportunities associated with development and construction which utilize a wide variety of real estate skills. Developers also employ professional architects, engineers, surveyors, draftspersons, and so on.

INVESTMENT

Real estate investors range from individuals who buy one or more small income properties, to large investment companies who hold national portfolios containing a wide variety of real estate. The following are some of the entities that invest in real estate:

1. Individuals
2. General partnerships
3. Limited partnerships
4. Small corporations
5. Large public corporations
6. Lending institutions
7. Insurance companies
8. Real estate investment trusts (REITs)
9. Government
10. Syndicators
11. Farmers and ranchers
12. Mining, oil, and timber companies

SUMMARY

When you consider all the different choices available, you can not help but conclude that there is room for almost anyone who wants to make real estate their career.

The majority of people who make real estate their career start off by selling houses and then progress to selling other kinds of real estate.

However, many people do not want to sell anything. Fortunately, for them there are many real estate careers that require no selling. For example, the authors are involved in appraising, counseling, education, and government service. But they all started in sales.

One of the best ways to start is to find a school that will prepare you for your real estate license. Most likely you will learn about many other real estate careers, too, and will meet people who will provide you with their first-hand experiences.

CHAPTER 22

What You Need to Know about Insurance

When a property is acquired, the buyer and the lenders need protection from the possibility that the deed to the property is somehow clouded and the current owner does not have clear title to the property. How property is transferred is covered in Chapter 10. In spite of title searches, surveys, certificates of title, warranty deeds, and so on, there exists the possibility that for a variety of reasons the current owner will not have clear title to the property. Fortunately, title insurance is available to guarantee clear title in case some defect in the title is discovered sometime in the future.

Another risk property owners sometimes face is that the payment of the mortgage premiums is dependent on the earning capacity of one of the owners. Should this owner die or become disabled, the other owners or their families may not be able to make the mortgage payments. Mortgage life insurance and mortgage disability insurance are designed to protect against these possibilities.

Owners of real estate are also exposed to the risk that their property (real estate and personal property) will be damaged by fire, storm, flood, earthquake, and a variety of other hazards. In addition, owning property exposes the owner to personal liability should the property cause someone to be injured. These risks can be insured against with a variety of different types of insurance.

Insurance is a complicated subject. To sell insurance requires a separate license from that required for real estate, which, in turn, requires the applicant to acquire a body of specialized knowledge about insurance. Since most property owners are not insurance experts, our advice is that they should buy their insurance from someone who is well qualified to give them the advice they need.

TITLE INSURANCE

Title insurance is a form of insurance that protects the policyholder from undisclosed defects in the title that occurred prior to the issuance of the policy. For example, if a property is purchased and the seller had borrowed against the property, the commitment for title insurance would disclose that the lender has a claim against the property. If the loan was not identified until after the closing, an owner's title insurance policy would protect the owner against the claim.

Prior to the issuance of a title insurance policy, the title company searches the public records to identify all matters of record that might have an impact on the title. When the commitment of title insurance is issued, it identifies all of the matters of record that might have an impact on the title that are excluded from the title insurance. The beneficiary of the title insurance should review the exceptions to ensure that they are willing to take responsibility for the title considerations that will be excluded from the title insurance policy.

There are numerous types of title insurance policies, and the most common ones are an owner's title insurance policy and a mortgagee's title insurance policy. An owner's title insurance policy is typically issued at the time a property is acquired, and the maximum amount of the insurance is the purchase price of the property. A mortgagee's title insurance policy protects the lender. The amount of the mortgagee's title insurance policy is the amount of the loan. A new mortgagee's title insurance policy is typically required for each refinance of the property.

Fraudulent Transactions

An increasing concern in the real estate market is associated with fraudulent transactions. The fraud could be associated with the parties to the ownership transfer, the true price of the transfer, or the loan that supports a transfer. Anything that is abnormal associated with a transaction should raise concern that some level of fraud might be occurring. All parties associated with a fraudulent transaction are investigated as being part of the fraud.

In some of these situations identity theft could be involved. The identity theft could be associated with anyone connected to the real estate transaction. Anytime there is fraud involved in a real estate transaction it is a federal offense, which could involve the Federal Bureau of Investigation.

MORTGAGE LIFE AND DISABILITY INSURANCE

Mortgage life insurance comes in a variety of packages. It is beyond the scope of this text to explain the variety of policies that are available. Sometime lenders require mortgage life insurance. Their need can be satisfied with a decreasing term form of life insurance. The policy is designed to pay off the mortgage in the event of the death of the insured. It has no cash value and is not a form of savings. It is the least expensive form of insurance that will accomplish this objective. To it can be added a variety of additional benefits.

Mortgage disability insurance pays the mortgage payments when the named insured is unable to work because of a disability caused by accident or sickness. There are endless varieties of this type of insurance, some of which are the waiting period before benefits start, the length of time for which the benefits are paid, whether the benefits are to be paid for partial disabilities, and, if so, what is the definition of partial disability.

RESIDENTIAL PACKAGE POLICIES

In order to take some of the mystery out of buying insurance, the insurance industry developed seven standard policies that will cover most residences. They are called homeowner and tenants policies. Four of these packages (HO-1, HO-2, HO-3, and HO-5) are designed to insure owner-occupied single-family dwellings. The (HO-4) policy is to cover tenants who do not own the property they live in. There is a special policy for condominiums and cooperatives that are owner-occupied (HO-6). There is also a special policy to insure older homes (HO-8). The HO-7 covers mobile homes.

Each of these policies contain two sections. Section I covers the real estate and personal property for physical damage. All of these policies cover the property for the following perils:

- Fire and lightning
- Losses sustained while removing property from endangered premises
- Windstorm and hail
- Explosion
- Riot and civil commotion
- Damage from aircraft
- Damage from vehicles
- Smoke damage
- Vandalism and malicious mischief
- Theft
- Glass breakage of parts of the building

If you want coverage for additional perils that are not covered in the basic Homeowner I policy, you can move up to a number II, III, or V. Some of the additional perils that will then be covered depending on which policy you select are:

- Falling objects
- Damage from the weight of ice, snow, or sleet
- Collapse of the building or any part thereof
- Sudden and accidental tearing asunder, cracking, burning, or bulging of a steam or hot water heating system or of appliances for heating water
- Accidental discharge, leakage, or overflow of water or steam from within a plumbing, heating, or air-conditioning system or domestic appliance
- Freezing of plumbing, heating and air-conditioning systems and domestic appliances
- Sudden and accidental injury from artificially generated currents to electrical appliances, devices, fixtures, and wiring

Policies HO-1 and HO-2 are called *named perils* because they cover only the perils named in the policy. The more you pay, the more perils are covered.

There is a better type of policy called an *all-risk policy* (HO-3 and HO-5). Instead of naming all the perils, it works in reverse. It covers everything except those perils that are excluded. That list usually includes flood, landslide, mudflow, tidal wave, earthquake, underground water, settling, cracking, war, nuclear accident, and environmental damage. These policies vary from state to state, so it is important to check with your insurance agent as to what you are buying.

The premium cost of the policy depends on many things, including the rate schedule of which company you are dealing with (they are all different), where you live, the proximity of fire hydrants, your claim experience, the limits of coverage, the deductible, and so on.

Another choice you have is the basis of how the value of what is damaged will be calculated. The least expensive is when you get "actual cash value," which is the depreciated cost of whatever is damaged. If the paint on the house is 10 years old, you probably will get about half of what the new paint job will cost. The same goes for anything else that is damaged.

The other choice is "new for old" coverage. It will pay based on what it costs to replace what is damaged, not its depreciated value.

None of these polices cover flood damage. To cover flood, you need a special flood insurance policy that is underwritten by the federal government. Most insurance agents sell it. Unfortunately, many people suffer flood damage who do not have flood insurance. The cost of this insurance depends on what flood zone the property is in and what limits and deductibles are chosen.

Depending on where you are, earthquake insurance can be added to the homeowner policy or obtained on a separate policy. Again the cost depends on where you are and what limits and deductibles are selected.

This is a very brief overview of Part I of the standard homeowner policy. Most of what was covered also applies to tenants' policies (HO-4) and condominium policies (HO-6). The big difference is that they do not cover most of the building, which must be covered by separate policies. The only conceivable reason not to buy an all-risk policy is the high premium cost.

Section II of all these policies provides liability coverage for the insured and their families who live with them. One big exclusion is automobile liability, which must be covered with a separate policy. It is a very broad coverage that covers anyone who is hurt on the insured premises plus anyone who is hurt by the insured, the insured's family (who are living with the insured), and the insured's pets. In order for there to be coverage, there must be negligence, with the exception of a medical expense coverage that does not require the insured to be negligent in order for there to be coverage. None of this covers the insured or his or her family for any injury they personally have. The cost of this coverage depends on the location of the property covered and the limits of liability selected.

Again there are possible additions to the basic policy, such as worker's compensation to cover people who work for you around the house. It is also possible to add coverage for an in-house office.

COMMERCIAL PACKAGE POLICIES

Commercial packages are similar to residential packages, plus they have a variety of add-ons that are needed by businesses such as business interruption coverage; fidelity coverage; separate worker's compensation coverage; group health, life, and disability insurance for the employees; and so on. In-depth coverage of commercial insurance is beyond the scope of this book.

FLOOD INSURANCE

The National Flood Insurance Program is about 50 years old. It is a joint effort between the insurance industry and the U.S. government to make flood insurance available at a reasonable price.

Although flood insurance is relatively inexpensive, most Americans neglect to purchase protection. Only about one-quarter of the homes in areas most vulnerable are insured against flood loss, according to the Federal Insurance Administration (FIA). In those areas, flooding is 26 times more likely to occur than a fire during the course of a typical 30-year mortgage. The most recent example of this problem is the large number of uninsured homes that were damaged by the Katrina hurricane and floods in New Orleans in 2005.

More than 19,000 communities have agreed to stricter zoning and building measures to control floods, according to the Federal Emergency Management Agency (FEMA). Residents in these communities are entitled to purchase flood insurance through the National Flood Insurance Program (NFIP), a program FEMA oversees.

HOME BUYER (HOME WARRANTY) INSURANCE

In a relatively short period of time, home warranty plans have grown dramatically in popularity. Today, the plans are almost standard in California real estate transactions, where 8 of every 10 home sales are covered. Home warranty plans are essentially service contracts or insurance policies that cover the major systems and appliances of a home.

The following benefits of a home warranty insurance plan:

- Sellers avoid after-the-sale disputes in case something goes wrong with the home.
- Buyers have peace of mind and protection against costly home repairs.
- Real estate professionals report more satisfied clients and less liability for all parties.
- Buyers have more confidence in buying a resale home.
- Sellers can be protected against costly repairs during the listing and escrow period.

Home warranties typically cover the mechanical systems of a home such as plumbing, heating, electricity, water heater, and most built-in appliances. Structural components typically are not covered. Some home warranty policies cover garage door openers and roof repairs, with certain limits.

Additional coverage is available under most home warranties at an extra charge for a pool, a spa, air-conditioning, and freestanding appliances such as refrigerators, washers, and dryers. Limited roof leak coverage is also offered by some home warranty insurance programs.

A standard home warranty contract costs about $275. Extras include $75 for washer and dryer and $25 for a refrigerator. Pool and spa equipment add about $125; central air-conditioning is $50 and limited roof leak coverage is about $100.

Usually the seller pays for the coverage. But the cost is negotiable, and it should be addressed in the purchase agreement. The type of coverage, including what equipment is to be included and the maximum policy fee, should be also specified. Otherwise, the seller may provide only a basic home warranty insurance policy.

When a malfunction occurs that involves a system covered by the home warranty plan, the homeowner calls the insurance company and requests a service call. The cost of the service call, which varies from $35 to $95 per visit depending on your location, is paid by the homeowner. The warranty company assigns the call to an approved contractor, and the home protection company pays for the system repair or replacement. A home warranty insurance protection plan should not be considered as an alternative to having the property thoroughly inspected by licensed professionals. System defects discovered during the home inspection won't be covered by a home warranty plan. These repairs should be negotiated between the buyer and seller prior to closing.

SUMMARY

Title insurance guarantees the buyer of a property clear title. It provides peace of mind knowing that when the current owner is no longer available to help clear a title defect, the title insurance company has to clear the title no matter how much it costs to do so.

The purpose of mortgage life and disability insurance is to provide money if the insured dies or becomes disabled and cannot pay off the mortgage. A true mortgage life insurance policy has no cash value, and the face value decreases in proportion to the decrease of the unamortized portion of the mortgage.

Most residential insurances are package policies that consist of two sections. Section I covers damage to the property and the personal property on the insured premises. A named peril policy provides coverage for those perils named in the policy. An all-risk policy provides coverage for all perils except those specifically excluded. Coverage for flood and earthquake damage is usually provided by special policies. Policy buyers have a choice of actual cash value coverage or new for old coverage.

Section II provides protection against being sued for bodily injury and property damage caused by the negligence of the owners or the occupants of the premises. It does not provide coverage for automobile liability and a variety of other excluded coverages.

Flood damage coverage is sold separately and is administered and underwritten by the federal government.

Sellers can purchase home warranty insurance that is transferred to the buyer, which provides protection in case of the failure of many of the components of the home.

Insurance is complicated and, therefore, it is wise to obtain the help of a knowledgeable insurance agent when deciding what coverage is needed to protect your property and provide adequate liability coverage.

CHAPTER 23

Practice Examinations

EXAM 1

E1.Q1 Which of the following is *not* a remedy for defaulting a contract for no legal reason?
   A. Specific performance
   B. Recision
   C. Compensatory and liquidated damages
   D. Bankruptcy

E1.Q2 The purpose of earnest money is all the following *except*:
   A. To show the sincerity of the buyer
   B. To demonstrate the buyer's capability to raise sufficient funds to purchase
   C. To serve as liquidated damages to the seller in the event of the buyer's default
   D. To compensate the broker in the event negotiations fail

E1.Q3 "A contract whereby the buyer will retain the property title upon paying full purchase price in installments and the seller agrees to transfer title to the buyer upon receiving full payment from the buyer" defines a:
   A. Contract for deed
   B. Purchase money mortgage
   C. Wraparound
   D. Deed in lieu of foreclosure

E1.Q4 The purpose of recording a contract for deed is to provide constructive notice of:
   A. The vendee's right to payment by the vendor
   B. The vendor's right to receive title upon full payment
   C. The vendor's right to payment by the vendee
   D. The vendee's transfer of title to the vendor

E1.Q5 What is an advantage to the principal in having an exclusive-right-to-sell listing agreement?
A. A guaranteed sale and optimum amount of exposure to the marketplace
B. Being represented by a secure and confident broker
C. Receiving optimum showings and free advertising at the expense of the broker
D. Retaining the amount of compensation if they sell the property themselves

E1.Q6 "Specific performance" means:
A. A seller transfers title when the buyer completes payments
B. Monies agreed to be paid in the event of breach of contract
C. An agreement to take back, remove, annul, or abrogate upon breach of contract
D. The contract will be executed as originally agreed

E1.Q7 Amortized payments are:
A. Regular installment payments applied first to the interest and the remainder to the reduction of principal
B. Installment payments made that pay off the principal and interest with a large final payment completing the obligation
C. Payments that cover only for a specific term at the end of which the principal is paid
D. Installment payments that include tax and insurance payments

E1.Q8 A purchase money mortgage is a:
A. Transfer of title upon full payment to the seller
B. Junior mortgage
C. Pledge of leasehold rights to secure the mortgage
D. Share of the profits of the property to the lender that are used to secure the loan

E1.Q9 When FHA was founded, part of its mission was:
A. To guarantee repayment of the top portion of the loan in the event of default
B. To include tax and insurance payments as part of the mortgage commitment
C. To provide a stable, effective method of financing homes
D. To provide a uniform standard for property valuation

E1.Q10 Veterans Administration (VA) qualifications are based on:
A. Disclosed statements that set forth a true, effective annual percentage rate
B. A residual balance for family support
C. Effective gross monthly income only
D. Set maximum loan amount

E1.Q11 Which is the correct regulation regarding assumption of a VA mortgage?
A. It is assumable by any qualified buyer who issues a release of liability.
B. It must be held for a set number of years before it becomes assumable.
C. It is assumable only by another qualified veteran.
D. It is not assumable under any circumstances.

E1.Q12 The term *prepaid items* includes all *except*:
A. Insurance monies at time of closing
B. Tax monies deposited at time of closing
C. Payments over and above settlement costs
D. Settlement costs

E1.Q13 The underwriting process includes:
A. Writing the contract
B. Negotiating the terms of the agreement
C. Evaluating the borrower's ability and willingness to pay
D. Disclosing the APR, finance charges, amount financed, and the total of the payments

E1.Q14 Cumulative zoning permits which of the following?
A. Property uses that are not designated in the zone
B. Preexisting use of the property that differs from current specifications
C. Permitted deviation from specific requirements of the zoning ordinance
D. Permitted use that is different from the requirements of that area's zoning

E1.Q15 The purpose of community planning is all the following *except*:
A. To provide orderly growth
B. To maintain social benefits
C. To obtain economic benefits
D. To disclose and regulate interstate sales of unimproved lots

E1.Q16 Ms. T inherited a three-bedroom home and wants two women to share the home. One of the applicants is Hispanic and another is African American. She refused each of them because she preferred women of her own national origin with whom she could share common cultural backgrounds. She is in violation of the law because:
A. She lives in the home.
B. She did not use an agent.
C. She prefers to have women only.
D. She discriminated because of national origin.

E1.Q17 The Americans with Disabilities Act (ADA) requires access for all people to all services and buildings *except*:
A. Public accommodations
B. Commercial facilities
C. Private dwellings
D. Public transportation

E1.Q18 Under provisions of the ADA, the term *readily achievable* means all the following *except*:
A. Easily accomplished
B. Able to be carried out without much difficulty
C. Accomplished at any cost
D. Accommodating the needs of those with disabilities

E1.Q19 Which of the following is *not* a requirement for new multifamily construction for persons with disabilities?
A. Switches at heights to be operated from wheelchairs
B. Elevators or lifts in structures of two stories or less
C. Wide open spaces in kitchens and bathrooms
D. Reinforced wall sections for grab bars

E1.Q20 Which of the following does *not* define *familial status*?
A. An adult with children under 18
B. A person who is pregnant
C. A person who has custody or will have custody of a child
D. A person with disabilities

E1.Q21 The Fair Housing Amendment of 1988 expanded to include the protective class for:
A. Religion
B. Familial status
C. Sex
D. Race

E1.Q22 Discrimination because of race, color, national origin, sex, religion, handicap, or familial status is illegal in all of the following situations *except*:
- A. Advising a prospective buyer that a house has been sold when it is available
- B. Refusing to accept an offer to purchase because the offeror is of a certain religion
- C. Refusing to rent to a person confined to a wheelchair
- D. Refusing to show an apartment designated for older persons to a young, single parent with two young children

E1.Q23 Directing prospective minority purchasers to presently integrated areas to avoid integration of nonintegrated areas is called:
- A. Blockbusting
- B. Redlining
- C. Steering
- D. Qualifying

E1.Q24 A person is deemed to be "in the business of selling and renting dwellings" if any of the following occurs *except*:
- A. The person has participated during the past 12 months as a principal in three or more residential transactions.
- B. The person has participated during the past 12 months as an agent in two or more residential transactions.
- C. The person is the owner of a dwelling of five units or more.
- D. The person moves and sells his or hre own single-family residence three times within 12 months.

E1.Q25 The Fair Housing Act can be enforced through the administrative procedures of all *except*:
- A. The Office of Equal Opportunity
- B. The administrative law judge
- C. The U.S. attorney general
- D. The local housing court

E1.Q26 An individual who engages in multiple discriminatory practices can be fined by the administrative law judge:
- A. A maximum of $25,000
- B. A minimum of $10,000 per case
- C. $25,000 to $50,000 without limitation of time periods
- D. Up to $10,000 per violation

E1.Q27 The U.S. attorney general may file a civil suit whereby it is deemed that any person or group is engaged in a pattern of violation of the fair housing law. In addition, the court may do all of the following except:
- A. Issue an injunction or restraining order against the person responsible
- B. Impose fines up to $50,000 to "vindicate the public interest"
- C. Levy a maximum fine of $25,000
- D. Impose a first-time fine of $50,000 when a "pattern of practice" exists

E1.Q28 A state housing court may sentence a person guilty of violating the state fair housing law to affirmative action by:
- A. Rendering community service
- B. Going out of business
- C. Hiring a minority
- D. Serving a prison sentence

E1.Q29 Examples of individuals with a disability that impairs any of the life functions include all of the following *except*:
A. Persons with AIDS
B. Persons with alcoholism
C. Persons with mental illness
D. Persons with minor children

E1.Q30 A private club is exempt from the provisions of the 1968 Fair Housing Act *except* when:
A. It holds events open to the public.
B. It provides lodging for the benefit of its members.
C. It is not used for commercial purposes.
D. It uses property the club owns.

E1.Q31 Under what circumstances is a religious organization *not* exempt from the provisions of the 1968 Fair Housing Act?
A. When using its own property
B. When operating for the benefit of its members *only*
C. When restricting its membership to only one national origin
D. When maintaining that its membership is *not* restricted because of sex, familial status, or handicapped conditions

E1.Q32 In general, real estate license law requires the licensee to possess all *except*:
A. Skill and knowledge of real estate procedures
B. A reputation of honesty and fair dealing
C. Ethical conduct in business activities
D. A one-year residence in the state issuing the license

E1.Q33 To obtain an indicated value through capitalization, the following formula must be applied:
A. Gross income multiplied by capitalization rate = value
B. Net operating income divided by capitalization rate = value
C. Effective gross income divided by capitalization rate = value
D. Net operating income multiplied by the capitalization rate = value

E1.Q34 Which of the following is *not* a specific lien?
A. Judgment lien
B. Mortgage lien
C. Real estate tax
D. Mechanic's lien

E1.Q35 The type of ownership that protects the owner by state law from forced sale by certain creditors of the owner is known as:
A. Dower right
B. In severalty
C. Estate for years
D. Homestead

E1.Q36 The one who receives an option is the:
A. Optionor
B. Vendee
C. Lessor
D. Optionee

E1.Q37 A salesperson obtained a listing on April 15 with a termination date of August 15. On May 15, the property was flooded, causing major damage to the foundation and the structure's integrity. On June 15, the salesperson's broker died. On July 15, the owner filed for bankruptcy. On which date did the listing actually terminate?
A. May 15
B. June 15
C. July 15
D. August 15

E1.Q38 A dwelling located next to a landfill site exemplifies:
A. Physical deterioration
B. Functional obsolescence
C. External obsolescence
D. Physical obsolescence

E1.Q39 All of the following are accepted theories of urban development *except*:
A. Sector
B. Competition
C. Axial
D. Multiple nuclei

E1.Q40 A purchaser wants a loan that is privately insured against loss in the event of default or foreclosure. Which of the following would the lender be able to offer?
A. An FHA loan
B. A VA loan
C. A conventional loan
D. A private insurance loan

E1.Q41 Which lender would be the best source of funds for mortgaging a farm whose prospective purchaser has limited credit potential?
A. FmHA
B. A savings bank
C. FHA
D. A commercial bank

E1.Q42 The borrower of funds for a mortgage is known as the:
A. Vendor
B. Optionee
C. Mortgagee
D. Mortgagor

E1.Q43 An owner wants to enclose a 55-foot × 80-foot portion of his backyard with 6-foot stockade fencing. Four bids have been obtained for equally professional work and comparable-quality materials. If the owner wants the job done most economically, which bid will he select?
A. $12 per linear foot
B. $3,200 flat fee
C. $2 per square foot
D. $18 per square yard

E1.Q44 In appraising a property using the cost approach, all of the following information can be used *except*:
A. Depreciation on land
B. Physical deterioration
C. functional obsolescence
D. External obsolescence

E1.Q45 Regulation Z is a lending institution requirement governing:
A. Loans with more than five installments
B. A business loan
C. Agricultural loans above $30,000
D. Any real estate purchase

E1.Q46 A salesperson working for a broker is required to attend two sales meetings a week, complete seven hours a week of floor time, and make five cold calls per day. This agent is probably working under a contract as:
A. An employee
B. An office manager
C. An independent contractor
D. A consultant

E1.Q47 A salesperson lists a property as sole agent and will receive a commission regardless of who sells the property. This type of listing is:
A. An exclusive right to sell
B. An exclusive agency
C. A nonexclusive agency
D. An open listing

E1.Q48 A completed contract is called:
A. An executory contract
B. A bilateral contract
C. A unilateral contract
D. An executed contract

E1.Q49 "A contract can exist when the intentions of the agreement are shown by conduct of the parties involved" describes:
A. An implied contract
B. An expressed contract
C. A bilateral contract
D. An executed contract

E1.Q50 Four investors agree to purchase a small office building together. One invests $35,000. Two each invest $25,000. The fourth agrees to invest the remaining balance, which is 20 percent of the total value of the investment. Her contribution is:

A. $15,000
B. $17,000
C. $20,000
D. $21,250

EXAM 1 ANSWERS

E1.A1   D

Bankruptcy relieves a person of the liability of outstanding contracts.

E1.A2   D

Under *no* circumstances can earnest money be used to *compensate the broker.*

E1.A3   A

Contract for deed can stipulate full payment or a certain percentage of payments and other agreements to complete the remaining balances due before passing title. In the *purchase money mortgage,* title is transferred at the closing of the contract and permits the buyer to finance the purchase through the seller. *Wraparound* is a junior mortgage of any amount agreed on between buyer and seller. *Deed in lieu of foreclosure* is a transfer of title from a borrower (mortgagor) to the lender, precluding the need for the lender to foreclose the mortgage.

E1.A4   C

Vendor's right to payment by the vendee is declared to the public when the contract for deed or land contract is recorded. The vendee is the buyer who holds the obligation to pay the vendor and vendee.

E1.A5   B

It is perceived that *the broker is so secure and confident* in her own ability to procure a qualified buyer that she is willing to invest her own funds, time, and skills in marketing the property for which she will be compensated at the closing. An exclusive-right-to-sell listing does not guarantee procuring a buyer regardless of the exposure to the market. There is no optimum number of showings to produce a buyer, as each property and market is unique. Advertising costs are absorbed by the broker, who offers advertising as a service rendered for which compensation will be made upon a successful sale of the prop-

erty. "Retain the amount of compensation himself if the property owner sells the property himself" is an advantage of the exclusive agency listing.

E1.A6   D

The parties are held to the terms of the contract *as originally agreed on* and are required to perform. Seller's transfer of title upon receiving full payment is contract for deed. Moneys to be paid upon breach of contract refers to damages. To take back, remove, annul, or abrogate define recision.

E1.A7   A

The terminology for *regular payments of interest and principal paid over the full term of the mortgage* is amortized payment. Payment completed with one large final payment is a balloon payment. Payments covering interest only until final payment of total principal is a term mortgage. Payment for taxes and insurance along with principal and interest is impound or escrow account.

E1.A8   B

Purchase money mortgage is usually *a junior mortgage* when part of the mortgage is held by the seller in a lesser position to the first obligation. A describes a contract for deed. C defines a leasehold mortgage. D is called a participation mortgage.

E1.A9   C

FHA's primary purpose is *to provide a stable, effective method to support the financing of homes.* The VA has a mortgage program that guarantees repayment to the lender. A mortgage with payments that include tax and insurance payments is an escrow to impound mortgage. The uniform residential appraisal report form provides a standard of valuation for property

E1.A10   B

A residual balance for family support is calculated from the relationship between a relatively stable gross monthly income and the estimated house payments, minus long-term debts in proportion to the number of family dependents. A is a requirement of the Truth-in-Lending Act. C and D are requirements of the FHA.

E1.A11 A

A is correct.

E1.A12 D

Prepaid items are *not included in settlement costs*. The FHA requires the borrower to pay all prepaid items but permits the seller to pay the buyer's closing costs.

E1.A13 C

Loan underwriting *evaluates the buyer's ability and willingness to pay* (creditworthiness) and the property's worth. An attorney writes the contract; the agent and principal negotiate the terms of the agreement; the Truth-in-Lending Act requires the lender to disclose to the borrower prior to the closing the APR, the amount of the financial charges, the amount financed, and the total of all payments.

E1.A14 A

Cumulative zoning may permit uses *not designated for the area*. B is nonconforming use; C is a variance; D is spot zoning.

E1.A15 D

HUD enforces and regulates the Federal Interstate Land Sales Act (the sale of unimproved lots across state lines).

E1.A16 D

Under no circumstances and without any exception can anyone discriminate against another because of race, color, or *national origin*.

E1.A17 C

Private dwellings are covered under the fair housing laws. (The ADA applies to owners and operators of *public accommodations, commercial facilities and public transportation.*)

E1.A18 C

The ADA wants buildings and facilities to be designed, constructed, and altered to be accessible to all persons under all circumstances, but *not accomplished at any cost.*

E1.A19 B

Elevators or lifts in two-story structures are not required. Elevators are required in multilevel buildings for more than four units.

E1.A20 D

A *person with disabilities* has a physical or mental impairment that substantially limits the major activities of the person.

E1.A21 B

Family status and persons with a handicapped condition became a major component of the Fair Housing Law of 1988. *Religion, sex,* and *race* are protective classes added much earlier than 1988.

E1.A22 D

Property designed for older persons and persons with disabilities is reserved for those persons. It does not constitute discrimination to reserve such accommodations for the elderly (62 years and older) and those with disabilities. A, B, and C are violations of the law.

E1.A23 C

Steering falls under the general prohibition of refusing to sell, rent, or negotiate housing for discriminating purposes. Blockbusting occurs when residents of a neighborhood are persuaded to sell because a minority is moving to their neighborhood. Redlining is a technique used by lending institutions to discriminate in areas where the lender does not want to lend money. Qualifying determines the buyer's financial capabilities.

E1.A24   D

Selling one's single-family residence is considered a single, completed transaction that does not constitute a real estate business.

E1.A25   D

The *local housing court* settles disputes between landlords and tenants regarding eviction status.

E1.A26   C

A fine of *$25,000 to $50,000 without limitation of time periods* if it is proven that the person has committed multiple offenses. Up to $10,000 can be levied against first-time offenders; $25,000 can be levied if another violation occurs within five years of the first offense, and $50,000 if two or more violations occur within a seven-year period.

E1.A27   C

The U.S. attorney general is *not* limited to *a maximum fine of $25.000.*

E1.A28   A

In rendering community service the person could be required to advertise the fair housing regulations or sponsor a seminar for the public regarding fair housing law and procedures. B, C, and D are powers granted to higher courts.

E1.A29   D

Persons with minor children are included under the protective classes of familial status.

E1.A30   A

No exemption is permitted *for events in which the public is invited to participate.*

E1.A31   C

It is illegal to discriminate under any circumstance because of race, color, or national origin.

E1.A32   D

A residency period is not a requirement for obtaining a real estate license in all states.

E1.A33   B

Net operating income divided by the capitalization rate gives the estimated value using the income approach to valuation. Gross income minus vacancy and loss plus other reliable amounts of income generates the effective gross income from which expenses are extracted, resulting in the net operating income.

E1.A34   A

Judgment liens are general liens affecting all of a debtor's property. Specific liens affect only one designated property.

E1.A35   D

Homestead is land and its improvements that are declared by the owner as a legal homestead and that by state law offer the additional protection from forced sale by some creditors. Dower right is interest given in some states to wives whose husbands owned land during their marriage in severalty as sole ownership. An estate for years is interest in real property leased for an exact period of time for specific consideration.

E1.A36   D

The *optionee* is the party that receives and holds the option offered by the *optionor*. The *vendee* is the buyer in a contract for deed. The *lessor* offers the lease.

E1.A37   A

May 15, as major damages to the property create change in value, use, terms, and conditions of an agreement. Subsequently B, C, and D would also terminate the listing.

E1.A38   C

External obsolescence, formerly referred to as locational, economic, or environmental obsolescence, reflects the loss of value caused from conditions outside the property boundaries. Physical deterioration occurs with the wearing out of the premises. Functional obsolescence is loss in value caused from poor design and lack of utility.

E1.A39   B

Competition is not a theory of urban development but a principle of appraisal.

E1.A40   C

A conventional loan can be privately insured against default and foreclosure. FHA and VA loans are government loans; hence, they cannot offer private insured capability. A private insurance loan is not for mortgage purposes.

E1.A41   A

The Farmers Home Administration assists those with weak credit capabilities. Savings and commercial banks have specific criteria regarding credit, which must be met.

E1.A42   D

The *mortgagor* pledges to the mortgagee (lender) the real estate to secure the loan. The vendor is the seller in a contract for deed. The optionee receives the option.

E1.A43   B

$3,200 is the least amount charged. Each of the others totals $3,240.

E1.A44   A

Land does not depreciate in cost approach.

E1.A45   A

Loans *with more than five installments* are covered by Regulation Z.

E1.A46   A

Employees can be given assignments and directions to complete the assignment.

Independent contractors may accept assignments to complete as they design and plan. Office managers or consultants may be either employees or independent contractors.

E1.A47   A

An *exclusive-right-to-sell* listing gives the rights and obligations to the agent of the listing brokerage firm to market the property, and the principal agrees to pay the compensation to the brokerage firm when terms of the listing have been met. Exclusive agency compensates the brokerage firm only if the agency procured the buyer. *Non-exclusive* and *open listing* are the same and compensate whomever procures the buyer who satisfies the terms of the contract.

E1.A48   D

An *executed contract* is one in which all terms have been met and the contract is accomplished. An *executory contract* is one that is in the process of becoming complete. A *bilateral contract* is a promise for a promise by each party that each will act in exchange for the other party's promise to perform. A *unilateral contract* exists where one party performs to induce the other to perform.

E1.A49   A

An *implied contract* occurs by each party acting as if an agreed-upon contract does exist. An *expressed contract* is a written agreement. A *bilateral contract* is one in which each party agrees to perform for the other in specific terms. An *executed contract* is a completed contract where all terms are accomplished.

E1.A50   D

$35,000 + $50,000 = 85,000

100% − 20% = 80% = 0.8

85,000/0.8 = $106,250 × 0.2 = $21,250

EXAM 2

E2.Q1 A house has a market value of $475,000. The assessed value is 65 percent of the market value. The mill rate is 43.4 mills. What is the annual property tax?
A. $3,087.45
B. $20,596.50
C. $13,399.75
D. $20,615.00

E2.Q2 The responsibility of the secondary market is:
A. Transferring first mortgages among mortgagees
B. Marketing junior mortgages
C. Transferring mortgages among mortgagors
D. Transferring title from grantors to grantees

E2.Q3 The document that must be filed to remove a mortgage lien after final payment has been made is called:
A. Satisfaction of mortgage
B. Revocation of agreement
C. Alienation clause
D. None of the above

E2.Q4 The IRS has requirements that determine independent contractor status. These requirements include all of the following *except*:
A. The individual must hold a current real estate license.
B. The individual must have a written contract with the broker containing specific wording declaring nonemployee status.
C. The individual must file a certified record of quarterly increments paid to the IRS.
D. At least 90 percent of the individual's income as a licensee must be based on sales production rather than number of hours worked.

E2.Q5 In the event an installment contract fails to state an interest rate, the IRS will:
A. Allow the payee to determine the going rate with a 5 percent penalty
B. Impute a prescribed rate, computed monthly
C. Accept the rate set by the Federal Reserve at the time of filing
D. None of the above

E2.Q6 A buyer of U.S. real property interest and any corporation, partnership, or fiduciary required to withhold tax must:
A. File an IRS Form 8288 to report and transmit amounts withheld
B. File an IRS Form 1040 along with other annual filings
C. File an IRS Form 1031 prior to the settlement
D. File an IRS Form 1099 stating the amount withheld

E2.Q7 According to the Sherman Anti-Trust Act, a person found guilty of price fixing rather than negotiating prices for services rendered is punishable by:
A. A maximum $100,000 fine and three years in prison
B. A $25,000 fine for the first offense and one year in prison
C. A $50,000 fine for each offense and five years in prison
D. None of the above

E2.Q8 Which of the following is *not* a true statement?
A. Contracts for the sale of real estate are required to be in writing.
B. Real estate contracts set forth all details of agreements between buyer and seller.
C. A document accepted and signed by the seller and delivered to the buyer becomes a contract of sale.
D. After the buyer and seller have executed a contract for

sale of real property, the buyer acquires equitable title of the property.

E2.Q9 A contract by which an owner gives a prospective buyer the right to buy at a fixed price within a specific time period is known as:
A. A contract for deed
B. A leased fee
C. A leasehold
D. An option

E2.Q10 A mortgagor wants to calculate the outstanding balance remaining on her loan. Her interest payment last month was $491.73 at a rate of 7.5 percent. Her balance last month before she made her monthly payment was:
A. $78,676.80
B. $5,900.76
C. 6,556.40
D. $78,185.07

E2.Q11 The deed that conveys the least amount of protection to the grantee is:
A. A general warranty
B. A quitclaim deed
C. A contract for deed
D. A bargain and sale deed

E2.Q12 A property that includes in its ownership the appurtenant right to use an easement over another's property for a specific purpose is known as:
A. Eminent domain
B. Encroachment
C. Dominant tenement
D. None of the above

E2.Q13 The heredity succession of any heir to the property of a relative who dies intestate is known as:
A. Dower
B. Descent
C. Duress
D. Devise

E2.Q14 All the following are examples of involuntary alienation except:
A. Deed
B. Escheat
C. Eminent domain
D. Accretion

E2.Q15 Which of the following statements is not true?
A. All titles pass to the grantee when the title is executed and delivered.
B. A title transfer for Torrens property occurs when the deed has been examined and accepted for registration.
C. Deeds are recorded to provide protection against third parties.
D. The date of delivery in a closing in escrow is the date it was deposited with the escrow agent.

E2.Q16 A condensed history of all recorded instruments affecting title to a property is known as:
A. an attorney's opinion of title
B. Certificate of title
C. Certificate
D. Abstract of title

E2.Q17 A man inherits his father's home, but he finds that each property in the new subdivision is larger than his. He is prevented by zoning ordinance from adding a family room to his house. This is an example of:
A. Nonconforming use
B. Conditional use
C. Variance
D. Spot zoning

E2.Q18 All of the following are examples that could prevent title passing except:
A. Laches
B. Lis pendes
C. Cloud on title
D. Valuable consideration

E2.Q19 What is the protection a buyer or seller may obtain against loss of title through defects unknown at the time of closing?
A. Certificate of title
B. Attorney's opinion of title
C. Title insurance
D. None of the above

E2.Q20 Ownership by occupants of a building whereby each purchaser becomes a stockholder and receives a proprietary lease to specific space describes ownership in a:
A. Partnership
B. Cooperative
C. Condominium
D. Leasehold estate

E2.Q21 The joining together of two or more parties to create and operate a real estate investment defines:
A. Syndication
B. Condominium
C. Community property
D. Tenancy in common

E2.Q22 All of the following are physical characteristics of land *except*:
A. Improvements
B. Immobility
C. Indestructibility
D. Nonhomogeneity

E2.Q23 Which of the following is not part of metes and bounds descriptions?
A. Specific point of beginning
B. Linear measurements and directions
C. Sections or parts of sections
D. Return of boundary lines to the POB

E2.Q24 A subdivision plat divides land into:
A. Sections
B. Townships
C. Monuments
D. Blocks and lots

E2.Q25 An acre consists of:
A. One square mile
B. 43,560 square feet
C. 5,280 linear feet
D. None of the above

E2.Q26 Nonjudicial foreclosure requires all the following *except*:
A. The court must award title to the lender.
B. The mortgage must include a power-of-sale clause.
C. Notice of default must be recorded.
D. The public sale must be advertised in local papers.

E2.Q27 The type of mortgage foreclosure whereby the lender sues the borrower in court and obtains judgment and a court order to sell is known as:
A. Strict foreclosure
B. Judicial foreclosure
C. Nonjudicial foreclosure
D. Deficiency judgment

E2.Q28 A final payment of a loan that is larger than previous payments and repays the loan in full describes:
A. amortized payment
B. Purchase money payment
C. Iinstallment payment
D. Balloon payment

E2.Q29 The most profitable use to which a property may be adapted is known as:
A. Conformity in use
B. Contribution in use
C. Highest and best use
D. Anticipation in use

E2.Q30 All of the following are accepted approaches to value used in an appraisal *except*:
A. Depreciation
B. Cost
C. Sales comparison
D. Income capitalization

E2.Q31 The *Financial Institutions Re-form, Recovery, And Enforce-ment Act* (FIRREA) of 1989 requires:
A. Licensing of real estate appraisers
B. Certification of lending institutions
C. Licensing of real estate brokers
D. None of the above

E2.Q32 What is used by brokers and salespersons to set a listing price for a property to be marketed?
A. A market value report
B. A cost approach report
C. A sales comparison analysis
D. A comparative market analysis

E2.Q33 "The present worth of future benefits arising from the owner-ship of real property" defines:
A. Market value
B. Value
C. Appraisal
D. Increasing and decreasing returns

E2.Q34 The steps of the cost approach in an appraisal include all of the following estimates *except*:
A. Annual potential gross income
B. Land value
C. Replacement value of improvements
D. Depreciation

E2.Q35 Which of the following is not a principle of valuation?
A. Comparative market analysis
B. Substitution
C. Change
D. Anticipation

E2.Q36 Which of the following is not a characteristic a property must have in order to be of value in the real estate market?
A. Utility
B. Scarcity
C. Terms of sale
D. Transferability

E2.Q37 The act of combining two or more adjacent parcels of land re-sulting in an increase in value is known as:
A. Plottage
B. Assemblage
C. Pyramiding
D. None of the above

E2.Q38 Construction cost at current prices for items that are not the exact duplicate of the subject property but serve the same function is:
A. Reproduction cost
B. Reconciliation cost
C. Replacement cost
D. Refinance cost

E2.Q39 What is the value of a residen-tial property receiving a monthly income of $1,200 in a neighborhood generating a GRM of 120?
A. $14,400
B. $120,000
C. $144,000
D. $1,728,000

E2.Q40 The estimated value of a property generating an annual income of $90,000 with a 10 percent vacancy and loss rate, expenses of $54,000, and an 8 percent capitalization rate is:
A. $337,500
B. $405,000
C. $450,000
D. None of the above

E2.Q41 The method of analyzing the economic activity of a commu-nity that attracts income from outside its boundaries is known as:
A. Economic life
B. Market analysis
C. Neighborhood analysis
D. Economic-base analysis

E2.Q42 Broker A listed a property for $125,000 with a 7 percent commission. He has an agreement to compensate the listing agent in his office 20 percent of the gross commission. The listing is shared through the MLS with a commission to the cooperating broker of 4 percent of the sale price. Broker B, whose agent produced the buyer who paid full price, agrees to pay his agent 35 percent of the gross received by his firm. Which of the following statements is true?
A. The cooperating brokerage received $8,750; its agent received $3,062.50.
B. The cooperating brokerage received $7,000; the listing agent received $1,750.
C. The listing agency received $8,750; the selling agent received $1,750.
D. The listing agent received $1,750; the selling agent received $1,750.

E2.Q43 A new home buyer builds a rectangular concrete patio at the rear entrance to her home. She selects a 6-inch slab that runs 24 feet adjacent to the rear wall of the house and 16 feet into the yard. How many cubic yards of concrete are required to construct this patio?
A. 7.111 cubic yards
B. 10.6667 cubic yards
C. 17.7778 cubic yards
D. 26.6667 cubic yards

E2.Q44 Which of the following measurements is not true?
A. An acre contains 43,560 square feet.
B. There are 9 cubic feet in one cubic yard.
C. A section contains 640 acres.
D. A right triangle is half the base times the height.

E2.Q45 A property whose market value was estimated at $100,000 is in a community where property is assessed at 70 percent of the market value and has a tax rate of 26 mills. This year's tax is:
A. $182
B. $1,820
C. $18,200
D. None of the above

E2.Q46 A 400-acre parcel of land is developed into a 250-lot subdivision. Ten percent of the land is reserved for roads, 6 percent for parks/playgrounds, and 15 percent for open space. All lots are of equal size, containing:
A. 1 acre
B. 1-1/2 acre
C. 1-1/10 acre
D. 2-2/3 acre

E2.Q47 All of the following are types of contract *except*:
A. Express
B. Void
C. Voidable
D. Valid

E2.Q48 A contract that appears to be valid but gives neither party the right to sue to force performance is known as:
A. Unenforceable
B. Voidable
C. Executed
D. Executory

E2.Q49 Which of the following is *not* known as a major warehousing agency?
A. Fannie Mae
B. FmHA
C. Ginne Mae
D. Freddie Mac

E2.Q50 The clause in a mortgage agreement that permits the lender the right to declare the entire debt due and payable is called the:
A. Assignment clause
B. Alienation clause.
C. Amortization clause
D. Acceleration clause

EXAM 2 ANSWERS

E2.A1   C

$475,000 × 0.65 = $308,750
Assessed Value
$308,750 × 0.0434 = $13,399.75

E2.A2   A

The secondary market handles only first mortgages and *transfers mortgages among mortgagees.* Junior mortgages are marketed through private sources. Mortgagors are borrowers who created the mortgage. Transferring of title is a legal act of ownership privileges.

E2.A3   A

Satisfaction of mortgage is a certificate that when recorded gives notice that the mortgagee consents to this discharge of record. *Revocation* is the act of terminating or canceling an agreement to perform a specific task or privilege. An *alienation clause* gives the grantor the rights to transfer ownership or title.

E2.A4   C

There is *no* requirement for the individual to file a record of funds paid to the IRS to determine independent contract status.

E2.A5   B

The IRS will impute the interest at a prescribed rate, computed monthly, on installment contracts that neglect to include the specific and reasonable interest rate.

E2.A6   A

Form 8288 must be filed to report and transmit the appropriate amount of tax withheld. *Form 1040* is an individual tax report of taxable income. *Form 1031* is the report for tax-deferred exchange. *Form 1099* is the report of commissions earned as independent contractors.

E2.A7   A

A person may be found guilty of a felony punishable by *a maximum $100,000 fine and three years in prison.*

E2.A8   A

Contracts are required by the *statute for the prevention of fraud* to be in writing *to be enforceable.* Oral contracts may be valid but may also be ambiguous because the terms are not clearly defined in writing.

E2.A9   D

The right to purchase property within a definite time at a specified price is an *option. Contract for deed* is a contract for the sale of the property whereby the sales price is paid in installments by the purchaser in possession and the title is retained by the seller until payment as agreed is completed. *Leased fee* is the lessor's interest, and *leasehold,* the lessee's interest in leased property.

E2.A10   A

$491.73 × 12 (months) = $5900.76 (annual)
$5,900.76/0.075 = $78,676.80

E2.A11   B

Quitclaim deed conveys to the grantee only the interest held by the grantor with no warranties or obligations. *General warranty* conveys to the grantee good title, which no one else can claim. *Contract for deed* conveys title to the grantee upon the buyer's completing the installment payments as agreed. *Bargain and sale* conveys title with no warranties, but does declare that the grantor has the right to convey title with warranties if he or she so desires.

E2.A12   C

Dominant tenement receives benefits from a servient tenement and is usually attached to it. *Eminent domain* is the government's right to acquire personal property for public use. *Encroachment* is realized when a fixture or structure invades another's ownership and property use.

E2.A13   B

Descent is governed by state law; *dower* is the legal right of acquisition afforded a wife of her deceased husband. *Duress* is the use of lawful constraint that forces one to act or refrain from acting against his will. *Devise* is the transfer of real estate by will.

E2.A14   A

Deed is a voluntary alienation accomplished through sale or gift.

E2.A15   A

All *titles except* Torrens and closing in escrow pass to the grantee when title is executed and delivered.

E2.A16   D

Abstract of title is a complete summary of all grants, conveyances, wills, records, court decisions, and liens affecting the title of a specific parcel of land. *Attorney's opinion of title* or *certificate of title* is prepared by an attorney without preparation of an abstract giving his opinion of the title condition. *Torrens system* certifies the title by the owner's signature filed with the registrar's office and used to verify future transfers.

E2.A17   A

Nonconforming use implies that the existence of use preceded the zoning ordinance but the property is allowed to remain in its present use. *Conditional use* is granted an individual to use the property in a way not permitted by the zoning ordinance. *Variance* allows an individual to deviate from the zoning ordinance. *Spot zoning* is a reclassification of a small area of land for a different use than the surrounding land.

E2.A18   D

Valuable consideration is a monetary measure of value, which is a major element of a contract to convey title to property. *Laches* is a court doctrine that bars legal claim because of undue delay to assert a claim. *Lis pendens* is a recorded, constructive notice that action relating to a property has been filed in court. *Cloud on title* is any claim that might prevent the title from passing.

E2.A19   C

Title insurance provides coverage for the policyholder against certain defects itemized in the policy. *Certificate of title* and *attorney's opinion of title* verify the validity of the title according to the recordings but give limited protection to the owners should the unexpected occur.

E2.A20   B

Cooperative is a corporation that holds title to land and buildings occupied by its stockholders who retain proprietary leases. *Partnership* is an association of two or more persons to carry on business. *Condominium* permits individual owners to hold fee simple title to their unit and a specified share in common elements. *Leasehold estate* permits the tenant (lessee) to occupy space for a specified period of time under specified conditions.

E2.A21   A

Syndication is a group of two or more persons who form a business for investment acquisition, operation, and eventual reversion. *Condominium* is a group of individual unit owners who also hold a specified amount of interest in common areas and responsibilities. *Community property* is property ownership acquired by a husband and wife after the marriage has occurred. *Tenancy in common* allows each owner to hold individual interest in severalty.

E2.A22   A

Improvements are structures or permissions that affect the economic value of land.

E2.A23   C

A *section or part of a section* is a characteristic of the rectangular (government) survey.

E2.A24   D

Blocks and lots are parcels of the subdivision plats. *Sections* and *townships* are parcels of land using the rectangular (government) survey. *Monuments* are found in metes and bounds descriptions.

E2.A25   B

The actual measurement of an acre is 43,560 square feet. A mile is 5,280 *linear feet*. *One square mile* constitutes a section of land (640 acres).

E2.A26   A

The *court awards title to the lender* in a strict foreclosure.

E2.A27   B

Judicial foreclosure also requires the property be sold at public sale to the highest bidder. In a *strict foreclosure,* the court transfers the title of the property directly to the lender. *Nonjudicial foreclosure* is agreed on and written into the mortgage agreement. *Deficiency judgment* is levied against the original mortgagor for the amount due because of insufficient funds from the sale of the foreclosed property.

E2.A28   D

Balloon payment requires the final payment to complete the entire obligation. *Amortized payment* is a regular periodic payment applied first to interest, with the balance applied to the principal throughout the entire term of the loan. *Purchase money payment* is given by the mortgagor (buyer) directly to the mortgagee (seller) and may be amortized or balloon. *Installment payment* is paid directly by the purchaser who is in possession of the property to the seller who retains title until full payment is complete.

E2.A29   C

Highest and best use is the ultimate use for the property. *Conformity* is the maximum value realized if the land conforms to existing neighborhood standards. *Contribution* is the value of a component of the property in relationship to what it adds to the property. *Anticipation* is the fluctuation in value as a result of benefits or detriments to the property.

E2.A30   A

Depreciation is a component of the cost approach reflecting the wasting of an asset.

E2.A31   A

Licensing and certification of appraisers is required in all states but must meet the standard specified by the federal guidelines of FIRREA. Some states require *licensing of lenders,* and FIRREA requires monitoring of lending institutions. Licensing of *real estate brokers* has been required in all states for several years.

E2.A32   D

Comparative market analysis compares recently sold, similar properties within a neighborhood. The *market value* is the most probable price a property will bring in a competitive market with reasonable time to obtain a knowledgeable purchaser. The *sales comparison* approach estimates value of the subject property through adjustments of sales prices of comparables. *Cost approach* is based on substitution.

E2.A33   B

Value is defined. *Market value* is the most probable price a property will generate in a competitive market in a reasonable amount of time to seek a knowledgeable buyer. *Appraisal* is an estimate or opinion of value. *Increasing and decreasing returns* occurs when improvements to land and structures produce an increase in value until the improvement loses sufficient value to cause a decrease in value.

E2.A34   A

Annual potential gross income is a component of the income capitalization approach.

E2.A35   A

Comparative market analysis is used in brokerage to estimate the listing price of a property.

E2.A36   C

Terms of sale is an area of adjustment within the sales comparison approach in an appraisal.

E2.A37   B

Assemblage is the process of combining adjoining parcels; *plottage* is the increase in value resulting from the assemblage. *Pyramiding* is the process of acquiring additional properties by refinancing owned property and then reinvesting those newly acquired funds into additional properties.

E2.A38   C

Reproduction cost is construction cost at current prices for exact duplications. *Reconciliation* is the final step in the appraisal process. *Refinance* is obtaining a new loan to pay off an existing loan.

E2.A39   C

$1,200 (monthly income) × 120 (GRM) = $144,000 (value)

E2.A40   A

$90,000 (annual income) − 0.10 (v/l) = $81,000
$81,000 − $54,000 = $27,000 =
$27,000/0.8 = $337,500

E2.A41   D

Economic-based analysis is used to predict the impact on real estate of population and other variables based on basic employment (income generated from sources outside the community) and service employment. *Economic life* is the estimated period of time over which an improved property may be profitably utilized to yield a designated return. Market analysis is a comparison of properties comparable to the subject property. Neighborhood analysis is the valuation of a homogeneous grouping of individuals or businesses within a larger community.

E2.A42   D

$125,000 (selling price) ×
0.07 (gross commission) = $8,750
$8,750 (gross commission) ×
0.2 (listing agent share) = $1,750
$125,000 (purchase price) ×
0.04 (cobroker commission) = $5,000
$5,000 (cobrokerage commission) × 0.35 (cobrokerage agent commission) = $1,750

E2.A43   A

24 feet × 16 feet × 0.5 feet = 192 cubic feet
27 cubic feet = 1 cubic yard
192 cubic feet/27 =
7.111 cubic yards

E2.A44   B

There are 27 cubic feet
(3 feet × 3 feet × 3 feet) in a cubic yard.

E2.A45   B

$100,000 × 0.7 × 0.026 = $1,820.00

E2.A46   C

400 acres − 124 acres (31% of 400) =
276 acres/250 lots = 1.1040 acres

E2.A47   A

Express is a contract classification in which the parties state terms and show intentions of the contract in oral or written words.

E2.A48   A

Unenforceable particularly with oral agreements. *Voidable* may appear to be valid but may be signed under undue duress, by a minor, or by fraud or misrepresentation. *Executed* reflects that all promises have been completed. *Executory* indicates that something remains to be accomplished by one or both parties.

E2.A49   B

Farmers Home Administration (FmHA) makes and insures loans for farmers, ranchers, and homeowners who are unable to secure credit from other sources, but it is not a warehousing agency.

E2.A50   D

Assignment is the mortgagee's right as assignor to assign the mortgage to a new owner known as the assignee. An *alien-* *ation* clause, also known as a due-on-sale clause, gives the lender the right to declare due on sale or grant the purchaser the right to assume the mortgage. *Amortization* is the loan payment process whereby the regular monthly payments reduce the principal and require interest on unpaid balance.

EXAM 3

E3.Q1 A woman receives 95 percent of her income from real estate sales she generates. Although she does not hold a real estate license, she is earning her income legally, provided:
   A. She is employed by a licensed real estate broker.
   B. She sells property she owns.
   C. She is paid a contract fee, not a commission.
   D. She sells only nonresidential property.

E3.Q2 The term *of definite duration* in a lease refers to tenancy known as:
   A. At sufferance
   B. For years
   C. At will
   D. From period to period

E3.Q3 All the following conditions can be verified in county records *except*:
   A. Encroachments
   B. Mechanics' liens
   C. Land dimensions
   D. Names of legal owners

E3.Q4 Which appraisal analysis is used by real estate brokers to estimate the value of a residential property for marketing purposes?
   A. Feasibility analysis
   B. Cash flow analysis
   C. Competitive market analysis
   D. Income analysis

E3.Q5 A property owner watched his neighbor construct a residence on an adjacent property for four months. A week before the new property was completed, the owner filed a claim that the structure was built too near his property line and demanded that the new structure be moved. In all probability, the court will refuse the action because of:
   A. Novation
   B. Recision
   C. Laches
   D. Abandonment

E3.Q6 A broker decides to purchase a listing within her office to fit the needs of a particular buyer she knows who will pay more for the property within the next three months. Under these circumstances, which of the following statements is true?
   A. A broker cannot purchase a listing within her own firm.
   B. The broker is liable to the seller for any profit she realizes from the property.
   C. The broker must disclose not only that she is a real estate licensee but also that she is a principal in this transaction.
   D. As long as the broker pays full price for the property, no further responsibility exists.

E3.Q7 A five-year lease expired on March 31. The lessor discovered that the lessee had not yet vacated the premises on April 5. Which of the following describes the current tenancy?
   A. Tenancy at sufferance
   B. Tenancy in severalty
   C. Tenancy in common
   D. Tenancy for years

E3.Q8 A broker informed her agent that she had listed property owned by herself and a partner for $137,500. She encouraged the agents to preview the property as soon as possible and to present the property to buyers immediately. One of the agents contracted an investor about the property. When the agent brought in an offer on the property, it was disclosed that the broker and her partner did not yet

have title to the property. The broker is not allowed to deny the agency created because of:
A. Ratification
B. Subrogation
C. Estoppel
D. Reformation

E3.Q9 All the following are advantages of investment in real estate *except*:
A. Liquidity
B. Appreciation
C. Depreciation
D. Income

E3.Q10 An interest payment of $457.50 paid over a nine-month period of time for a straight note of $6,100 has a rate of:
A. 7.5 percent
B. 9.0 percent
C. 10 percent
D. None of the above

E3.Q11 A man gave a life estate to his daughter for the life of his seven-year-old granddaughter, who has disabilities. The daughter died while the grandchild remained alive. The property now:
A. Reverts to the man
B. Passes to the daughter's heirs
C. Becomes escheat property to the state
D. Passes to the grandchild

E3.Q12 A property owner has soil tests performed on his land. The results indicate that the soil is excellent for agricultural purposes. The land is zoned for industrial use. It is logical that the owner would be successful in filing for a change in the zoning for his land to have a:
A. Variance
B. Conditional use permit
C. Nonconforming use
D. Down zoning

E3.Q13 Property for a valid tax-deferred exchange must meet all the following requirements *except*:
A. It must be property held for income and investments.
B. It must be like-for-like property.
C. The income will be taxed as a progressive tax coinciding with the increments paid.
D. Funds may be held in escrow, but the property to be purchased must be designated 45 days before the closing.

E3.Q14 Income tax deductions are allowable for interest on first and second homes provided the loan balance does not exceed the cost basis, which is the:
A. Cost of the residence plus improvements
B. Cost of the residence without improvements
C. Cost of the combined residences without improvements
D. Value of the combined residences including improvements

E3.Q15 In addition to the cost basis for income tax deductions, another provision regarding the primary and secondary residence is:
A. The combined value of the principal and the secondary residences cannot exceed $1 million.
B. The value of the principal residence cannot exceed $1 million.
C. The indebtedness for the principal of both residences cannot exceed $1 million.
D. The indebtedness on all properties owned cannot exceed $1 million.

E3.Q16 Upon the death of a man on October 17, 1992, the value of his estate property was calculated at $550,000. His income at the time of his death placed him in the 28 percent tax bracket. Therefore, the amount of federal estate taxation owed is:
A. 0
B. $28,000
C. $126,000
D. $154,000

E3.Q17 Applying the following data, the taxable gain on a residence sold last month with no other property purchased is:

Cost of home 1	$75,000
Improvements	$10,000
#1 sold for	$125,000
Cost of home #2	$155,000
#2 sold for	$185,000
Cost of home #3	$225,000
Improvements	$25,000
Sales cost on #3	$15,000
#3 sold for	$287,000

A. $92,000
B. $145,000
C. $180,000
D. $203,000

E3.Q18 An investor who purchased a three-family home for $180,000 and made $18,000 in improvements with depreciation of $95,000 has an adjusted cost basis of:
A. $67,000.
B. $85,000
C. $103,000
D. None of the above

E3.Q19 Jack and Jill Johnson sold their home when Jack was 57 years old. Soon after the sale, Jill died. Jack remarried and purchased a home with Joan for $125,000 and added $10,000 for improvements. When Joan turned 55 three years later, they sold their house for $195,000 with sales costs of $10,000 and decided to travel around the world for two years before purchasing again. Their taxable gain is:
A. 0 (none)
B. $50,000
C. $60,000
D. $70,000

E3.Q20 The tax rate for a community whose budget is $550,000 and whose tax roll is $10,355,000 is:
A. 0.0531 per dollar of assessed value
B. 0.0531 per $100 of assessed value
C. 0.1882 per dollar of assessed value
D. 0.1882 per $1,000 of assessed value

E3.Q21 A purchaser agrees to buy land from a seller for $85,000. After the contracts are signed but before the closing, the seller changes his mind and refuses to sell the property. The purchaser sues the seller but proceeds to buy another, similar parcel for $93,000. To settle the lawsuit, the court awarded the purchaser $8,000, known as:
A. Punitive damages
B. Land damages
C. Prospective damages
D. Compensatory damages

E3.Q22 Sam writes to his sister Sally that he is accepting her offer to purchase his condominium for $75,000 in three months. This contract is:
A. Unilateral, implied, executed
B. Bilateral, express, executory
C. Bilateral, express, executed
D. Unilateral, implied, executory

E3.Q23 A written offer to purchase stated the purchase price of a property as $155,000 numerically, but with the words stated *one hundred fifty thousand dollars*. The correct interpretation of the offer's ambiguity is:
A. Words take precedence over numerals.
B. Numbers take precedence over words.
C. The offer is invalid.
D. The lesser amount is acceptable.

E3.Q24 A broker decided that she would type a clearer copy of an agreement to purchase for the seller's attorney. In doing so, she misspelled the name of the purchaser and made an error in the sales price figure. She had both parties sign her typed copy as well as the handwritten one. The attorney, noting the errors, is correct in relying on which data for accuracy?
A. Handwritten
B. Typed
C. Neither
D. Whichever favors his client

E3.Q25 The basic distinction between misrepresentation and fraud in a contract is:
A. The requirement of intent
B. The amount of consideration involved
C. The type of contract
D. There is no difference

E3.Q26 Offer and acceptance of a contract to purchase real estate is evidence of:
A. Intent to purchase
B. The value of the property
C. Mutual agreement
D. The legality of the parties

E3.Q27 A salesperson accepts an offer to be presented to the client for the purchase of the client's house. Before the agent contacts the seller, the purchaser contacts the agent and withdraws the contract. This is an example of:
A. Revision
B. Reciprocal
C. Regression
D. Recision

E3.Q28 All the following can make a valid contract unenforceable *except*:
A. Statue of limitations
B. Laches
C. Legal change of name
D. Estoppel

E3.Q29 The right of all citizens to inherit, purchase, or sell property was given by the:
A. Civil Rights Act of 1969
B. Civil Rights Act of 1866
C. Court decision in the *Jones v. Mayer* Supreme Court case
D. Civil Rights Act of 1988

E3.Q30 The federal Fair Housing Act prohibits all of the following *except*:
A. The broker's refusal to show property to a financially unqualified customer
B. A broker's discrimination against clients and customers
C. Discrimination by blockbusting and redlining
D. Discrimination in access to multiple listing services

E3.Q31 All the following are methods required in appraisals *except*:
A. Direct sales comparison approach
B. Gross rent multiplier approach
C. Cost approach
D. Income approach

E3.Q32 Which of the following statements is true about the major weakness in the gross rent multiplier?
A. The data is not current.
B. It is not a recognized method.
C. It does not take expenses into consideration.
D. It uses unsupported data.

E3.Q33 A devise is:
A. Personal property given by will
B. Real property given by descent
C. Real property given by will
D. Money given by will

E3.Q34 Which one of the following types of wills needs no witnesses?
A. Formal
B. Noncupative
C. Holographic
D. None of the above

E3.Q35 A woman who owned a farm with several hundred acres of timberland wanted to give half of her land to the university in her town. She spoke with several persons about her desire but never took appropriate action to accomplish this task. She died intestate. Her property now:
A. Passes to the state
B. Passes to the university
C. Is distributed between the town and the university
D. Is distributed according to descent

E3.Q36 A property with a five-year-old first mortgage is being prepared for a foreclosure sale. Other liens against the property are town taxes, a mechanic's lien dated three years after the first mortgage, a private second mortgage, and a lien for a sewer assessment that remained unpaid since a year ago. At the public

sale, the purchaser will need to satisfy:
A. All liens
B. All senior liens
C. All junior liens
D. No liens other than the first mortgage

E3.Q37 The interest amount of a first monthly payment at 8.5 percent on a mortgage for $76,500 is:
A. $541.88
B. $650.25
C. $750
D. None of the above

E3.Q38 An income-producing property generating $50,000 annually was expected to provide an 8 percent return on the investment. When it sold, the highest return achievable was 11 percent. The difference in the value is:
A. $1,500
B. $170,454
C. $454,545
D. $625,000

E3.Q39 The function of most appraisals is to:
A. Create market value for similar properties
B. Determine the market conditions for the best value
C. Compare the conditions of the marketplace
D. Estimate the market value of the subject property

E3.Q40 All of the following are examples of personal property *except*:
A. An in-ground swimming pool
B. Air rights
C. Annual crops
D. An installed stockade fence

E3.Q41 A mobile home is classified as real property when it:
A. Has a fence around the lot
B. Is attached to a permanent foundation
C. Was sold by a real estate agent
D. Has been connected to a central water supply

E3.Q42 All of the following are examples of fixtures except:
A. Lumber for construction delivered to the site
B. Trees to be cut for lumber
C. Shrubs to be planted on the site where they are delivered
D. Compost for use on the premises

E3.Q43 Who is empowered to discount a mortgage?
A. The mortgagee
B. The mortgagor
C. An investor
D. Secondary market agencies

E3.Q44 The highest loan-to-value ratio is available for:
A. Commercial buildings
B. Complexes for offices and retail combinations
C. Single-family residences
D. Farmland

E3.Q45 A property owner who fishes in the stream that runs through his own land enjoys the legal right of ownership known as:
A. Littoral rights
B. Easements appurtenant
C. Mineral rights
D. Riparian rights

E3.Q46 The type of ownership of real property reserved for husbands and wives is known as tenancy:
A. By the entirety
B. In common
C. For years
D. In severalty

E3.Q47 Liquidated damages are appropriate contract remedies in all of the following situations *except* one in which:
A. A construction contractor fails to perform on time as agreed.
B. Money is awarded by a court to an injured party to compensate for loss suffered.

C. A buyer forfeits the earnest money when she refuses to purchase the property.
D. A seller fails to leave an item on the premises as agreed in the contract for sale.

E3.Q48 Mr. Holmes agrees to sell his property to Ms. Purchaser and signs the agreement contract on Tuesday evening. An agent for Holmes willingly delivers the contract to Purchaser within one hour of the seller's signing. Four days later, Holmes receives a call from his employer canceling his transfer, so Holmes decides not to sell. In the meantime, Purchaser has made arrangements for the transfer of her household goods to be packed and delivered within three weeks and has signed a mortgage commitment. All the following are options available to Purchaser *except*:
A. Novation
B. Specific performance
C. Recision with restitution
D. Compensatory damages

E3.Q49 All of the following contracts are assignable upon agreement *except* a:
A. First mortgage sold in the secondary market
B. Lease agreement with a transfer clause for the lessee
C. Qualified appraiser accepting an assignment to appraise a specific property
D. Lessor selling a leased property to a buyer

E3.Q50 *Familial status* involves all of the following *except*:
A. Families with children who are under the age of 18
B. Families with an 18-year-old living at home
C. Persons in the process of obtaining legal custody
D. A pregnant woman

EXAM 3 ANSWERS

E3.A1   B

As an owner, *she can sell her own properties* without a license. A, C, and D require a real estate license in order to sell legally.

E3.A2   B

Tenancy for years is a lease for a specific period of time agreed to before the lease is accepted. *Tenancy at sufferance* is a holdover after the lease has expired and without the landlord's permission. *Tenancy at will* is leasing a premise to a tenant with the landlord's permission. *Tenancy from period to period* is an agreement to rent from one short period to another.

E3.A3   A

Encroachments would be observed on the property. B, C, and D are maintained in public records.

E3.A4   C

Competitive market analysis is a comparison of properties like the subject within the neighborhood of the subject. A, B, and D are appropriate for income-producing properties.

E3.A5   C

Laches is an equitable principle that prevents the exercise of a right because of an unreasonable delay to assert the right. *Novation* is the substitution of a new agreement for an old one. *Recision* is a legal termination of a contract. *Abandonment* is a voluntary surrender of property without any vesting interest in another person.

E3.A6   B

The broker's fiduciary responsibility is to inform the principal of all interest in the property. Since the agent did not disclose the possibility of selling to her prospective purchaser, *the agent is liable to the seller for the amount of profit gained* in her sale to the investor.

E3.A7   A

Tenancy at sufferance is a holdover tenancy whereby the tenant remains in possession of the space even though the lease has expired. *Tenancy in severalty* is ownership by a single individual. *Tenancy in common* is concurrent ownership by two or more individuals who have undivided interest in the whole property. *Tenancy for years* is a lease for a specified time period.

E3.A8   C

Estoppel means that one party is prevented by his or her own acts from claiming a right to the detriment of another person who was entitled to rely on such conduct and has acted accordingly. *Ratification* is confirmation of a previous voidable act. *Subrogation* is a lawful substitution of a third party acting in place of one who has a claim against another party. *Reformation* is equitable remedy used to reframe a written contract where mutual error was made.

E3.A9   A

Liquidity is not an attribute of real estate investments. B, C, and D are benefits of real estate investments.

E3.A10   C

$457.50 = $610 (annual interest = 10%)
$0.75 \times $6,100$ (note)
(9 months is 75% of one year)

E3.A11   B

It *passes to the daughter's heirs* to hold for the life of the grandchild.

E3.A12   B

A *conditional use permit* is special permission to use the land in a manner that otherwise is not allowed under the present zoning classification. A *variance* is a permanent exception to zoning. *Nonconforming use* is a use that preceded the current zoning use. *Down zoning* is a lesser use.

E3.A13   C

Income taxed as a progressive tax is a requirement of installment sales. A, B, and D are requirements for tax-deferred exchange.

E3.A14   A

Cost of the residence plus the improvements constitutes cost basis for tax purposes. Value of a residence and its cost are usually different amounts.

E3.A15   C

Indebtedness on a principal or secondary home incurred before October 13, 1987, has no interest limitation.

E3.A16   A

$550,000 is less than the exemption for federal estate taxation.

E3.A17   C

$ 75,000	Cost of original home
+ 10,000	Improvements
+ 30,000	Added to proceeds to buy home #2
+ 40,000	Added to proceeds to buy home #3
+ 25,000	Improvements to home #3
$ 180,000	Adjusted cost basis
$ 287,000	Sales price
– 15,000	Sales costs
$ 272,000	Seller's net
– 180,000	Adjusted cost basis
$ 92,000	Taxable gain (if no other residence purchased within 24 months)

E3.A18   C

$180,000 + $18,000 – $95,000 = $103,000

E3.A19   B

Since Jack had taken advantage of the $125,000 exclusion, the couple is not entitled to it again.

A.$195,000 – $10,000 = $185,000 (seller net)
B.$125,000 + $10,000 = $135,000 (cost basis)
$185,000 – $135,000 = $50,000 (taxable gain)

E3.A20   A

$550,000 (budget needed) =
0.0531 per dollar of AV
$10,355,000 (assessed valuation)

E3.A21   D

Compensatory damage is sufficient to compensate the injured party for the amount of loss sustained. *Punitive* damages are awarded the plaintiff over and above the basic compensation for property loss. *Land* damage is the amount of compensation to be paid for land taken under the power of eminent domain. *Prospective* damages are for damages not yet accrued but anticipated as a result of evidence.

E3.A22   B

Bilateral (promise for a promise); *express* (in writing); *executory* (not yet completed).

E3.A23   A

Words take precedence.

E3.A24   A

A *handwritten* document has precedence over a typed document, which in turn has precedence over a printed one.

E3.A25   A

The intent of the discrepancy determines the difference. Misrepresentation does not involve intent.

E3.A26   C

Mutual agreement or meeting of the minds on terms and conditions specified is a major component of a valid contract.

E3.A27   D

Recision is an action to void, to repeal, to take back. *Revision* changes the offer. *Reciprocal* is a mutual action. *Regression* is the loss of value because a property is placed in an area of less expensive property.

E3.A28 C

A *legal change of name* (i.e., married name, change in spelling) does not make a valid contract unenforceable. A, B, and D may cause a contract to be unenforceable.

E3.A29 B

The *Civil Rights Act of 1866* remained obscure until the court decision of the *Jones v. Mayer* Supreme Court case. The *Civil Rights Act of 1968* added religion and sex as protective classes. The *Civil Rights Act of 1988* added familial status and handicapped condition as protective classes.

E3.A30 A

A broker is correct in showing properties only to *financially qualified* customers. B, C, and D are prohibitions.

E3.A31 B

Gross rent multiplier is an appraisal variation method that serves as support for data of the other three methods (A, C, and D) that are required.

E3.A32 C

Specific expenses are not considered in calculating the GRM. The gross income is multiplied by the GRM, which is derived from the general market without consideration of operating expenses.

E3.A33 C

Real property given by will is one of three types of property acquired through an estate. *Personal property given by will* is a bequest. *Real property given by descent* follows the statutes of the state where the property is located. *Money given by will* is a legacy.

E3.A34 C

Holographic wills need no witnesses. *Formal* wills are usually witnessed by two or more persons. *Nuncupative* is a deathbed will usually for personal items.

E3.A35 D

Property in her estate *is distributed according to descent,* the laws of intestate succession of the state in which the property is located.

E3.A36 B

The purchaser at a foreclosure sale takes title subject to *all liens senior to the mortgage.*

E3.A37 C

$76,500 \times 0.085 = \$6,502.56/12 = 541.88$

E3.A38 B

$50,000/0.08 = \$625,000$
$50,000/0.11 = \$454,546$
$625,000 - 454,546 = \$170,454$

E3.A39 D

An appraisal is an *estimate of the market value of a subject property.* To estimate the value, conditions and actual comparable sales are considered.

E3.A40 C

Annual crops are considered personal as they are not permanent. A, B, and D are examples of real property.

E3.A41 B

A mobile home on wheels is treated as personal property.

E3.A42 C

Property that is personal or real may be considered a fixture depending on the intent of its use. Clarification of items in a contract is key to avoiding misunderstanding and conflict.

E3.A43 A

The mortgagee creates the discount when the mortgage is sold on the secondary market for less than its face value.

E3.A44   C

A single-family residence with VA qualifications offers 100 percent financing; conventional financing requires a loan-to-value ratio of 80 percent; insured mortgages are offered at higher ratios.

E3.A45   D

Riparian rights are attributed to flowing waters (nonnavigable); *littoral* rights pertain to navigable waters (nonflowing, large lakes or the ocean).

E3.A46   A

Some states recognize community property ownership; others offer joint tenancy with survivorship (although not reserved for a husband-and-wife ownership).

E3.A47   B

This exemplifies compensatory damages.

E3.A48   A

Novation is the substitution of a new contract for an old one.

E3.A49   C

Appraisal services are considered personal and therefore are not assignable. Assignable contracts transfer all interests of one contractual party to a third party.

E3.A50   B

An 18-year-old is of majority age. Families with minor children are within the scope of "familial status."

EXAM 4

E4.Q1 An agent proclaimed to home-owners in her farm area that a group home for the mentally handicapped coming to the neighborhood next summer would certainly cause property values to decline and encouraged the owners to list their properties as soon as possible. The agent is guilty of:
A. Steering
B. Redlining
C. Farming
D. Blockbusting

E4.Q2 *Parole evidence* rule is verbal evidence used to:
A. Modify a written contract
B. Show that a clearly written contract means more than it shows
C. Clarify an ambiguity in a written contract
D. Substitute for a written contract

E4.Q3 Reviewing the legal papers after the closing on a large parcel of land, the new owner noticed that the lot number and map did not match the legal description of the property. He would make a request to the court for a deed of:
A. Reformation
B. Recision
C. Restitution
D. Revocation

E4.Q4 The basic distinction between a condition and a covenant is:
A. Forfeiture
B. Restriction
C. Encumbrance
D. Variance

E4.Q5 Which lien would be paid first in a foreclosure sale?
A. A mechanic's lien recorded February 5, 1994
B. A delinquent mortgage recorded March 3, 1990
C. A delinquent mortgage recorded April 19, 1993
D. Delinquent municipal taxes due January 1, 1992

E4.Q6 Which of the following is *not* a true statement about attachments?
A. It is a final order by a court requiring a defendant to pay the plaintiff a specified amount of money.
B. It is a lien placed on the property of the defendant before judgment is rendered.
C. It assures the plaintiff that property exists that can be levied against in the event that a judgment is rendered.
D. It is available only for unsecured claims based on a contract.

E4.Q7 A listing agent verifying that there is no recorded notice of a pending lawsuit involving the property to be listed would be looking for:
A. Judgments
B. Attachments
C. Lis pendes
D. Liens

E4.Q8 A family leasing a chalet in the mountains for the month of February has signed a lease for:
A. An estate for years
B. A periodic tenancy
C. A freehold estate
D. A tenancy at sufferance

E4.Q9 All the following have the power to terminate an easement *except*:
A. Expiration date stated
B. Change of mind by servient tenement
C. Quitclaim by dominant and servient tenement
D. Merger

E4.Q10 When a buyer assumes the seller's mortgage, the settlement costs will be itemized for the buyer in all the following ways *except*:
A. Credit to the buyer; debit to the seller
B. Debit to the buyer; credit to the seller
C. Reduction of the amount needed for the purchase
D. Proration of taxes and insurance as applicable

E4.Q11 A property owner signs a deed transferring a parcel of land to his son as a wedding gift. Before the wedding, an argument occurs, resulting in the man's change in plans. He decides not to convey the land at this time. He places the signed deed in his safe. Several years later, upon his death, the deed is discovered. Ownership of the land:
A. Is now conveyed to the son
B. Remains as part of the man's estate
C. Remains as part of the son's property
D. Cannot be conveyed to the son

E4.Q12 RESPA requires the buyer to:
A. Receive credit for all monies paid prior to closing
B. Receive an explanation of all settlement charges
C. Use an attorney recommended by the lender
D. Pay no finance charges prior to the closing

E4.Q13 A standard title insurance policy includes coverage for all of the following *except*:
A. Boundary disputes with an adjacent property owner
B. Special assessments shared by the subdivision owners
C. Competency of the parties holding title
D. Former deed holders' rights

E4.Q14 A woman wants to convey property she owns to her granddaughter. She signs the deed and keeps it in her strongbox. For years, she continues to refer to that particular property as belonging to the granddaughter. The family is aware of the woman's wishes and encourages her to convey the property while she is alive. The woman continues to declare that she has already done so. Which one of the following statements is true about the land?
A. The property belongs to the granddaughter, since everyone has been informed and agrees.
B. The property must be surveyed before the granddaughter can assume its ownership.
C. The woman has life use of the property, but the title is held by the granddaughter.
D. The property continues to be owned by the woman, as the title has not yet been delivered to the granddaughter.

E4.Q15 Salesperson A misrepresented the fact that the property she was showing to a prospective purchaser never has had any structural damage, knowing full well that the property had burned and received extensive damages four years ago. The agent is liable:
A. Only if the buyer challenges the statement
B. Only when the buyer makes a legitimate offer to purchase the property
C. Even though the buyer does not show interest in the property
D. Only if the misrepresentation was committed maliciously and intentionally

E4.Q16 A broker's fiduciary duties lie
with the:
A. Seller
B. Client
C. Buyer
D. Cooperating brokers

E4.Q17 Which of the following is *not* in
a fiduciary relationship?
A. Owners of a property listed
by the same firm
B. Owners of property and their
listing broker
C. Purchasers for property and
the salesperson they hired
D. Purchasers for property and
their agent's broker/employer

E4.Q18 A listing agent is required to do
all of the following *except*:
A. Clear defects in the property
B. Disclose any material defects
in the property
C. Discover defects in the
property
D. Exercise due care of the
property even though defects
exist

E4.Q19 Commission rates are
determined:
A. At the time of closing
B. By state statutes
C. By the salesperson listing the
property
D. Through negotiation at the
time the property is listed

E4.Q20 A salesperson has a primary fi-
duciary relationship with:
A. The property owner
B. The property purchaser
C. The broker for whom the
agent operates business
D. The broker who listed the
property

E4.Q21 A broker's trust account is for:
A. Operating expenses
B. Reserves
C. Compensations due agents
D. Deposits from clients and
customers

E4.Q22 An agent who holds the right
to sign documents for the prin-
cipal is:
A. A real estate agent
B. The designated broker of the
listing firm
C. An attorney-in-fact
D. An attorney-at-law

E4.Q23 A real estate agent can lose her
license in all the following situations *except*:
A. Representing a property
owner without a written listing agreement
B. Misrepresenting material
facts about a property
C. Transferring her license to
another broker before the
closing of a sales transaction
D. Allowing her board membership to lapse

E4.Q24 An eager saleswoman obtains a
listing whereby the seller insists
on receiving $100,000 himself
and authorizes the agent to retain the remaining amount as
her compensation. The comparative market analysis indicates
that $110,000 is a fair market
value at this time. The compensation rate for the agent's firm is
5.5 percent. To be a legal listing,
the sales price must be:
A. $100,000
B. $105,500
C. $110,000
D. None of the above

E4.Q25 A broker received a letter from her
former neighbor requesting that
she put his property (adjacent to
her lot) on the market for
$175,000. He agrees to pay
$5,000 above the usual fee the
broker charges if the property
closes within 60 days. The broker
places the property on the market
immediately, knowing it should
sell very quickly because property
values in that area now average
$200,000. An agent in the bro-

ker's office purchases the property with the intent of selling the property to a friend who is looking for a good investment. The property transfer takes place within 45 days from the listing date. Within 30 days, the agent sold the property to her friend for $220,000. How does the original property owner benefit from such a transaction?
A. The owner benefits only to the extent of the original sales request for $175,000 minus the compensation as agreed.
B. The owner will net the difference between the actual selling price and the amount of compensation paid to the broker.
C. The owner will net the difference between the actual selling price and the compensation as agreed, plus the profit the agent received from the sale.
D. The owner may net all proceeds, as there is no legal listing agreement between the broker and the property owner.

E4.Q26 An agent buys a property with the intent of selling it quickly at a profit to an investing customer of hers. Upon its sale to the investor, the profit the agent realizes must be:
A. Placed in escrow for 30 days
B. Given to the original seller from whom she purchased the property
C. Hers free and clear as long as she discloses the fact to the investor
D. Shared with her broker at the same ratio as her commission

E4.Q27 A broker can supply all of the following documents to a potential buyer *except*:
A. A copy of the owner's deed.
B. The owner's property tax data
C. Maps of the owner's property
D. A copy of the listing contract

E4.Q28 A buyer gives $5,000 and agrees to purchase a seller's property at a specified price in 180 days. This indicates that the buyer has obtained:
A. An option
B. A mortgage
C. A lease
D. A contract for deed

E4.Q29 A vendee is one who:
A. Offers to buy at some time in the future
B. Offers to sell at some time in the future
C. Lends money for the sale some time in the future
D. Buys the property with the title passing some time in the future

E4.Q30 In a bilateral contract, the exclusive-right-to-sell listing must be signed by:
A. Buyer and seller
B. Vendor and vendee
C. Broker and seller
D. Broker and agent

E4.Q31 When the foreclosure sale fails to pay the debt in full, the mortgagee has the right to:
A. Call the sale null and void
B. Claim other assets of the mortgagor
C. Assume the expense itself
D. Pass the debt on to the new owner

E4.Q32 A mortgage that covers several parcels of land from which lots may be sold individually, reducing the mortgage amount, is known as:
A. A shared appreciation mortgage
B. An amortized mortgage
C. A blanket mortgage
D. A package mortgage

E4.Q33 An owner who recently lost his primary employment is facing foreclosure procedures on his house. Which of the following actions would be most beneficial to him in protecting his credit?
A. Judicial foreclosure
B. Nonjudicial foreclosure
C. Strict foreclosure
D. Deed in lieu of foreclosure

E4.Q34 A promissory note is evidence of all of the following *except*:
A. Written proof of title
B. Recognition of an acceptance
C. Written evidence of a promise to repay a loan
D. A promise to perform a specified act an agreed-on time

E4.Q35 Which of the following is *not* a fiduciary agent?
A. A broker
B. A lender
C. A principal
D. An attorney

E4.Q36 Mary Sue reviewed her mortgage papers and discovered that when she sells her property, the mortgage must be paid in full and is not assumable. Her mortgage contains:
A. An acceleration clause
B. An escalation clause
C. A defeasance clause
D. A redemption clause

E4.Q37 An unsecured loan is known as a:
A. Mortgage
B. Lease
C. Debenture
D. Devise

E4.Q38 A period of time during which an investor gains most benefit from a property is known as:
A. Redemption
B. Physical life
C. Economic life
D. Value extension

E4.Q39 Securities are regulated by state statutes known as:
A. Uniform commercial codes
B. Blue-sky laws
C. Interstate land sales
D. Unit ownership acts

E4.Q40 A major advantage in owning a condominium unit rather than a cooperative unit is:
A. More readily available financing
B. More real estate taxes
C. A limited number of occupants in the complex
D. Greater resale opportunities

E4.Q41 The remaining balance on a $100,000 mortgage amortized for 30 years at 7 percent after the third monthly payment of $672.44 is:
A. $99,731.12
B. $99,910.90
C. $99,640.45
D. $100,000

E4.Q42 All of the following are true statements about private mortgage insurance *except*:
A. Lower down payments are required.
B. The loan-to-value ratio is higher than with most other mortgages.
C. Total principal is included with the final payment.
D. The lender obtains additional security to insure against default.

E4.Q43 Three discounts points are charged on a $175,000 loan amounting to:
A. $1,750
B. $5,250
C. $58,333
D. None of the above

E4.Q44 How many points does a lender need to charge a borrower who obtains an 8 percent mortgage if the lender receives an 8-5/8 percent yield?
  A. One
  B. Three
  C. Five
  D. Eight

E4.Q45 Under what circumstances can an owner refuse rental to a person who speaks a different language from that of the owner?
  A. When the renter is a boarder in the owner's own dwelling
  B. When the owner is renting a unit in a two-family complex
  C. When the property is housing members of the owner's family
  D. When the owner has not advertised in writing nor used an agent or agency

E4.Q46 All of the following are true statements about FHA rules and assumptions *except*:
  A. FHA loans obtained since December 1989 for investment property are assumable.
  B. FHA loans that originated prior to December 1986 have no assumption restrictions.
  C. FHA loans for a primary residence that originated since December 1986 must be reviewed during the first 12 months of the loan's existence.
  D. FHA loans obtained since December 1989 for primary residential purposes are assumable by well-qualified buyers.

E4.Q47 Which of the following statements is true regarding FHA loans?
  A. Interest is paid annually in one lump sum.
  B. The property must be appraised up to a minimum of 97 percent of the purchase price.

C. The insurance premium must be paid at the time of closing.
  D. When the purchase price exceeds the appraised value, the difference may be added to the down payment.

E4.Q48 All of the following are true statements regarding VA loans *except*:
  A. The Department of Veterans' Affairs is authorized to guarantee mortgages for qualified veterans and certain individuals who have completed six years of service.
  B. VA loans are available at low interest rates with no down payment.
  C. The VA insures loans for the purchase of mobile homes and the land they sit on.
  D. VA lends money to veterans in areas where financing is not reasonably available.

E4.Q49 The major difference between FHA and VA loans is:
  A. An FHA mortgagor must be a nonveteran.
  B. The FHA does not limit the amount of the purchase price.
  C. The VA requires that the seller pay all points.
  D. The VA requires a loan origination fee in cases where no down payment is rendered.

E4.Q50 FIRREA empowers all of the following *except*:
  A. BIF to insure all loans issued by the Department of Veterans' Affairs.
  B. OTS to monitor and regulate the savings and loan industry.
  C. RTC to assume the management of insolvent savings and loan institutions.
  D. FDIC to manage insurance funds for both savings and loan associations and commercial banks.

EXAM 4 ANSWERS

E4.A1   D

Inducing panic selling (*blockbusting*) by claiming that values will drop as a result of certain groups entering the area is illegal. *Steering* is directing certain persons toward or away from a certain area. *Redlining* is refusing to lend or insure in certain areas. These are also illegal actions. *Farming* is a method of developing real estate business legally.

E4.A2   C

It can also be used as evidence of fraud or undue influence.

E4.A3   A

It corrects a mistake in an agreement or deed to conform to the original intent.

E4.A4   A

Conditions are treated as covenants by the courts to prevent forfeiture in the event of a breach.

E4.A5   D

Municipal taxes are paid in full first.

E4.A6   A

A judgment is the final order of the court. Attachments are usually reserved for situations when it is believed the defendant will flee or dispose of the property prematurely.

E4.A7   C

It is constructive notice that a party other than the owner has interest claimed in the subject property.

E4.A8   A

A definite period of time agreed to as a term of the lease.

E4.A9   B

The termination must be for legal reasons. In some states, a specific term of years is appropriate, whereas others permit easements forever.

E4.A10   A

Credits are the amounts a party is entitled to receive; debits are amounts to be paid.

E4.A11   B

Inasmuch as no delivery occurred, the deed remains as part of the man's estate.

E4.A12   D

The buyer may choose his own attorney and the lender may select its own closing agent. RESPA is full disclosure to the buyer and to the seller of all distributions made at the closing of title.

E4.A13   A

Title insurance covers known and recorded facts but does not resolve known differences in ownership rights and privileges.

E4.A14   D

Until the conveyance of title is delivered to the granddaughter, the property continues to be owned by the woman.

E4.A15   C

An agent is liable under any circumstances for misrepresentation of material facts whether intentionally, innocently, or negligently.

E4.A16   B

The client could be either the buyer or the seller who has hired the agent (broker). Those fiduciary duties are shared with co-operating brokers as subagents.

E4.A17   A

Clients are principals who have no relationship to each other, even though they each hired the same broker.

E4.A18   A

Clearing defects is the responsibility of the property owner. The agent observes the defects and can give business counsel regarding the owner's options for remedial action. All physical defects must be disclosed. Defects become negotiable items of contracts to purchase if not cleared up during the listing process.

E4.A19 D

Commission rates are set by each designated broker but are negotiable at the time of the listing agreement hiring the broker.

E4.A20 C

The salesperson (agent) owes primary fiduciary duty to the broker of the firm with which he is affiliated.

E4.A21 D

Other people's money is to be kept separate from all other accounts

E4.A22 C

Through power of attorney, the principal authorizes his agent to sign specified documents on behalf of the principal.

E4.A23 B

Misrepresentation of material facts is illegal. Written listing agreements are required to be enforceable, but oral agreements are permissible, though risky. Transferring one's license properly is legal. Sales transactions continue under the license of the listing broker in all cases. Membership with a trade association is not a requirement of licensure.

E4.A24 C

The fair market value indicates $110,000. When the property sells, 5.5 percent compensation is due the listing broker.

E4.A25 C

The letter of request does not constitute a written listing agreement. It is unenforceable. Whatever profit realized as a result of this sale is due the original owner unless full disclosure and agreement provided otherwise.

E4.A26 B

Undisclosed profits are to be given to the original property owner when immediate profit is realized.

E4.A27 D

The listing contract is confidential between the principal and the agent. A, B, and C are public documents recorded in town records.

E4.A28 A

An option holds the seller bound to the agreement and reserves the final right to purchase for the buyer without obligating him to do so. In most cases, the deposit is forfeited if the sale is not completed.

E4.A29 D

It is the buyer in a land contract or contract for deed transaction.

E4.A30 C

A written bilateral listing contract to sell requires the signature of the owner/seller(s) and the broker. The sales agent's signature is advisable but optional.

E4.A31 B

In most situations, the mortgagee can seek a deficiency judgment against the mortgagor. If the loan is nonrecourse or if an antideficiency law exists, deficiency judgment is not possible, resulting in a loss.

E4.A32 C

Commonly used in subdivisions, close attention must be rendered to each lot for accuracy in measurements. Shared appreciation mortgage allows the mortgagee and mortgagor or the buyer and seller to share in the appreciation a property realizes at a specific point in time. Amortized mortgage permits payments to include principal and interest throughout the life of the mortgage. Package mortgage includes real and personal property.

E4.A33   **D**

Deed in lieu of foreclosure presents a disadvantage to the lender, as it does not cancel junior liens.

E4.A34   **B**

It is an acceptance of an unconditional promise from one party to repay another at a specified time.

E4.A35   **C**

To create a fiduciary relationship, a principal employs the services of an agent as representative.

E4.A36   **A**

It contains a due-on-sale clause requiring the mortgage to be paid in full upon sale.

E4.A37   **C**

A *debenture* is a long-term note or bond not secured by any real estate, but is an agreement to pay a specific amount at a specific rate of interest at a particular time ahead.

E4.A38   **C**

It is the time during an investment that the property maintains a profitable use.

E4.A39   **B**

The purpose of the state's blue-sky law is to prevent fraud.

E4.A40   **A**

Condos are financed as single units, independent of each other; coops are an integral part of the entire complex. Some states are changing the regulations.

E4.A41   **A**

First month
$100,000 × 0.07 = $7,000/12 = $583.33
$672.44 − $583.33 = $89.10
$100,000 − 89.10 = $99,910.90
(first month remaining balance)

Second month
$99,910.90 × 0.07 = $6,993.76/12 = $582.81
$672.44 − $582.81 = $89.63
$99,910.90 − $89.63 = $99,821.27 second month RB

Third month
$99,821.27 × 0.07 = $6,987.48/12 = $582.29
$672.44 − $582.29 = $90.15
$99,821.27 − $90.15 = $99,731.12 third month RB

E4.A42   **C**

The entire mortgage is amortized so principal is paid along with interest throughout the life of the mortgage. Most lenders will adjust the rate when the remaining balance and equity meet the ratio of uninsured conventional mortgage amounts.

E4.A43   **B**

$175,000 × .03 = $5,250

E4.A44   **C**

One point is charged for every eighth of a point difference.

E4.A45   **D**

Under no circumstances and without any exception can one discriminate because of race, color, or national origin. Language is part of one's national origin and culture.

E4.A46   **A**

FHA loans for investment purposes are no longer available since December 1989.

E4.A47   **D**

Also, the FHA has established minimum loan amounts in various parts of the country.

E4.A48   **C**

The Department of Veterans' Affairs does not insure loans, but it guarantees the lender's position.

E4.A49   B

The VA loan may not exceed the appraised value of the home; the FHA sets the maximum loan it will insure but does not limit the total purchase price.

E4.A50   A

The BIF (Bank Insurance Fund) insures banks deposits; the SAIF (Savings Associations Insurance Fund) insures savings and loan deposits.

Glossary

Absolute Net Lease A lease providing that the tenant pays all the customary expenses of running and maintaining the property, including water and sewer charges, insurance, and taxes. Known variously as a net lease; net, net lease; net, net, net lease; or triple net lease.

Abstract of Title A condensed history of title to real estate, consisting of a synopsis or summary of the material or operative portion of all the conveyances, of whatever kind or nature, which in any manner affect the real estate or any estate or interest in it, together with a statement of all the liens, charges, or liabilities to which the real estate may be subject.

Acceptance A manifestation of the desire and will to be bound by the terms of an offer.

Acid Mine Drainage Waste from mining operations that seeps into the ground; a major source of pollution.

Acknowledgment The process whereby the signers of a document take an oath before an authorized officer, such as a notary public, establishing their identity.

Acre A unit of land that measures 43,560 square feet, or 4,840 square yards, or 160 square rods.

Actual Authority The power conferred on an agent by the principal. Real estate brokers traditionally receive only limited powers from the sellers they represent.

Actual Eviction When a landlord forces tenants, through physical or legal action, to vacate the premises they are occupying.

Ad Valorem Taxation Taxes based on a fixed percentage of a property's value, usually determined by an assessor who is a community official.

Adjustable-Rate Mortgage (ARM) A type of mortgage that permits the lender to adjust the interest rate periodically, on the basis of movement in a specified financial index. The term also refers to other types of ARMs.

Administrator/Administratrix A person chosen by the court to be the legal representative of a deceased person's estate in cases where the individual dies without a will or without having named an executor.

Administrator's Deed A deed signed by an administrator under the authority of the probate court.

Adverse Possession A special means of acquiring property, established by statute, whereby possession of a property is based on open, continuous, hostile physical control by an adverse possessor, and where the current owner has notice of the adverse possession as it is occurring.

Affirmative Easement An easement that gives to the owner of the dominant tenement the right to use the servient tenement, or to do some act thereon that would otherwise be illegal.

Agency A legal relationship between an agent and a principal wherein the agent is contracted to represent the principal in specific dealings with a third party.

Agency by Estoppel An agency created when agents overstep their authority but an action (or failure to act) by the principal leads others to believe the authority existed.

Agency Disclosure Form Form(s) signed by parties to a real estate transaction stating that they have been advised exactly whom the agent represents.

Agent A person who represents another person, called the principal, in business and legal affairs with third parties.

Agricultural Pollution Groundwater pollution caused by runoff of pesticides, fertilizers, animal waste, and other pollutants associated with farming and ranching activities.

Air Rights Lease A lease creating a leasehold in the air rights of a property.

Amortization The process of paying a debt through a series of equal payments (including principal and interest) at equal time intervals. Over the payoff period, the amount of each payment credited to loan reduction increases as the interest on the unpaid balance decreases.

Amortization Mortgage A type of mortgage where the borrower is obligated to pay all of the principal plus the interest over the period of the mortgage loan.

Annual Percentage Rate (APR) The true or effective rate of a loan including all the costs and charges. The federal Truth-In-Lending Act requires this rate to be calculated to the nearest ¼ percent to allow consumers to accurately compare various loan offers.

Appraisal (adjective) Of or pertaining to appraising and related functions, such as the practice of appraisal services.

Appraisal (noun) The act or process of developing an opinion of value; an opinion of value. An appropriately supported, objective, and unbiased opinion of a defined value, as of a specific date, of an adequately and accurately described property, made by a qualified person who has no undisclosed present or future interest in the property.

Area 1. The surface of any object or space measured in square units. 2. A neighborhood or other specified geographic space. 3. In residential design, a term indicating use, such as "work area."

As Is Also: **As Is Condition** A clause in a sales contract stating that the buyer agrees to accept the property in the exact condition that it is in and the seller makes no representation as to the condition of the property.

Assessed Value A value assigned to a property by the tax assessor to be used as a basis for taxation; usually a percentage of market value.

Assessment Appeal Board The government body that hears appeals of assessments.

Assignment 1. A valuation service provided as a consequence of an agreement between an appraiser and client. 2. The transfer of a property from one party to another.

Assumption 1. That which is taken to be true. 2. A statement made by appraisers in an appraisal report of something they believe to be true without having verified whether it is or is not true. 3. When a new owner agrees to take over responsibility for paying an existing mortgage and this action is permitted under the terms of the loan.

Attorney in Fact Someone who has been authorized to act on behalf of another in legal matters under a power of attorney.

Automatic Extension Clause A clause, in a sales contract or lease, that automatically extends it, unless either party notifies the other that they wish to terminate the agreement.

Automatic Valuation Models (AVMs) A computer model that computes the estimated market value (sale price) of a house, based on the selling price of computer-selected comparable sales and adjustments made by the computer.

Avulsion A loss of land resulting from the shifting of a river, stream, or other body of water on the boundary of a property.

Bail Bond Security that is posted with the court to guarantee that people who are accused of crimes will appear for their trial.

Bail Bond Lien A lien on real estate used as collateral in a court action instead of a cash bond.

Bargain and Sale Deed A type of conveyance deed used to transfer the legal ownership of real property, usually containing no warranties.

Base 1. In a geometric shape, the lower straight line used as part of the equation for calculating the area of the object. 2. For tax purposes, the amount of capital invested in a property, which is subtracted from the sale price of the property to permit capital gains or capital appreciation calculations.

Beneficiary 1. The recipient of the proceeds of an insurance policy. 2. One who receives benefits from gifts of another, in essence, a will or trust.

Bequest Property that is given in accordance with a will.

Bilateral Contract A contract whereby there is a mutual promise for the performance of certain acts; each party is both a promisor and a promisee.

Binder A preliminary agreement and down payment certifying the good faith of a purchaser.

Biological Contaminants Indoor air pollutants including bacteria, mold and mildew, viruses, animal dander, cat saliva, mites, cockroaches, and pollen.

Blockbusting An illegal practice of persuading homeowners to sell their properties based on fear that people of a different race or religion will move in and lower property values. Property is bought cheaply by blockbusters and then resold at a higher price.

Bog A type of spongy, wet ground made of decaying matter found in humid climates or wetlands areas.

Broker Protection Clause A listing agreement clause stating that the property owner will pay the broker the commission called for in an expired listing agreement if, within a specified period of time after the expiration of the listing, the property is sold, leased, rented, optioned, or exchanged to anyone who was introduced to the property during the listing period by the broker, sales associate, or cobroker.

Building Codes The set of governmental regulations that specify minimum construction standards. Often there are separate codes for the electrical and plumbing systems.

Building Permit Authorization required by local governments for new buildings or major alterations of existing buildings. Usually the permit must be displayed on the building site during the period when the construction is being done.

Bundle of Rights The bundle of rights is often illustrated by a bundle of sticks. Each stick in the bundle represents a separate right or interest inherent in ownership. These individual rights can be separated from the bundle by sale, lease, mortgage, donation, or other means of title transfer. The complete bundle of rights, called the "private rights" is often divided as follows: (1) the right to sell one or more of the interests in the property; (2) the right to occupy the property; (3) the right to lease or not lease property to someone other than the owner of the property; (4) the right to mortgage the property; (5) the right to give away (donate) all or part of the property; (6) the right to do none of these things.

Capitalization Rates A rate that reflects the relationship between the value of a property and its net operating income (NOI) in capitalization.

Carbon Monoxide An odorless, colorless, extremely toxic indoor air pollutant composed of a gas produced by combustion from unvented kerosene and gas heaters, leaking chimneys and furnaces, downdrafting from woodstoves and fireplaces, gas stoves, automobile exhaust from attached garages, and tobacco smoke. Exposure in a closed space can cause death.

Cash Equivalency A price expressed in terms of all cash as opposed to a price that is expressed in terms of cash and securities, notes, mortgages, other property, or any other thing that cannot readily be converted into cash at face value.

Cash Rent 1. The amount of rent paid in cash to the landlord. 2. A farming term for a fixed amount of rent for a farm.

Certificate of Execution A document that is presented to a property owner who pays a debt, removing a mechanic's or materialman's lien from a property.

Certificate of Occupancy A document issued to a builder by a local building department certifying that a building is free of building code violations and fit for occupancy by owners or tenants.

Certificate of Title A signed document made by a title examiner that is usually presented to the buyer along with the deed. It certifies that the seller of a property has good title.

Cession Deed A form of quitclaim deed whereby a property owner conveys street rights to a municipality or the state.

Cesspool Part of a waste disposal system that functions similarly to a septic tank; a covered cistern of stone, brick, or concrete block.

Chain of Title The list of conveyances, in chronological order, from the original owner to the present one.

Chemical Storage The storage of chemicals in drums made of steel or other materials. Illegal storage occurs when chemical users store chemicals in drums to avoid paying for their legal removal.

Circumference Measurement of the perimeter of a circle.

Civil Rights Protection under law for people of various races, religions, and nationalities to prevent exploitation or the denial of personal freedom regarding civil action.

Civil Rights Act of 1964 The first major legislation at the federal level designed to directly prohibit acts denying or limiting personal rights to people of various minority groups, based solely on race or creed. It included the first fair housing provisions.

Civil Rights Act of 1968 Federal statutes that prohibit discrimination in the sale and rental of real estate.

Closing (Closing meeting) A meeting at which the seller gives the title to a property to the buyer in exchange for the agreed-on purchase price; also called settlement. The deed is delivered to the buyer, and the seller's money is distributed as detailed in a closing or settlement statement.

Cloud on the Title A claim or encumbrance on a property that can impair the owner's title if it is not removed by a quitclaim deed or court action. Consumers may buy owner's title insurance to protect themselves from any cloud on their title. See also **Title Insurance.**

Coastal Wetlands Land along the coast where saturation with water is the dominant factor determining the nature of soil development and the types of plant and animal communities living in the soil and on its surface.

Codicil A written amendment to a will.

Commercial Easement A common type of easement. An example is an easement that permits putting up advertising billboards on the land.

Commingling In real estate, the mixing of client funds in a broker's personal account. This practice may cause a broker to lose his or her license, although commingling does not always result in misappropriation of funds.

Commissioner's Deed A deed given by a member of a government commission that has the power to establish and enforce regulations within a specific jurisdiction and for a specific activity and grant deeds.

Comparable Sale A property used in the sales comparison approach in the appraisal of real estate. Often it is compared to the subject property and adjustments are made to its sale price to reflect the differences between it and the subject property.

Comparative Market Analysis A tool used by RESPs to estimate the value of houses they are trying to list for sale or convince a potential buyer to make an offer on.

Compensation A sum of money paid to make amends for an injury. In condemnation law, it is the amount paid to the owner when a property is taken without the owner's consent.

Compensatory Damages Money awarded a claimant in a legal action that results in a finding for the plaintiff, whose purpose is to make the plaintiff whole.

Competitive Market Analysis (CMA) An analysis usually made by a real estate broker or sales associate prior to listing a property for sale. It uses recent nearby sales and competitive listings to estimate an appropriate offering price for the property.

Comprehensive Environmental Response Compensation and Liability Act (CERCLA) Environmental legislation that provides specific regulations regarding liability for environmentally hazardous substances released or found on real property.

Condemnee The owner of property taken by condemnation (eminent domain).

Condemnor The party taking property by condemnation (eminent domain).

Condominium (Condominium Ownership) A form of ownership in which each owner owns the fee simple interest to his or her individual unit and a percentage of the fee to the common areas.

Conflict of Interest A legal concept applying to professionals holding that undisclosed involvement with the property or principals to a transaction may disqualify a person from acting in the best interest of their client. Avoiding conflict of interest is a prime requirement of most professional ethics. See also **Agency Disclosure Form.**

Consideration 1. The valuable item given as an inducement to enter a contract, usually money, commodity exchange, or other compensation. 2. The actual selling price of a property.

Constructive Eviction Any act by which the landlord interferes with a tenant's right of quiet enjoyment and use of leased premises.

Contract Rent The actual rent paid for a property, which is not necessarily the market or economic rent.

Contractual Lien A claim or charge on a property that is created by agreement of the parties, such as a mortgage lien.

Conventional Mortgage A mortgage made by a lender, such as a savings and loan association, bank, insurance company, or pension fund, that is not insured by the FHA or VA.

Conveyance Tax A state tax on the sale of real estate, usually paid at the time when the new deed and mortgage are recorded.

Cooperating Broker A broker who sells or leases a property originally listed by another broker, shares the resulting commission with the listing broker, and is called a cobroker on the sale.

Cooperative (Cooperative Ownership) Property in a form of ownership in which each owner owns shares in a corporation that owns the entire property. The shareholder obtains the exclusive right to occupy part of the property. The property is financed by a mortgage that covers the entire property.

Corporate Franchise Tax Lien A state lien against a person, partnership, or corporation property for failure to pay state corporation franchise taxes.

Corporation An entity created by law that is treated as an individual with its own rights and liabilities. It is usually owned by stockholders. Its functions and duration are limited by its charter or set forth in its certificate of incorporation. It is subject to specific statutes that are set by each of the states and territories.

Correction Deed A recording document that rectifies a mistake made in a deed.

Cost Approach One of the three traditional approaches to value used by real estate appraisers. It is based on the theory that the value of a property is the sum of the value of the land plus the reproduction cost of all the improvements, less depreciation from all causes.

Covenant of Against Encumbrance A statement by the grantor of a deed that there are no encumbrances against the title, except those that are stated in the deed.

Covenant of Further Assurances A promise made by the grantors that they will perform any acts necessary to correct defects in the title being conveyed and any errors or deficiencies in the deed itself.

Covenant of Quiet Enjoyment A special clause in a deed or agreement whereby the grantor guarantees that the grantee will have the right to a property free from the interference of other parties who may claim an ownership interest in the property.

Covenant of Right to Convey A written statement made by the grantors that they have the legal capacity to convey the title.

Covenant of Seisen A statement by the grantors that they hold the title that they specify in the deed and that they convey it to the grantee.

Covenant of Warranty A statement that the grantors will warrant and defend the title to the grantees against the lawful claims of all persons whomsoever.

Covenants, Conditions, and Restrictions (CC&Rs) The restrictions governing the use of real estate, usually enforced by a homeowners' association. They are often created by the developer of a project to en-

sure that the project is maintained as it was planned.

Curtesy That portion of a wife's estate that a husband is entitled to in some states.

Dedication The voluntary donation of a private property for public use.

Deed of Conformation A document used to correct an error in a previously executed and delivered deed.

Deed of Reconveyance A document used primarily to release a title from the lien of a mortgage when the debt secured by the mortgagee has been paid in full.

Deed of Release An instrument whereby a mortgaged property is absolved from the lien of the mortgage, usually given when the mortgage is paid off.

Deed of Surrender A document used in some states by life tenants to convey their life tenant estate or their reversionary or remainder interest.

Deed of Trust The vehicle by which a trustor conveys property to a trustee for a beneficiary. A deed of trust may also be used in financing situations where title is conveyed to a disinterested third party and held in trust for the benefit of a lender, to secure the borrower's debt.

Deed Restrictions Limitations on the use of property for a specified period or forever that are written in a deed, which apply even after the property is sold. Illegal restrictions, such as those against race or religion, are not valid.

Deficiency Judgment The judgment for the portion of debt a borrower is responsible for if a foreclosure sale does not recover all the money due for the foreclosed mortgage.

Delivery (Delivery To and Acceptance By) 1. Final legal transfer of a deed from seller to buyer, so that the seller cannot recall the deed. 2. The official point at which a title passes to the grantee.

Depreciation The difference between the reproduction cost of improvements and their value. It is the loss in value suffered by improvements to property and personal property caused by physical deterioration, functional obsolescence, and external obsolescence.

Descent To pass real estate title by succession or to pass title without a will.

Devise Real property given by last will and testament.

Devisee Person to whom real estate is left in a will.

Devisor Person who leaves real estate by will.

Diameter In a circle or sphere, the length of a straight line drawn from a point on the perimeter to another point on the perimeter passing through the center and dividing the form exactly in half.

Director's Deed A document used in some areas when a public agency sells surplus land.

Dower The legal rights that a widow has to her husband's estate.

Dry Closing A preclosing meeting to verify that all the necessary steps have been taken and all the required documents prepared to proceed with a real estate closing.

Dual Agency A situation in which a broker or salesperson represents both parties to a real estate transaction. In some states, this practice is illegal. Many Realtors think it is a bad practice, even where it is permitted by law or by the National Association of Realtors Code of Ethics, due to the possibility of conflict of interest. It always requires full disclosure to all parties.

Duty of Confidentiality The requirement that agents keep confidential any information received from their clients and not reveal it to potential buyers or renters of the property, including information gathered from a competitive market analysis they may have performed in order to establish a listing price.

Duty of Disclosure The obligation of brokers, sales associates, and cobrokers to disclose to their clients any relationship they may have to any other party in the transaction or any interest they may have in the property to be transacted.

Duty of Honest Accounting The obligation of brokers to honestly handle and account for the principal's funds and to avoid practices such as commingling of funds.

Duty of Loyalty The obligation of an agent to always act in the best interests of their principal, even when it is not in their own best interest.

Duty of Obedience The obligation of agents to obey the instructions they receive from their principals, even when they do not agree with these instructions, except when the instructions are not legal.

Duty of Reasonable Care and Skill The obligation of an agent to be professional and accurate when marketing a property, showing a property, representing the principal, and presenting offers.

Earnest Money Deposit A sum of money paid by a buyer at the time of entering into a contract that indicates the intention and ability of the buyer to carry out the contract. It is usually applied toward the purchase price, and all or part may be forfeited if the buyer fails to go through with the contract.

Earthquake A geological hazard causing tremors, cracking, shaking, and destruction of the ground, from shifting tectonic plates in the earth's crust, especially over fault lines, such as the San Andreas fault in California.

Easement A liberty, privilege, or right that one has to use land for a specific purpose distinct from ownership of the soil, such as the right to cross X to get to Y.

Easement Appurtenant An easement attached to the dominant estate; it is passed with the conveyance of the dominant estate and continues to burden the servient estate.

Easement by Agreement A simple easement, usually not recorded, whereby one property owner gives another the right to use his or her property for some specific purpose, such as fishing in a pond.

Easement by Condemnation The type of easement created through the governmental power of condemnation, via a taking of that portion of the fee that is affected by the easement. In some cases, such a taking has little or no detrimental effect on value; therefore, the owner does not receive much (if anything) in the way of just compensation.

Easement by Express Grant A type of easement whereby the owner of a property prepares a deed that delineates the easement being given, executes the deed, and delivers it. The easement is expressly granted and should be recorded.

Easement by Necessity Also: **Easement by Implication** This type of easement is created by traditional usage, and necessity, but not recorded in the deeds of the properties involved. When the subordinate property is later sold to a third party, the easement by implication continues.

Easement by Prescription A way to acquire title to property by immemorial or long-continued enjoyment, it refers to personal usage.

Easement by Reservation Also: **Easement by Exception** An easement created by owners in a property they sell, subject to their continued use of the property for some specific purpose, such as access to a beachfront.

Easement in Gross A limited right of one person to use another's property when the right is not created for the benefit of land owned by the owner of the easement; it is not attached to any particular estate or land, nor is it transferred through the conveyance of title. Examples would include pipelines and telephone lines.

Economic Rent The rent that a property would command in the market at any given time, if it were vacant and available for lease, even though the actual rent may be different.

Effective Date of the Appraisal (Value Opinion) A mandatory date that must be stated in every appraisal report. It is the date to which the value estimate applies. It can be the date of the last inspection or any other date clearly specified in the appraisal report.

Effective Tax Rate The ratio between the market value of a property and its annual taxes; used by assessors and appraisers as a method of comparing the taxes on properties located in several communities with different assessment percentages and tax rates.

Electromagnetic Radiation The emanations from electrical and electromagnetic sources such as microwaves, high-voltage electric lines, televisions, and other sources. It is as yet uncertain whether or not such radiation is harmful and, if so, in what doses or exposure. Enough people believe that there are problems associated with this type of radiation that houses in close proximity to high-voltage electric lines may suffer some penalty in the market.

Eminent Domain The right of the government to acquire private property for public use by condemnation, which is the legal mechanism for taking private property, with just compensation being paid to the owner.

Employee A person who works for another person (the employer) and is paid hourly wages or a salary. The employer controls the employee's job description, hours, and responsibilities.

Employer One who hires, manages, and pays an employee or employees.

Employment Contract A document given by an employer to an employee, delineating the employee's responsibilities, job description, and compensation. It may also include such items as a review schedule and vacation policies.

Encroachment An intrusion of one person's property onto the property of another. It may be a wall, a fence, or a cornice or casement window that extends onto adjoining property.

Environmental Protection Agency (EPA) An agency of the federal government whose task is the oversight and implementation of environmental law, with a focus on maintaining and improving the quality of the environment and avoiding or abating further damage to it from release of hazardous substances.

Equalization (Equalization Factor) An adjustment used on a regional or statewide basis to equalize the tax burden among the citizens of the area for ad valorem taxation.

Equitable Lien A lien against real property created without a property contract, based on fairness and justice as interpreted by the courts, as when a seller accepts a deposit for real estate and refuses to transfer the property.

Equitable Right of Redemption The right of an owner and mortgagor of property to redeem the property from a forced sale by foreclosure, by meeting the payment requirements on the debt.

Equitable Title A person's right to obtain absolute ownership to a property that has legal title in someone else's name.

Erosion The wearing away of rock and earth caused by running water, glaciers, and wind.

Escheat One of the powers of government with reference to property ownership. The ownership of property reverts to the state when it is abandoned or when an owner dies without any heirs. It has its roots in English common law. Now many state statutes reinforce it in detail.

Escrow (Escrow Account) 1. A bank account established by an agent into which escrow funds are deposited. In many states, licensed brokers are required to have escrow accounts. 2. An account established by a mortgage lender into which a portion of each mortgage payment is set aside to pay taxes, insurance, and other expenses as required by the terms of the mortgage.

Escrow Agent (Escrow Officer, Escrow Holder) An agent or other disinterested party to a transaction who holds monies in escrow for distribution at a closing or settlement.

Escrow Closing A traditional manner of handling real estate closings in some jurisdictions whereby all the paperwork is signed and all the checks are drawn and held until after the transaction has been recorded, whereupon the money and documents are distributed to the appropriate parties by the escrow agent.

Estate and Inheritance Tax Lien In situations where there is an inheritance tax payment due, property from the deceased's estate is often encumbered with a tax lien to ensure satisfaction of the debt. Once the debt has been paid by the heirs, the property is cleared of the tax lien by the taxing authority.

Estates at Will An estate that can be terminated any time by the landlord or tenant.

Estoppel A legal doctrine stating that a person is forbidden to contradict or deny his or her own previous statement, act, or deed when an innocent third party has relied on the statement, act, or deed. For example, if a lender gives the wrong mortgage balance to a purchaser of a property when the purchaser is going to assume the mortgage, and the purchaser relies on this figure, the lender will have to abide by the figure given in error.

Eviction A court action for the physical removal of a person, usually a tenant, from a real property.

Exclusive Agency Listing A contract stating that the agents will receive a commission if a property is sold as a result of their efforts, but not as the result of the efforts of the principal.

Exclusive Right to Sell Listing An agreement between the owner of a property and a broker that the broker will receive a specified commission whenever the property is sold, regardless of who is ultimately responsible for procuring the buyer.

Executed Contract A contract that has been "signed, sealed, and delivered" is considered to be executed.

Executor (Executrix) A person who is appointed as the one to carry out requests in a will.

Executor's Deed A court-approved deed where the grantor is the executor.

Executory Contract A sales contract, after the acceptance but before the closing.

Executrix A female executor of an estate.

Express Contract A verbal or written contract spelling out clearly the mutual agreements between the parties, who will take what action or actions, and how they will be compensated.

Extraordinary Assumptions An assumption, directly related to a specific assignment, which, if found to be false, could alter the appraiser's opinions or conclusions.

Familial Status An exclusion of the fair credit laws that prohibits denying credit to people living with a parent or other familial relation.

Fannie Mae Created by the federal government as a government agency called the Federal National Mortgage Association and later chartered as a private corporation, now called Fannie Mae. Its stock is publicly traded. Its primary purpose is to buy mortgages from primary lenders and sell them in the secondary mortgage market. Originally it dealt primarily in FHA- and VA-insured mortgages. Now it buys and sells many types of mortgages.

Farmer's Home Administration (FmHA) A government agency under the U.S. Department of Agriculture. Its primary purpose is to provide credit to farmers and other people in rural communities.

Fault Creep A geological hazard caused by underground stresses along a split or fault in the earth. Fault creeps can shift several inches each year, causing a variety of problems to structures.

Federal Deposit Insurance Corporation (FDIC) An agency that insures depositors against loss of deposits in commercial and savings banks up to a maximum amount (currently $100,000, per depositor, per bank or $250,000 for IRA accounts).

Federal Home Loan Mortgage Corporation (FHLMC, Freddie Mac) This federal agency was created in 1970 and is commonly known as Freddie Mac. Its primary purpose is to buy conventional mortgages from savings and loan associations, thus giving them the liquidity they need to remain active in the mortgage lending field. It also buys some FHA- and VA-insured loans. It raises money by selling mortgage-backed securities and certificates.

Federal Housing Administration (FHA) A federal agency that is now a division of the Department of Housing and Urban Development (HUD). Its major activity is to promote good housing by insuring residential mortgage loans. The FHA has made a major contribution to improving housing throughout the country by the establishment of minimum property standards. The agency is involved in a variety of programs to improve housing, especially for low-income families.

Federal Interstate Land Sales Full Disclosure Act Regulates interstate land sales of unimproved lots. The act is administered by the Secretary of Housing and Urban Development (HUD) through the office of Interstate Land Sales Registration. Its purpose is to prevent fraudulent marketing schemes that may transpire when land is sold "sight unseen."

Federal Reserve System (the Fed) A governmental financial body that functions outside of the control of the president and directly influences the supply of money and interest rates by a variety of market manipulations, including the liquidity requirement for banks in the Federal Reserve System.

Federal Tax Lien A lien on property because the owner has failed to pay some kind of federal tax, such as federal estate tax, income tax, or payroll tax.

Fee Simple The best and most complete title an owner can have to a piece of real property.

Fiduciary A person who acts in a relationship of trust or confidence with respect to another person, involving sums of money or other assets.

Fiduciary Responsibility A trust relationship such that the trustee has special information, obligations, and duties that require faithful performance by the trustee on behalf of the beneficiary (trustor). Usually, access to and responsibility for money or other assets are involved.

Final Estimate of Value (Final Value Estimate) An opinion made by an appraiser after all the steps of the appraisal process and after the final reconciliation as to what the appraiser thinks the value of a property is.

Flood Plains The flat surfaces along the banks of rivers and streams that are subject to flooding.

Foreclosure Legal proceedings following default by the mortgagor, where a mortgagee (usually a bank) makes the mortgagor sell the property in order to repay the loan.

For-Profit Corporation A corporation created to run businesses and engage in a wide variety of other activities. The stock of for-profit corporations can be publicly traded or privately owned.

Fractional Interest(s) Also: **Divided Interest(s)** 1. An interest in some part of a whole property. 2. Ownership interests that are less than fee simple, such as air rights, subsurface rights, easements, right-of-ways, or any other partial interest.

Freddie Mac Created by the federal government in 1970 as a government agency called the Federal Home Loan Mortgage Corporation and later chartered as a private corporation now called Freddie Mac. Its stock is publicly traded. Its primary purpose is to buy mortgages from primary lenders and sell them in the secondary mortgage market. Originally it dealt primarily in mortgages written by Federal Savings and Loan Associations. Now it buys and sells many types of mortgages.

Freehold Estate(s) An estate in real property which is held for at least the life of the owner in fee simple, conditional fee, or fee tail.

Friable Asbestos An inhalant form of asbestos created when asbestos insulation or other asbestos-containing products are broken up or removed, or crumble. Friable asbestos is exceedingly toxic to humans, with prolonged exposure causing a condition called asbestosis and even moderate exposure contributing to the development of certain types of lung cancers. Asbestos removal must therefore be undertaken with great caution, as the abatement procedure itself creates the most damaging form of this substance.

Full Amortization An adjustable-rate mortgage that has a monthly payment sufficient to amortize the unpaid principal balance (at the interest accrual rate) over the mortgage term.

Gauss The unit used to measure electromagnetic radiation, named after a noted German mathematician, Carl F. Gauss.

General Agent (General Agency) A relationship whereby the principal gives the agent the power to bind them for specific business transactions.

General Data Data that originates outside the property. It is divided into primary data, which is generated by the appraiser or some agency and is not known by the public, and secondary data, which is published and available to the public.

General Liens As differentiated from specific liens, these include judgment liens, federal tax liens, and estate liens on property.

General Listing An open or nonexclusive listing of a piece of property for rental or sale.

General Partnerships Partnerships made up solely of general partners who are responsible for management and are personally liable for debts and obligations of the partnership.

General Power of Attorney A relationship that gives the agent the right to consummate all manner of business on behalf of the principal.

General Warranty Deed Used to convey the highest and most complete ownership interest in real property.

Geological Hazards Hazards associated with the earth and subsurface of the soil including earthquakes, fault creeps, and other destructive natural forces.

Gift Deed A deed that is given without the grantor receiving any consideration.

Government National Mortgage Association (GNMA, Ginnie Mae) is a federal agency that is a part of the FHA. It specializes in the purchase of FHA-insured mortgages in the secondary mortgage market that were made at below-market interest rates or that have higher than normal risk. Such mortgages could not be profitably purchased by the private sector.

Graduated Rent A step-up or graduated rent lease. When the amount of the increase is tied to an index it is called an indexed lease.

Grant Deed Type of conveyance used in California, Idaho, and North Dakota in place of a warranty deed. Grant deeds are not as complete as warranty deeds, as they specify particular warranties rather than providing a full general warranty.

Grantee A person who receives a transfer of real property by deed.

Granting Clause The legal mechanism that creates a grant of property to a grantee, usually in a deed.

Grantor A person who transfers real property by deed to a grantee.

Gross Rent All rental receipts received from an income-producing property.

Ground Lease A lease for land only, exclusive of any buildings that may be on it.

Ground Rent Rent paid for the use of vacant land. If the property is improved, it is the portion of the total rent that is attributable to the land.

Guardian's Deed A deed to property given by the guardian of a minor or incompetent person on orders of the probate court.

Habendum Clause One of the standard clauses in a deed that defines the extent of ownership.

Handicapped People who have a physical or mental disability that impairs their functioning particularly relative to physical access to buildings. Handicapped access is covered by several new laws against discrimination.

Health and Safety Laws Specific laws, ordinances, or codes prescribing safety and sanitary standards and regulations designed to protect and preserve the health and safety of the community.

Highest and Best Use The utilization of a property to its best and most profitable use. It is that use, chosen from among reasonably probable and legal alternative uses, which is found to be physically possible, appropriately supported, and financially feasible to result in highest land value.

Holdover Tenant A tenant who retains possession of a leased property after his or her lease has expired.

Home Equity Loan A mortgage loan that is usually subordinate to a first mortgage and that allows homeowners to obtain loan proceeds at their discretion up to an amount previously agreed on by the lender, based on the owner's equity in the property.

Homeowners' Association (HOA) 1. An association of property owners in a residential area formed for the purpose of improving the area both physically and socially. The association may own or maintain some physical facilities. 2. An association that is formed as part of the process of establishing the ownership of a property such as a condominium or planned unit development. The association is responsible for the regulation and maintenance of the commonly owned property.

Homestead 1. The fixed residence of a family, including the surrounding land and buildings. 2. Artificial estate giving certain statutory exemptions against the rights of creditors. 3. The traditional gift of the federal government of a piece of property 160 acres in area to settlers of the Western regions of the country as an inducement to move there in the mid-1700s and 1800s.

Horizontal Subdivision The zoning provisions that allow the condominium form of ownership.

Housing for Older Persons (Housing for the Elderly) 1. Housing created under special laws to promote and facilitate specific domiciles for elderly persons. As such, it is specifically exempt from the provisions of the Civil Rights Act pertaining to age discrimination. 2. A special classification of housing that is designed with features needed by elderly residents.

Hypotenuse In a triangle, the two short sides are called the legs and the long side is called the "hypotenuse." In a right triangle, the formula states that the hypotenuse is equal to the square root of the sum of the two shorter sides.

Hypothetical Conditions That which is contrary to what exists but is supposed for the purpose of analysis. It assumes conditions contrary to known facts about physical, legal, or economic characteristics of the subject property, or about conditions external to the property, such as market conditions or trends, or about the integrity of the data used in an analysis.

Implied Contract An unwritten agreement that is a contract based on the acts of the parties involved. Often, home improvement work is performed under an implied contact, that is, that the contractor will be paid upon its completion.

Improvements 1. Objects or structures attached to the land. 2. The site preparations required for building that include grading, landscaping, driveways, utility connections, and others. 3. Additions in structure, function, or utility made to a property to increase its value.

Income Capitalization Approach An approach to value used by appraisers to measure the present value of the future benefits of property ownership.

Independent Contractor A self-employed person who performs services without being controlled by the person or organization for whom the services are rendered. For a real estate salesperson to be an independent contractor, he or she must be free to act independently and without obligations such as floor time, meeting attendance, fixed hours, and so on. The independent contractor should be paid gross amounts without tax deductions for his or her services.

Indexed Lease A lease that is tied to an external published rate, such as the consumer price index (CPI) or the cost of living index. The terms of the lease usually call for escalations of rent or a percentage increase based on the changes in the specified index.

Indoor Air Pollutants Airborne materials that contaminate indoor air. Some examples include tobacco smoke, asbestos, mites, and animal dander.

Infectious Medical Waste The portion of medical waste from hospitals, nursing homes, and medical laboratories that contains blood or blood products, human tissue, and other matter deemed potentially infectious to humans.

Installment Contract A type of real estate sale based on an agreement between buyer and seller wherein payment is made in specified installments (usually monthly). Equitable title and possession of the property pass to the buyer at the beginning of the contract, and legal title passes after all the required payments have been made.

Intended Users The client and any other party identified, by name or type, as users of the appraisal, appraisal review, or appraisal consulting assignment opinions and conclusions, as identified by the appraiser based on communication with the client at the time of the assignment.

Interest 1. A right or share in something. 2. Money paid for the use of borrowed money. 3. Money paid to savers by thrift institutions for keeping their money at that institution.

Interpleader (Interpleader Action) 1. An action filed in court by an escrow agent asking the court for instructions regarding dispersal of monies they are holding. 2. A court action that can be filed by a real estate broker holding a commission that is claimed by several parties.

Interspousal Deed A deed between a married couple.

Interstate Land Sales Offerings of land or building sites for sale to purchasers who are from other states. Due to past problems, federal disclosure laws require that purchasers in such transactions be given a three-day grace period after signing contracts, during which they may withdraw, thereby invalidating the sale.

Intestate A person who dies without leaving a will or who leaves a will that is invalid.

Involuntary Alienation The loss of property through a variety of unsought-for occurrences, such as eminent domain (condemnation), foreclosure, adverse possession, or destruction by natural forces.

Involuntary Lien A lien against property other than a mortgage (which is a voluntary lien). Typical involuntary liens are a mechanic's lien or a tax lien.

Joint Tenancy An estate or tenancy shared equally by two or more parties with the right to survivorship. When a joint tenant dies, his or her interest goes to the surviving tenants rather than to the deceased's heirs.

Joint Venture When two or more people combine their property, skills, and funds and become partners in a single business purpose.

Judgment Lien A lien placed on property as a result of a court decision. Used as a way to guarantee that the owner of the property will comply with the decision of the court.

Judicial Deed A deed supplied by a court and signed by an officer of the court. It is often the deed given in a sale under foreclosure proceedings.

Judicial Foreclosure A court action that offers a property for sale under foreclosure due to a breach of a mortgage contract. It includes provisions for the original owner to try to redeem the property. A redemption date is set by which time the owner must redeem the property by paying off the debt and court costs, or lose the property.

Just Compensation The amount paid to a property owner when a property is condemned. In theory, the payment leaves the owner no richer or poorer than before the condemnation.

Laches Like the statute of limitations, laches defines a period of time during which different types of legal actions must be filed. However, no specific time period is indicated. Under laches, the time frame is based on whether or not the action was filed in a reasonable period of time and if late filing harmed the other party. For example, as soon as property owners become aware of an encroachment onto their property, such as by a fence or other structure, prompt notification is required under laches to stop the encroachment. They cannot delay, permit completion of the structure, and then file, as this will do additional harm to their neighbor.

Land 1. The solid portion of the earth's surface substantially in its undisturbed condition. 2. Unimproved property without site improvements such as roads, utilities, and the like. 3. That portion of a real property that is not structures or other improvements.

Landslides A geological hazard caused by disturbance of the substructure of land, often from excess water saturation after flooding, leading to sudden falls and slides down slopes to the land areas below.

Land Trusts Open space land held in trust by a municipality or other jurisdiction for the use of people in a community. Many communities in the Northeast have land trusts which predate the Constitution.

Lead Paint A leading source of toxic lead from flakes and chips that are ingested by children and can cause irreversible brain damage. Lead paint is still found in substandard and low-income housing, although lead is no longer used in the composition of household paints.

Leaking Underground Storage Tanks (LUSTs) Underground tanks holding toxic and hazardous substances, which are improperly sealed and are leaking into the subsoil. LUSTs are identified as part of environmental site inspections, and a variety of abatement procedures are used to stop the leakage.

Leased Fee The interest in a property that remains with the owner after he or she has granted someone else the right to occupy the property. This right to occupy is usually granted by a lease for a specific period of time.

Leasehold The interest in a property of a tenant (lessee) created by a lease. It is usually the right to occupy and use the property for a stipulated period of time in exchange for the payment of rent. It is usually subject to terms and conditions that are set forth in a lease.

Leasehold Estate 1. Nonfreehold interest in a property created by a lease. 2. The interest of a tenant or lessee in a property created by a lease. To the extent that the contract rent is less than market rent, there is value attached to the leasehold. 3. Right to occupy and use a property for a specific period in exchange for rent, subject to terms and conditions set forth in a lease.

Leasehold Estate at Sufferance The leasehold interest of tenants who continue to occupy the premises they originally leased, despite the termination of their lease, and without a renewal.

Leasehold Estate at Will An interest in real estate that gives a tenant the right to occupy a property for an unspecified amount of time, usually at the mutual convenience of the tenant and landlord.

Leasehold Estate for Years A typical leasehold estate that provides that a tenant has possession and use of property for a specified period of time at a contract rental. A lease does not usually end upon the death of either the lessee or the landlord, but is inheritable by their heirs.

Leasehold Interest The value of a tenant's interest in a lease. When the value of the right to occupy the premises and the rent being paid are equal, there is no leasehold value. When the value of the right to use the property is greater than the value of the rent being paid for this right, the difference is the leasehold value. Appraisers estimate the value of the leasehold interest by calculating the rent savings over the term of the lease (the difference between the contract rent and the market rent) and discounting the difference into a present value.

Lease Option A type of lease that allows tenants to buy the property they lease at a preset price at some point during the lease, at the termination of the lease, or at some other specified date in the future.

Lease Purchase A term referring to a type of sale of real estate to an investor whereby the investor leases the property back to the original owner. It is a relatively common way for owners to exchange equity in their property for profit or operating capital for their business.

Legacy A special gift of money or other personal property made in a will to a recipient called a legatee.

Legal Description A method of identifying the boundaries of a property. There are a variety of different systems approved by the laws of different states.

Legal Purpose A provision of contract law that holds that a contract must be for legal purposes in order to be valid and enforceable.

Legatee A person to whom a legacy in a will is given.

Lessee (Tenant) The party to a lease (tenant) who receives the right to use or occupy a property in return for the payment of rent.

Lessor (Landlord) The party to a lease who owns the fee title and gives a tenant (lessee) the right to use or occupy the property in return for the payment of rent.

License 1. Permit or authorization issued by a governmental office, granting explicit permission to engage in some action that would otherwise be illegal. 2. A right granted by the owner of a property to someone else for an action to take place on the property without providing an interest in the property.

Lien A claim on property that encumbers the property and makes it security for the payment of a debt.

Lienee The person whose property is subject to a lien that encumbers it.

Lienor The person or entity that holds a lien on property as collateral for a loan.

Life Estate A term in real estate law that refers to the interest of a person in real property that lasts for his or her own life only, and does not pass to their heirs upon the person's death.

Life Tenant The holder of a life estate.

Light Pollution Excessive and intrusive light at times of the day when it disrupts normal activities or comfort, usually from neighboring uses.

Limitations Clause A clause in a transfer document that reserves certain rights for the owner, which continue after the transfer.

Limited Liability Company (LLC) This is similar to a corporation in that it provides liability protection to the owners. It is best suited for businesses with a limited number of owners. Owners are known as members. When there is more than one owner, the entity is treated as a partnership for tax purposes.

Limited Partnership(s) An association of some partners in a business venture where they have no day-to-day control and no liability beyond their investment. Control is usually held by a few general or managing partners who are paid a fee for these services.

Liquidated Damages A provision in a real estate sales contract that limits the liability of a designated party to the agreement to a specified sum if that party defaults on his obligation under the contract.

Liquid Waste The liquid portion of household waste such as sink, toilet, and shower water drainage.

Lis Pendens The jurisdiction, power, or control that a court acquires over property involved in a suit, pending the continuance of the action, and until a final judgment has been given.

Listing Agreement (Listing, Listings) 1. A contract between a principal and broker hiring the broker-agent to perform a particular act. Typically, it is a contract between a property owner and a broker that authorizes the broker to offer the property for sale or rent in return for a commission. 2. A document that describes a property being offered for sale or rent. 3. A property listed in a listing agreement.

Listing Expiration Date The termination date on a listing agreement.

Living Trust A trust arrangement made during the lifetime of the owner of the property whereby a trustee is appointed who manages the property for the benefit of the designated beneficiaries.

Lot and Block System A map that divides a parcel of land into lots and is the basis of legal descriptions. It is used in most of the United States except in the original 13 states.

Marketable Title A representation made as part of the documentation in a real estate transaction that permits the property to transfer.

Market Area The geographic territory within which a product being marketed can reasonably expect to find a buyer.

Market Value The price (highest or most probable) that a property will sell for in a competitive market when all the conditions for a fair sale exist. These conditions include buyers and sellers who are knowledgeable about the property and the market and who are typically motivated and free of unusual stimulus and acting in their own best interest. It also assumes that there is sufficient time available to market the property and that typical financing will be available.

Mechanic's Lien (Materialman's Lien) A special lien created by state statute to protect those who work on real estate and provide material and labor for construction, improvement, and repairs. In many states, a mechanic's lien has priority over other liens and mortgages, even when they are recorded after those liens. Many state statutes give mechanics a specified time after the work is performed to record a lien.

Metes and Bounds 1. The boundary lines of a property including terminal points and angles. 2. A system of property description used primarily in New England whereby land records predate the government survey system.

Military Affidavit An affidavit that is required as part of a regular foreclosure procedure that states that the person who signs the affidavit has personal knowledge that the owner of the property being foreclosed is not in the military service.

Mill 1. A type of building equipped with machinery for grinding grain into flour. 2. A building or group of buildings used to manufacture or process trees into lumber. 3. To process trees into lumber or grain into flour. 4. Other industrial facilities that process raw materials into end products, such as ore into steel.

Mill Rate A multiplier, that is multiplied by the assessed value of property to calculate ad valorem taxes.

Mineral Lease A type of lease that permits the exploration for minerals and their mining if found. Often the rent consists of a specified amount plus a percentage of the value of anything that is mined.

Mineral Rights The rights to minerals beneath the ground such as coal, iron, and gold with or without ownership of the surface of the land.

Minor A child by legal definition. In most states the age of majority is 18 years.

Month-to-Month Lease A lease given to a tenant who rents for one month at a time, renewable automatically until one of the parties to the lease notifies the other of the desire to terminate it.

Mortgage The pledge of property to a lender to secure the payment of the debt. There are a variety of forms that are determined by custom and state statutes. They must be in writing and often are recorded in the land records. They are temporary in nature and end when the debt is paid off by the mortgagor.

Mortgage Deed A written document verifying that a real property has been given as security for a loan.

Mortgagee The lender who loans money, the payment of which is secured by a mortgage.

Mortgage Lien The voluntary alienation of fee simple ownership, using it as collateral for a debt, which is described in a corresponding note.

Mortgagor The person who borrows money secured by a mortgage.

Multiple Listing Clause Part of a listing agreement that provides that the property will be offered to the public through the MLS system.

Multiple Listing Service (MLS) A system whereby a group of brokers agrees to work together and cooperate to sell each other's listings. When a listing is taken, it is displayed in the MLS publications or online or both, and cooperating brokers are invited to become subagents of the listing broker.

Mutually Rescinded Contracts A contract that is abandoned by both parties by mutual agreement.

Narrative Appraisal Report Presentation of an estimate of value, featuring a book-like layout. Typically, a narrative report consists of many pages and is divided into sections, including exhibits and photographs of the subject. This is the most complete type of appraisal presentation.

National Priorities List (NPL) The EPA's list of the most serious uncontrolled or abandoned hazardous waste sites identified for possible long-term remedial response using money from the Trust Fund. The list is based primarily on the score a site receives on the Hazard Ranking System (HRS). The EPA is required to update the NPL at least once a year.

Natural Forces Destruction of property by waves, landslides, and the like.

Nearby Hazardous Property An environmental risk factor that must be considered when buying or selling property.

Negative Easement An easement used to prevent the use of a property in some way. Examples are light and air easements, which prohibit construction of improvements in a manner that would block the light and air of another property. A common type of negative easement is a scenic easement that prevents building in a manner that would block a view.

Net Lease Also: **Net Net Lease; Net Net Net Lease; Triple Net Lease** A lease by which a tenant pays maintenance and operating expenses for the leased property in addition to rent.

Net Listing A listing under which the broker receives all monies above the minimum sales price predetermined by the owners and broker. This form of listing is now illegal in many states.

Noise Pollution Excessive and often ear-damaging noise from a wide variety of sources, especially in industrial concerns. Residential property located too close to major highways, railroad tracks, and nearby industrial uses may also suffer from significant noise pollution.

Nonconventional Mortgage A mortgage that is insured by a federal agency such as the VA or FHA.

Nonfreehold Estates An estate in real estate without seisin (ownership). The most common form of nonfreehold estate is a leasehold estate.

Nonjudicial Foreclosure The "power of sale method" of collateral property recovery. The lender has the right to sell the property to satisfy the debt without going to court to get permission to do so.

Note The negotiable portion of a mortgage loan transaction, being the promissory instrument signed by the mortgagor, for which the property is the collateral. Since the note is negotiable, only one copy is signed.

Not-for-Profit Corporations (Nonprofit Corporation) A corporation that is formed for a purpose other than making a profit. Such groups are often used for charity purposes or may be political, fraternal, or educational organizations. These corporations do not have shareholders or stock. They have members who elect a board of directors to run the affairs of the corporation. In many other respects, they operate like a regular corporation.

Offeree The person to whom an offer is made.

Offeror A person making an offer.

Office of Thrift Supervision (OTS) A part of the U.S. Treasury. Its mission is to supervise savings associations and their holding companies in order to maintain their safety and soundness and compliance with consumer laws.

Online Appraisal A type of appraisal offered online by computer. Often it is free.

Open Listing (Nonexclusive Listing) A listing to sell or rent property given to more than one broker. The first broker who finds a party ready, willing, and able to buy or rent at the asking price, or at a mutually agreeable negotiated price, receives a commission as specified in the listing agreement. Unless required by state law, an open listing does not have to be for a finite period of time.

Optionee A person who receives an option.

Option Listing A practice that is frowned on because it gives the broker or sales associate an option to purchase a property at the listing price. The problem is one of conflict of interest, as the agency relationship requires the broker to obtain the highest price for the property.

Optionor A person who gives an option for a fee.

Ostensible Agency Also: **Ostensible Authority** or **Attorney in Fact** An agency relationship, with full privileges and binding in nature, created by actions or failures to act, regardless of whether the agency relationship is clear or disclosed to the parties involved.

Outdoor Air Pollution Toxic and unhealthy conditions in the atmosphere including a wide variety of precipitates from industrial uses, smog, smoke, and automobile exhaust.

Ownership in Severalty Individual and undivided ownership of a piece of property.

Partial Amortization Mortgage A mortgage whereby payments, made as scheduled over the whole term of the mortgage, are not sufficient to completely cover both interest and principal reduction; as a result, there still remains an unpaid balance of the principal at the end of the term.

Partial Performance When some but not all the provisions of a contract have been met. It is up to the injured party to pursue completion of the contract or accept partial performance instead.

Partial Taking The taking of a portion of a property by the government under its power of eminent domain. The compensation received by the owner is the difference between the value of the whole property prior to the taking and the value of the remaining property after the taking.

Party Wall Agreement(s) An agreement regarding a common wall in buildings that separates two units into separate ownerships. It is commonly found in row houses and town houses.

Party Wall Easement A common wall in a building that separates two units in separate ownership.

Percentage Leases A lease that contains a provision that requires the rental or a portion of the rental to be based on a percentage of the gross sales, income, or profit of the tenant.

Perimeter 1. The total boundary of a site or building. 2. The circumference of a circle.

Period (Periodic Tenancy) A leasehold estate that is automatically renewed for successive periods until proper notice to terminate is given either by the landlord or tenant.

Perpendicular At right angles to. The base of a right triangle is perpendicular to one of the legs, creating a 90° angle.

Pesticide A generic term for a wide group of rodenticides, insecticides, and herbicides that are toxic to pests and often to humans as well.

Phase I Environmental Inspection The first level of environmental inspections performed to evaluate the present condition of the site and determine the likelihood of an environmental problem.

Phase II Environmental Inspection The second level of environmental inspection, required when the Phase I report shows evidence of environmental problems. Includes on-site environmental sampling and laboratory analysis of materials gathered.

Phase III Environmental Inspection The most complete type of environmental inspection, performed to determine the degree, extent, and rate of any on-site release of toxic materials, and to evaluate the potential impact on human health or safety. Recommendations for remedial actions are formulated from the data obtained.

Pi (π) Pi is the constant 3.1416 used in calculations involving circles. The formula for the area of a circle is πr^2, where r is the radius of the circle; the formula for the perimeter of a circle is $2\pi r$ where r is the radius of the circle.

Picocuries (pCi/L) The standard measurement for Radon-222 contamination is picocuries per liter.

Planned Unit Development (PUD) A type of land development that is specially provided for in a community's zoning regulations, allowing the developer more flexible use of the land. Part of the land is divided into lots, which are individually owned. The balance is set aside for use by all the owners of lots within the subdivision and is owned either by the community or by an association formed for the lot owners in the subdivision.

Points Monies paid to the lender over and above normal closing costs on a mortgage. Each point is 1 percent of the face amount of the mortgage. One or more points may be charged by a lender at the time of closing as an additional fee for making the loan. Points may be paid by the buyer, by the seller, or by both parties. By deducting points from the proceeds of the mortgage, the lender increases the effective interest rate (APR) on the mortgage.

Police Power The power of the government to control the use of real estate for the general welfare of the public. It does this through zoning regulations, building codes, environmental regulations, and the like. It also includes the government's right to acquire property by condemnation.

Power of Attorney A document that gives one person the authority to act for another in legal situations.

Preliminary Title Report 1. A written report issued by a title insurance company after investigation to determine if a good and marketable title exists for a piece of property. 2. A binder for title insurance.

Prepaid Items Expenses relating to property, such as taxes, insurance, and rent, which are paid in advance. If the property is sold, these items are often prorated between the buyer and the seller.

Principal 1. The capital portion of a debt or investment as distinguished from interest, income, or profit. 2. One who employs another (the agent) to act in his behalf. 3. The head of a real estate company. 4. A party to a transaction acting for himself.

Principle The basis of an ethical consideration.

Private Mortgage Insurance (PMI) Mortgage insurance that is written by companies not a part of the federal government. It ensures that the borrower will make timely mortgage payments on conventional mortgages.

Procuring Cause Being the direct cause of a real estate transaction. In order to be entitled to a commission, brokers or salespersons must often prove that they were the direct cause of the transaction being consummated.

Profit a' Prendre The right to take part of the soil, gravel, water, minerals, or other products from the land of another. While it acts like an easement, it is considered an independent property right.

Promissory Note A document that is a promise by one party to pay a specified amount to a second party.

Property Rights The rights associated with a piece of real estate are divided into the rights of the government and private property rights, which consist of a bundle of rights including the rights to use the property or transfer the rights by sale or gift.

Prorate (Proration, Prorating) Apportioning of those items in a closing or settlement that are owed between buyer and seller, such as prepaid fuel, uncollected rent, or taxes. It is the custom for each of the items to be calculated separately and included as part of the settlement statement used at the real estate closing. The net result of the prorations is paid by either the buyer to the seller or vice versa.

Protected Class All those classifications of people who are protected under various civil rights, fair housing, and fair credit laws.

Puffing The act of exaggerating the good qualities of something that is being offered for sale or rent.

Purchase Contract A contract between a buyer and seller of real property that defines the terms of the sale.

Purchase Money Mortgage Also: **Owner Financing** A mortgage on real property given to the seller by the buyer to help reduce the amount of cash they need to complete the sale. Payments are made monthly to the seller rather than to the bank. Sometimes, a purchase money mortgage is given for the down payment and becomes a second or subordinate mortgage on the property.

Purchase Option A common clause in a lease that gives the lessee the right to purchase the premises at some time in the future for an established price, or a price that will be determined in an agreed-upon manner, such as by an appraisal.

Quadrilateral A four-sided geometric shape.

Quiet Enjoyment The right of owners or tenants to the use and possession of their property without interference.

Quitclaim Deed A deed that conveys all of the ownership of the seller to the buyer without guaranteeing the quality of the title.

Radiation 1. The emission of particles or rays by the nucleus of an atom. 2. The emission of heat waves into the surrounding air from an object that is warmer than the air. 3. The rays of energy from the sun.

Radius Also: **Ray** A straight line connecting a point on the circumference of a circle with the center of the circle. The radius is used in the formula for calculating area, which is πr^2, where r is the radius of the circle.

Radon-222 A colorless, odorless, naturally occurring gas produced by decomposition of radioactive minerals in the ground. Radon is a recognized health hazard, particularly for lung cancers. It has the same effect as smoking on the lungs. Radon seepage into the atmosphere is not generally harmful, but when it builds up in an enclosure such as a house, via a sump or through the cracks of a basement floor, concentrations may become dangerous. Brokers must disclose known radon problems in any property they are showing or listing.

Ratification The confirmation of an act committed on someone's behalf that might be voidable if not affirmed.

Ready, Willing, and Able A term often used or implied in a listing agreement that describes the buyer who must be produced by the broker in order for the broker to earn a commission. The buyer must offer the full listing price without unfilled contingent conditions. In the event that such a buyer is found, the commission is earned even if the offer is rejected by the seller.

Real Estate Also: **Realty** 1. An identified parcel or tract of land, including improvements, if any. 2. Land and all attachments that are of a permanent nature. Real estate as distinguished from personal property. At one time real estate was the sole source of wealth, and thus achieved a special place in the law because of its importance.

Real Estate Appraisal See **Appraisal.**

Real Estate Investment Trust (REIT) A real estate mutual fund, allowed by income tax laws to avoid corporate tax. It sells shares of ownership and must invest in real estate or mortgages. A REIT allows small investors to participate in the ownership of large potentially profitable real estate.

Real Estate Settlement Procedures Act of 1974 (RESPA) Enacted to protect buyers of one- to four-family homes from fraud, it requires lenders to provide full and accurate information about interest rates and other costs prior to the closing in a closing statement or settlement statement.

Real Property The rights and benefits derived from the ownership of real estate.

Recasting a Loan Renegotiating the interest rate, terms, or other conditions of a loan during the life of the loan.

Reconciliation The final step in the appraisal process, in which the appraiser combines the estimates of value produced from the sales comparison, cost, and income approaches to arrive at a final estimate of market value for the subject property.

Recording 1. The process of inscribing certain legal instruments such as deeds, mortgages, leases, and liens into permanent books available for inspection by the public. 2. A record of the transactions and related documents involved in real estate sales that is maintained for the benefit of the public.

Recording Act Each state and territory has an act that requires that these documents be recorded in the area where the property is located.

Recording Fees (Recording Charges) Fees associated with recording the details of a real estate transaction. Some localities have recording fees that may or may not be related to the amount paid for the real estate.

Recovery Account Also: **Recovery Fund** A fund maintained and managed by the state that reimburses the public for losses caused by licensed real estate brokers and salespeople as a result of their wrongful actions.

Rectangle A four-sided geometric figure having 90-degree angles at all of its corners.

Rectangular (Government) Survey System Also: **Public Land Survey System (PLSS)** A system established in 1785 by the federal government, providing for surveying and describing land by reference to principal meridians and base lines.

Redemption Date The right of a defaulted property owner to recover his or her property by remedying the default by a date set by the court in a foreclosure procedure.

Redlining The illegal practice of a lending institution denying loans or restricting their number for certain areas of a community.

Referee's Deed in Foreclosure The document by which real property is transferred in some foreclosure sales.

Referee's Deed in Partition The document that is used to transfer partial interest in a dissolution of joint ownership or joint tenancy.

Regulation Z Implements the Truth-in-Lending Law requiring credit institutions to inform borrowers of the true cost of obtaining credit.

Release of Lien An instrument that discharges a lien when payment of the debt is made together with interest and costs.

Remainderman The person who is to receive possession of the property after the death of a life tenant. Many people wish to allow a surviving spouse to occupy property for the rest of the spouse's life, with a child being the remainderman.

Replacement Cost The cost of erecting a building to take the place of or serve the functions of a previous structure. Replacement cost often sets the upper limit on value; it is often used for insurance purposes.

Reproduction Cost The normal cost of exact duplication of a property as of a certain date. Reproduction cost differs from replacement cost in that replacement requires the same functional utility for a property, whereas reproduction is an exact duplicate, using the same materials and craftsmanship.

Respirable Particles Small volatile airborne particles of matter that may be inhaled. These range from pollen and dust to hazardous materials such as friable asbestos and other contaminants.

Restrictive Covenants A private restriction on the use or transfer of property. Restrictive covenants are illegal if they prohibit transfer of a property based on race or religion.

Reverse Annuity Mortgage (RAM) A loan under which the homeowner receives monthly payments based on his or her accumulated equity rather than a lump sum. The loan must be repaid at a prearranged date or upon the death of the owner or the sale of the property.

Reversion The right of a lessor to possess leased property upon the termination of a lease. A lease is valid for an established term, after which the lessor receives the reversion.

Right Angle The joining point of two perpendicular lines resulting in a 90-degree angle.

Right of First Refusal A right usually contained in a lease or contract that entitles a tenant or partner in a real estate venture to purchase the property if the owner decides to sell, at the same price as any offer received by the owner.

Rights of Ownership The bundle of public and private rights that together make up the bundle of rights of property ownership. Ownership of all the private rights is called fee simple ownership.

Riparian Rights Rights pertaining to the use of water on, under, or adjacent to one's land. In most states, riparian rights provide that property owners cannot alter the flow of water to their downstream neighbors.

Sale(s) The transfer of a property title in exchange for some sort of payment.

Sales Associate A person licensed to sell real estate who works in the office of a real estate broker.

Salt Marsh A type of boggy land area included under wetlands provisions in environmental laws.

Sandwich Lease Lease held by a lessee who sublets all or part of his or her interest, thereby becoming a lessor. Typically, the sandwich leaseholder is neither the owner of the fee estate nor the user of the property. The sandwich lessee tries to profit from the rent differential of the other leases.

Satisfaction of Judgment The completion of an obligation created by a court ruling by the payment in full of the amount required by the judgment.

Satisfaction of Lien 1. The completion of an obligation, such as a mortgage, by the payment in full of the debt. 2. The name of the document that is issued by a mortgagee when a mortgage is paid off.

Scenic Easement An easement granted to nearby property owners that restricts construction on adjacent property of those uses that will detract from the attractiveness of the area or block scenic views of neighbors.

Second Mortgage A mortgage that is a junior lien on the property. Its security interest comes after the preceding mortgage or mortgages.

Secondary Mortgage Market A group of large, quasi-governmental agencies and other investors that purchase existing mortgage loans. After a mortgage loan is originated, it can be sold into the secondary market to provide funds for more mortgage originations. This means that mortgage loans can be made by lenders regardless of how many local deposits they have.

Security Instrument A mortgage whereby property owners pledge their real property as collateral for a loan.

Seller's Lien A lien against property held by the seller, which is removed when certain specific conditions are met by the buyer.

Septic System A sewage system consisting of a septic tank, distribution box, and leaching field, used in areas where sewers have not been installed or hooked up.

Settlement Also: **Real Estate Closing** The consummation of a real estate transaction, at which time the purchase price is paid by the buyer to the seller, and adjustments (prorations) are made between them for prepaid rent, taxes, and unpaid expenses.

Settlement Statement Also: **Closing Statement** A statement drawn up by a broker, escrow agent, or qualified others, that provides a breakdown of all the costs involved in a real estate sale.

Sharecropping A type of lease whereby the tenant agrees to farm the land and, as all or part of the rent, shares the crop with the landowner.

Shared Appreciation Mortgage (SAM) A loan where the mortgagee receives a share of the profits in addition to mortgage interest.

Sheriff's Deed A deed given to the purchaser at a court-ordered sale to satisfy a judgment, without warranties.

Site A parcel of land that is improved with grading, utilities, driveways, and utility hookups and is suitable for building purposes.

Special (Specific) Agency An agent with limited authority to transact business for a principal. Real estate brokers are often special agents, as they are usually only permitted to show property and present offers to owners who must decide whether to accept an offer or not.

Special Assessments Real estate tax assessments that are levied against properties in the community that receive special services not provided to other properties in the community.

Special Power of Attorney An authorization by a principal to an agent giving the agent responsibility and authority to carry out specific acts.

Special Warranty Deed A deed in which the grantor warrants, or guarantees, the title only against defects arising during the period of his or her tenure and ownership of the property and not against defects existing before that time, generally using the language, "by, through or under the grantor but not otherwise."

Specific Data Data that includes details about the subject property, comparable sales, rental properties, and relevant local market characteristics.

Specific Date Every appraisal must be as of a specific date that is defined by the 2006 USPAP as being a specific day.

Specific Liens Encumbrances for specific debts owed by a property owner.

Specific Performance A legal action in which the court requires a party to a contract to perform the terms of the contract when he or she has refused to fulfill obligations. Used in real estate because each parcel of land is unique. In other types of property transactions, a court may award compensation as damages in terms of money; by contrast, in real estate the court may insist on specific performance.

Square 1. In the Rectangular (Government) Survey System, an area measuring 24 miles by 24 miles, also called a check. 2. In roofing or siding, a section that measures $10' \times 10'$, or 100 square feet. 3. A geometric shape with four equal sides and four right angles of 90 degrees each.

Statute of Frauds State laws that require that certain real estate contracts must be in writing to be enforceable. It applies to deeds, mortgages, and other real estate contracts, with the exception of leases for periods shorter than one year.

Statute of Limitations A certain statutory period after which a claimant is barred from enforcing a claim by suit. If a practice continues beyond the statute of limitations, the person who is adversely affected may be barred from trying to prevent it.

Statutory Lien An involuntary lien against a property by the operation of a statute, including taxes, a court judgment, or a mechanic's lien.

Statutory Right of Redemption The right of the owner to recover the property after its sale in a foreclosure proceeding by paying off the debt plus the appropriate fees and charges.

Steering An illegal practice of some brokers and salespeople of channeling clients to buy or rent only in those areas where there are other residents of similar ethnic, racial, or religious backgrounds.

Step-up Rent Also: **Step Up Lease; Escalation Clause** A lease that permits increases in rent at set, predetermined intervals, usually based on a published index.

Storage Drums Typically, 55-gallon drums that may be used to hold a wide variety of materials, some of which are environmentally unsafe. A property with a large number of storage drums may have serious environmental problems.

Straight Loan A loan that is made at a fixed interest rate, which calls for periodic interest payments for the term of the loan and a final balloon payment of the principal amount.

Strict Foreclosure An action taken by a court after a period of redemption, terminating all the interests of the property owner and turning the property over to the creditors without the sale of the property at auction.

Subagent An agent hired by another agent, often through an MLS system, to help sell or rent a listed property.

Subject Property The appraised property that must be identified in such a way that there can be no confusion about what is being appraised.

Sublessee A person or other entity who rents space from a primary tenant or lessee.

Sublessor The primary tenant of rented space who allows a secondary tenant (sublessee) to occupy or use the premises in exchange for rent.

Sublet A lease executed by the lessee of a property to a third person for a period of time shorter than the leasehold.

Subprime Lending A general term that refers to the practice of making loans to borrowers who do not qualify for market interest rates because of problems with their credit history.

Subsurface Rights Ownership rights in a parcel of real estate to the water, minerals, gas, oil, and so forth that lie beneath the surface of the property.

Suit for Possession A court action whereby the rightful owner or tenant of a property sues the possessors to require them to vacate the property.

Swamp(s) 1. Wetlands protected from development by environmental legislation. 2. To totally inundate with water.

Syndication 1. A group of people, companies, or organizations who join together for the purpose of making an investment in an asset or property. 2. Creation of a group venture in an asset by bringing together investors.

Tax Certificate The document that is given at a public tax auction to the highest bidder for property sold to pay off delinquent taxes.

Tax Deed The type of deed given to a purchaser at a tax sale.

Tax-Exempt Properties Certain real properties owned by tax-exempt institutions such as universities.

Tax Lien An encumbrance on property for unpaid taxes.

Teaser Rate Loan A type of loan where the interest rate for a short initial period of the loan is well below market interest rates. After the initial period the interest increases to a higher rate.

Tenancy at Sufferance A leasehold estate that is created when the tenants continue to occupy the property after they are supposed to move out, according to the terms of the lease.

Tenancy by the Entirety The joint ownership, recognized in some states, of property acquired by husband and wife during marriage. Upon the death of one spouse, the survivor becomes the owner of the property.

Tenancy in Common An ownership of realty by two or more persons, each of whom has an undivided interest without the right of survivorship. Upon the death of one of the owners, his or her ownership share is inherited by the party or parties designated in his or her will.

Termiticides Chemicals that are toxic to termites and other insect pests.

Testamentary Trusts Trusts established by a will for the benefit of beneficiaries. If real estate is involved in the estate, a trustee will manage the real estate for the benefit of the legatees.

Testate Having made and left a valid will.

Testator A man who makes a will.

Testatrix A woman who makes a will.

Time Is of the Essence A clause in a contract to indicate that timely performance is a requirement of the contract, and delayed performance can be entirely rejected.

Timesharing Also: **Timeshare Ownership; Interval Ownership** Ownership interest in real property that is an undivided interest for a fixed or variable time period. Common in vacation property.

Title Insurance Coverage issued by a title insurance company to property owners or lenders that indemnifies them against losses caused by any defects in the title to real property that are discovered after the closing. The lender's policy does not typically cover the buyer. However, owner's title insurance may usually be purchased along with lender's title insurance at a small additional fee, since the title abstract work will already have been performed.

Transferable Development Rights (TDRs) Rights of development or subdivision that have been obtained for a property and are transferable with the title to the property.

Transfer of Title The conveyance of title to a real property from one person to another.

Trapezoid A four-sided geometric shape with two sets of parallel lines and one right angle of 90 degrees.

Treasury Bill Also: **Treasury Bond; Treasury Note** Government securities traded by the Fed to stabilize currency and interest rates.

Trespasser A person who wrongfully enters onto someone else's property.

Triangle A closed three-sided geometric shape with three interior angles.

Trust Deed A deed that conveys title of a property to a trustee. It is a deed that establishes a trust.

Trustee 1. A person or organization that holds property in trust on behalf of another party. 2. Anyone acting in a fiduciary or confidential relationship for another.

Trustor A person who creates a trust and names a trustee to manage property or business for the benefit of his or her beneficiaries upon the person's death or disability.

Truth in Lending Act (Regulation Z) The purpose of the act is to ensure that every customer who has a need for consumer credit is given meaningful information with respect to the cost of that credit. In most cases, the credit cost must be expressed in the dollar amount of the finance charge, and as an annual rate computed on the unpaid balance of the amount financed. Other relevant credit information must be disclosed so that the customer may compare the various credit terms available from different sources and avoid the uninformed use of credit.

Tsunami Tidal wave caused by an undersea earthquake.

Underground Storage Tanks (USTs) Environmentally dangerous storage units that have historically been poorly insulated and sealed, and that can leak toxic materials into the ground. Current regulations require all USTs to be identified and noted on property descriptions. It is considered prudent to have them sealed and certified or remove them from the property.

Uniform Residential Appraisal Report (URAR) A widely recognized and accepted appraisal report form designed to report an appraisal of a one-unit property or a one-unit property with an accessory unit (including a unit in a planned unit development), based on an interior and exterior inspection. It is approved by Fannie Mae, Freddie Mac, FHA, and others. It carries the form numbers Fannie Mae 1004 and Freddie Mac 70.

Uniform Settlement Statement (HUD-1) The required closing document for residential real estate transactions of one- to four-family homes according to the Department of Housing and Urban Development.

Uniform Standards of Professional Appraisal Practice (USPAP) A set of professional appraisal standards established by the Appraisal Standards Board of the Appraisal Foundation. The standards address the development and reportage requirements for appraisals and analyses, as well as issues of ethics and practice.

Unilateral Contract A one-sided contract wherein one party makes a promise so as to induce a second party to do something. The second party is not legally bound to perform; however, if the second party does comply, the first party is obligated to keep the promise.

Unilateral Recision A breach of contract by one of the parties. The other party may have recourse in court or may simply abandon attempts to have the contract completed.

United States Department of the Treasury The governmental department in charge of money and the money supply.

Universal Agency A category of agency, whereby the principals give the agent extremely broad authority to act on their behalf.

Urea Formaldehyde Foam Insulation (UFFI) A previously popular insulating material that was blown in between wall joists. It has been found to be toxic and is considered environmentally unsafe.

Vacancies Buildings or rental units that are not rented.

Valid Escrow Also: **Valid Contract** A legally binding agreement, authorized by law and incapable of being set aside.

Vendor's Lien Also: **Seller's Lien; Purchase Money Mortgage** Created when a seller of property takes a note and mortgage from a buyer or vendee for part of the purchase price.

Vertical Lease A contract that allows mining and other activities in the subsurface of a property.

Voidable Contract A contract that seems to be valid on the surface but may be rejected or disaffirmed by one or both of the parties. A common example is where one party is a minor and elects to void the contract.

Void Contract A contract that has no legal force or effect because it does not meet the essential elements of a contract.

Volcanic Eruption A destructive and dangerous geological event with massive upheavals of the earth and the expulsion from a volcano of molten lava and other materials from the earth's core.

Volume The cubic area of an object, such as a sphere.

Voluntary Alienation Also: **Voluntary Lien** The granting of a mortgage by an owner in exchange for the proceeds of a loan.

Voluntary Lien A lien created by the property owner. The most common voluntary lien in real estate is a mortgage. It is voluntary because it is contracted by the agreement of both of the parties.

Warranty Deed One that contains a covenant that the grantor will protect the grantee against any and all claims. Usually contains covenants assuring good title, freedom from encumbrances, and quiet enjoyment.

Waste Heat A by-product of many chemical and industrial processes that has negative environmental impact, especially on water sources.

Wetlands 1. Land periodically covered by water, such as salt marshes, bogs, wet meadows, mud flats, and ponds subject to environmental legislation. 2. Land containing high quantities of soil moisture where the water table is at or near the surface for most of the year. 3. Boggy land specifically protected under environmental legislation.

Zoning The division and separation of a community into zones, usually under the management of a zoning board. The use for which a property in a zone may be developed is specified in the zoning regulations.

Zygocephalum A real estate term for any inaccurate measurement of land. Historically, it was the amount of land a yoke of oxen could plow in a single day.

Index